IAIN MACLEOD

Nigel Fisher

IAIN
MACLEOD

Introduction by Lord Boyle of Handsworth

ANDRE DEUTSCH

First published May 1973 by
André Deutsch Limited
105 Great Russell Street London WC1
Second Impression May 1973
Third Impression June 1973

Printed in Great Britain by
Tonbridge Printers Ltd.
Tonbridge Kent

ISBN 0 233 96324 3

TO MY WIFE
WITHOUT WHOSE HELP
THIS BOOK WOULD NOT
HAVE BEEN WRITTEN

Contents

❦

List of Illustrations

◦◦◦◦◦◦◦

Acknowledgements

~~~~~~~~~~

I AM grateful to Lord Boyle of Handsworth for kindly agreeing to write the Introduction to this book and to Baroness Macleod of Borve, Sir Michael Fraser and my wife for their invaluable help in reading and correcting the manuscript.

My thanks are due, too, to Alan Thompson who researched five of the chapters, to John Barnes who researched two chapters, to J. W. M. Thompson for his work on the *Spectator* chapter and George Hutchinson for his advice on this chapter, and to Nicholas Scott, Dudley Turner and Edward Gilly for their help with the Ministry of Labour chapters.

I am very grateful to Toby Winterbottom and to the talented team of young men he assembled who did some honorary but valuable basic research in the early stages – simply because they were admirers of Iain Macleod. They are Peter Dixon, Robert Jackson, Peter Sinclair, Anthony Speaight and Thomas Tickle. Others who helped with the research in various ways were Colin Craig, Nigel Maslin, David Mellor, Keith Raffan and Michael Young.

I owe a special debt of gratitude to Mrs R. Kloegman, who typed the whole of the manuscript twice with scarcely a mistake and with remarkable speed; and I wish to thank Mrs Phyllis Arnold of Bangor, Co. Down, N. Ireland, for permission to reproduce the silhouette she drew for me of Iain Macleod from photographs.

The following kindly either talked to me about Iain Macleod – some of them, especially Harold Macmillan and Lord Butler, being very generous in the amount of time they gave me – or sent me valuable written material for inclusion in the book:

Lord Aldington, Earl of Avon, Mrs M. J. Baylis, Charles Beasley, Dr Reginald Bennett, Humphry Berkeley, Viscount Boyd, Lord Boyle, Sir Bernard Braine, Samuel Brittan, Lord Butler, James Callaghan, Lord Caradon, Robert Carr, Christopher Chataway, Arthur Cockfield, Lord Colyton, Aidan Crawley, Sir Henry d'Avigdor-Goldsmid, Alan Dawtry, Robin Day, Sir Alec Douglas-Home, Mrs Helen Hope, Dr. Matthew Forster, Hugh Fraser and Lady Antonia Fraser, Wayne Fredericks, Ian Gilmour, Sir Alexander Glen,

Sir George Godber, Lord Grey of Naunton, John Grist, Lord Hailes, Lord Hailsham, Colin Harding, Ian Harvey, Sir John Hawton, Barney Hayhoe, Edward Heath, Mrs David Heimann, Terence Higgins, Lord Hill, Colonel Rowland Hill, Peter Hordern, Dame Patricia Hornsby-Smith, David Howell, Patrick Jenkin, Roy Jenkins, Sir Charles Johnson, Sir Glyn Jones, Eric Knight, Selwyn Lloyd, Charles Longbottom, P. B. Lucas, Rhoderick Macleod, Torquil Macleod, Harold Macmillan, James Margach, Sir Alan Marre, Sir John Martin, the late Hugh Massingham, Reginald Maudling, the Dowager Viscountess Monckton, Sir Leslie Monson, David Montagu, Duncan Morison, Howard Morby, Dr. Michael Mungavin, Michael Noble, Sir Arthur Norman, J. E. Pater, Earl of Perth, Lord Poole, Sir Hilton Poynton, Lord Reigate, Lord Robens, Dr. Cedric Robinson, Dame Enid Russell-Smith, Duncan Sandys, Brendon Sewill, Sir Geoffrey Shakespeare, Miss Hilary Spurling, Sir Alexander Stanier, the late Viscount Stuart, Henry Thurlow, Sir Richard Turnbull, Sir William Urton, Peter Walker, Alan Watkins, David Watt, Professor Wheatcroft, Harold Wilson, Richard Wood, Ralph Wynn, Miss Felicity Yonge.

This list is not exhaustive and I am grateful to many others who kindly sent me information, some of which I was able to use.

I am much obliged to Bernard Tate of the BBC for allowing me to see the full transcripts of interviews with Brian Connell for a memorial programme to Iain Macleod in September 1970; to John Tawney for showing me the transcript of a tape-recorded interview which Macleod gave for the Oxford Colonial Records project; to Sir Michael Blundell for permission to print a private letter he wrote to Macleod and extracts from his book *So Rough a Wind* and to Sir Roy Welensky for permission to quote from his book *4,000 Days*.

I am most grateful to Mr L. Thomas, of Lombard Banking, for permission to reproduce the Emwood Cartoon, and to Lady Macleod for permission to reproduce the Vicky Cartoon. Thanks are also due to the following: Thames Television, the *Nursing Mirror*, P.I.C photos Ltd., Mr Barnet Saidman, the Keystone Press Agency, and the Thomson Organisation Picture Service.

Introduction

IAIN MACLEOD was a man of government who knew that politics are about power. His wit, his combativeness, his ability to pack a punch in a question, or in a peroration, were all devastating. But what engaged him most was policy-making, taking real decisions, participating in the work and deliberations of a government backed by a parliamentary majority.

Macleod's memorable victory in debate over Aneurin Bevan back in 1952, which launched his ministerial career, owed much to his outstanding natural ability as a parliamentarian, but much also to his years of patient, accurate work in the Research Department, preparing for the time when a Conservative government would be returned to office. I agree with Nigel Fisher when he perceptively writes that Macleod 'did not care to think ahead in areas where he could not visualise a concrete situation', and there may be truth in the judgement that, partly for this reason, he 'was never entirely at home with the problems of the economy'. Yet it is equally true, as the later chapters of this book show clearly, that no prospective Chancellor of the Exchequer can have worked harder to prepare himself for a major reform of our whole system of taxation. Millions of people will have felt that his death was a tragedy not only for the Conservative party but for the nation as a whole.

Macleod was a great rhetorician. He could rouse a party conference, and he nearly always *commanded* the House of Commons – something hard to achieve, yet of priceless value to any government or opposition. His secret was partly preparation, and he would have endorsed John Bright's reply to a supporter who complained that a speech 'smelt of the lamp': 'Young man, I have never heard a speech worth listening to that didn't'. But part of his effect was also due to rigorous selection and concentration. I was often struck by the brevity of his party conference speeches, and it was always the tremendous sense of force behind his key sentences that made the greatest impact.

Nigel Fisher has rightly emphasised Macleod's courage: his physical courage in the face of constant pain and discomfort, and also his moral and political courage. It was in everyday political life, when things weren't going easily for him, that I admired this courage most of all. As Chairman of the Party, at a time of acute political difficulty, he never flinched from meeting the press, nor tried to be above the battle, and as Leader of the House he did not shirk the awkward duty of sometimes appearing to play the role in Cabinet of spokesman for the Opposition. Along with Macleod's courage went his outstanding loyalty to his friends, a loyalty which – as Nigel Fisher shows – never wavered just because they were under fire. And it was often at moments of acute disagreement with his friends, as I for one remember well, that he most wanted to talk with them.

Macleod had a deep understanding of politics, and he combined two qualities which, added together, surely make up the true politician. He had political beliefs and convictions; he thought that politics mattered, and that the 'game' had an object. But Macleod also knew, as well as anyone in his generation, that a politician has to accustom himself to the inevitable fluctuations of political fortunes, and to wait calmly for his opportunities. Macleod felt political and personal elation, or depression, more intensely than most people. I can remember most vividly his joy (this is not too strong a word) when, on a single day during the 1961 party conference, a pro-European motion was decisively carried, and a motion to restore capital punishment was rejected; whilst the heavy defeat of his friend Peter Goldman at Orpington some months later caused him real personal sorrow. But he seldom allowed elation or depression to obscure his political clear-sightedness. And he would sometimes say to younger friends within the party: 'Don't stick your neck out unnecessarily, don't take up too many unpopular causes all at once; wait for the climate of opinion to change – as change it will.' And he never fretted in opposition. 'These are the dog days', he used to say to his Shadow Cabinet colleagues, when progress seemed disappointingly slow; he knew it was no good attempting to build up an election atmosphere too soon.

Another of Macleod's strengths – I am inclined to think the greatest of them all – was that he was always responsive to the feelings of ordinary voters, and yet politics for him were never just a crude matter of 'giving people what they want'. I can recall, sometime in the mid-1950s, a discussion about the impending 'End of Empire', and the unreality of talking (as some people at that time used to do) about 'self-government within the Empire' as though this were a meaningful concept. Macleod replied, 'Yes – but the emotion that has always been associated in our party with the Empire really does matter'. He saw, hard-headedly, the danger of this emotion having nothing worthwhile to attach itself to, and of its becoming something negative and defensive. Again, I think Macleod may have surprised some of his friends by going out of his way, shortly before the famous meeting at Selsdon Park, to make a speech about public concern over law and order, and yet it may well have been politically wise to do so at that particular moment.

But Macleod never thought it was good enough to lead public opinion simply by following it. In the words of the obituary tribute to Macleod which appeared in the *Economist* (I think the best press obituary of a politician I can ever remember reading): 'Iain Macleod understood acutely the people in his party, and in the country, that he represented. He did not despise what they wanted. But he missed few chances of persuading them that they might want something a little better.'

Macleod wanted a broad-based Conservative party embracing a wide range of opinions and preferences and appealing to a wide variety of temperaments. He had, as Nigel Fisher rightly emphasises, a special empathy for the younger members of the party. No political office gave him greater pleasure than his presidency of the Greater London Young Conservatives, and the last words I ever heard him utter at a Shadow Cabinet meeting, the afternoon I sent in my formal resignation, expressed his conviction that 'the YCs are a political youth movement which would be the envy of any political party within the Western world'. He liked enthusiasts, and indeed any speaker who addressed himself seriously to the question: 'What, here and now, are we trying to achieve?'. He liked *good* people – and I used to feel that, among the many strands of his personality, there was a particularly strong admiration for those who were active in social service, and that this fitted in with his dislike of abstract ideas that he could not 'feel upon the pulse'.

Lastly, it would be wrong to sketch Macleod's personality as a politician so as to suggest that his interests were confined to policies and to party affairs. The Cabinet itself also fascinated him. For instance, Macleod greatly admired David Eccles, not just because of his work for education, but even more because of his general contribution to the work of the Cabinet; and Macleod used to say that one could never be sure, in advance, who would prove of Cabinet timber and who would not. (But he was equally insistent that no Cabinet could afford passengers – they had to go.) I think he knew inwardly that he himself was never again so strong in Cabinet after he had ceased to sit as the representative of a department of major political significance – first the Ministry of Labour, and then the Colonial Office.

Macleod identified himself from the very beginning of his parliamentary career as a 'liberal Conservative' and, as Nigel Fisher reminds us, he was a founder member of the One Nation group. There is an interesting point, by the way, about how this important group ever came to be founded. The original initiative arose directly as the consequence of a most unfortunate debate on housing in which Aneurin Bevan was felt to have scored heavily over the official Opposition spokesman. New policies, or new party groups, are far more often the result of a damaging debate than people outside Parliament (including some academics) may realise.

What were Macleod's beliefs that made him a Conservative? First, and he himself would have laid by far the greatest stress on this, whereas British socialists – not only extremists, but justly admired and respected men like Tawney in the 1930s and Gaitskell in the 1950s – said that 'Socialism is about equality', Macleod always preferred to stress *opportunity*. One might, indeed, say that 'the opportunity State' was the precursor of 'A Better Tomorrow' as the slogan that united us all within the Conservative party in the late 1950s and the early 1960s. Macleod often used to say that he wanted younger people to have 'more equal opportunities of proving themselves unequal', and he was therefore sympathetic towards all those of his colleagues who wanted to put educational progress right in the forefront of Conservative strategy. It also followed from his belief in the ideal of opportunity, rather than that of equality, that he was a consistent and determined supporter of working towards greater selectivity, rather than uniformity, in social welfare policy.

Macleod's second Conservative belief was a strong, though not extreme, commitment to the objective of a freer market economy. One has to remember that, when Macleod entered Parliament in 1950, Britain's economy was still the most tightly controlled in Western Europe. I can well remember his delight at the growing success of R. A. Butler's policies in freeing the economy during the years immediately after 1951. And it always bothered him that the British boom of 1954–55, perhaps the most promising since the war (because it was so largely an investment boom), had to be brought to an end because of a balance of payments deficit which turned out to be less than £100 millions. Macleod always had a particularly lively sense of the extent to which British government policy was hemmed in during the 1950s and 1960s by the exiguousness of 'the reserves' – the elusiveness of that 'fairy gold', as one civil servant happily called it, which was never there when governments most needed it.

But while Macleod's economic instincts favoured 'a dash for freedom', he was, as I have indicated, no *laissez-faire* extremist. He believed in regional policy. He wasn't in principle opposed to occasional government intervention in the affairs of a particular industry, provided that the Cabinet itself took the key decisions; he always remembered the decidedly successful intervention by the Macmillan Government in assisting the cotton textile industry. What he *did* oppose was a proliferation of institutions, creating a general climate of 'intervention', with the government's own role not clearly defined. He was against statutory wage control, but specifically repudiated the idea that a Conservative government could dispense with all forms of incomes policy whatsoever. It was in about 1965 that he made his famous remark on Powellite economics: 'I'm a fellow-traveller, but I prefer to get out one or two stops before the train crashes into the buffers at the terminus'. He remained a fellow-traveller, but it is my definite impression that he tended to get out rather earlier as the years went on.

The third reason why Macleod was a Conservative was that he held definite views on the acceptable limits of government power and influence. When it was a matter of remedying avoidable social evils, no one could have been firmer than Macleod in accepting political responsibility. But he had an intense dislike of what he used to call the 'nanny State'; he set a particularly high value on widening individual freedom of choice as something that was clearly desirable in itself; and he had little sympathy, to put it mildly, with the sort of view expressed by a member of the Labour front bench who complained that the reason for the 1959 defeat was that 'the ethical reach of our policies was beyond the grasp of the British electorate'.

Macleod's instinctive libertarianism led him, bravely and consistently, to support a number of 'liberal' causes throughout his career: he was against hanging, for divorce law reform, and against the notion that it is the function of the criminal law to try to enforce morality as such. (I once got him to read Professor Herbert Hart's *Law, Liberty and Morality*,[1] and he told me that he agreed with every word of it.) But these same feelings also led him in certain directions where not all 'liberals' would have followed him. For instance not only was he a strong supporter of the introduction of commercial television, but it went decidedly against the grain with him that the government of which he was a member should take action against 'pirate radio'; and it is safe to say that the Pilkington Report, which contrasted 'competition in audience rating' with 'competition in good broadcasting', was just about his least favourite Report to appear during his twenty years in Parliament.

There is, of course, a case for holding a somewhat different view. Let us imagine a society which widens opportunity, increases choice, progressively removes avoidable social evils, and makes a significant contribution to the narrowing of the gap between rich and poor nations. These would all be notable achievements, and yet I wonder whether they comprise *all* that many of us mean when we speak of 'A Better Tomorrow'. Surely there is something else that one can only call 'the quality of life' which matters as well. There must be a place for conservation in our schemes of values, as well as for economic efficiency. Book publishers, and broadcasting authorities, do have a responsibility for offering a service to authors, and to creative talent, as well as to consumers. Students are right to ask, 'How are the disciplines for which we're being trained going to be used?' and one sympathises with their unwillingness to be railroaded through O level, A level and first degree without regard to the question 'What is this all *for*?' Economists are right to want to get away from too much concern with 'aggregates' and from speaking of 'demand' as though it were, in Joan Robinson's trenchant phrase, some kind of 'neutral stuff'.

I have little doubt that Macleod, if he were still alive, would sympathise with at least some of these points, and that he would be impressed to find them raised by many younger voters who are certainly not committed Labour supporters. But he did feel rather strongly that there were areas of life where the ordinary preferences of non-intellectual citizens, exercised in ways that did not interfere with the freedom of their neighbours, ought to be respected. In the words which I have quoted from the *Economist* 'he did not despise what they wanted', and he felt an instinctive

1. Oxford University Press, 1968.

hostility towards mandarins who knew a little too confidently what was good for the rest of us.

Macleod, then, was a libertarian who believed that there were fairly strict limits to the functions which any government should attempt to perform. Nevertheless he also believed, equally firmly, that within these limits government was there 'to be used as an instrument of action' (I quote from *The Making of the President: 1960* by Theodore White,[1] a book Macleod much admired). And this leads to the consideration of the question: why did he have the reputation, rightly, of being a 'liberal' Conservative?

The first answer is that Macleod was deeply concerned, throughout his political career, over two key domestic issues – poverty and unemployment. He had compassion. And in this connection one thing always impressed me during our twenty years together in the House of Commons. We all know what a fighter he was – yet, whether in power or in opposition, he never liked debates on unemployment to become too partisan. People have occasionally asked me during this past year whether I think Macleod, if he had lived, would have been more worried about unemployment than about the pace of inflation. I think that, last winter, that would certainly have been true; I am less sure whether it would still be true at this present moment (September 1972). Macleod did have an exceptional capacity for viewing economic problems in practical human terms. Even when scoring a notable personal victory, as over the bus strike in 1958, his principal day-to-day concern was to be kept informed whether or not people were managing to get to work. And his sharp reaction to any debating point which he considered illegitimate, because it exploited human suffering for political purposes, had a quality of spontaneity which nearly always carried conviction. Almost his very last intervention from the Opposition Front Bench involved an angry exchange with the then Prime Minister, and a subsequent apology to the Speaker. But his defence, before withdrawing, earned him (I judged) the sympathy of the greater part of the House: 'I always say frankly what I did say. I used the words complained of. I thought it unforgivable to bring children's deaths into a political argument and to make capital out of it'. When Macleod used the word 'unforgivable', he meant it.

Secondly, Macleod's compassion, and his strongly felt concern for the fair treatment of individuals, extended beyond those fellow-citizens who

1. Cape 1961.

have come to be defined as 'patrials'. As Colonial Secretary, he was – by his own admission – the last member of the Macmillan Cabinet to be persuaded of the necessity for the introduction of the Bill to control Commonwealth Immigration in 1961. And he was passionately opposed to the subsequent Act of 1968. A part of his very strong objection was based, with much justification, on the smallness of the quota for the Kenya Asians that was announced along with the change in the law; and he would certainly have felt relieved if he could have known that a Conservative government would double this quota, and that they would subsequently, and without any equivocation, show themselves determined to honour this country's obligations to accept those United Kingdom citizens who are being expelled from Uganda.

Whilst Macleod came, reluctantly, to accept the need for strict control of immigration from the Commonwealth, he always made it clear that, for his part, he would prefer to lay the greatest emphasis on the fair and equal treatment of those immigrants already here. And it must be stressed as firmly as possible that the notion of stigmatising children born and educated in this country as not 'part of Britain' but 'part of Asia' was, to Macleod, not just wrong, but 'hateful' – a word I heard him use in Shadow Cabinet in this very context. All his deepest and most instinctive beliefs were fully in line with that centuries-old tradition of commitment to the ideal of equal citizenship, which is surely the most justified reason for pride in British nationality.

The third reason for Macleod's reputation as a 'liberal' Conservative was, of course, his tenure of the Colonial Office. Macleod will always have a special place in British history as one of the two or three greatest Colonial Secretaries, and Nigel Fisher has devoted three chapters of his book to a full and admirable account of this key part of his career. I remember a senior member of the colonial service once saying to me that he and most of his colleagues had never for one moment expected that, whatever Macleod's own personal inclinations, a Conservative government returned in autumn 1959 with an increased majority would then proceed to speed up the movement towards African independence. I pointed out to him that during the whole run-up to the 1959 election, the only area of policy in which Conservatives had found themselves on the defensive was African policy, with particular emphasis being laid by the Opposition on Suez, the Devlin Report, and the truly horrible disaster at Hola Camp. (Macleod, like Quintin Hogg, had grasped imaginatively the full ghastliness of Hola, just as Enoch Powell in a memorable speech had laid bare the precise errors which caused the tragedy.) Political parties in the first flush of victory much prefer to make their peace with recent events, and few Conservatives expected that Macleod, on his appointment as Colonial Secretary, would carry on exactly where his predecessor had left off. Many back-benchers remembered his victory in debate over Aneurin Bevan, and they hoped that he would prove able to deal on more than equal terms with his opposite number Jim Callaghan. At the same time Macleod himself rapidly arrived at the view, surely a correct one, that any policy other than a speeding-up of the movement towards independence would be 'bound to lead to terrible bloodshed in Africa'. And I do not think it is too much to claim (in Nigel Fisher's words) that, as a result, 'Macleod saved Africa for the Commonwealth'.

One important aspect of Macleod's policies as Colonial Secretary was the enthusiasm they evoked at home among younger political supporters, especially at the universities. In fact Macleod commanded, at this period, an intensity of admiration which is very rare in British politics; even some of those who were most strongly committed in a radical direction would go to one of his meetings and find themselves compelled, not just to recognise the area of common ground over policy, but also to think again about the nature of the Conservative party. Macleod, like Lord Butler, helped to make a number of right-wing social democrats feel they could (at any rate sometimes) vote Conservative; I have also the strong impression that his period as Colonial Secretary in a Conservative Government, coming soon after the Hungarian tragedy of 1956, strengthened belief in the continued viability of our political system, and lessened the appeal of Marxist ideology for a number of able minds.

Nigel Fisher gives a detailed account of the long drawn-out wrangle over the constitution of Northern Rhodesia which persisted throughout Macleod's last year in the Colonial Office. We are reminded that in the end, and after Macleod's departure, the matter was eventually settled in February 1962 'on very much the same basis as Macleod had recommended a year earlier. The delay had achieved nothing for anyone. It had alienated the Africans without pacifying Welensky, [and] the Federation was now doomed'. I well remember listening to much of the Lords Debate in which Lord Salisbury made his celebrated and unworthy 'too clever by half' speech. What impressed me most was the contribution of the speaker who immediately followed Lord Salisbury, a Conservative Peer who had been a member of the Monckton Commission;

he pointed out that the fundamental weakness of Welensky's position as Prime Minister of the Federation was that, for all the Federation's multi-racial pretensions, his own party had conspicuously failed to make a multi-racial appeal. There is just one point I would add to what Nigel Fisher has written. I remember that Macleod became increasingly annoyed during the summer of 1961 at the way not only Sir Roy Welensky, but also Sir Edgar Whitehead, the Prime Minister of Southern Rhodesia, was being brought into the consultative process. Perhaps this was inevitable; yet in retrospect I still feel sympathetic to Macleod's view that, given the existence of the Central African Federation, the Prime Minister of the Federation had a *locus standi* when any change in the constitution of Northern Rhodesia was under consideration, to which Whitehead had no legitimate equal claim.

Macleod's speech to the 1961 Conservative Party Conference, shortly after he had ceased to be Colonial Secretary, was one of the finest he ever made. Nigel Fisher has described the impressive peroration, with its invocation of 'the brotherhood of man'. There was also an interesting inversion of Disraeli, of which Macleod was quite unconscious. Disraeli, in his Crystal Palace speech of 1873, told his audience that 'social and not political improvement' was the aim they ought to pursue; better sanitation, improved social provision, and a trade union law which removed the taint of criminal conspiracy from collective action – all these things were of more immediate urgency than any further extension of the franchise. Macleod's message in 1961 was the opposite. He pointed out that no amount of colonial development and welfare, and no rate of economic improvement, could be an adequate substitute for a government with which the majority of a nation felt identified. Along with Macleod's compassion, and his commitment to equal citizenship, went a deep sense of the primacy of self-respect. He knew that it was always right to try to narrow the gap between the value which men and women – of whatever race or creed – place on their own personalities, and the value placed on them by the society within which they lived.

Macleod always maintained that the best test of any society was the way that society treated people. He believed in compassion for the unfortunate and for those in need; opportunity for the young and for the enterprising; justice and fair-dealing for all, including minorities; and toleration coupled with understanding for everyone, especially among the younger generation, whose ideals were generous and constructive. Both as a Minister and as a political force he caught the imagination of the country.

This biography by Nigel Fisher not only records the facts of Macleod's life with accuracy, but it portrays the man himself with extraordinary fidelity. It is also a moving testament of a political friendship, and I am sure Macleod would have liked it. But there is just one memorial he would have valued still more – the thought that his own strongest convictions would continue to evoke a matching response within the party, and the House of Commons, which he served so well.

EDWARD BOYLE

CHAPTER I

Early Life 1913-1939

ᎧᏇᏂᏇᎧ

IAIN MACLEOD was a complex character – a fascinating mixture of the Celtic romanticism of his ancestry and the down-to-earth pragmatism of his Yorkshire upbringing. He combined idealism with realism and an acute appreciation of what was politically possible. He had the qualities of courage and compassion. He liked young people and talked to them as equals, so they liked him. Ian Gilmour thought that it was as much the element of poetry in him as the liberalism of his political views which helped to attract the young and uncommitted to him and to the Tory Party. Randolph Churchill's son, Winston (MP for Stretford), wrote of him: 'No politician bridged the generation gap more forthrightly than Macleod. The appeal he held for the young was intense.' His influence upon them was certainly deep and may well be lasting.

'The last of the orators in the Tory Party' was Harold Macmillan's tribute to his fellow-highlander, and it is true that it is usually the Celts who stand out in their ability to influence the English by the spoken word. John Grigg the political journalist (formerly Lord Altrincham) wrote of him: 'He was the finest orator in the country since Aneurin Bevan died . . . His freakish memory enabled him to deliver carefully prepared speeches without notes and he delivered them with a punch and sense of timing that no one in recent years could rival . . . His elocution was unhurried but relentless: every word was made to tell. And the physical disability from which he suffered was turned to good account in that his body (or, on television, just his head and shoulders) had a terrible fixity which matched the concentration of his words.'

'When the ball rolls your way, grab it' was a Macleod maxim which illustrated an important facet of his personality. He was intensely ambitious and, from the time at the Staff College at Camberley in 1943 when he first realised his own capacity, he was quick to seize any opportunity which would further his political career, but never at the cost of his convictions. The Liberal Leader, Jeremy Thorpe, said of him in the House of Commons: 'His conscience was his only guide and master.'

As a young man Macleod was a wild tearaway until he entered politics; but he quickly became a professional, and this enabled him to implement in practice many of the ideas and ideals which were an essential part of his political philosophy. His clarity of mind, prodigious memory and strong determination carried him through the rough water which he often created by his own impatience and intellectual intolerance.

His selfless loyalty to his friends was one of the characteristics which made men love him. His ill-concealed contempt for the prejudiced and the stupid made others dislike him. No one could be indifferent to Iain Macleod.

'I do not run in a race to run second,' he once told me. Yet in the end he had to settle for second place.

*

Iain Macleod was born at Skipton in Yorkshire on November 11, 1913.

His father, Norman Macleod, was a doctor, born and bred in Lewis in the Western Isles. He married his second cousin, also from Lewis, so that Iain came of Highland stock on both sides of the family.

Dr Macleod had done well. He was the brightest child in a crofter's family, the son of a fisherman and fish curer in the small village of Kershader in the parish of Lochs. He had left school at fourteen to help on the croft, but the local schoolmaster took an interest in him, lent him books and helped him to study. Macleod took the opportunity and obtained a bursary at the Nicolson Institute at Stornaway and later a scholarship to Glasgow University.

It was quite usual in Lewis in those days, and still is even now, for the cleverest child in a crofter's family to be helped by the other members of it to qualify for a profession; and the rest of the family must have made sacrifices to supplement Norman Macleod's scholarship award of fifteen pounds a year.

Macleod had decided to work for a theological degree at Glasgow and enter the Church. But on the way south in the train he sat in a carriage with some other theological students from the Highlands and found them a dull lot. There was noise and laughter from the next carriage and Macleod walked down the corridor to investigate. He found it was occupied by some young medical students, also on their way to Glasgow University. Their company was gayer and more congenial than in the .

carriage he had just left, and there and then he made up his mind to read medicine instead of theology.

He never practised in Lewis. After qualifying in 1903, he went to India as a doctor on a tea plantation. He stayed in Assam for four years, made a little money and came back to Scotland where he married in 1910. On the recommendation of another Lewis man, Dr Bain, Macleod took a junior partnership in Dr Alec Waugh's Yorkshire practice and the family lived at Skipton in Airedale for the next thirty years.

Although his parents were distantly related, Iain's mother, Annabel, came from a different background. Her forebears were yeomen farmers and her father, Rhoderick Ross, was a much respected Lewis doctor. Her mother, born Isabella Macdonald, was the heroine of a romantic novel about the Isle of Lewis called *The Princess of Thule* by William Black; and her maternal grandmother was a Macaulay, through whom she was kin to the historian, Lord Macaulay.

Norman and 'Lab' Macleod had four children. They were a happy, close-knit family, which meant much to Iain all through his life. The eldest, Rhodabel, born in 1911, was a vital, attractive, intelligent girl who married a mill-owner called Thomas Garnett and lived near Skipton all her life, so that Iain always had a Yorkshire base to return to even after his parents had left the county. He was devoted to his sister, who must have been an exceptional person because any conversation about the Macleod family always seems to come back to Rhodabel and everyone loved her. She died in 1962 and is buried a few yards from Iain in the churchyard at Gargrave. It was only after her death that Iain consciously assumed the leadership of the family.

Two of her married daughters still live near Gargrave and this was a source of pleasure to Iain, who had a great sense of family continuity. He had two younger brothers, Torquil, who was born in 1917, and Rhoderick three years later.

The family home for the first twenty-five years of Iain's life was Clifford House. This square, solid, Victorian building stands in a garden in the middle of Skipton. It was a comfortable house, large enough for Dr Macleod to use as a surgery as well as a home, with a centre stair-well between the first and ground floors. At the age of seven Iain fell through the stairs on to a piece of coral on a card table in the hall below. This first encounter with a card table nearly killed him and he was ill for some time as a result of it.

Life was not luxurious at Clifford House, but the Macleods had two cars, two maids (from Lewis) and a family nanny. This was usual in those days for a busy doctor's household. They lived comfortably and it was a secure upbringing for the children. Iain is remembered by his contemporaries as a happy little boy.

In addition to the indoor staff, Dr Macleod employed Harry Thurlow, who was chauffeur, handyman and jack-of-all-trades and assisted him in keeping the books of the practice. In course of time he became a friend of the family as well as their employee and was treated as such. When Iain was working in London before the war and playing bridge and poker at Crockford's, he sometimes lost more than he could afford and on one occasion Thurlow paid out ninety pounds for him on an IOU. It was soon reimbursed, but presumably Iain had not liked to go to his father for the money. The incident illustrates the close and continuing relationship between Thurlow and the Macleod children.

Norman Macleod made Clifford House a centre of hospitality for Lewis people living in the north of England. They met there for the *ceilidhs*, so dear to the hearts of Lewis men far from home.

Dr Macleod is still talked of with affection in Skipton, where he was much respected and a person of consequence in the town. He was a good doctor, hard-working and conscientious and a real friend to his patients. During Iain's childhood he was building up a large practice, especially among the poorer people whom he often under-charged and, if times were difficult, did not charge at all. He was a competent surgeon who wasted no time. It is said that his record for an appendicitis operation was five minutes.

In 1938 Dr Macleod sold the Skipton practice. He died in a nursing home in Bradford in 1947 from heart failure following an operation.

Because he had been so busy with his practice, Dr Macleod had seen comparatively little of the children except on holidays and they were brought up mainly by their mother, who kept the whole family together.

Mrs Macleod was a remarkable person of very strong character. She was a good woman, kind and intelligent, whose whole life was based on Christian principles and even in the last decade of her life friends of all ages sought her company and her advice. She talked well and mostly about the future even when she was herself very old. She was not involved in politics, though she understood them and was always well informed. She did an immense amount of work in Skipton for the British Legion and the local hospital and started one of the first clinics for poor children.

She was very generous with money, especially to her family, but at the same time frugal, as a good Scotswoman should be. She believed in saving the pennies, and is remembered in Skipton to this day as a house-wife who 'painted round the furniture'.

Mrs Macleod always thought she was right. On one occasion she met a woman whose accent she thought was Scottish and said, 'How nice to meet a Scotswoman in the south of England' to which the woman replied that she was from Ulster. After she had left, Mrs Macleod com-mented, 'Damn fool woman, doesn't know where she comes from.' It was a favourite phrase and was repeated at her ninetieth birthday party. This had been arranged for her – including a piper to play after dinner – by Iain's wife, Eve. When Mrs Macleod heard the first skirl of the pipes, she turned to her neighbour and said, 'Damn fool girl, doesn't know there are no pipes on the Island (Lewis), only on the mainland.'

Dr and Mrs Macleod argued incessantly, but they were completely devoted to each other. They often spoke in Gaelic when they did not wish the children to understand.

Iain Macleod was closer to his mother than to his father. He enjoyed teasing her, but he loved her deeply and was very unhappy when she died during the general election campaign of 1970. In answer to a letter of sympathy, he wrote to my wife, 'It is so desolate to be no one's child.' He cancelled every speaking engagement for a week and went up to Gargrave for his mother's funeral in the parish church where his own was to take place seven weeks later. The Vicar recalls that he stood by her grave, next to his father's and his sister's, gazing intently down the lovely dale, along the crest of Sharphaw to Skipton and the moor beyond. This was his home and these were his people, at rest in the peace of Gargrave. But it held only half of his heart.

His roots were in the Highlands and Islands, as well as in the Yorkshire dales and, although none of the Macleod children ever learned Gaelic, they spent every summer and many Easter holidays in the Isle of Lewis, where Dr Macleod had bought a large, homely, holiday house from Lord Leverhulme in 1920. The estate was called Scaliscro and consisted of a shooting lodge and 9,000 acres. It was purchased for the remarkable price of two shillings an acre. It was twenty-four miles from the nearest shop and in those days could only be reached by a sea crossing of sixty-one miles from the Kyle of Lochalsh.

There were nearly forty fishing lochs on the property, good snipe shooting, some grouse over dogs and a little stalking. Dr Macleod also kept sheep at Scaliscro, from which a local firm spun the wool and made blankets and even an occasional suit for the Macleod family. Iain Macleod caught his first trout there and thirty years later his son, Torquil, caught his first fish in the same burn.

The household at Scaliscro was nearly self-supporting, with brown trout for breakfast, home-made scones for tea, and grouse or their own mutton or venison for lunch and dinner. Iain knew every loch on the estate and would often return with twenty or thirty trout from a day's fishing. He was taught to shoot by day and to play bridge in he evenings. Dr Macleod was himself a very good player, who had been Northern champion in his time, and he first began teaching Iain (auction bridge in those days) when the boy was only nine. He was an apt pupil and used to spend hours dealing dummy hands and working out imaginary games.

Most evenings were spent reading, but guests sometimes introduced other activities. Alasdair Alpin MacGregor, in his book *The Golden Lamp*,[1] tells the story of the gambling bug which infected Scaliscro in the summer of 1932. MacGregor had gone to stay with the Macleods, and a succession of wet, blustery days provided an excuse for long sessions of vingt-et-un, which were often continued far into the night. The maximum stake was twopence so no fortunes were won or lost, but Iain's extraordinary memory enabled him, after a few deals, to know precisely the order in which the cards lay in the dealer's hand, unless they had just been reshuffled. He probably inherited this advantage from his father, who used to see thirty patients without taking a single note and then return to his surgery at the end of the day and write up every detail.

One holiday the family had been visiting friends and were driving home afterwards. A heated discussion developed in the car and Iain was losing the argument. In a schoolboy huff he said, 'If no one agrees with me, I will get out and walk.' Without a word, Dr Macleod stopped the car and opened the door. They were thirteen miles from home. It was past midnight when Iain arrived back, foot-sore and weary, and everyone else had gone to bed. The incident was never mentioned again.

The Lewis home made the Macleod children very conscious of their Highland background. Iain thought of himself as Scottish, except in the cricket season when he considered himself a Yorkshireman. He loved the West Riding and drew strength from it, but his heart and his romantic nature were deeply influenced by Scaliscro and by his Highland ancestry, and many of the poems he was to write were about the Western Isles. He wrote 'The Harris Hills' in 1941.

1 Michael Joseph, 1965.

The Harris Hills

The Yorkshire hills are friendly hills
And sleepy to the sight.
Grey-washed with cottages and farms
And full of sudden light.
But the Harris hills are elfin hills
Blue-etched against the night.

The rolling downs are casual hills
And tug your heart away
With the breathless lilt of singing birds
And the strong sweet scent of hay.
But the Harris hills are shot with gold
About the break of day.

The hills of Wales are sullen hills
Where none should walk alone:
With towering crags and deep ravines
And gaunt cold bursts of stone.
But the Harris hills stand sentinel
Above my Lewis home.

Iain Macleod began his education at St Monica's Convent School at Skipton. This consisted of about one hundred girls and a kindergarten which included four or five small boys. He often said he was the only old girl of St Monica's who became a member of the Cabinet.

He stayed there for a year, until he and a friend were expelled for tripping up the Reverend Mother with a skipping rope and for tying some of the little girls by their plaits to the school railings. After this episode he went to the 450-year-old Ermysted Grammar School at Skipton for one term, before being sent as a boarder to St Ninian's Preparatory School at Moffat.

St Ninian's, a school of 60 or 70 boys in the Dumfriesshire hills, had been founded 50 years earlier and was presided over by an old-fashioned and somewhat puritanical headmaster, the Rev Frank Wingate Pearce, who believed that every Christian gentleman should have read at least one of the Gospels in Greek, so the boys had to struggle through St Mark, the shortest of the four.

Golf, trout fishing or walks were allowed on two afternoons a week, but the regime was spartan and the day always began with a cold bath or, in the summer, a length of the swimming pool.

Mr Pearce, a kindly but formidable man, six and a half feet tall, was a stern disciplinarian who made frequent use of the cane, and Iain, who had a well-developed sense of mischief, was often in trouble. On one occasion the boys were gathered round the headmaster's wife, who was correcting their French exercises, when Iain, awaiting his turn, collected a lot of red berries from a potted plant and laid these neatly in a furrow between Mrs Pearce's bun and the top of her head. The other small boys watched with bated breath and barely suppressed laugher until, inevitably, Mrs Pearce inclined her head and the berries cascaded to the floor. Such *lèse majesté* could only have been perpetrated by Macleod and it provoked several stinging blows on the back of his small hand from Mrs Pearce's strong and be-ringed fingers.

Iain accepted all corporal punishment, of which he received his full share, without flinching. He was a tough, pugnacious little boy, always in a fight and usually against someone much larger than himself. He was very small for his age, and on one occasion when he was playing against a rival preparatory school called St Mary's, the St Ninian's pack heeled the ball near the St Mary's line. Iain grabbed it, tucked it into his chest, ran straight through the legs of the scrum and scored a try. He recalled the incident later as one of the moments of purest pleasure he had ever experienced.

Everyone at St Ninian's had to learn to swim and any boy thought capable, but not keen, was thrown in bodily at the deep end and left to get on with it. A school friend remembers Iain, half-drowned and almost totally submerged, triumphantly achieving the required length at his first attempt.

His work was less distinguished and, like his appearance, untidy. He was usually among the first half-dozen in a class of fourteen, but he did not over-exert himself and was not thought to have more than average ability. All his life Iain could never sing in tune and in a letter to his mother he wrote, 'To-night is our carol performance. I have not been forbidden to sing . . . yet!'

Iain Macleod left St Ninian's in July 1927 and went to Fettes that autumn. He was there till 1932. These were grey years in Scotland, with the General Strike only just over, unemployment rising steeply and the shipyards empty on the Clyde. But it is unlikely that the boys at Fettes were conscious of the misery and hopelessness of existence in the tenements of Edinburgh and Glasgow. Their own surroundings were very different. Although the school building has too many gargoyles and pinnacles, the grounds are beautiful and there is a fine view of the Edinburgh sky-line from the classrooms.

Like most public schools at that time, life at Fettes was inward-looking. Discipline was strict and it had the reputation of being a tough school, with the main emphasis on success at organised games. Cold baths in enamelled tubs were still in use when Iain first arrived there. But fagging was not arduous and consisted mainly of cleaning the prefect's shoes and his study and making toast for his tea. The food was so poor that it left most boys either quite indifferent to the good things of life or more than usually appreciative of them. Iain was in the second category.

For many boys at Fettes, rugger was a religion. Iain was good at most games without being outstanding at any of them. He got into the School 2nd XV at rugger and the 2nd XI at cricket. He was a fearless and tenacious scrum-half and became a useful wicket-keeper, but as a batsman he never scored many runs. Cricket was not rated as highly at Fettes as at an English public school and, as Iain wrote later, was only played at all because in summer the ground was too hard to play rugger. He became a house prefect, but described himself in a television interview in 1970 as having been 'basically a 2nd XI sort of chap' at school.

Many Fettesians in those days despised indifferent games players, but although Iain could hold his own with the best performers, he was always friendly to those who could not. He was already a keen student of cricket and rugby football and later added racing to his interests. He spent much of his time at Fettes studying *Wisden*, often in form hours, and his amazing memory ensured the fantastic knowledge he acquired and always retained of this and indeed almost all sports.

Scholars at Fettes were segregated in School House and received their education free. They were looked down on as 'charity' boys by some of the others, but Iain did not take this snobbish view and had several friends, including Ian Harvey, who later became a junior Minister, among the foundation scholars.

He made no particular mark at work and, although he eventually reached the Modern Sixth, no one considered him intellectually outstanding. On his own admission, he was lazy. His house tutor described him as 'reliable but unremarkable'. His academic interests were History and English, for which – without exerting himself unduly – he showed some aptitude. Sir Michael Fraser (now Deputy Chairman of the Conservative

B

Party), who was in the same house at Fettes, has described him as an
'early developer' who had outgrown school in his last two years there.

In appearance, Iain had a round, almost cherubic, face, and an unusually
deep head. He was untidy, his top hat furry and unbrushed and his
umbrella like the proverbial 'gamp'. His hair was often too long and his
nails were bitten. He appears to have been more self-sufficient than most
boys; but many of his school friends have recalled his sense of humour,
sometimes dry, sometimes impish, but never unkind, and his physical
courage. While he was at Fettes he had a bad attack of rheumatic fever
which left him in pain for some time, though he seldom admitted it.
Later, pain was to become the background to his life. It has been suggested
that, owing to the rheumatic fever, he was unable to throw a ball, and that
it was for this reason that he became a wicket-keeper and a scrum half,
since in those positions he could scoop rather than throw.

He loved poetry and was a leading member of the Shakespeare Society,
which met on Saturday evenings in the headmaster's study to read the
plays. In his last year he and Ian Harvey shared the Shakespeare essay
prize, which they received from the hands of Sir John Simon, himself an
old Fettesian. He was also a member of the school debating society, in
which he made speeches on a wide variety of subjects, none of them
political.

The report of his first speech, in 1929, on the motion that 'No one
should give up his seat to a lady', reads: 'I. N. Macleod, in a very good
speech which had the merit of being short and to the point, said that
women had stolen all men's most cherished possessions and that the best
way to deal with them was to show their inferiority by offering them
seats. But why not share the seat?'

Later that year he supported the motion that 'boxing is a brutal and
barbarous sport'. The debate took place on the day of the annual boxing
competition and the opposition was led by Knox Cunningham (who was
later to become a QC and MP for South Antrim), an old Fettesian and
by then a Cambridge boxing blue. Macleod maintained that, even at
school, boxing was brutal and that one of the heavyweights had recently
knocked two sparring partners unconscious just to practise for that
evening's competition. He did not care which House won, as his own was
out of the competition, and he was no judge of boxing – so he was only
there to see blood and blows and this attitude was typical of any boxing
audience. Perhaps rather surprisingly at Fettes forty years ago, the motion
was carried.

Macleod also supported a motion that, 'this house would not hang a murderer'. He always opposed capital punishment, but on this occasion, as for many years in the House of Commons, he was on the losing side.

A mock election was held in October 1931, in which he was allocated the Mosleyite 'New Party' candidature. Out of eight candidates, who included a nationalist, a prohibitionist and a communist, the conservative won with forty-five votes and Macleod was third with twenty-three votes. He had no political aspirations at that time and no strongly held political views. He was, perhaps, an instinctive Conservative with liberal sympathies, but he saw no future in the Liberal Party as a force in contemporary politics.

He did not write much verse at Fettes, but one unsigned poem was published in the school magazine in his last term, and he confessed to its authorship thirty years later when he was the principal guest at Founder's Day in 1957. It was not a very good poem but it showed his love for the school and his pride in having been there.

Iain Macleod went up to Gonville and Caius College, Cambridge in the autumn of 1932. He read history, but this occupied little of his time. His principal recreations were bridge, poker and racing. He played rugby football for his college and a little golf and tennis, neither very well. He also did some amateur acting, which he enjoyed and which may have had significance for the future. No one can be an effective public speaker without the instinct and ability to act. Indeed, Iain said later that he might have become an actor but for the fact that, while he was in his second year at Cambridge, his hair-line receded to such an extent that he looked as though he was fifty years old. He was as bald at twenty-one as he was when he died.

At the end of his three years he obtained a respectable second class honours degree. But he had not done much work. At the University and during the pre-war years which followed, he made little attempt to apply his mind or to attain the academic distinction which was within his reach if he had devoted more time to it.

This was a disappointment to his father. Dr Macleod had made his way as a young man by his own unaided effort and he felt that life had been too easy for his son. He knew Iain had the capacity and he disliked seeing it wasted. But Cambridge in the 1930s was a very different place from the Glasgow University of thirty years earlier. It was also quite different from Cambridge itself thirty years later. In the years between the wars most undergraduates went to the older universities because it was traditional for upper and middle-class boys to do so. No intellectual distinction was required. It was almost impossible to fail the entrance qualification and the main requisite was the willingness and ability of one's parents to pay the bills. Of course, there were many young men who worked hard to equip themselves for a career, but the majority went to Oxford and Cambridge, not to attend lectures and achieve good degrees, but to complete their education by enlarging their experience of the world. The use of leisure was, for them, more important than the pursuit of knowledge. Iain Macleod was in this category.

A friend of those days remembers meeting him one morning in the courtyard of Caius. Iain had just paid a visit to his tutor, who had advised him that the best university degrees were not obtained at the bridge table or on Newmarket Heath. His tutor had quoted the name of another Caius undergraduate as a model of the hard work and academic prowess which would take him to the top of any profession. Twenty years later Macleod, newly appointed as Minister of Health, was being conducted round the department by the Permanent Secretary and introduced to the staff. In one office he recognised a middle-grade official, whose face he could not immediately place, but whom he soon remembered as the young man who had been held up to him at Caius as an example of certain success in later life. The recollection appealed to his dry sense of humour and he told me the story with pleasure some years afterwards.

Macleod's social life at the university was spasmodic. He was a good conversationalist and could be the best of company, but he was unusually self-sufficient and spent much of his time in his own room reading poetry. He never lost his fondness for it and could quote almost any poem he had ever read for the rest of his life. He knew the whole of T. S. Eliot by heart. G. K. Chesterton was also a special favourite, and he always kept a copy by his bed. It was a range of taste which perhaps illustrates the intellectual and the romantic in his character.

Poetry and rugby football are an unusual combination, but in the winter vacations he enjoyed playing scrum half for the Skipton 'A' team. He always recalled an old Skipton supporter, who attended every match and who, when play had only been in progress for five minutes, used to begin the chant, 'Come on Skipton, they're tired', a battle cry which he kept up throughout the game. This delighted Iain. It seemed to symbolise his own approach to life.

At Cambridge he took little interest in politics, joined no political club or party and spoke only once in the Union – against the Ottawa Agreements.

The debate had started at 8.15 and by 11.00 p.m. he had still not been called. He described the speech in a letter to his sister:

> At last the President, an Indian called Dhavan, made a remarkable noise which sounded like Mr Maclooood. I concluded this was me, so I moved forward, glanced modestly at my feet and tried to remember what I was going to say. There were nearly 400 people there. I decided to risk a joke in doubtful taste, which got a laugh. After five minutes I launched in to a vicious and quite unpremeditated attack on Stanley Baldwin. It went down rather well. The *Granta* review said 'Mr I. N. Macleod (Caius) is promising' which, though short, was satisfactory; and the *Cambridge Review* made my speech sound better than it was.

Twenty years later Iain and Geoffrey de Freitas were having a drink together in the smoking room of the House of Commons and de Freitas, who had been president of the Union in 1934 when they were both undergraduates, asked Macleod why he had not taken a more prominent part in the Union debates. 'I did try once,' Iain replied, 'but there was a sharp and I thought unfair report of my speech and, as I was a shy boy, I did not persist.' De Freitas enquired who had written the report and Macleod answered, 'I never knew because I did not recognise the initials. They were G. de F.' Almost certainly Iain invented this story on the spur of the moment to tease Geoffrey de Freitas, but if so it was entirely in character and typical of his perverse sense of humour.

He had no thought at that time of politics as a career. If he had had a vote, he would probably have voted Conservative, but only just and certainly without enthusiasm or involvement.

When Dr Michael Mungavin, a friend from university days, wrote many years later to congratulate him on becoming Minister of Health, he replied:

> I'm a bad advertisement for industry at Cambridge. I can't remember doing any work there, and even less till the war; and then six years as an indifferent soldier. Anyway, however it's come about, Caius – the best medical College – has the youngest Minister. Some outsiders must win races from time to time just to keep the bookies happy.

He often went racing, mainly at Newmarket, and won money at the Cottenham point-to-points, chiefly by obtaining inside information from acquaintances who owned horses and ran them there. He developed a remarkable knowledge of racing form and knew and remembered the times and performances of all the prominent Newmarket runners. But racing was a sideline.

Bridge was his real love. Most of his friends could not play with him because he was already in a different class. He usually played with Colin Harding, who became a lifelong friend, and in October 1934 they decided to issue a challenge to Oxford. At this time there was no Cambridge bridge club, so Iain created one. He elected himself as president and Colin Harding as secretary. He then wrote a letter to the *Isis* and received an immediate reply from Charles McLaren, now Lord Aberconway, who wrote accepting for a team of four, consisting of himself, Michael Noble Terence Reese and Ted Peel.

The match was played at the Savile Club in London and lasted for a whole weekend. Oxford won easily. It was the first of a series of annual matches between the two universities and probably the only one to include two future Cabinet Ministers and also, in Terence Reese, the most successful future international bridge player in Britain.

On the eve of another match at Cambridge, Iain had clearly consumed too much alcohol and was in a comatose condition. His friends were discussing the possibility of getting someone else to take his place, when he awoke and declared roundly, 'Macleod drunk is better than any substitute sober'.

By the age of twenty-two he was playing international bridge, and in the Camrose Cup (for the four United Kingdom countries) he always played for England, not Scotland. Soon after leaving the university he and Colin Harding were invited by the French Bridge Federation to play in matches against France at Cannes and Deauville, with all expenses paid. Iain enjoyed these trips; but he was no linguist and his French accent, like Winston Churchill's, was deplorable. On one occasion he asked for 'encore du glace', but pronounced it so badly that the waiter thought he was speaking in English and brought him an empty glass!

When Iain Macleod was in his last year at Cambridge, the English Bridge Union sent a team down to play the university. One of its members was Bernard Westall, the Chairman of De La Rue. The company's business was expanding rapidly at that time and Westall was looking for bright young men to take into the firm. He was impressed by Iain's personality and his ability at bridge, and there and then offered him employment with De La Rue as soon as he came down from Cambridge.

Macleod had nothing else in view and accepted. He joined the company in 1935 at a salary of £3 a week.

In those days De La Rue had three different lines of business – the very profitable bank-note side and the less profitable playing card and commercial printing activities. Iain became a trainee in the company's commercial printing department under the office manager, Leslie Newman, in premises in Bunhill Row.

As a chairman's introduction, he was at first looked upon with some reserve and suspicion. But he was soon accepted and quickly made friends with the other employees. A van driver, who drove him on a special job for three weeks, recalls that he used to get into the van, put a box of fifty cigarettes on the seat and say 'help yourself'. He always paid for coffee or a meal when they stopped. He was a heavy cigarette smoker at this period but gave them up later and only smoked cigars in moderation.

Another young recruit called Arthur Norman (later to be a Chairman of the CBI) joined the firm at the same time. He worked hard, stuck to his last and later became managing director, and now chairman, of the company. Iain Macleod was less assiduous. He played bridge almost every night and sometimes almost all night. Not surprisingly, he often arrived late in the morning, usually too tired to work. The chief recollection of those who were with him in De La Rue was of a young man who was always falling asleep at his desk. Sometimes it was not even his own desk.

In those days the firm printed a spiritualist paper called *Psychic News*, the editor of which was Hannan Swaffer. One morning Macleod, who had been up all night and was sleepier than usual, retired to the editor's office for a rest because Swaffer was not expected in till 11.30 and his room was quieter than the main office where Macleod normally sat. Unfortunately on this occasion Swaffer came in early to find an unknown young man fast asleep in his chair. He stormed out at once to complain to Leslie Newman. Macleod was quickly woken by a friend and just had time to slip back into the main office before Swaffer and Newman returned to the now empty editorial room. When Newman expressed incredulity and said Swaffer must have imagined the whole incident, Macleod commented drily that the mysterious intruder must have been *spirited* away.

Every departmental manager complained that he did no work in the office and eventually the chairman was forced to acknowledge that he was making an inadequate contribution. Bernard Westall and Iain parted with mutual respect and 'by mutual agreement'. In fact, he was fired. He had obtained the job because of his ability at bridge. He lost it two years later for the same reason.

It may be said that his priorities were wrong; but for a young man of twenty-two the temptation to spend more time doing what he enjoyed and making a large income from it than he spent in the office making £3 a week must have been considerable. He retired with some relief to the card tables at Crockford's and soothed his conscience and his father's displeasure by announcing his intention of reading for the Bar. It is doubtful if his legal studies were pursued with any greater diligence than his work at De La Rue. At any rate, in the two years which remained before the outbreak of war, there is no record that he ever passed a Bar exam.

He was living at this time in an eighth floor flat at Duncan House, Dolphin Square, which he sometimes shared with his brother, Torquil. There were frequent parties which sometimes went on most of the night. It was a gay, carefree existence. But there was another side of Iain's nature. His love of poetry and of acting were often combined to illustrate his brilliant memory. He would ask a friend to choose a difficult and little-known poem which he had not read before. He studied it with immense concentration for a few minutes and then closed the book and recited, indeed performed it perfectly. No doubt this satisfied a streak of exhibitionism in his make-up; but he had a genuine passion for words and he understood the magic of the English language. The timing and arrangement and the music of words meant much to him, although he had no appreciation of music as such.

It was during this period that Macleod and three others – Jack Marx, Harrison-Gray and S. J. Simon – devised the Acol system, which was named after a small bridge club in Hampstead. They worked night after night into the small hours, scrawling hands on scraps of paper and tablecloths. The development of a new system for good bridge players requires a clear, analytical mind. It took a year to test, modify and refine and by that time Acol was a very good system indeed. It was an approach forcing method with light opening bids and light informative doubles. For a year after its innovation, it was almost unbeatable and much of it is still used over thirty years later by good bridge players. It was efficient and scientific with limited risk elements, but it was not a 'romantic' system. Indeed it was publicly criticised by Kenneth Konstam as being dull and unadventurous – to which Iain made a witty reply in verse in the *British Bridge World*.

Iain Macleod was a fine bridge player and, although he never competed enough at the highest level to become a really great player, he was certainly one of the masters of the game and in the 1930s was regarded, with Terence Reese, as a prodigy. He had a good card sense and great powers of concentration. He was also intensely competitive. If he had stayed in the game, he would certainly have become a regular member of Britain's international team.

Macleod was an attacking, aggressive player, but he was not intuitive or psychic. It was efficient bridge, not inspired bridge. He played with courage, flair and imagination, sometimes to the point of recklessness, but it was a recklessness firmly based on technical knowledge and self-confidence. He would bid his cards very high – always avoiding the use of the plural ('2 heart', '4 no trump') – and then often stop abruptly when he judged that he had pushed his opponents too far to make their contract. He could size up a hand and calculate the odds very quickly and was always prepared to gamble, and perhaps go down badly, but only if he thought the risk was justified.

Many of his contemporaries regarded him as a gambler, and he certainly enjoyed playing poker and chemin de fer and betting on race horses. There were occasions when he played for more than he could afford and Michael Fraser recalls a high game of poker when Iain was losing steadily through the evening: 'Eventually I could not watch any more and left Iain at the table, hunched, indrawn and apparently emotionless – and then met him again six hours later, triumphant, with a great victory under his belt.'[2] That is the picture of a gambler, but I am not sure that it was the whole picture. At bridge and perhaps to a lesser extent at poker, he always believed that it was not luck but his own skill which could make him a winner. And it usually did. After leaving the university he and Terence Reese used to play at Crockford's and Lederer's Club in the Bayswater Road. At ten shillings a hundred he might win or lose £100 in an evening and before the war he was probably making an average of £2,000 a year, free of tax, which in those days was a considerable sum for a young man of twenty-three.

Iain Macleod was attractive to women, mainly no doubt because of his quick mind and his beautiful speaking voice, but he was often rough in his treatment of them. Most of his time and attention at this period was

2 BBC programme on Iain Macleod, Sept. 25, 1970.

devoted to wine (or whisky), women and cards. He was, in fact, a playboy, without purpose or ambition, content to enjoy the world as he found it and with little thought of improving it. The war was to change this. Before it began he was almost a professional bridge player. By the time it ended he was on the road to becoming a professional politician.

CHAPTER 2

The War 1939-1945

∽∾∾∾∾

EVELYN BLOIS was the daughter of a clergyman. Her father, Gervase, was a younger son of Sir John Blois, 8th baronet, and her mother, Hester, was a daughter of the 3rd Lord Hampton. The Blois family are one of the oldest in the Eastern counties of England, where they have owned property from the time of Richard I, in the twelfth century, to the present day.

The family lived at Hanbury in Worcestershire, where Eve had the conventional country upbringing of a girl of her background in the years between the wars. Horses played a large part and she was an enthusiastic rider. In summer, there was country-house tennis, in winter hunting and, as she grew up, hunt balls. She went to a girls' boarding school called Lawnside at Great Malvern and later, as was the custom in those days, she was presented at Court.

In 1937 she married Mervyn Mason, who was drowned in a convoy off the coast of Ireland early in 1940. After Munich she went to work for the LCC Ambulance Service and was posted to Kingston House in London on the outbreak of war. In September 1939, she interviewed Iain Macleod amongst others and accepted him as an ambulance driver while he waited to get in to the Army. It was their first meeting.

Eve was a beautiful girl with Wedgwood blue eyes and a lovely complexion. Iain was entranced. Twenty-five years later, after a marriage which, like any other, had had its troubled patches, he said to my wife: 'Every man has many dream loves, but only one true love.' Eve was his.

While Macleod was at Kingston House there was a spy scare. A note, apparently in code, had been found on the floor of the ambulance station and was handed over to the security authorities. They took it seriously and sent several intelligence officers to Kingston House to make enquiries. There was great excitement and everyone who worked there was closely questioned. The note read 'A . . . A to K, xxx, Qxxx' and when Macleod's turn came to be interrogated, he recognised it at once as part of a bridge hand which he had scribbled down and later thrown away.

Iain enlisted as a private soldier in the Royal Fusiliers on September 11th, and three months later he was posted to an OCTU at Colchester. The young cadets assembled one bitterly cold December evening at Liverpool Street Station, clad as instructed in stout shoes, a mackintosh and a cloth cap. A Cambridge friend who was going to the same OCTU recalls that Macleod's rather gnome-like figure, draped in a raincoat which was far too long and a cap several sizes too large, was a sight to remember.

The first winter of the war was intensely cold, and when he went to bed Iain used to wear two sweaters over his pyjamas, a pair of football stockings, a thick scarf and a balaclava helmet. He did not take kindly to army discipline and habitually flouted the minor restrictions. The cadets were only allowed to visit the local public house at weekends, but he went there almost every evening.

Other cadets took copious notes of the long lectures on tactics. Macleod took none. On one occasion the lecturer illustrated an interminable talk about the attack, which included intention, method and route, by giving as an example the various ways of getting to Ipswich to visit a maiden aunt. Most of the cadets covered sheets of paper, but when someone looked at Macleod's notebook, it contained only three words: 'Aunt in Ipswich.' When asked if that was all he had written about the whole lecture, he replied: 'Yes, it conveys perfectly what the man was talking about. I shall remember the rest.' Perhaps not surprisingly, he did not obtain very high marks, but he knew the minimum amount of work necessary to pass and his sense of humour and faint contempt for the more stupid regulations helped to enliven the course and make it tolerable for his colleagues.

In April 1940 he was commissioned as a Second Lieutenant in the Duke of Wellington's Regiment and sent to a holding battalion at Wetherby. His reception in the officers' mess on the first day of his regimental soldiering was discouraging. There were four officers sitting in the only four chairs reading the only four newspapers. Not a word was spoken for five minutes. At length a major glanced up and in a broad Yorkshire accent enquired: 'Young lad, 'ast tha just cum in?' Macleod thought he was to be made welcome and perhaps given some information about his accommodation or duties. 'Yes, sir,' he replied brightly. There was a pause. 'Well, shut bloody door,' said the major and returned to his newspaper.

Within a month he was in France. The retreat to Dunkirk had already begun and Macleod was ordered to put up a road block near Neufchatel. Like any wise infantry officer, his immediate concern was to dig a trench in case of air attack or shelling and the first thing his men unearthed was a skull from the First World War. This gruesome beginning was described in a poem he wrote at the time:

> There were endless files of men passing by,
> And the big tanks rumbling
> To the bridges on the Somme:
> And the great guns grumbling
> In the sky,
> Far away – far away.
>
> We were digging in the ground,
> Tearing through the earth and stones,
> While the slow hours slid away:
> When a spade struck home on bones,
> And we found,
> Ghosts of men – ghosts of men.
>
> And these dead things seemed to sneer
> 'Ye are here, ye men of war,
> Digging trenches – digging graves
> Dying where we died before:
> We were here:
> Long ago – long ago.'
>
> Were they English, were they Huns?
> Came no answer but the sobbing
> Of the breezes in the pines:
> And the low dull throbbing
> Of the guns:
> Coming near – coming near.

The road block was constructed out of a pile of logs laid across the road, which were to be wired together; but before the men could get them securely tied, a German armoured vehicle drove round the corner and crashed into the road block, sending some of the logs flying. One of them hit Iain's leg and his thigh was badly fractured, almost pulverised. He used a bayonet as a splint until he reached a dressing station. He was evacuated by destroyer from St Nazaire on June 8th and sent to hospital at Exeter. He did not return to France until D-day, almost exactly four years later.

Macleod's subsequent ill-health may have been partly the result of this injury because, although the bone set, he limped and suffered more or less permanent pain for the rest of his life. The slanting of his pelvis, to make walking easier, may have upset the normal carriage of the spinal column and perhaps this contributed to the arthritis which gave him so much discomfort in later years. He was unable, eventually, to turn his head at all and this forced him to give up driving a car. The last time he drove himself was in 1957.

Macleod's war injury was not, however, the direct or main cause of his later illness. He had an inherited tendency to gout and an unusual condition called ankylosing spondylitis. This is a chronic inflammatory disease affecting the spine, which causes considerable pain, a progressive limitation of movement in the back and neck and toxaemia. It is a form of rheumatoid arthritis and at one time Macleod was put on to cortisone drugs. These temporarily relieved the pain and stiffness and induced a false sense of well-being, but did no lasting good. It is difficult to wean patients from the use of steroids, but Macleod accepted his doctor's advice and the drug was gradually withdrawn. He resisted any later suggestions to re-introduce it, even when he was at a very low ebb, and he certainly endured much pain and discomfort throughout the last twenty years of his life.

The illness waxed and waned and both Eve Macleod and his doctor had the impression that he was in less pain in the last year or two, as he seemed to be taking fewer pain-killing pills; but he scarcely ever referred to it, even to the family, and it was always difficult to know how severely he suffered. He hated talking about his health and, if one enquired, he usually replied with his unforgettable throaty chuckle: 'Oh, mustn't grumble.' His doctors' notes contain constant references to his courage and endurance and it was a surprise to them that he was able to continue in high office for nearly twelve years. He never spared himself and never allowed his pain to interfere with his work. He had learnt to live with it.

When he was discharged from hospital, Iain was posted to the 2/7th Battalion at Halifax and at about the same time Eve, now a widow, transferred to the Bradford Ambulance Service. They were married at Halifax on January 25, 1941.

Some friends lent them a car and some petrol coupons, and they spent their honeymoon at the Devonshire Arms Hotel at Bolton Abbey. One day they drove south to Cheltenham races where they lost all their money. By the last race Iain had only one pound left. He put it on an outsider which won at 25/1, so they were able to return to Yorkshire in comfort instead of penury. At this time they were living on his pay as a Second Lieutenant of eleven shillings a day.

Whether because of his ability or his injury at Neufchatel, or a combination of both, Macleod was soon seconded from the Duke of Wellington's Regiment to the staff of the 46th Division, and early in 1941 he arrived at the divisional headquarters at Wye, near Ashford in Kent, as Staff Captain to the DAAG.

He impressed his senior officers by the speed at which he was able to read and absorb Army Council instructions and select from them whatever was relevant. He did not find it necessary to work long hours.

On the weekly evening off duty which staff officers were allowed, he usually went to London, where he played cards at Crockford's until it was time to take the early morning train back to Ashford. On his return he had a bath and a shave, but no sleep, and was at his desk by nine o'clock, apparently untired and capable of an efficient day's work. He had always made the evening's expenses and a profit of between £20 and £50.

The DAAG, for whom Macleod worked, was Alan Dawtry, now town clerk of Westminster. One evening in the mess Iain had too much to drink and wanted to play stud poker, which Dawtry, who was sober, wisely refused to do. Instead, he retired to his bedroom and locked the door to avoid further argument. This infuriated Macleod, who first fired a revolver shot through the door, which fortunately did no damage, and then battered the door down with a heavy piece of furniture. The effort and the alcohol proved too powerful a combination and he proceeded to pass out on Dawtry's bedroom floor. The following dialogue took place next morning at breakfast:

Macleod: Good-morning, sir.
Dawtry: Good-morning, Iain.
   Silence, then, after a pause:
Macleod: I think you owe me an apology.
Dawtry: What for?
Macleod: For not playing stud poker with me last night.

Many years later Iain told the story to a mutual friend and added: 'If I had killed Alan Dawtry, he would never have become town clerk of Westminster and I should never have become a member of the Cabinet.'

When Dawtry wrote to congratulate him on his appointment as Minister of Health, Macleod replied:

My dear Alan
Bloody silly, ain't it? I'm glad I missed you.
Yours ever, Iain

It was the only occasion during the war on which he made use of his service revolver.

Later in 1941 Macleod rejoined the Duke of Wellington's Regiment and served with the 2/7th Battalion, which was on coastal defence duty in the area of Dungeness. His company commander remembers his remarkable application and attention to detail. His thinking was clear and logical and nothing was left to chance. He had an exceptionally good relationship with his men and was sympathetic and conscientious in dealing with their problems.

The usual after dinner relaxation in the officers' mess was a game of bridge at three pence a hundred, but Macleod always concealed his brilliance at the game and never referred to the fact that he was an international player. Another officer, who was no expert, said he had never played with a nicer or more encouraging partner.

At Christmas 1941 he and his brother, Torquil, wrote and produced a regimental pantomime in which they also acted. It consisted of a series of satirical sketches, ridiculing the Army Establishment. It was performed in a public hall at Littlestone and many of those present thought it one of the funniest and most witty shows of its kind, amateur or professional, which they had ever seen. It was the first of several revues which Iain Macleod was to write and produce during the war for the amusement of his brother officers.

Iain's only son, named Torquil after his brother, was born in Buckinghamshire on February 20, 1942. For the next two years Eve stayed with her parents, or with Iain's, or took furnished rooms to be near him, so he was able to see her and the baby quite often until he went to Normandy on D-day.

There were many postings, including a course at Newmarket, for which he had volunteered in order to get some racing. One assignment was as Staff Captain to an Independent Brigade Headquarters at Dover Castle. His work there was not demanding and he got through it very quickly each morning. He would then take a miniature chess set from a pocket of his ill-fitting battledress, split his mind in two and play chess against himself.

When this palled, he wandered over to the Brigade Major's office to offer his help. His methods were unorthodox. He had discovered a large wicker laundry basket in an attic of the Castle and he used this as the receptacle for all the letters he thought unimportant. He left them to answer themselves, which they usually did, and the basket soon became quite full. Sometimes his judgement was at fault and a letter arrived which clearly required a reply but which referred to several others of earlier dates. He then turned the basket upside down and delved hopefully in to the pile of paper for the relevant correspondence. It was a procedure he enjoyed and he would pick out the more fatuous instructions to read again, occasionally putting them to music and singing them in his croaky, tuneless voice. The Brigade Major, fresh from the Staff College and still under its influence, had to weigh up these acts of indiscipline against the advantage that they clearly did much to raise the morale of the office clerks.

For some time there had been no Brigadier at Dover Castle, but eventually a message was received, stating that the new incumbent would arrive that day on the evening train from London. The Brigade Major (now Colonel) Rowland Hill took Macleod to the station to meet him. They dined well beforehand and then, as the train was late and the night cold, sought sustenance and warmth at the station bar. Inevitably, as the delay lengthened, their consumption of whisky increased and they were in cheerful mood when the train at last arrived. The Brigadier was dragged from his carriage, his luggage strewn carelessly on the platform, and was given a perhaps overfulsome welcome. They all clambered into the staff car and Macleod indulged in a light-hearted and often slanderous description of the Brigade personalities his new commanding officer was soon to meet. He finished with a comment on Rowland Hill: 'The Brigade Major,' he said, 'is an Old Etonian and must be checked constantly from assuming that he is not as other men are. In fact there is only one thing worse than an Old Etonian in a small headquarters and that is a Wykehamist. Wykehamists may be good civil servants but they are altogether too pernickety to be anything but a bore in the army.' The Brigadier spoke for the first time: 'Before going to Sandhurst,' he observed, 'I was a Winchester Scholar.' There was a silence until they arrived at the castle, by which time the night air had had its effect and the Brigadier's first job on assuming command was to help the Brigade Major put the Staff Captain to bed.

Despite this unpromising start, it was a happy unit. Macleod taught his brother officers to play poker, which he claimed was pure science. His theory was that luck and bluff had little part in it and success depended upon a perfect memory. When payment of his mess bill could be delayed no longer, they sent him up to London at their expense and he never returned from Crockford's empty-handed.

In October 1943 Iain Macleod was selected to attend the 12th War Course at the Staff College. This was the turning-point in his career. Until then he had lacked ambition and his life, though agreeable, had been without purpose. He had coasted along and there had been no incentive to do more than the minimum. His mind had been under-used because he had not himself realised its exceptional capacity.

In peace time the Staff College course took two years. In the war it was compressed into four months; and the standard of those attending it was far higher. Iain Macleod summed up its significance for his own future in a television interview in April 1970: 'I'd never been pushed into competition with people of first class ability before and it was there that I found, genuinely to my very great surprise, not only that I could keep up, but that I could beat them.'

An officer who was in the same syndicate for part of the time has confirmed this. He was impressed by the clarity with which Macleod saw the problems and by the practical solutions which he suggested. Another officer at Camberley described Iain's work there as brilliant. But he still found time to spend many of his weekends playing cards for high stakes at Crockford's. On one occasion when a poker game had, rather unusually, been financially unsuccessful, he commented to a friend that he could always recoup his poker losses at the bridge table.

By coincidence Torquil Macleod was on the same course and he and Iain were again recruited as co-authors, this time of the Staff College revue. The Commandant sent for them both and laid down the ground rules they were to follow. He instructed them that there was to be neither language nor incident which could shock his sixteen-year-old daughter. Although they adhered meticulously to this condition, the revue, which included some witty lampooning of the directing staff at Camberley, was a tremendous success. It was called *The Blues in the Night*.

When Iain and Torquil were relaxing over their whisky after the production and congratulating themselves upon its reception, Iain suddenly observed that, if conditions were right after the war, he thought the sky would be the limit so far as he was concerned. Twenty-five years later Torquil asked him what had started him on the road to success in public life and Iain replied, 'You have probably forgotten, but it was

The Blues in the Night.' He meant, of course, the Staff College and I have no doubt this was true. Once he realised he could compete at the highest level, it was a short step to aim for the highest prize. He had never thought of going into politics until he attended the Staff College. Within months he was talking of it as his postwar objective.

Iain Macleod graduated from the Staff College in February 1944 and had had one day of the leave then due to him when a telegram arrived instructing him to report, as a Major, to an address at Ashley Gardens in Westminster. He found that he was to be DAQMG on the planning staff of the famous 50th Northumbrian Division, which had been brought back from Sicily to take part in the invasion of Europe. It was not an easy Division to join because, after two and a half years in the desert, those in charge of the divisional services had far more practical experience than most of the officers teaching at the Staff College. Macleod concealed any lack of expertise and worked hard to learn his job.

Sir Alexander Stanier commanded one of the Brigades in the 50th Division. He wrote to me later that, after a visit to Divisional Headquarters, he had told his own staff: 'I was lucky enough to find two staff officers, Major Urton and Major Macleod, who understand our problems. Major Macleod seems able to give the answers to all the most intricate questions.' He added in his letter that 'Iain, as always, remained in the background and allowed others to reap the praise.'

Macleod learnt, by accident, where the invasion was to take place. He was going through a file at 2nd Army Headquarters when he came across a receipt for a map marked 'Top Secret Overlord' (the invasion code name). To most people the receipt would have had no significance, but he recognised the map sheet number as one, based on St Lô, which had been used in a Staff College exercise. He now knew that the landing was to be in Normandy, not the Pas de Calais. He removed the receipt and burned it.

In the spring the Division moved from East Anglia to the south coast and there were many rehearsals with the Navy at Studland Bay in Dorset. In the last two days of May the invasion force began to assemble in the Southampton area. D-day was to be on June 5th. In fact, it was postponed for one day owing to bad weather and even then General Eisenhower took a calculated risk in launching the invasion in rough seas. The Air Force gave complete cover and there was not a single German plane in the sky until the evening of June 6th, when the landing had been successful.

Iain Macleod slept soundly during the night crossing and came on deck at first light. He described the scene in an article in the *Spectator* twenty years later:

> The coast of Normandy began to take shape through the haze. And then one saw the ships and the planes . . . It was as though every ship that had ever been launched was there and as if every plane that had ever been built was there. There had never been such a rendezvous for fighting men; there never will be again. And I remember reciting, out of sheer delight at being part of that great company, 'And Gentlemen in England now abed. . . '

The assault began and Iain described in a letter home how the invasion forces 'seemed to be smashing at the beach defences and countless squadrons droned in one after another to bomb. The enemy batteries blazed back but did very little damage. Then, over the ship's loudspeaker, came the order "Assault parties, man your craft" and the army began to take a hand. The small assault boats rolled off through the swell to the beaches and the attack went in. The infantry were magnificent. They went up the beaches under fire as if they were doing an exercise on Ilkley moor. Due to their speed and determination, the casualties were incredibly light.'

As a martial gesture Macleod thought he would load his revolver, but he found that his batman, who knew more about war than he did, had filled the ammunition pouch with boiled sweets instead of bullets. They were far more useful.

Soon he and Colonel Bertie Gibb, who was ADOS in charge of ordnance supplies, climbed down the scrambling nets into their assault landing craft and made for the beach. They stepped out of the LCA into waist-deep water and waded ashore.

Macleod wrote:

> The beach was alive with the shambles and order of war. There were dead men and wounded men and men brewing tea. There were men reorganising for a battle advance and men doing absolutely nothing. There were even some German prisoners waiting patiently. There was a whole graveyard of wrecked ships and crafts and tanks. It was like an absurdly magnificent film by Cecil B. de Mille. It was like war.

They walked across the beaches and climbed the dunes behind. It was strangely quiet. They did not realise till later that the villages on each side of them were still held by the Germans. They had taken a sand track between and walked inland for a mile and a half. Later some shots were fired into their orchard headquarters by a small nest of Germans who had been overlooked.

Macleod's jeep (called 'Evelyn') had stuck in the sand, so he set out on a motor-cycle to find the forward brigades and make contact with their staff captains. By dusk nearly every objective had been taken and patrols were already moving in to Bayeux. The 50th Division had taken half the prisoners on the whole front.

Macleod had a meal of tinned steak, tinned Christmas pudding and whisky, and was about to get some sleep in the corner of a barn when Tom Black, another staff officer, came in to see him. They went outside and looked back towards the sea. Some German fighters were raiding the beach and the red tracer bullets were following them into the sky. It was exactly midnight and Iain realised that he had lived through D-day. He had not been scared. He had enjoyed it. Before the day began he had been convinced he would be killed. Now, with equal lack of logic, he felt certain he would live through the war.

Despite the constant build-up of troops, there seemed to be plenty of room in the bridgehead; and the RAF's complete mastery of the air was reassuring. After a day or two Macleod never bothered to look up when there were planes overhead; they were always our own. The comfort of life at divisional headquarters surprised him. He had a jeep, a Humber car and an office caravan with his wireless sets and telephones. His clerks were clicking away at their typewriters in a lorry beside him and the mess lorry was in the next field. He could even have a gin and French and dine off linen. Conditions were very different in a front-line company or armoured squadron like my own, and Iain was the first to acknowledge his good fortune.

The well-dressed officer in the bridgehead only wore battledress on formal occasions. A polo sweater, corduroy trousers and suede shoes were more usual and Iain had soon collected a remarkable assortment of clothes, some of them left behind by Germans who had been taken prisoner. Between battles he played poker dice or drove to the nearest town, where the French festooned his car with flowers and gave him a wonderful reception which on one occasion included three bottles of brandy free of charge.

Even battle periods were not always arduous for the DAQMG. A few days after 21st Army Group landed, a staff conference was held and a dumping programme of artillery ammunition was ordered for the first set-piece battle. Macleod expected to have to sit up all night working out every detail as he had been taught at Camberley. The reality was very different. He said afterwards that the senior officer concerned simply took his pipe out of his mouth and said 'Yes'. Everything else then followed automatically and the ammunition reached the right place at the right time without Macleod having put pen to paper.

After the Caen battle died down and the Americans began their great advance, Iain wrote home at the beginning of August to say that the battle for France was already won. His letters were full of excitement and optimism. He was enjoying every moment and told his mother, 'I wouldn't be anywhere else for a fortune.'

It must have been about this time that he visited my battalion headquarters. I had always assumed that our first meeting was in February 1950 when we both entered Parliament, but he told me later that we had had a talk and a drink together in Normandy six years earlier, and as his memory was so much better than my own, I am sure he was right. We had never met at Cambridge, although we were there at the same time.

It was in the bridgehead that he first mentioned, to Bertie Gibb, that he would like to go into politics after the war. He drafted a letter applying to be put on the Conservative Party's candidates list and they went through it together and made some small amendments. He referred to the subject again two months later during the advance into Holland. His companion on this occasion was Major William Urton (later to be General Director of the Conservative Central Office) who, unknown to Iain, was a Conservative agent by profession. 'Which side would you be on?' Urton enquired. 'Conservative, of course,' was the reply; and at that moment an enemy plane dropped a load of anti-personnel bombs, so they both dived into a convenient slit trench. When they climbed out a few moments later, Bill Urton asked, 'What would be your aim?' and Iain answered, 'to be Prime Minister.' Like the personnel bomb, it was a near miss.

Meanwhile the advance across France had been amazingly fast. The battlefields of the first world war, where millions of men had fought and died for four years, were taken in a day, sometimes with scarcely a shot fired. Small pockets of German resistance were often by-passed or simply overlooked in the tidal wave of the advancing allied armies. On one occasion Iain sent his batman to a farm to buy some provisions and he returned with six eggs and eleven German prisoners.

In November the 50th Division was withdrawn from the battle. In three years it had suffered over 22,000 casualties. Now the Division returned to Yorkshire and Iain to his home county. He was just too late for the birth of his daughter, Diana, on October 8, 1944, and had not even heard of her safe arrival until he read it in *The Times* ten days later at Nijmegen, but he was back in time for her christening in Worcestershire.

In the early summer of 1945 Iain was on leave at Scaliscro with Eve and the two children. The general election was announced while he was there, but there was no Conservative organisation and no Conservative candidate. Dr Macleod was himself a Liberal but he was also an admirer and supporter of Winston Churchill and he thought the Government should be represented in the election in the Outer Hebrides. So he called an inaugural meeting of the non-existent Conservative Association to nominate a candidate. But there was nothing democratic about the selection process in the 1945 election in the Western Isles – because there was no competition. The only people who attended the meeting were Dr Macleod and Iain, so they elected Dr Macleod as chairman and Iain as the candidate. Conservative Central Office were informed, though not consulted, and Dr Macleod sent a telegram to Mr Churchill announcing Iain's selection. The Prime Minister's endorsement and good wishes arrived by return of post. It was a remarkable start in politics for a young man who within seven years was to become a Minister of Cabinet rank and the youngest Privy Councillor in Britain.

The Outer Hebrides stretch for 150 miles from the Butt of Lewis to Barra Head. The smaller islands are populated mainly by sheep, and the high level of unemployment, up to 25%, often leads either to alcoholism or emigration. No Conservative candidate has any chance of election and Iain stood as a National Government candidate in the hope of attracting a few additional votes. His election address was a short and simple document, containing ten policy points, five national and five local, and bearing the slogan 'A vote for Macleod is a vote for Churchill'.

The same party of young hecklers attended every meeting Iain addressed and asked the same questions at each, so that towards the end of the campaign they had established a friendly personal relationship with the candidate. On his way to the last meeting in a country district Iain came across the opposition car which had broken down by the roadside. He stopped and offered his habitual hecklers a lift, so that they could, as usual, interrupt his speech. They were delighted and disarmed by his humour and gave him an unusually fair hearing that evening.

The result of the election was a foregone conclusion. The Labour candidate, Malcolm Macmillan, was elected with a majority of 1600 over the Liberal, who came second. Macleod was bottom with 2756 votes in a poll of 13,000. He used to say that only his cousins voted for him, 'but I've got a lot of cousins in the Western Isles'.

Years later, in a letter to James Margach of the *Sunday Times*, Iain wrote:

> As a G.P. my father had no politics and we, as children, heard none at home. But he was in fact a life-long Liberal and invariably so voted at all local and national elections until 1945 when he voted (I presume!) for me. My mother, however, is and always was a true Conservative and they used to vote together, cancelling each other out. It is not, I think, fanciful to see both strains – Radical and Conservative – in my political make-up.

There were two other significant influences which contributed to his complex personality as well as to his political philosophy. James Margach drew attention to them in his excellent booklet *Here Come the Tories*, published just before the 1970 election. Macleod was the product of the Western Highlands by birth and of Yorkshire by upbringing and he combined a Celtic vision and imagination with the shrewd toughness and pragmatism absorbed in his boyhood in Airedale.

Iain Macleod had enjoyed his first taste of politics, but he was still in the Army and after the election was over he returned to his duties as DAQMG of the 50th Division, now stationed just outside York.

In August Divisional Headquarters was sent to Norway, where Iain lived in the Royal Norwegian Automobile Club at Oslo. One of his responsibilities was the control of supplies, including a large stock of wine captured from the Germans, who had looted it from France. He wrote later in the *Spectator*'s Notebook: 'All I did was to sign the chits and fix the prices. One shilling for red and white wines, 3s. for a bottle of champagne, 5s. for brandy and the top price of 7s. 6d. for Cointreau and Benedictine because I only had a few thousand bottles of them.'

The news of his wine store soon circulated in Oslo and a deputation of Norwegian Government Ministers called to see him to ask if he could release some wine for the civilian population for Christmas. He asked if a million bottles would be enough and when they gasped a grateful acceptance, he reached for a message pad and wrote out the order. 'My popularity flows, it never ebbs,' he told a friend.

As part of the Christmas celebrations just before Divisional Head-quarters returned home at the end of December, Iain wrote, produced and acted in another successful revue. And when they arrived at Dunbar, he organised a haggis supper for the mess, with plenty of whisky to wash it down. It was his last contribution as a soldier and perhaps a fitting one for a Highlander in an English Regiment. He always retained an affection for the Regiment and in 1954 presented an inscribed silver ink-stand to the 7th Battalion, which is now among the silver of the West Riding Battalion at the drill hall in Huddersfield. He was demobilised in January 1946 after six years in the army.

It had been an important period in his life. He had married and had two children. The ill-health and pain which he was to endure till he died had already begun. He had discovered, with surprise, his own ability; and he had found an interest in politics which would increasingly absorb his mind and his energies. For the first time in his life he had a high purpose and an ambition, which he knew he had the capacity to achieve.

CHAPTER 3

The Conservative Research Department and the Enfield Constituency 1946-1950

⟨∼∿⌒∿∽⟩

BY 1945 there had been a Conservative majority in Parliament for four-teen years. It was time for a change. The allied victory owed so much to the inspiration of Winston Churchill's leadership that most people ex-pected him to win the election, as Lloyd George had won the 'khaki' election of 1918; but the middle-aged still remembered the 1930s, and the younger voters wanted new men and new ideas more likely to reflect their own hopes and ambitions for the future. Such was the political ignorance of some of the electors that they imagined they could have a Socialist House of Commons and that Churchill would still be Prime Minister of Britain. When the Forces vote was counted, a Labour Govern-ment had been elected with a large majority. At the time this shocked traditional Conservatives. In retrospect, it was natural and probably inevitable. Iain Macleod always said it was not the electorate who were wrong; the Conservative Party had not yet adapted its outlook to postwar Britain and had mainly itself to thank for its own defeat. The Labour Party seemed more likely than the Tories to bring in a brave new world and the voters decided to take a chance.

After six years of war the world had changed. Taxation was high and the upper class was contracting under severe economic pressures. The large houses were being sold or broken up, and the green baize door which segregated the employer from his servants was vanishing. The upheaval of war had brought about a social revolution and had produced, if not a classless society, at least a social structure where the old differences were less noticeable and less important. But this change was not generally reflected in the membership of the Conservative Party in the first postwar Parliament.

58

Many of the older Tory members had retired or been defeated and there were new and younger faces on the opposition benches; but the Socialist victory had been so complete that most of the 1945 Conservative entry consisted of the representatives of county or suburban constituencies, where the Party was still traditionally entrenched, and they were usually of the same social pattern as their predecessors. This was not surprising.

The Conservative constituency associations had disintegrated or been deliberately dissolved during the war and the local party organisations were virtually non-existent. In the Chislehurst division of Kent, which I contested in the 1945 election, there were only sixteen voluntary workers, most of them elderly. A new candidate was probably chosen by the chairman of the association, as in Lewis, or at best by an *ad hoc* committee hastily convened from local residents, the majority of whom had been too old to serve in the Forces. They had a prewar outlook and in the county divisions were likely to choose political representatives who were younger editions of themselves. In the suburbs and the seaside resorts they tended to select candidates in a socially higher bracket than their own. In most cases a good war record and a good social background were the main requisites for nomination. It was an advantage to have been at Eton and to have served in the Brigade of Guards. Personal wealth still influenced some constituency committees because a rich candidate was often prepared to pay his own election expenses and to subscribe substantially to the funds of the local association[1]. In these circumstances the Conservative membership in the new House of Commons consisted largely, though not of course exclusively, of brigadiers and colonels and landowners or their sons. They represented the selection committees which had chosen them, but they were unlikely to alter the policies or the appearance of the Conservative Party.

The need for change was, however, recognised by some of the Conservative leaders, and especially by R. A. Butler, and was readily accepted by the younger men like Iain Macleod who helped him to adapt the party to the new political and economic environment. An instinctive sense of continuity had made Macleod a Conservative. His Highland ancestry had made him a Tory romantic. His background and upbringing identified

---

1 This was altered by the Maxwell Fyfe Committee, which reported in July 1949 (following a resolution moved by the author at the Conservative Party Conference at Brighton in 1947) and limited subscriptions to £50 p.a. for M.P.s and £25 p.a. for candidates; election expenses to be paid by the Associations.

him with the new type of classless politician who, in the next generation, was to reach the highest echelons of government.

He was the son of a doctor, not of a landowner; he had been to Fettes, not Eton, and to an unfashionable college, not Trinity or Christ Church; he had served in a line regiment, not in the Brigade of Guards. More important, he had nothing to unlearn. He was not inhibited by past policies or by social conditions he had never experienced. No change of approach was necessary, because he had not started with any preconceived ideas. He was learning politics at the beginning of a new chapter and, as he became interested, it was not in prewar Conservatism but in the new ideas which Butler and others were beginning to evolve. The ground was fallow and he could sow his own political seed.

The area in which the Conservative Party was weakest and to which it had given least thought was social policy. Butler had already put the 1944 Education Act on the Statute Book. He was now turning his attention to the other domestic issues which required a new approach. Among them were housing, health, pensions and national insurance; and it was with these problems that Macleod was soon to be concerned. It was chance that his interest and background synchronised with the work he was given to do and that this was in a sphere where new thought and new policies were emerging. It was chance, too, that his introduction to politics was under the general guidance and direction of Butler, who was the man most consciously seeking a Conservative answer to the new conditions in Britain.

Macleod always had a great affection and admiration for Rab Butler, whose ideas he found attractive and stimulating and entirely in tune with his own. Largely under Butler's influence as chairman of the Conservative Research Department, the whole outlook of the Tory Party changed and developed after the war; and the subsequent success of the outstanding team of younger men which he assembled round him owed much to his inspiration and reflected his own thinking. The Conservative Party has never adequately acknowledged the debt it owes to this exceptionally gifted, sometimes ambivalent but always progressive and forward-looking man.

Harold Macmillan's remarkable book, *The Middle Way*,[2] was the forerunner and greatly influenced those who were beginning to take an interest in politics in the prewar years; but Butler philosophically and Woolton organisationally did more than anyone to modernise the party

2 Macmillan, 1939.

and to make it attractive to the men who entered Parliament in the exceptional 'class of 1950'. In later years Macleod himself was to provide, because of his greater power of communication, an even more significant inspiration to the younger generation.

Soon after he was demobilised from the army, he applied for a position in the Conservative Party secretariat. His sister, Rhodabel, had facilitated this by mentioning Iain's name to Eleanor Yorke, who then spoke to her brother, Ralph Assheton, (later Lord Clitheroe) at that time Chairman of the Party.

The Conservative Research Department had been set up at Old Queen Street in 1929 and had worked on long-term policy throughout the 1930s. When the party went into opposition following the 1945 election, it became essential to revive and develop this organisation as a vehicle for the evolution of policy. But, in addition, ex-Ministers missed the civil service briefings on day to day issues to which they had long been accustomed, and a Parliamentary Secretariat was established to meet this need, under the direction of Henry Hopkinson (later to become Lord Colyton).

David Clarke, who was the director of the Research Department, interviewed Macleod early in 1946. He had already recruited Reginald Maudling, whose political thinking was more mature, and he considered that Enoch Powell, who joined the Secretariat at about the same time, had the greater intellectual force. He put Macleod third of the three in ability. Clarke acknowledged subsequently that he had underrated Iain's capacity and had not forseen his rapid political development. When asked for his comparative assessment ten years later, he said he thought Macleod the best politician of the three. Iain himself never made comparisons, although he sometimes said that if their different qualities and abilities could have been combined in one man, the result would have been the complete politician. But in 1946 Macleod's previous record and his limited knowledge of politics did not suggest an outstanding contribution. He seemed likely to become a competent member of the Secretariat. Clarke did not rate him higher than that.

As in the Western Isles, there was very little competition. The existing staff was so small that anyone who was at all suitable was appointed. Three or four relatively inexperienced young men were serving more than twenty parliamentary committees and Clarke was relieved to have a Scotsman to act as secretary of the Scottish Unionist Committee. It was Macleod's first assignment. A little later he took over national insurance, but he was not made responsible for health until Aneurin Bevan's Bill was already through the House.

He got on well with his party committees and became increasingly absorbed in the parliamentary side of his work. He was more interested in the immediate political problems than in long-term planning and seemed more of a politician and less of a specialist than many of his colleagues. He was never a technocrat.

It was a busy time because there was an immense amount of legislation, on which Shadow Ministers and Members needed detailed briefing for their work on the standing committees of Government Bills. Macleod soon proved his competence. His political interest and knowledge developed quickly and his enthusiasm increased noticeably when he realised that employment in the Secretariat was no bar to becoming a parliamentary candidate. He was clearly ambitious and membership of the House of Commons was the next step. R. A. Butler, in comparing Iain with his contemporaries, said later: 'What struck us most about him was that he was at that time the most intense and ambitious of the lot.'[3]

Henry Hopkinson regarded him as 'the quickest and wittiest' of his team in the Secretariat and Jim Thomas, (later Lord Cilcennin) who was then Deputy Chairman of the Party, told Selwyn Lloyd that they had found 'a real fizzer' on the staff called Iain Macleod.

As a member of the Secretariat he did not contribute to the Industrial Charter or the other early policy documents, which were the work of the Research Department under Butler's supervision. But he fully endorsed and agreed with them and, after his adoption as a Conservative candidate, he was an ardent advocate of the new thinking they represented.

Speed was often essential in the Secretariat and Macleod worked very quickly. Butler noted that 'he was so quick . . . he seemed able to write a minute or produce a brief in record time and he was extremely clear'. His methods were unusual. While others made notes before dictating, Michael Fraser, who shared a room with him for a time, recalls that Iain used to sit, almost lie, with his feet on the desk, gazing abstractedly out of the window. He had the telephone switched off and his concentration was complete. He was constructing the memorandum in his head. He then rang for a secretary and dictated it lucidly and without hesitation in its final form. Corrections were seldom necessary. It was a way of working which perfectly illustrated his quick, clear mind and his brilliant memory.

3 *24 Hours*, BBC, July 21, 1970.

He worked hard but he did not work long hours. He liked to start late and finish early, and he and Reggie Maudling often had convivial lunches together at Crockford's, where he was still playing bridge in his spare time. He virtually gave up the game soon after becoming Minister of Health and even in Research Department days he was playing much less frequently. He was becoming increasingly fascinated by politics and especially by the House of Commons itself.

The Research Department and the Secretariat, although run from the same building, were at first separately organised. They were amalgamated in the autumn of 1948 when the Library and Information Department of the Conservative Central Office was added to form the Research Department as it has operated ever since. It was still not a large organisation. When the party was in office it had only about twenty-five officers, and even in opposition a maximum of thirty-five. R. A. Butler was its chairman and the three joint directors were David Clarke, Henry Hopkinson and Percy Cohen.[4]

It was only after the amalgamation that specialist sections were formed. Maudling was made responsible for the economic subjects, Ursula Branstom for foreign affairs, Brigadier Blunt for defence and Gerald Sayers for the Commonwealth and colonies. Macleod and Powell became joint heads of home affairs, which included housing and all the social services. They shared an office in 34 Old Queen Street, which was an overflow from No. 24. Powell left the Research Department in the summer of 1949 to devote more time to his Wolverhampton constituency, and from then until the 1950 election campaign Macleod was in sole charge of the home affairs section.

He played a considerable part in the drafting of the social service sections of the party's first complete postwar policy document *The Right Road for Britain*, which was published in July 1949. This brought together the whole spectrum of Conservative policy by adding to the industrial and agricultural charters the new social service policies with which Macleod had been mainly concerned. A shorter and distilled version of it called *This is the Road* became the party's manifesto for the 1950 general election.

After he entered Parliament Macleod continued to contribute to the development of party policy by working, under Butler's direction, on the

4 When Hopkinson entered the House of Commons in 1950 and Clarke became Principal of Swinton College a year later, Michael Fraser and Cohen were joint directors until Cohen's retirement in 1959 when Fraser assumed the sole directorship of the department.

1955 election manifesto, *United for Peace and Progress*, which was edited by him, Michael Fraser and Peter Goldman. And from 1957 to 1959 he was chairman of the policy study group and a member of Harold Macmillan's Steering Committee, which was responsible for the 1959 election manifesto *The Next Five Years*. As Chairman of the Party from 1961 to 1963 he formed a chairman's policy committee to prepare for the 1964 election, but this was rather oddly constituted (I was a member of it myself!) and, so far as I remember, did not do very useful work. Nevertheless, although for his first two years in the party organisation Macleod was mainly concerned with day to day matters, for the next fifteen years he was closely and personally involved in the evolution of longer-term Conservative policy.

Macleod was always a quick and voracious reader, mostly of poetry and detective stories, and during his four years at Old Queen Street he developed an avid taste for political biography, especially of Victorian statesmen. This may have influenced his style of speaking at large meetings and party conferences. It must certainly have taught him some of the ways and means of achieving political objectives. Although his personal contacts with Winston Churchill were few, he was a great admirer of Churchill's power of oratory, which was cast in a Victorian mould. But Macleod was always flexible and, as the style of speaking in the House of Commons changed and became less formal, he instinctively adapted his speeches to the mood and atmosphere of Parliament without ever losing the ability to move and inspire a larger and less sophisticated audience.

Apart from Michael Fraser, whom Iain had known since his school-days at Fettes, his closest friends and associates at Old Queen Street were Reggie Maudling and Enoch Powell. Macleod's friendship with Reggie Maudling was close and enduring. Over the twenty-five years of their association they had no serious differences; their political philosophy and their approach to important issues were the same and although they were sometimes in a sense rivals, this never affected their personal friendship. Indeed, they had a private and informal pact that if at any time both were candidates for the leadership of the Party, whichever appeared to be leading in the race at that moment would not be opposed by the other.

Maudling was no doubt less ambitious than Macleod or Powell, but his easy-going manner is misleading. His relaxed, almost lethargic appearance conceals a quick mind and a firm purpose, and those who imagine that his enjoyment of the good things of life indicates indolence or lack of interest in public affairs are very wide of the mark. As Macleod did, he works quickly and understands how to delegate. He has an exceptionally acute intelligence and understands very well what is politically possible. His limitation as a politician is his relative inability, as compared with Macleod or Powell, to move an audience to cheers or tears.

Iain Macleod and Enoch Powell were also friends in the Research Department days, when Enoch sometimes stayed with Iain for weekends at Enfield. Both men were ambitious, brilliant, courageous and sincere, and each had the power of communication. They were perhaps the only two Conservative politicians of their generation who understood the importance of words and how to use them to inspire their fellow country-men. No doubt Powell had the more formidable intellect of the two, but it was also more rigid and more ruthless. Macleod admired Powell's work and thought he had the finest and best-trained mind in the House of Commons.

In an article in the *Spectator* in 1965, he wrote: 'I am a fellow-traveller but sometimes I leave Powell's train a few stations down the line before it reaches, and sometimes crashes into, the terminal buffers. I am certainly less logical in my political approach, but I would argue that Powell suffers sometimes from an excess of logic.' He thought Powell's speeches 'carefully drafted and usually written out in full before delivery' were meant to provoke and to irritate. There was an element of over-statement in them which was not accidental. He respected Powell's religious con-victions which he described as 'the faith sometimes of a martyr, sometimes of a fanatic'.

For nearly twenty years the paths of these two men ran together, diverged and rejoined; but after Powell's first speech on race relations and immigration in March 1968, as a result of which he was asked to leave the Shadow Cabinet, they drifted apart and Macleod said he would never again sit in a Cabinet with Powell. But he knew well how difficult life could be made for anyone out of favour with the establishment and he took the trouble to be seen in public with Powell at the 1968 party con-ference. Despite this gesture, he thought Powell's speeches on race issues were horrifying and literally hateful in every sense of the word. They seemed to him unbalanced, intolerant and inhumane and, as Powell grew more extreme in his views and more fanatical in the expression of them, the two men became almost completely estranged.

In a uniquely discordant public comment on the day Macleod died – that when they entered public life no two men were closer together and that by the time of Iain's death no two were further apart – Powell expressed, bluntly and honestly, no more than the truth, though it was insensitive to choose that moment to proclaim it. It greatly distressed Iain's family, but he might himself have considered it a compliment.

*

Iain Macleod always believed that chance played an important part in the development of any career and it certainly did on many occasions in his own. Just as his candidature in the 1945 election was due to the chance that he was on leave in the Western Isles at the time, so his adoption for Enfield, which he was to represent in Parliament for twenty years, only arose because he happened to be playing in a bridge tournament at Harrogate when he received a telegram from David Clarke, offering him the position in the Secretariat for which he had recently been interviewed. He cabled his acceptance and told his bridge partner, Dr Fraser Allen, who was then in practice at Enfield, that he must now make his home in or near London. Allen immediately invited Iain to stay until he could find somewhere suitable to live. He also mentioned that the Conservative Party in Enfield were looking for a new parliamentary candidate. By chance again, the chairman of the Enfield Association, Mr Douglas Waite, was a patient of Dr Allen's, who knew his telephone number. Iain telephoned Waite that evening:

'I hear you are looking for a new Tory candidate and as I am coming to live in Enfield, I thought you might like to include me on your list.'

'But we've already got forty-seven names.'

'Then forty-eight won't matter.'

There was a pause and a dry chuckle:

'Come and see me, young man, when you arrive here.'

He did so and his visit began a friendship which lasted until Waite's death.

Macleod was the only applicant among the forty-eight who was not on the official Central Office list of approved candidates. It was an unusual way for a future Chairman of the Party to begin his parliamentary career, and but for Waite and the Enfield Young Conservatives the opportunity might not have materialised.

Macleod had reached the short list of four candidates, but Waite was so certain that he would be the winner that he failed to inform the Executive Council of the selection committee's decision that, if the second candidate came within ten per cent of the winning candidate, both would go forward to a special general meeting of the association for the final selection. Of the thirty-two Young Conservative members of the executive, thirty-one had voted for Iain, but he had still only come second, although within ten per cent of the top candidate. When Waite announced that, under these circumstances, both would go before a special general meeting, there was an uproar and forty people walked out in disgust, alleging that the selection had been rigged and that Macleod's name should not be further considered. But Waite stuck to his guns and at the general meeting which followed, Iain made the first of the real Macleod speeches and easily carried the day. The other three candidates on the short list all became MPs and two of them are still in the House of Commons.

At the time of Macleod's adoption in April 1946, Enfield had not been divided into East and West; it was still one constituency. The Labour majority in 1945 had been over 12,000, so it was not a hopeful prospect. At the adoption meeting, the president of the association observed gloomily that he was sure Macleod was 'the sort of man who would do his best to reduce the majority'. It was not exactly a clarion call to battle But two years later the redistribution of seats divided Enfield into two constituencies which entirely changed the situation. Macleod had the more Conservative western half and a splendid team of Young Conservatives, which included Colin Turner, later M.P. for Woolwich. They were all ardent supporters and worked very hard for him before and during the election campaign.

The Macleods found a house called Ladykirk on the Ridgeway at Enfield, which they bought with the aid of a mortgage. They lived there for the next thirteen years until Iain became Colonial Secretary and had to move to London.

Douglas Waite took Macleod round the borough to meet all the people who mattered and on one occasion remarked that he ought to see 'Mrs . . . . .'s beautiful garden'. Iain replied glumly: 'Another bloody garden.' But he worked hard to become known in Enfield, and Eve was a great help and asset to him. There are probably few political wives who have worked so consistently and selflessly in their husbands' constituencies. She took a real interest in people's individual problems and always knew (and cared) when a party worker was ill or had just had a baby. She supported all the worthwhile causes and organisations in the borough and she was and still is a member of the local Bench. Mrs Waite always said that Eve was responsible for fifty per cent of Iain's success and, if she meant as a constituency member, it was certainly an understatement. After he became a Minister and had less time available for Enfield, Eve fulfilled almost every engagement he could not manage. It became a family joke and when she departed without him to attend a local function, Iain used to remind her with the two words 'also representing' that she should mention that she was deputising for him. But she was not merely a substitute. She was herself a good speaker as well as an attractive, sympathetic personality. For years she virtually carried the constituency.

Macleod's interest in sport made him the automatic president of every games club in the district and he enjoyed watching matches in which the Enfield football club, the Saracens rugby club or the Enfield and Cock-fosters cricket club were taking part. He was a governor of Enfield Grammar School and went to its meetings whenever he could; and he made a point of attending the Conservative Association's functions, however small, including the annual dinners of the branches and of the Conservative Clubs.

Almost every Sunday the Macleods attended the morning service at the Church of St Mary Magdalene, Windmill Hill, where Iain was a sidesman for fifteen years and sometimes read the lesson. He believed in religious observance and respected Christianity, but religion did not play an important part in his life. He would have liked to believe and envied those who could – indeed he sometimes said that he would like to die a Roman Catholic – but he was unable to achieve sufficient faith to accept personally all the tenets of the Church. Although the expression may seem contradictory, he could perhaps best be described as a Christian agnostic.

Since the war Members of Parliament have become glorified welfare officers in their own constituencies and people expect to be able to bring any personal problem, however inappropriate, to their Member for his help or advice. Exceptionally, Macleod never held the political 'surgeries' which the rest of us consider obligatory. He took the view that he lived locally and that anyone could call and see him by appointment, so a 'surgery' was unnecessary. But he took infinite trouble to help his constituents in their difficulties.

The Enfield public as a whole were proud that their MP was a national figure, whom they read about in the newspapers and saw regularly on television. Some of his party workers were less enthusiastic. They admired their Member, but found him difficult to get to know. He was not interested in 'small talk', did not suffer fools at all, let alone gladly, and had few social graces of a superficial kind.

His old friends understood his habit of 'withdrawing' mentally during a conversation, but others found it disconcerting. One evening he was sitting next to a distinguished colonial governor at a dinner in London and said suddenly: 'I have been writing a memorandum for the Cabinet' (he meant composing it in his head), 'so I have only been giving you a quarter of my mind. Now I have finished it and I can give you my whole attention.' It was not a very flattering conversational gambit.

When he was leaving the Enfield Parish Church one morning, the vicar introduced him to two prominent members of the local Labour Party, to whom he talked in a friendly way for a minute or two. He then went into one of his typical 'withdrawals' and totally ignored a group of leading Conservative ladies, walking straight past them and not even acknowledging their 'good-mornings'. The matter was raised at the next meeting of the Executive Council.

He was notoriously absent-minded about his clothes and would often wear a different coloured sock on each foot. At a party conference at Brighton he appeared in the BBC studio one evening wearing a dinner jacket and pin-striped trousers for a television performance.

Sometimes he offended people by allowing too little time to talk to them. One one occasion a constituency cocktail party was arranged at someone's private house especially to enable him to meet a number of new arrivals, who were thought likely to become active party workers. He entered the room, spoke briefly to two people near the door and left. A few days later he commented to the Association chairman that the party had been an excellent idea as 'it gave me the opportunity to circulate and meet so many new people'.

Aneurin Bevan often created the same sort of impression among his party activists in Ebbw Vale as Iain Macleod did at Enfield. Both were meticulous over constituents' problems and both evoked much public enthusiasm. But neither was universally popular with his own local workers and supporters. Associations can be represented either by an assiduous but probably undistinguished back-bencher who gives much time to his constituency, or by a member of the Cabinet (or Shadow Cabinet) who is also in demand as a party speaker throughout the country. They cannot have both. Except for his first two years in Parliament and the short period when he was editor of the *Spectator*, Iain Macleod was a party leader for the whole of his twenty years as an M.P. and he could not devote as much time to Enfield as he would have wished.

Although he lived in his constituency during most of his political career, he did not recommend this to others: 'A member is apt to be drawn into all the hundred and one small disputes and differences of opinion. I think it is wiser for him to be near, but not on the door step.' He held strong views on the political relationship between a Member and his supporters. In an article for the Enfield Conservative magazine he wrote: 'An M.P. is the standard-bearer for his constituency, but he is not its lackey. He would be expected to speak for the party which elected him, but this must never mean that he should be expected to vote for or to support any cause that he believes is wrong. Fortunately the Tory Party, in this difficult field, has always been wiser than its opponents.'

During the six years between his discharge from the army and his appointment as Minister of Health, Ian Macleod was still playing bridge whenever he could spare the time – one evening he left Crockford's with his pockets full of gambling chips, in order to address a Churches meeting – on the subject of gambling! He supplemented his slender salary at the Research Department by writing a weekly bridge article for the *Sunday Times* for which he was paid £500 p.a. It took him half an hour to write this each weekend. He also set and judged the bridge competitions run by the paper.

One evening in 1947 he was playing in an important match at Crockford's and he asked Eve if she would go and watch the game. At great inconvenience she arranged to do so and sat patiently (though uncomprehendingly as she is not a bridge player) by the table for two or three hours. No one paid the least attention to her and eventually, tired and discouraged, she took the last bus and underground back to Enfield. Some hours later Iain arrived home by taxi and greeted her rather petulantly: 'I asked you to come and watch me play and I was very disappointed when you didn't.' His concentration had been so intense that he was quite unaware that she had been sitting a few feet away from him for most of the evening.

In 1951 Iain wrote *Bridge is an Easy Game*[5], on which he earned royalties of about £80 p.a. for the next twenty years. The title is revealing. It was a witty, humorous, rather arrogant title for a difficult game, but it is not an arrogant book and was not designed to show the author as a brilliant player. Macleod was always intolerant of pretentious people whether at the bridge table or elsewhere, but he had no false modesty and when he was asked many years later whether competition bridge was something he had

5 Falcon Press, 1952. In the fly-leaf of the copy which he presented to the Library of the House of Commons, Iain wrote: 'To my colleagues in the House of Commons—this strange cuckoo for the miscellaneous shelf.'

loved doing or something that he did superlatively well he replied, 'it was just something that I did superlatively well.' *Bridge is an Easy Game* is a sound, well written book; warm, intelligent and readable. It is a teaching book which medium standard players can understand and profit from, but it was not intended for beginners. It was written to help and encourage the reasonably good player to improve. If he had had time, Macleod should have followed this publication by others, but active politics were occupying his full attention and it was nearly ten years before he published another book.

On February 23, 1950 he was elected to Parliament for Enfield West with a majority of 9,193 votes.

CHAPTER 4

The House of Commons
1950–1952

THE Labour Government had been elected in 1945 with a massive majority of 146 seats in the House of Commons. But in the years which followed its popularity waned, and in the 1950 election it could only cling precariously to office with an overall majority of six.

There was a large new Conservative entry of exceptionally high quality, which included Julian Amery, Robert Carr, William Deedes, Lionel Heald, Edward Heath, Charles Hill, Harry Hylton-Foster (who later became Speaker), Aubrey Jones, Iain Macleod, Reginald Maudling, David Ormsby-Gore (later Lord Harlech), Enoch Powell, Christopher Soames, Harold Watkinson and Richard Wood. All these became senior Ministers. There were also some notable 'characters' like Geoffrey Hirst, Gerald Nabarro and Ted Leather who, though never Ministers, were independent minded Parliamentarians and made a real contribution in the House of Commons.[1]

Of the ninety-three new Conservative Members, twenty-four later became Privy Councillors and no less than forty-one became Ministers. Thirteen are now peers, fifty-five have died, retired or been defeated and only twenty-five of us are still in the House of Commons. Aneurin Bevan described it as 'the finest Tory vintage in history'.

The House of Commons, when Macleod entered it, was rougher and more demanding than at any time for the next twenty years until the passage, in 1971, of the Industrial Relations Bill. After six years of socialism, with large doses of nationalisation and other indigestible legislation, the Tories had come within an ace of regaining power. It did not seem likely that the Labour Government could survive for long on so slim a

---

[1] Among others in the 1950 entry who were to make a mark in the House of Commons or outside it were Cub Alport, Reginald Bevins, Cyril Black, Bernard Braine, Pat Hornsby-Smith, Montgomery Hyde, Gilbert Longden, Laddie Lucas, Angus Maude, Richard Nugent, Ian Orr-Ewing, Jackie Smyth and John Tilney.

majority and we were determined to force them out as soon as possible.

In retrospect, the tactics we adopted were unattractive. At the time they seemed rather fun and a legitimate part of the game. We 'paired' sparingly, kept the House sitting late night after night, and sometimes all night, and in the process endangered the physical health of some of the older members. We forced unexpected divisions and often reduced the Labour majority almost to vanishing point. On one occasion we all left the House early, ostentatiously carrying our brief cases and evidently bound for home. Thinking there would be no further divisions, many Labour Members drifted away, but the absent Conservatives had assembled in the nearby houses of colleagues who were 'on the bell'[2] and hurried back to vote when the pre-arranged division was called. The ruse succeeded and we defeated the Government by eighteen votes on a minor Order to reduce the weekly cheese ration from three ounces to two ounces.

Bob Boothby spoke openly of 'harrying the Government' and that is exactly what we were doing. It was effective but it was unwise; because when we were ourselves returned eighteen months later with a majority of only seventeen, the Socialists, justifiably, paid us back in our own coin. 'The Bing Boys', a left-wing group on the Labour benches, led by Geoffrey Bing, the Member for Hornchurch, developed the technique of the fillibuster to a fine art, reminiscent of the tactics of the Irish Members in the previous century. Now it was the Conservatives who had to 'keep a house' and over the next two years many of us went very short of sleep.

Eventually public opinion brought about a welcome relief. The electorate was not impressed by lurid newspaper reports of the hours we kept in the House of Commons and people were shocked when they read that men who were seriously ill were being brought in ambulances from the Westminster Hospital to vote in the division lobbies. It did not sound an efficient way to run the country and it wasn't. Gradually it dawned on the politicians that the public thought we were behaving like irresponsible schoolboys. When this was realised the tactics changed and the atmosphere slowly improved. But the years 1950 to 1953 had been a rough apprenticeship.

Macleod was quickly off the mark in the new Parliament. He made his maiden speech on March 14, 1950, only six sitting days after the House

2 Members living within a few minutes by car of Parliament Square can have a bell installed in their house which rings whenever a division is called in the House of Commons.

assembled. He spoke briefly, for thirteen minutes, but he spoke with knowledge. Much of the speech was directly comparable with the first chapter of *One Nation*, to be published later in the year, and many of the points in the speech were repeated and amplified in the pamphlet.

The occasion he chose was a supply day debate on the supplementary estimates of £148 million, and he drew attention to the fact that two-thirds of this, nearly £100 million, was attributable to the Health Service. The Chancellor of the Exchequer, Sir Stafford Cripps, in leading for the Government, had announced that there would be a ceiling on National Health Service expenditure for the next year, but Macleod pointed out that the cost of the scheme had already grown from £152 million a year to £400 million; that it was bound to rise still farther;[3] and that the Chancellor and the Minister of Health were in the same position as Alice and the Red Queen – they had to run as fast as they could to stay in the same place.

He questioned the priorities in the Service and pointed out that the bill for the general dental services was exceeding the bill for the general medical services. 10,750 dentists were being paid more than 21,000 doctors. He thought this an indefensible position. He also questioned the priorities within the dental service itself and said that in many areas the school dental arrangements had virtually broken down. He supported the view, which had recently been expressed by Anthony Eden, that we should not help, indiscriminately, everyone alike. It was another twenty years before this principle was to be implemented under the present Government by giving most help to those in the greatest need.

The Times commented: 'Among the maiden speeches which added to the quality of a notable debate, there were thoughtful contributions from Dr Charles Hill and Mr Ian [sic] Macleod', and there was quite a full report of the speech on the parliamentary page. The popular press ignored it and whereas the *Daily Telegraph* gave Charles Hill several paragraphs, it reported Macleod in five lines. The *Guardian* did not mention his speech at all.

Despite the lack of newspaper interest, Macleod had made a good start, which established him in the House as one who could speak with authority on the sort of subject not then fashionable in the Tory Party. He used to say that the best way to get to the Front Bench quickly was to be a practising barrister representing a Scottish seat because there were never enough with these qualifications to fill the positions of Lord Advocate

3 The National Health Service now costs £2,000 million a year.

and Solicitor-General for Scotland. He might have added with almost as much accuracy that the surest way for a Conservative to get on in those days was to specialise in the social services.

Conservatives tended to concentrate on foreign and Commonwealth affairs, defence, agriculture and finance; and, at any rate in 1950, there were few with any real knowledge of the social services. There was therefore less competition, and within two years Macleod had become successively secretary, vice-chairman and chairman of the Conservative Parliamentary Health and Social Security Committee. It was unusual for a new member with so little House of Commons experience to rise so rapidly to the chairmanship of a back-bench committee. It gave him an advantage in the House itself because, as an officer of the Committee, he was usually called earlier in debates on these subjects than most of his back-bench colleagues, including Enoch Powell. In his biography of Powell,[4] Andrew Roth wrote: 'The Powell–Macleod competition was visible to the naked eye. Their habit of popping up together to speak earned them the nicknames of Tweedledum and Tweedledee from Dr Edith Summerskill.' And she sometimes confused the two. Perhaps these opportunities in the House made Powell jealous. At any rate, when Iain was made Minister of Health, Roth comments that for a few weeks Powell 'turned sour on Macleod, virtually cutting him dead'.

Although he sometimes described his maiden speech as 'a pedestrian affair', Iain wrote in the *Spectator* fourteen years later that he had repeated it at intervals over the next two years and found himself Minister of Health: 'Get a good speech and stick to it,' he advised, 'it's the shortest way home.' And indeed his speeches as a back-bencher, which averaged six a session, were mostly on social service, and especially health service, subjects. The exceptions were speeches on the Army Estimates, the Bishops' Retirement Act, and the Bermondsey Corporation in the spring of 1951.

Macleod loved the House of Commons and was never in awe of it: 'Respect and affection, yes,' he wrote, 'exhilaration and depression, yes; fear, no.'[5]

One of Iain Macleod's lesser known appointments was that of director of the London Municipal Society, a post he held between 1950 and 1952, under the chairmanship of John Hare (now Lord Blakenham). It had become a somewhat neolithic institution and there was plenty of scope for

4 *Enoch Powell: Tory Tribune*, Macdonald, 1970.
5 The *Spectator*, November 27, 1964.

Macleod's clarity of mind. Hare was much impressed by his skill and efficiency and the administrative experience he gained there must have been helpful when he became a Minister. He was responsible, as director, for the Conservative Party organisation in the LCC elections, and many of our candidates recall how encouraging he was to those with little experience. Weekend conferences were held to assist them, and at one of these Macleod took the part of a Labour councillor. Our candidates had to answer his speech and try to catch him out at question time. His performance was so convincing that many in the audience were red-faced with rage over the arguments he advanced, and Humphry Berkeley, then Political Education Officer for the London area, records that he had no idea, until then, of Iain's acting ability.

After his four years in the Parliamentary Secretariat and the Research Department, in which he had specialised in the social services, it was not surprising that Macleod's interest in them continued to occupy most of his time and attention after he entered Parliament. His work outside the Chamber was largely concerned with the evolution of party policy in this field.

Some other new members were thinking along the same lines. Soon after the 1950 election Angus Maude and Cub Alport (at that time MP for Colchester, now Lord Alport) discussed the failure of the Conservative leadership to devise and project a consistent policy for the development and financing of the social services. After a further talk with Gilbert Longden these three decided to invite a few other newly elected colleagues to form a discussion group. The first recruits were Robert Carr, Richard Fort and John Rodgers. Rodgers then enrolled Edward Heath and shortly afterwards Iain Macleod was invited to join the Group. The eight members then met for lunch at 16 Queen's Gate, and Macleod informed the others that he had been asked to write a pamphlet on the social services for the Conservative Political Centre. This was to be published before the 1950 party conference and Macleod suggested that it should become a joint production of the Group, each member of which would contribute a section to it. He also proposed that Enoch Powell, who had a special knowledge of housing, should be invited to join them. These nine thus became the original members of the group. Later the number was increased to twelve and eventually to twenty-four; but during Macleod's time the average number attending each meeting was eight or nine.

Macleod and Angus Maude were appointed joint editors of the CPC booklet, and Macleod took the chair at the first meeting. At later meetings, which were held to discuss the drafts for each chapter, the chair was taken by the author of the chapter under consideration. By the time the House rose at the end of July, the drafts had been corrected and agreed and Angus Maude completed the editing and press preparation during the summer recess. But no title had been decided upon. Eventually Maude thought of *One Nation*, agreed it on the telephone with Macleod, and sent it to the printers. It became the name not only of the pamphlet but of the group. R. A. Butler agreed to write a foreword. *One Nation* was published in October 1950 with the usual nervous caution that no one was to assume that anything in it was official party policy. This was of course true, but it greatly influenced future Conservative policy for the social services and it also contributed, with Harmar Nicholls' notable conference speech, to the adoption, in opposition, of the 300,000 houses target. This demand amounted to a revolt from the floor of the conference. Labour's housing programme, never impressive, had reached its peak in 1948, and the annual provision of new houses had since dropped to 178,000. Prefabricated units were still in use. By 1950 people expected more both in quality and quantity. The platform's acceptance of 300,000 houses a year was a major policy commitment which, though undoubtedly right in social and political terms, was later a source of difficulty to Butler who, as Chancellor of the Exchequer after the 1951 election, had to allocate a somewhat disproportionate amount of the national resources to its achievement. Ironically, in view of their later rivalry for the leadership of the party, the realisation of the housing target greatly enhanced the reputation of Harold Macmillan, who was at that time Minister of Housing and Local Government.

Macleod was often referred to in the press as the chairman of the One Nation Group, but in fact it never had a chairman. The chairmanship rotated at each meeting. Owing to his knowledge of social policy, however, Macleod did act as a stimulating discussion leader and his influence on the early work of One Nation was considerable.

Soon after Parliament re-assembled in the autumn of 1950, the Group decided to meet regularly every Thursday evening. Enoch Powell became the secretary. He kept the minutes of the Group and made the arrangements for the meetings, which usually took the form of a dinner and discussion in Dining Room A at the House of Commons. Other members sometimes sensed an underlying jealousy between Macleod and Powell, but at this period their views were in harmony and they worked closely together, each influencing the other. Both were regular attenders and seldom missed a meeting. From time to time the Group invited one or other of the Party leaders to dine with them. Rab Butler came on two or three occasions and Eden and Macmillan once each, but there was a reluctance to have guests as it was felt that they tended to inhibit the discussions.

The first change in the membership of One Nation took place after the 1951 election. Edward Heath had been a junior Opposition Whip in the 1950 Parliament and now became a Government Whip. It was decided that membership of the administration was incompatible with that of an independent group and would lead to a conflict of loyalties. Heath therefore resigned and was succeeded by Reginald Maudling, who was a member for only a short time because he became a Junior Minister soon afterwards. On May 8, 1952 the minutes record: 'Note taken that Iain Macleod had ceased to be a member of the Group on appointment as Minister of Health.' He was invited back as a guest whenever an 'old boys' dinner was held and he rejoined One Nation in 1963 when he resigned from the Government after declining to serve under Sir Alec Douglas-Home.

The Group sought to influence the party's thinking in any way it could. For instance, it decided in advance which candidates to support for election as officers of party committees, including the 1922 Committee, and voted accordingly when the elections took place. Even 'plumping' for the election of the 1922 Committee's executive was not unknown.

One Nation was trying consciously to make the Conservative Party more classless in its outlook and more progressive in its policies. The members of the Group were dissatisfied with the look of the Conservative Party and what it seemed to stand for. They felt there was a lack of social purpose and a lack of concern for people as individuals. They wanted a more positive approach to these problems than the Conservative Opposition had so far shown.

Iain Macleod sympathised with many of the Labour Party's ideals, but rejected its tendency to think and talk of people in terms of classes or categories. He believed the unit of concern should be the family, and he wanted to see as many people as possible owning property in its widest sense, with a minimum standard for the unfortunate provided by the State. In the first chapter of *One Nation* he wrote:

There is a fundamental disagreement between Conservatives and Socialists on the questions of social policy. Socialists would give the same benefits to everyone, whether or not the help is needed, and indeed whether or not the country's resources are adequate. We believe that we must first help those in need. Socialists believe that the State should provide an average standard. We believe that it should provide a minimum standard, above which people should be free to rise as far as their industry, their thrift, their ability or their genius may take them.

He also rejected the socialist view that private charity has little place in a public service. The health chapter of the booklet set out the One Nation policy for the hospitals, the doctors, the dentists, the ophthalmic service and the pharmaceutical service. It dealt also with the role of the local health authorities, with future extensions of the health service and with the principles the group considered should be followed for financing it. Most of the policy points advocated by One Nation have since been implemented.

Macleod was interested in the problems of ordinary people, what they wanted and what they needed; and he was deeply and genuinely concerned about unemployment because he realised that, below a certain level of security, people could not exercise personal choice or control their own lives. But he never believed in the socialist concept of equality, which he thought an impossible proposition. He thought the objective should be 'to see that men had an equal chance to make themselves unequal'. He liked the idea of a society classless in its thinking, diverse but not divided. As with Disraeli's 'two nations', the rich and the poor, *One Nation* was the essence of his approach to politics. It was much more to him than the name of a pamphlet or a group. It summarised a philosophy and proclaimed an ideal.[6]

In January 1952 the Conservative Political Centre published a forty page booklet entitled *The Social Services: Needs and Means* by Iain Macleod and Enoch Powell. It contained evidence of radical thinking, including charges for hospital beds and for prescriptions, and attracted much favourable comment in the press. *The Times* devoted two-thirds of a column to reviewing it, and in the first leading article on January 17th

6 Iain Macleod's forward thinking is well illustrated in a lecture, entitled '*Sanitas Sanitatum* —The condition of the people', which he delivered to the Conservative Political Centre in 1954 and which set out not only his approach to the problems of his department (he was then Minister of Health), but his social thinking over a wider range and indeed his whole political philosophy. The lecture is a long one and is therefore included as an appendix to this book.

commented: 'Some clear thinking is the chief merit of a provocative booklet issued to-day . . . they (the authors) conclude rightly that the question that should be asked is not "should a means test be applied to a social service" but "why should any social service be provided without a means test".' 'Peterborough', in the *Daily Telegraph*, observed that he had spent a profitable weekend reading *Bridge is an Easy Game* and went on to refer to the new pamphlet which had 'attracted attention'. Peterborough concluded: 'To both the Welfare State and bridge Mr Macleod seeks to apply system. Acol's advantage is that it requires no legislation.'

When Winston Churchill returned to Downing Street in October 1951, some were surprised that he did not recognise the ability of more of the younger men, like Macleod, who had made their mark in the short 1950 Parliament. Very few were given junior appointments. Despite this there was none of the frustration which had been apparent for the same reason on the Labour benches in the 1945 Parliament. The Tory Party tends to command greater loyalty from its rank and file than the Labour Party, and in any event the stars of the future could afford to wait. Some of the older men in office would not remain there for long; when he became Prime Minister, Anthony Eden would no doubt draw on the younger talent; and with their patron, R. A. Butler, as Chancellor of the Exchequer, the bright young men knew that it was only a matter of time before their turn would come. Meanwhile, they could add to their experience by taunting the Socialist ex-Ministers for their failures and by improving the Bills brought forward by their own Government.

Under any circumstances Macleod would certainly have been one of the first of the new entry to be promoted to the Front Bench, but as in the case of Maudling and others, this would normally have come about with the offer in due course of a parliamentary secretaryship. Macleod's dramatic appointment as Minister of Health, without previous experience as a junior Minister, was – as with the candidature for Enfield – a combination of luck and the ability to seize an unexpected opportunity when the ball rolled his way.

The chance came with the Second Reading debate on the National Health Service Bill, which took place on March 27, 1952. The Bill imposed the prescription and dental charges which the Labour Government had written into their own 1949 Bill but had not implemented. These supplemented the charges for false teeth and spectacles which were introduced by Hugh Gaitskell in his 1951 budget. The Bill was introduced by the Minister of Health, Captain Harry Crookshank, who combined this portfolio somewhat uneasily with the Leadership of the House of Commons. Crookshank was followed by the Shadow Minister, Dr Edith Summerskill, from the Opposition front bench. As chairman of the party's Health Committee, Macleod would normally have been the first back-bencher to be called on the Government side of the House, and when he vacated the Chair, Mr Speaker Morrison suggested to the Deputy-Speaker, Sir Charles MacAndrew, that he should call Macleod when Dr Summer-skill sat down. But Charlie MacAndrew was a kind-hearted man. He knew that a new Member, Ingress Bell, was waiting anxiously to make his maiden speech; he said that he would like to put Bell out of his misery by calling him next. The Speaker agreed, so Bell followed Summerskill. Aneurin Bevan, who had been Minister of Health in the Labour Govern-ment and was the architect of the Health Service, then rose to speak from the Opposition side of the House. He and Harold Wilson and John Freeman had all resigned from the previous Government, ostensibly in protest against the imposition of the 1951 Health Service charges, so Bevan was now on the back benches, but as a Privy Councillor he had priority and was called at once. By interposing Ingress Bell the Deputy Speaker had unwittingly given Macleod a golden opportunity. He had expected to follow Edith Summerskill, but he now had a far more exciting prospect – the chance of replying to the greatest debater in the House of Commons on Bevan's own ground, the National Health Service. It was also Macleod's own ground. His extraordinary memory enabled him to carry in his head the facts and figures which were the product of years of research and which he could now use with devastating effect in his duel with Bevan. He threw away the notes he had jotted down for a reply to Dr Summerskill and concentrated on listening to Bevan and preparing in his mind a speech which would demolish the former Minister. It was a David and Goliath opportunity, but there was no one in the House except Macleod who would have had the ability and background knowledge to exploit it. And now destiny dealt him another card. Winston Churchill had come into the House to hear Nye Bevan. But for this he would not have heard Macleod.

When Bevan sat down, the Prime Minister was rising slowly to leave the Chamber, but his attention was caught by the opening sentence of Macleod's speech: 'I want to deal closely and with relish with the vulgar, crude and intemperate speech to which the House of Commons has just listened.'

It was an arresting start and, instead of leaving at once, Churchill remained, perched on the edge of the bench, waiting to hear if the next few sentences would be as good as the first. Macleod proceeded to deal shortly and effectively with the Liberal attitude to the Bill and then with that of the official Opposition. Edith Summerskill had left the Chamber but he demolished Hilary Marquand who had unwisely interrupted him from the Labour Front Bench. By this time the Prime Minister had sat back in his seat opposite the despatch box and was listening attentively. Macleod turned to deal with Bevan. He welcomed him back to the House after a brief indisposition and commented that 'a debate on the National Health Service without the Right Honourable Gentleman would be like putting on Hamlet with no one in the part of the first grave-digger.' He had intended to say that a Health Service debate without Bevan would be like playing Hamlet without the ghost. Instead, at the split second of its utterance, he substituted first grave-digger for ghost. It brought a roar of appreciative laughter from the Conservative benches.

As it happened, I was sitting on the parliamentary private secretaries' bench immediately behind the Prime Minister, so I heard the exchange between him and Patrick Buchan-Hepburn, the Chief Whip, (later Lord Hailes) which followed: 'Who is this? enquired Churchill. 'Macleod, sir.' There was a pause, then: 'Ministerial material?' suggested the Prime Minister. Buchan-Hepburn had learnt to be watchful of Winston's enthusiasms and replied cautiously: 'He's still quite young' – to which Churchill, who had himself been Home Secretary at the age of thirty-three, snapped back: 'What's that got to do with it?' With the passage of time the story has been improved and I have read a delightful version of it that Buchan-Hepburn's comment on Iain's age was 'too young to be eligible', to which Churchill is alleged to have retorted: 'too eligible to be too young.' In fact, when Macleod was made Minister of Health a few weeks later, no one was more delighted than Buchan-Hepburn.

Meanwhile Macleod was outlining the history of the prescription charges and their intended introduction by the Labour Government in December 1949. The cost of drugs and the number of prescriptions had gone up since then and the case for the charge was correspondingly greater. He recommended Members to read Bevan's earlier speeches in full: 'It is true that if we read now we can find, like raisins in a bun, arguments put forward by the Right Honourable Gentleman as to why this charge was impracticable, but he knew something at the time that nobody else did. He knew that he was going behind the back of his

Cabinet and his leader to defraud the House of Commons.' Bevan inter-jected indignantly that his was an unworthy statement and there were Socialist cries of 'withdraw'. But Macleod replied calmly, 'I have nothing to withdraw. The Right Honourable Gentleman has been a long time in this House and I do not think he objects at all to this form of debating.' He then attacked Bevan for failing to carry out an undertaking he had given the House about the dental service. Bevan again intervened to justify his position, but Macleod rejected his explanation as 'entirely inaccurate': 'The Right Honourable Gentleman made a great reputation in the last two Parliaments by always speaking at the end of the health debates and never answering any points. He is much less effective when he comes down into the arena. He does not know the figures.' Macleod then supplied them. There were attempted interruptions by other Labour Members, at which Macleod delighted the crowded Tory benches by commenting: 'I appreciate that the Right Honourable Gentleman is in need of care and protection.' This brought Bevan to his feet again and there were two more sharp exchanges between them. Macleod dismissed Bevan's last point with: 'That is utterly ineffective. The Right Honourable Gentleman does not know what he is talking about.' No one had spoken like this to the architect of the Health Service since he created it. Macleod continued: 'The Right Honourable Gentleman went down about a month ago to explain his conduct in this House to his constituents – something which I gather is in the nature of an annual event. . . .' He quoted Bevan as having given an assurance in Ebbw Vale that, in the debates on the Health Service cuts, he would not be restrained by any previous commitments made by anyone. Macleod commented that they could not complain of Bevan's enthusiasm, since he had made it quite clear that he was not going to be restrained even by the commitments he had made himself. Coming to the 1951 Bill, Macleod recalled that 'the Opposition held on the floor of the House one of what are laughably referred to as their private Parliamentary meetings. This was a great convenience for Members because, although explanations of these meetings in the press are unusually full, they are rarely verbatim and they do not include the Division lists. But we can see exactly what happened at the end of the day a year ago when these proposals were before the House. We can see exactly how much the froth and speeches were worth. The general tenor of Honourable Members who spoke against the Bill was, shortly, that they disliked the Bill a great deal but that they preferred the Bill to a Tory Government.'

Mr Fernyhough (Labour, Jarrow): 'Hear, hear.'

Mr Macleod: 'I am glad the Hon. Gentleman agrees, because it has obviously escaped him that he has ended with both the Bill and a Tory Government.'

This was an early example of the technique of trailing his coat which Macleod was later to perfect. He always enjoyed drawing his opponents into an injudicious interruption and then delivering a *coup de grace*.

It was now seven o'clock. By a quirk of parliamentary procedure, leave had been given earlier to interrupt the debate at this hour to enable Anthony Wedgwood Benn to move the adjournment of the House under Standing Order No. 9 in order to consider the action of the Commonwealth Secretary in deposing Seretse Khama as chief of the Bamangwato tribe in Bechuanaland. The Health Service debate was not to be resumed until ten o'clock when Macleod would continue his speech. Half an hour after the African debate had started, John Vaughan-Morgan (now Lord Reigate) who saw Iain in the 'Aye' lobby and went up to congratulate him, was surprised to notice that he was still trembling with tension. It was not the impression he had given in the Chamber. In the interval he sought Charles Hill's opinion as to whether he should go on with the attack upon Bevan or take a more constructive line in the last part of the speech. Hill rightly advised him to be constructive and, as he wanted to do this in any case, he accepted the advice. It was wise counsel, especially as, when the debate was resumed, Bevan was not in his place. Perhaps he had some other engagement outside, but it was an error of judgement not to return because it looked as though he had had such a trouncing that he dare not come back for more. Indeed the House put this construction on his absence and this enhanced Macleod's triumph. Chance had given him a great opportunity. It was not chance but capacity which enabled him to grasp it. Six weeks later he was made Minister of Health.

Macleod attributed his promotion to the influence of James Stuart, a former Chief Whip, who was Secretary of State for Scotland in Winston Churchill's second Administration. Stuart had recommended the appointment and this may well have carried weight because Churchill, rightly, relied greatly upon Stuart's advice in matters of this kind. In any event Macleod wrote to thank him for having made the suggestion. It is of interest that Stuart also gave Alec Douglas-Home his first important post by asking for him as Minister of State at the Scottish Office when the 1951 Government was formed.[7] But although Stuart's advocacy of

7 *Sir Alec Douglas-Home*, Kenneth Young, Dent, 1970.

Macleod's claims must certainly have helped, there is no doubt that the Prime Minister wanted to make a change at the Ministry of Health at that time and had been much impressed by Macleod's performances against Bevan in the House of Commons. Harry Crookshank was a skilled and effective parliamentarian, but the double post of Minister of Health and Leader of the House of Commons was more than he could conveniently cope with and he now gave up his department and combined the Leadership of the House with the sinecure position of Lord Privy Seal.

The Times leading article of May 8th read as follows:

> The appointment of Mr Iain Macleod as Mr Crookshank's successor at the Ministry of Health could not be better. Chairman of the Conservative Party's Committee on insurance, health and pensions and a prominent member of the 'One Nation' Group of Conservative backbenchers who have interested themselves specially and effectively in the social services, Mr Macleod has in recent debates in the House of Commons displayed a knowledge of the Health Service and an understanding of its problems which are shared by few on either side of the House. It is of no small importance, since Mr Bevan is the foremost Labour spokesman on Health questions, that Mr Macleod has already shown himself well equipped to meet Mr Bevan on what he regards as his own ground.

The *Economist* of May 10th, which regarded the other changes in the minor ministerial re-shuffle as 'routine', commented: 'The tribute that may fairly be paid to Mr Crookshank's successor is to say that the appointment is no surprise'

If it was no surprise to the *Economist*, it was certainly a surprise to Iain Macleod. A few days earlier he had annoyed Patrick Buchan-Hepburn by declining to represent the party at the Council of Europe. It was an honour which most young members would have accepted with alacrity, but Macleod had been a delegate the previous year and had found the experience boring. The Chief Whip told him that his refusal would be reported to the Prime Minister. Soon afterwards Iain received a curt message asking him to go to 10 Downing Street the next morning at eleven o'clock. He remarked to Eve: 'I can't think why Winston has sent for me. He isn't small-minded enough to waste his time ticking me off about the Council of Europe.' Eve drove him to Downing Street and waited in the car outside. He emerged fifteen minutes later looking grey and shaken. 'Please drive me to the nearest telephone box,' he said. When

Eve asked him why, he replied, 'I have just been made a Privy Councillor and Minister of Health. I have to take over the department and I've no idea where it is, so I think I'd better look up the address in a telephone book.'

When they got home that evening, before the public announcement of Iain's appointment had been made, he told Eve to telephone their local doctor, Gordon Moores, who was also a close personal friend. She rang the number, pretending to be a secretary, and asked if the doctor could speak to the Minister of Health. Puzzled and a little perturbed, Moores hurried to the telephone – to hear Iain's voice at the other end of the line. 'You bloody fool,' he said. 'I almost believed it was the Minister.' 'And so it is,' replied Macleod.

He had been in Parliament for just over two years and was still only thirty-eight. It was the first break-through of the new generation into major Conservative politics.

CHAPTER 5

Minister of Health 1952-1955

❧❀❧❀❧

ON the day of Macleod's appointment as Minister of Health, Pat Hornsby-Smith, already Parliamentary Secretary in the department, had heard through an open door: 'God, we've got the whizz kid; do you think he'll turn us upside down?' But Iain had no such intention. His predecessor, Harry Crookshank, was an experienced Minister who knew the corners as well as the corridors of power. Macleod had yet to learn them and to learn, first, his own department. His health was already giving him trouble, even in 1952, and on his first day at Savile Row he asked for a pillow for his arthritic shoulder, to ease the discomfort he was suffering.

At first he made little impact on most of his officials, who found him difficult to get to know and somewhat impersonal. The Permanent Secretary, Sir John Hawton, thought the new Minister was diffident, modest and unsure of himself. This initial impression contrasted strikingly with the assurance and certainty which, within a year or two, had become one of Macleod's characteristics. As he had never been a junior Minister, he did not know how a government department worked, but he learnt very quickly.

After a fortnight he went to the monthly meeting of the departmental regional officers and gave a little talk. He said that he wanted the Health Service to enjoy a period of tranquillity, with no drastic reorganisation. He would do his best to ensure that the service got a fair share of whatever funds could be made available for the social services. Dame Enid Russell-Smith,[1] who was present, noted that he made an admirable impression and that 'we hadn't had such leadership since the days of Aneurin Bevan.' She thought it the speech of a young man with his way to make and that he would do well.

The elections of 1950 and 1951 had been fought, at least partly, about the memories and myths of the 1930s. Many Labour Party supporters

1 Dame Enid Russell-Smith, Under-Secretary, Ministry of Health, 1946. Deputy Secretary, 1956.

feared that a Conservative victory would mean a return to unbridled capitalism at home and war-mongering abroad. The *Daily Mirror* head-line 'Whose Finger on the Trigger?' was intended to alarm the electorate at Churchill's expense and no doubt it frightened a number of un-committed voters who might otherwise have supported the Conser-vatives.

Labour had very little idea of the extent to which the Tory Party had changed. Some believed there would be a revival of class politics and that the Welfare State would be dismantled. The run on the reserves in the summer and autumn of 1951 was dramatic and even the Labour Govern-ment had had to undermine its own health service by the introduction of selective charges. Many people feared a further dose of austerity. The prospect of an age of affluence seemed remote and, when it dawned, it was a major political advantage for the Conservative Party which partly accounted for the unique increase in its representation in Parliament at four successive elections between 1950 and 1959.

Winston Churchill was seventy-six when he became Prime Minister for the second time in 1951, and some of the old fire had gone. He was well aware of his reputation as the enemy of organised labour and of the popular view that he was more interested in adventures abroad than in welfare at home. In fact, he wanted to preserve the fabric of the Welfare State, which had been projected by his great war-time Coalition and implemented by the Labour Government which followed it. He was anxious for peace and continuity in domestic politics and for conciliation and a better understanding with the unions. For these reasons, after the death of Oliver Stanley in 1950, he appointed Rab Butler as Chancellor of the Exchequer, instead of Oliver Lyttelton, and Walter Monckton as Minister of Labour instead of David Maxwell Fyfe. In dealing with organised labour he cultivated the right-wing triumvirate of Deakin, Lawther and Williamson, who had great influence with the TUC, and he instructed Monckton to avoid strikes over wage claims, especially that of the railwaymen.

The Conservative election slogan had been 'Set the people free', and in a remarkably short time de-rationing and de-control redeemed this promise. The Government was assisted by the turn-round in the terms of trade between 1952 and 1955, which gave Butler a little elbow room, but the housing commitment was an embarrassment to the new Chancellor who still had to keep a watchful eye on public expenditure. This was especially true of the expensive Health Service, the cost of which was constantly rising. Hugh Gaitskell had already done some pruning in 1951 with his charges on false teeth and spectacles, and both parties tried to adhere to Stafford Cripps's £400 million spending ceiling.

The Health Service was particularly vulnerable to cost inflation, so a reduction in its scope seemed inevitable. In March 1952 Crookshank had introduced the one shilling prescription charge, the one pound dental treatment charge and part payment for surgical boots, abdominal supports, wigs and elastic hosiery. Children and expectant and nursing mothers were exempt from the dental charge and those on national assistance were exempt from all the charges.

The National Health Service Act had become law on November 6, 1946, but the Service was not brought into operation till nearly two years later. Conservative parliamentary opposition to the Bill had seemed reactionary and was in fact ineffective. Aneurin Bevan's most bitter battle had not been with the politicians but with the medical profession, represented by the negotiating committee of the BMA and its able and articulate secretary, Dr Charles Hill. Hill's distinctive voice as the war-time 'radio doctor' was known to and loved by millions and he was a powerful advocate for the profession. Bevan took the view that he would negotiate with the doctors over their terms of service but not over the structure of the Health Service itself.

The doctors were worried that there would be a conflict of interest in the state-run service – that demands for economy, the classification of patients into groups, standardised treatment and increased paper work and bureaucracy would combine to interfere with clinical freedom and with the duty of a doctor to his individual patient. In fact, the syndicalist structure of the Service did much to prevent this, and the doctor/patient relationship was unimpaired.

For the doctors a state-salaried service, making them into civil servants, was anathema. Their point was conceded by an amending Bill which provided for a capitation fee basis of remuneration; and a small fee-paying element was permitted both for doctors and private rooms in hospitals. But the sale of GP practices was abolished and the hospital service was completely integrated under regional boards. The outcome, as between the Minister and the profession, could fairly be described as a draw, and nearly 19,000 out of the 20,000 doctors in Britain joined the Health Service.

When the Service was inaugurated many hospitals had been short of money for years. They had had to budget on a shoe-string, with their funds restricted to the amount they could raise by donations, voluntary efforts such as flag days and fêtes, and through the rates. The inflationary pressures of the postwar period and the shortages of money, material and personnel, especially nurses, made matters worse.

Its architect, Aneurin Bevan, described the National Health Service as 'the most civilised achievement of modern Government' and, broadly, this was true; but there was insufficient money for the service and it could not be radically improved while it was under-financed.

There were serious practical shortcomings especially in the early years. Nearly half the hospitals in England and Wales had been built more than sixty years before. In 1948 504,000 hospital beds were available in Britain. By 1955 there were still only 507,000 and not a single new hospital had been completed since the war. As a result, most hospitals were over-crowded. Urgent cases were never denied immediate treatment, but minor surgery, such as tonsilectomy, was subject to long delays. Mental, chronic and infirm patients were especially badly affected. Capital expenditure on new hospital building and improvements amounted to £10½ millions in Macleod's last year as Minister of Health, but this was still sadly inadequate and long overdue. Group practices for doctors were not organised on a large enough scale and only a small number of health centres were provided, although they had been regarded initially as one of the key features of the new service.[2]

Throughout Macleod's three years as Minister, lack of money was the dominant and inescapable limitation. When, years later, as Shadow Chancellor of the Exchequer, speaking at the Brighton party conference in 1965, Macleod coined the phrase 'money is the root of all progress', he may well have been thinking wrily of his period as Minister of Health. But as a relatively junior Minister outside the Cabinet, he had to accept the position as he found it. He knew that Health Service budgeting had to be subject to the national budget and the pressures on Rab Butler from other departments, especially Housing, were very strong.

Moreover, when Macleod took over the Ministry it was declining in political importance. Much of its pensions work had already gone, and the housing and town and country planning divisions had been taken over by Macmillan in 1951. The department was no longer a Cabinet post. It was

2 Only about one centre a year was established in England between 1948 and 1963. From 1964 to 1968 the average rose to nearly twelve a year and in 1969 to 50. Almost 500 more centres are included in local authority plans for the next few years. By 1978 there may be about 1,100 as compared with 103 at the end of 1968.

either a stepping stone for a young Minister on the way up or a back-water for someone who had earned a Ministry of his own but would go no further. In the ten years between 1950 and 1960 there were eight Ministers of Health and in that decade Macleod's 3½ year tenure was the longest.

Bevan drew attention in the House of Commons to the weakness of Macleod's position:

> In February and March this year there was an argument between the Minister of Health and the Chancellor of the Exchequer. It was not an unusual argument . . . it is an argument in which I used to be engaged myself. It is also an argument in which every spending Department has to engage. . . . In some respects the Rt. Hon. Gentleman lost the argument; so did the President of the Board of Trade, so did the Minister of Supply, so did the Minister of Education, because the Minister of Housing and Local Government said to them: 'Look here, boys, you stand back a bit. I am advancing here.' That is exactly what happened . . .[3]

It was true Macleod's tenure of the Ministry of Health was dominated by lack of money and the need for strict cost control and it was prejudiced by the Government's pre-election pledge to build 300,000 houses a year. Homes, no doubt rightly, were given priority over hospitals.

Within the Service itself competing claims for scarce resources had to be carefully weighed. The money for one new hospital could finance ten or twelve smaller but useful projects. Sadly but fairly, Macleod probed and pruned the rival claims of the twelve regional hospital boards.

Soon after he had taken over the Ministry, a personal tragedy hit Iain Macleod's family. On June 28, 1952, Eve collapsed with meningitis and polio. She was taken to the National Hospital for Nervous Diseases in Queen's Square, where she was dangerously ill for many weeks and at first paralysed from the waist down. Gradually she recovered the use of one leg and the partial use of the other, but she could not return to Enfield until October, and even then she had to use a wheel-chair.

Despite the preoccupations of learning the department by day and attendance in the House of Commons each evening, which was necessary owing to the small Government majority, Iain contrived to visit her every day.

3 *Hansard*, Vol. 515, Cols. 1711/1712. May 18, 1953.

It was a difficult time for him and the care of the children, aged ten and eight, was a main anxiety. His sister, Rhodabel, was able to have them in Yorkshire after the first week, and in the interval he arranged for Mrs de Brissay, who ran a children's guest house at her home in Suffolk, to take them at short notice. She met him with Torquil and Diana at Liverpool Street Station. It was clear that there had been some improvisation, and the packing looked precarious, with a trail of sweets from a broken paper bag. At the end of their stay Iain went down for the week-end to collect them. He spent the day sitting on the beach with his own and the other children. From time to time they all disappeared; he had taken them to buy sweets and doughnuts. Mrs de Brissay wrote of him later '. . . there was something so simple and human about him . . . no man in these circumstances could have been more easy and delightful to meet and help.'

Enoch Powell had resented Macleod's early appointment as a Minister of Cabinet rank when he himself was still left on the back benches, and this caused a temporary estrangement between the two; but he reacted generously to Eve's illness and the problems he knew it must create for Iain. Macleod wrote later: 'Enoch strode into the room and threw a key on my desk. "There's a room ready in my flat," he said, "come and go as you wish." And the door banged behind him.'[4] It was typically abrupt and shy, gruff yet kind.

By November Eve was well enough to go on a six weeks' cruise to South America with Rhodabel. She was home by Christmas and able to resume her life as a Minister's wife; but one leg remained partly paralysed and she has had to walk with two sticks ever since. Iain gave her a small car with special hand controls on the steering column for the accelerator and the brake.

As Minister of Health Macleod was not an innovator. He left the Health Service much as he found it. It was a period of consolidation. The service had survived its teething troubles and was running well. Aneurin Bevan's widow, Jennie Lee, wrote later: 'When Iain Macleod became Minister of Health he was generous enough to tell Nye how little he found it right, or possible, to change, once he had had a close-up of the Health Service as it was at that time.' She added 'how much public life has diminished for all of us when anyone so able and dedicated dies prematurely.'[5]

4 *Spectator*, July 16, 1965.
5 Lady Lee to the author, August 19, 1970.

Speaking at Taunton on September 29, 1952, Macleod set the tone of his administration when he said that he would like to be the first Minister of Health who did not pass any legislation. Not only had too much been passed but too many instructions had been issued: 'It is about time we stopped issuing paper and made the instructions work. I want to try and recreate local interest in the hospital and above everything to get a complete partnership between voluntary effort and the State.'

He was as good as his word. No major legislation was passed, and although the Dentists' Bill was drafted and introduced in 1955, while he was still the Minister, it was not enacted until 1956 when he had already gone to the Ministry of Labour.

Iain Macleod's interest in the voluntary side of the work of the Health Service may have owed something to the lack of public funds at his disposal for more dramatic improvements, such as new hospital building; but he also saw that it had an important part in its own right and his personal interest may have been prompted by Eve who was already doing much for the League of Hospital Friends of which she subsequently became, and still is, deputy chairman. She certainly contributed significantly to Iain's work at this period.

In his first party political broadcast on October 30, 1952, Macleod stressed the importance of voluntary effort in the Health Service. He said there had been less local pride in the hospitals since the state took them over:

I won't be content until every hospital has its own voluntary organisation, League of Friends or whatever you like to call it. Has your hospital got one? If not, why not? And don't forget old people's homes and, most important of all, the mental hospitals – cheerless and bleak as many of them still are. It is here, where the patients can do so little for themselves, that voluntary work can bring its richest and most satisfying reward.

Macleod's main concern was to humanise the Health Service. He swept aside the traditional Labour view that all voluntary effort was an excuse for reducing Government spending. In an address to the League of Friends in January 1953 he returned to the problem of mental patients and the need for voluntary work to help them. He pointed out that they occupied forty-two per cent of the hospital beds in Britain; that 5,000 mental patients were still awaiting admission, and that half of them were children.

In the House of Commons in February he went further:

It is a great tragedy that in the more carefree days of the Health Service, before a ceiling of expenditure was imposed by Sir Stafford Cripps, more money was not allocated to the mental health field. The percentage of investment has been climbing since then, but I am by no means satisfied with it yet . . .

And in another speech in May he put fairly and squarely the issue of priorities:

Suppose we have a vast trading surplus; suppose all the things we want to see in fact come true; suppose the Chancellor approaches the Minister of Health and says, 'You can have another £40 million for the Health Service'. It costs that to get rid of the charges. Is this really the first use to which a Minister of Health ought to put that sum? I know where I would look if I had that sum or one tenth of it. I should not look to free dentures or free medicines, but to the mental health of this country. It is a strange system of priorities that puts free dentures and free medicines before the care of the mentally ill.

On October 10, 1953, he announced to the House the end of all restrictions on voluntary effort. In future the League of Hospital Friends would be able to hold meetings inside hospitals and the hospital staff would co-operate and play their part. He believed there was great scope for voluntary work which required no special training; and he told Lady Monckton, the chairman of the League: 'I know when I go into a hospital whether it has a League of Friends or not – there is a different atmosphere.'

Another voluntary organisation in which Macleod took an interest was the Multiple Sclerosis Society, which was formed in 1953. He spoke at its inaugural meeting. It was almost the first occasion when a Minister had given public support to a new voluntary body of this kind. He also supported and encouraged the Family Planning Association.

Mr J. E. Pater, an Under-Secretary at the Ministry of Health, in charge of hospitals, thought that no Minister of Health in his time had done as much to encourage the voluntary side of the hospital work. And Macleod never failed to link the plea for voluntary effort with the mental hospitals which most needed it.

In the spring of 1954 the Ministry of Health estimates proposed that the capital programme for mental health should be doubled. On May 8th Macleod laid the foundation stone for the first hospital to be started since

1939. Significantly, it was a mental hospital and would provide a thousand additional beds. In his speech on this occasion Macleod claimed that the previous year had seen a reduction of five hundred in the mental waiting lists; but progress was still too slow, and in February 1954 the Minister had appointed a Royal Commission under the chairmanship of Lord Percy (a former president of the Board of Education) to enquire into the problem. This commission, which did not report till 1957, was to revolutionise mental health in Britain.

In proposing the toast at a BMA dinner later in the year, the Duke of Edinburgh mentioned that the Minister of Health was to reply and added, 'I hardly dare say that the last time I met him was in a mental hospital!'

Macleod's visits to hospitals were both frequent and welcome because of his interest in what he saw and in the people he met. One official contrasted them with Enoch Powell's visits as Minister some years later, remarking that 'Mr Powell gave the impression of being a good inspector, Mr Macleod of being a man who cared.' The human side of hospital problems always concerned him, and in March 1953 he issued a ministry circular urging hospital authorities to allow parents to visit their children every day instead of once a week, which had been the previous limitation in most hospitals.

Macleod's first responsibility as Minister of Health was to administer the charges introduced by Harry Crookshank, which came into force in June 1952. Politically they were of symbolic importance to the Labour Party. Macleod regarded them not only as a financial saving but as a way of implementing the One Nation principle that priority should be given to those in real need:

'From some health charges, good may come,' he said at the Constitutional Club on May 30, 1952. 'If the charge on prescriptions enables the GP to give more freely of his skill and time to those who really need his care, that will be a great gain.' No doubt the hitherto unlimited right to free medicines had produced overcrowding in doctors' surgeries and, in consequence, often inadequate time for more serious cases.

On July 2 the Opposition moved a Prayer to annul the charges, and Macleod made his first important speech as a Minister in replying to the debate. He was accurate and factual, and his peroration was enthusiastically received by the Conservative benches. Macleod was always good in the House of Commons and only once said anything that afterwards embarrassed him. This was when, replying to Dr Edith Summerskill, he referred to 'filthy diseases like yaws'.

The charges reduced the Treasury's liability by £20 million a year; but, financially, it was like trying to hold water in a sieve, because at the same time Mr Justice Danckwerts was awarding the doctors salary increases which cost £40 million a year, retrospective to 1948. This represented a major victory for the doctors. When Iain was invited to play bridge by members of the profession after a BMA conference in Birmingham, he replied: 'Delighted, but I warn you I'll take your Danckwerts awards off you.'

Nevertheless, Macleod held the position. The Health Service bill for 1952/53 was £518 million. By the time he left the department three years later it had risen to £585 million, due mainly to inflation; but he had, perforce, kept the cost remarkably steady and as a percentage of the gross national product it was no higher at the end of his three years as Minister of Health than it had been at the beginning.

By 1954 the Opposition had dropped the health charges as their main line of attack, and had switched to hospital building and pay beds. The Labour Party claimed that those with money could leap-frog the hospital waiting lists, but Macleod pointed out that pay beds represented only one per cent of those available, and when Bevan announced that they would be abolished by the next Labour Government, Macleod described this pledge as 'sheer, blithering irrelevance to the problems of the National Health Service'.[6]

Owing mainly to the Danckwerts award, which virtually coincided with the date of his appointment, Iain Macleod had less trouble from the general practitioners than his predecessors or his successor. But there were other reasons for the better atmosphere during his time at the Ministry. He was himself, like Kenneth Robinson later, the son of a GP, and Skipton was almost the birth-place of organised group practice, with his father's as the nucleus of one of the two groups which were formed there. He often visited the hospitals in the area, and in November 1954 he devised and introduced a party political television broadcast called 'Home Town'. Its theme was the effect upon ordinary people of the Government's plans for education, health, housing and pensions. Its location was Iain's own home town of Skipton. He used his friends there, including Ralph Wynn, then Chairman of the local Conservative Association, as his cast, and

6 Conservative Annual Conference at Margate, October 1954.

The original 'One Nation' group, 1951 (Edward Heath is missing). Left to right: Lord Alport, Sir John Rodgers, Sir Gilbert Longden, the Rt. Hon. Iain Macleod, Richard Fort, Angus Maude, the Rt. Hon. Robert Carr, the Rt. Hon. Enoch Powell

As Minister of Health, 1952. Macleod with nursing staff on a tour of inspection

A family group. Iain, Torquil, Diana and Eve

rehearsed them personally for their parts in the programme. It was one of the first of the friendly, informal political broadcasts which have since become usual.

One of the chores of any Minister of Health was attending and addressing many of the endless dinners of various national organisations, and Sir George Godber (now Chief Medical Officer in the Department of Health and Social Security) recalls that Macleod and Robinson achieved a better rapport with medical audiences on these occasions than any of the sixteen other Ministers for whom he worked. Sir Cecil Wakeley, a former President of the Royal College of Surgeons, has described Macleod as a 'true friend to doctors . . . no other Minister has done so much for medicine and for the medical profession as a whole.'[7]

Iain Macleod looked hard at the cost effectiveness of general practitioners, and one answer seemed to lie in the new concept of health centres. On September 16, 1952, he opened one of these at Bristol, designed to serve a housing estate of 25,000 people. It included surgeries, maternity and child welfare clinics and the district headquarters of the local domiciliary services. To get all the X-ray and other equipment under one roof would clearly save money, but Macleod had reservations about undermining the GP/patient relationship: 'It would be foolish to build large numbers of health centres,' he said, 'until it is known what type of centre is likely to be most useful and popular with patients and at the same time acceptable to doctors. It is better to allow a few health centres of different types to be tried first in areas where there is real need.'

Macleod often argued for a closer liaison between the GPs and the hospitals. Treatment had become so expensive that it should be reserved for patients who really needed it, and doctors should not send their patients into hospital unless the attention they required could only be given them as in-patients. In a speech at Cardiff he commented: 'Too many people are in hospital who ought not be there; too many people who ought to be there, are not.'

The Minister's preoccupation with cost effectiveness was also illustrated by the favourable arrangements he made for partnerships, including special allowances for under-doctored areas. The Cohen Report – an official survey of general practice set up in December 1950 – was published in June 1954 and showed that the number of doctors in partnership had gone up by over a thousand, and that the proportion of the urban

7 Sir Cecil Wakeley to the author, November 5, 1970.

population living in under-doctored areas had fallen from sixty per cent to forty-six per cent.

On May 18, 1953 he announced a study into the rise in the cost of proprietary drugs. Prescribing costs accounted for 10 per cent of the total NHS bill and therefore warranted scrutiny. On June 17 he spoke to a large gathering of general practitioners from all over Britain in the Great Hall of the British Medical Association. His theme was the high cost of doctors' prescribing and he asked for their help in reducing this. When he sat down Dame Enid Russell-Smith recalls 'the astonishing sight of hundreds of doctors clapping and cheering a Minister of Health'.

At about this time one of the leading pharmaceutical companies was advertising a new drug 'at a reasonable price', which turned out to be 3s 6d a tablet. It was probably a fair price after years of research, development and clinical trials and the large expenditure, perhaps running into millions of pounds, which had been spent in producing it, but the price did not seem reasonable to some of the doctors who were prescribing it. When Dr Cedric Robinson of Skipton, a childhood friend of Iain's, pointed this out to him, he at once arranged for every doctor in Britain to be told what the price really was.

Nevertheless, Macleod tried to be fair and he was careful not to criticise the profits made by manufacturers of new proprietary medicines. He recognised that it was the money they spent on research which had made possible the tremendous advances in the conquest of disease over the previous twenty years.

In 1954 he paid a visit to Blackpool, to look at the vehicle, personal appliance and artificial limbs work being carried out there for the department. He subjected the officer in charge of the equipment section to long and detailed questioning about leg calipers, which went far beyond the usual ministerial interrogation. He explained that he was influenced by Eve's disability and he showed a keen subjective interest in the problems of the disabled, especially those affecting their personal dignity. He thought conventional calipers were ugly, inefficient and humiliatingly conspicuous, and asked for studies to be put in hand immediately to see what could be done to improve their design. The new Salford caliper is the result of the impetus Macleod gave to his work. Officials constantly noted the humanity of his outlook and his searching personal interest in the services for which he was responsible.

During a polio outbreak in 1952, Felicity Lane Fox, herself a polio victim, wrote to him to plead that more attention should be given to the prevention and cure of this disease. He replied in long hand on September 10th:

Dear Miss Lane Fox,

For the moment I am only acknowledging your letter and will write again in detail rather later. I, too, have the best of reasons for hating and fighting polio. My wife was attacked by it a few weeks after I became Minister and has been in hospital ever since. Probably, with a caliper, she will walk again, but we do not know.

Thank you for writing to me.

Yours sincerely – Iain Macleod

A new drive to eliminate tuberculosis was launched in March 1954. The death rate was already falling, but this campaign was the first to use techniques of mass radiography for screening. In a broadcast on May 3rd the Minister declared:

Money spent on the prevention of disease will pay a far higher dividend than money spent on the cure of a disease. Tuberculosis, for example, is still one of the black spots. Certainly the death rate is going down . . . but, though we are discovering cases earlier and treating them more efficiently, there are still too many cases. . . . In this sphere, as in so many others, a major factor in good health is good housing. So we Tories have deliberately put housing first.

In the same year Macleod made two statements about cancer. Commenting on a report issued by the standing advisory committee on cancer that there was a relationship between smoking and lung cancer, he said he had released the information immediately but that no action would be taken until more evidence was available. At the party conference in October he undertook to inform the country as soon as the evidence seemed conclusive, but he declined to speculate in advance of proof. The report had no effect on his own cigarette consumption. At that time he was almost a chain smoker and even when he saw the lobby journalists to answer questions on the report, he smoked throughout the press conference. Later he gave up cigarettes completely, but he continued to smoke two or three small cigars a day until shortly before he died.

Macleod's relations with the dentists were never as agreeable as with the doctors, chiefly because they considered their scale of remuneration inadequate. The doctors had had their Danckwerts award; the dentists had not. Indeed their fees had been cut by Aneurin Bevan.

The initial problem, however, was numbers. There were far too few qualified dentists in practice. Ideally, there should have been 40,000. In fact there were 10,000 and their work-load was increasing. Recruitment, too, was far too low. Macleod suggested that more use should be made of 'assistants', who were competent to deal with scaling and the extraction of deciduous teeth, leaving the qualified practitioner time for the more difficult work. But the dentists objected to this because it meant a dilution of professional standards. Macleod had to bide his time.

During 1954 the pressure for more pay grew stronger. In March the Minister, accompanied by the department's chief dental officer and Dame Enid Russell-Smith, attended a dinner of the London Dental Committee, whose members were so critical of the Ministry officials that Macleod, in his speech of thanks, invited his audience to abuse him as he took full responsibility for his officials. Afterwards Dame Enid asked the chairman what the trouble was. 'Oh,' he replied, 'that wasn't intended for you; that was for my rank and file. They think we aren't belligerent enough.'

The atmosphere was cool when it was not positively hostile until Sir Wilfred Fish, the Chairman of the Dental Board, eventually intervened. In his usual forthright way Sir Wilfred asked the Minister why he and the British Dental Association did not stop their unedifying slanging match and have dinner together.

'They would never invite me,' said Macleod.

'Nonsense,' replied Fish, 'would you accept an invitation if you received one tomorrow?'

'Certainly,' said Macleod.

He received it and accepted it and relations between the profession and the department improved from that day. But soon there were more solid grounds for a better understanding. In December 1954 Macleod appointed a committee to enquire into dental recruitment and in April 1955 he announced a dental pay rise review.

The way was now clear for the Dentists Bill, Macleod's only piece of legislation as Minister of Health, which he introduced on second reading on November 4, 1955. Its main purpose was to enable dental assistants, under supervision, to undertake scalings, fillings and minor extractions. The Bill also made it easier for Commonwealth and foreign dentists to practice in Britain and in these ways relieved the pressure of work under which the profession had suffered for years.

Meanwhile the dental treatment charge for adults had brought a real gain in the treatment of children who were exempt from payment of it. Until the charge was imposed too much work had been devoted to the adult population at the expense of the children; but in the three following years there had been an increase of one hundred and fifty per cent in the number of children's treatment courses. This welcome change was enhanced by a Ministry circular issued at the end of 1952 which encouraged dentists to work in the school dental service on a sessional fee basis. By March 1953, two hundred dentists had volunteered for this work.

The most difficult of Macleod's ministerial problems was the hospital service. New buildings and improvements to old buildings were greatly needed, but they were expensive, and the money, materials and labour available for the construction industry were being used to meet Macmillan's housing programme. Quite apart from capital expenditure, Macleod had to control current costs with anxious care. In December 1952 he asked hospital boards to watch their staff levels and they were expected to refer any increase in establishment to the Minister. He required a cut in staff of five per cent for the year 1953.

By the summer of that year he was able to announce that hospital improvements would go up by £15 million. But there was still no money for new building and the Opposition began to mount an intense attack on this vulnerable area of the Ministry's responsibilities.

It was not until May 1954 that Macleod, in reply to criticisms by Arthur Blenkinsop, could report to the House that 'the outlook in the capital field is a great deal more encouraging than it has been for some time.' He announced that £12.3 million would be available for capital expenditure on hospitals in the year 1954/55. It was the largest sum allocated for this purpose since the Health Service began. But it was not a programme for new building.

After some particularly fierce newspaper criticism Pat Hornsby-Smith went into Macleod's office one morning with the worst of the press cuttings. 'Cheer up,' he said, 'it's going to get a lot worse than this over the year, but about February 1955 I shall announce our first real hospital building programme.' He was as good as his word. On December 3, 1954, Dame Enid Russell-Smith recorded 'The Minister had succeeded in getting a better allocation of money for the Health Service and I noted his increasing influence with his colleagues.' On February 9, 1955, Macleod announced the new building programme.

There were still many reservations – that there would be no increase in capital expenditure in 1955/56, that it was projected into the future and that it could be cancelled, if necessary, by the Chancellor; but, despite these Treasury safeguards, the programme represented a fifty per cent increase in capital investment by 1958 and a real break-through for Iain Macleod.

1955 was a difficult year, with economic restrictions in July and again in October, but the hospital commitment was confirmed. On October 31, after Butler's 'pots and pans' budget, Macleod was able to say:

> That programme stands; every hospital, every bed, every ward in it. I am deeply grateful to the Chancellor that he has been able to keep the green light fixed on that particular programme. . . . We are now coming into a period of building twice as much as the Socialists undertook.

He had won his most important battle with the Treasury.

A month later Macleod was able to announce that the Guillebaud Report was almost ready for publication.[8] He had appointed this enquiry into the Health Service in April 1953 and been criticised by Bevan at the time for 'seeking another instrument by which he might mutilate the NHS'. This was indicative of the emotional atmosphere which still surrounded the Service at that time.

On the Tory benches it was widely assumed that Guillebaud would find reckless extravagance. In fact he could see little evidence of waste. Indeed, the report commented that substantial improvements had been achieved in the scale and quality of the services provided. If anything more money, not less, should be spent, especially on the hospitals.

Guillebaud could make no radical recommendations with regard to the structure of the service or to economies in its administration. Much of the credit for these conclusions must be accorded to Iain Macleod.

Just before he left the Ministry of Health, Macleod was involved in a controversy which aroused high passions at the time and, in the light of today's tragic drug problem, is even more topical now.

On June 13, 1955, he had announced in the House of Commons the banning of the manufacture and use of heroin on the grounds that we should play our part 'in combating a substantial social evil all over the world although there may be little evidence of addiction in this country. . .'

Great Britain was then the largest manufacturer of heroin, and the ban

8 The Report was published in Jan. 1956, just after Macleod had left the department.

arose because the previous Labour Government had been asked by fifty-four nations what they proposed doing about this dangerous drug. Aneurin Bevan had referred the question to the NHS Standing Advisory Committee, which included the presidents of the royal colleges, three representatives of the BMA and the president of the General Medical Council. In due course this entirely professional committee reported to the Minister, advising a total ban.

There was an immediate and widespread reaction by the doctors and the BMA claimed that the ban was 'aimed at curtailing the freedom of a registered medical practitioner to prescribe.' Of course it was nothing of the sort; but shoals of pathetic letters deluged the department and the correspondence columns of *The Times* from patients who had been told by their doctors of the pain they would suffer if deprived of heroin. The Standing Advisory Committee's contention that there were far less addictive substitutes was denied. Dame Patricia Hornsby-Smith recalls: 'Never had I seen canvassing used to such effect. The doctors put the fear of God (and of pain) into their patients and members of both Houses.'

Macleod remained unmoved, and on December 1 Dame Enid Russell-Smith recorded that 'The Minister scored a notable success by persuading his colleagues to stand firm on the question of limiting the manufacture of heroin when all but he were badly shaken by a very hostile leader in *The Times*. The decision was announced that afternoon and seemed to have a calming effect.' But meanwhile Lord Elibank had launched a major campaign, which culminated in a debate in the House of Lords on December 13, a week before Macleod left the department.

There was a formidable line-up of peers against the ban which included Lord Jowitt, a former Lord Chancellor, and Lord Waverley, a former Home Secretary. For the ban were Lord Woolton, Lord Mancroft and Lord Moran. Unfortunately two of the most eminent members of the Standing Advisory Committee, Sir Henry Cohen (now president of the General Medical Council) and Sir Russell Brain (a former president of the Royal College of Physicians), were not at that time members of the House of Lords. Macleod, steeped in the evidence, had to sit silent on the steps of the throne, unable to intervene;[9] and the Government were forced to withdraw the ban on a technicality, much stressed by Lord Jowitt, that it should be imposed by a Bill instead of by Orders under the Dangerous Drugs Act. In the result no Bill was introduced and an opportunity was

9 Privy Councillors are allowed to sit on the steps of the throne and listen to, but (if they are not members of the House of Lords) not take part in, debates in the House.

lost to reduce the drug addiction problem which has since become so serious.

During his first year in the department Macleod seemed to the civil servants to have very little influence with his government colleagues, but thereafter his political stature steadily increased. Respect, indeed admiration, came more quickly in the Ministry and he soon astonished his staff by the amount of material he could read and absorb. He was never content to study the carefully prepared summary on the top of a bulky file. He would untie the tape and read every material document. Not all Ministers take the trouble to read every submission on a file. But sometimes civil service advice is conflicting and if a conscientious Minister detects this he can send for the dissentient official and examine the reasons for his view. This may change or modify the Minister's decision.

Sir John Hawton considers that no Minister before or since had such a retentive memory. Macleod was able, weeks later, to quote the exact words of anything he had read or the precise statistics from a massive report. This was sometimes disconcerting and, on the rare occasions when an official was forgetful or disingenuous, it could be fatal.

Pat Hornsby-Smith remembers an incident when, after a long and protracted negotiation, a memorandum to settle the matter was put to Macleod for his approval. 'But didn't we write to them months ago and say . . .?' he asked. 'Oh, no sir,' replied the official. Macleod rang for his secretary and the file and turned back to the letter he had seen. He read out what he had already quoted verbatim from memory and added: 'You wrote it, you signed it, you cannot have forgotten it.' This was devastating and officials soon learnt that they could not take a chance on slipshod work for the new Minister.

Sir George Godber recalls Macleod's ability to receive awkward deputations and deal with difficult subjects with no papers in front of him and without any prompting from his officials. And Sir Alan Marre (now the Parliamentary Commissioner) remembers an occasion when the Minister apologised to a deputation for not having with him the documents they had sent, adding that it was a peculiarity of his not to rely on papers at meetings. It soon appeared that he was as familiar with their arguments and supporting figures as they were themselves. Like President Kennedy, he could receive a complicated brief of three or four foolscap pages, study it for ten minutes and never look at it again. Days or weeks later he might ask whether 'the third sentence on the second page is still correct.'. Once he had absorbed an argument or a subject, he never had to be reminded of it afterwards.

Macleod was a good administrator and a good negotiator. His skill at bridge may have helped. Sir John Hawton has said that 'in dealing with people he knew where all the cards lay after the first few exchanges'. He was remarkably quick in mastering a new subject in detail and in every department in which he worked senior officials have paid tribute, always using the same phrase, to his 'clarity of thinking'.

Iain Macleod's keen interest in, and knowledge of, cricket and rugby football was soon apparent to his officials. Throughout his whole ministerial career whenever a Calcutta Cup match was being played at Twickenham he usually contrived to take the afternoon off; and if it was at Murrayfield he always ensured that a speaking engagement in Scotland had been arranged for that evening. When a Test Match was in progress he had to be kept constantly informed of the latest score, and if it was taking place at Lords or the Oval he would not spend as much time in the office as usual. His Private Secretary at the Ministry recalls that, while on a political engagement at Merseyside, he picked up a local paper which was running a competition to pick the next England Test side. In due course the first prize, awarded for his entry, arrived at the Ministry of Health.

Mr Holliman, his government driver throughout his time in the Department, catered for another of Iain's interests. On one occasion when he had just sat down after delivering an important speech, Holliman approached the platform and put an official looking memorandum on the table. It read: 'Minister, if you do not fill in your football pools *now*, we shall miss the last post.'

During his time at the Ministry of Health, Macleod used to 'pair' with Nye Bevan. One night they had arranged to pair because Iain was giving a party outside the House for his mother. When the day came, the Labour Party had imposed a 3-line whip[10] and instructions were issued that no Labour MP could leave the House of Commons. Bevan adhered, literally, to this ruling but he refused to let Macleod down by cancelling the pair. He therefore stayed at the House till late at night but never voted once, so that Iain could attend the party for his mother. By this time the two men had become friends. Macleod admired Bevan and always spoke of him in the most affectionate terms. Sir John Hawton, who knew them both well, thought they had many of the same qualities. Macleod was not so

10 Members must be present or 'paired' for a 2-line whip, but no pairing is allowed for 3-line whips.

picturesque a figure but both were brilliant communicators, of high intelligence and with a very clear approach to their problems. Each impressed Hawton as an individualist, rather than as a party man.

Macleod had a good relationship with his parliamentary secretary. He gave her specific responsibilities in which he did not interfere and kept her fully informed about the evolution of general policy. Few Ministers fulfilled as many outside engagements, but Pat Hornsby-Smith did her full share and between them they covered most of the country.

Civil servants know more than is sometimes realised and brief their Ministers very fully, so Macleod always knew the good points and the bad and every aspect of each problem before he arrived on a visit. He was sometimes impatient and would cut a long-winded explanation short with, 'I know all that. What are your proposals for dealing with it?' This saved time but it did not make friends, and the same criticism was made of Macleod in other departments. He never tolerated fools and too often showed it.

Eve Macleod was a great help to him in this department, in the work of which their interests so often coincided. Officials paid constant tributes to her courage in standing for hours at a time, supported by her two sticks, to receive the guests at the innumerable receptions and cocktail parties. On one occasion Dame Enid Russell-Smith noted 'Mrs Macleod's plucky gaiety in winding her sticks with magenta ribbon to contrast with her blue dress'. Her practical knowledge of the voluntary side of NHS work, unique in a nationalised service, was helpful to Iain and no doubt prompted much of his own interest. She was also an enthusiastic supporter of the nursing profession and opened their conference and exhibition at the Seymour Hall in 1954. The nurses loved her.

When Macleod first went to the Ministry of Health he told Sir George Godber that if he had had his choice of departments he would have chosen Health. It was the subject he had specialised in and his remark was certainly true at the time, although later he was to feel that he had done his most important and rewarding work at the Colonial Office. He was interested above all in the practice of politics, but there can be no doubt, in the words of Sir Alan Marre, of the 'humanity of outlook with which he sought to fulfil his responsibilities' as Minister of Health.

'Much as I admired Iain's work as a Minister,' wrote Sir George Godber, 'I mainly look back on him as a friend, and I don't suppose you can pay higher tribute to a Minister than that from a civil servant.'[11]

11 Sir George Godber to the author, August 14, 1970.

CHAPTER 6

Minister of Labour and National Service (1) 1955-1957

~~∿∽∿~~

WINSTON CHURCHILL retired as Prime Minister in April 1955 and was succeeded by Anthony Eden, whose only immediate major change in the Government was the appointment of Harold Macmillan as Foreign Secretary. Iain Macleod was disappointed not to be moved. He had served with success at the Ministry of Health for three years and he hoped for promotion to the Cabinet. Indeed his confidence was such that he accepted a number of speaking engagements as Minister of Health which he thought his successor would have to fulfil. He admitted ruefully to Eve that there were amongst these some he would never have undertaken had he realised at the time that he would have to discharge them himself!

After serving as crown prince for fifteen years under the shadow of the greatest statesman of the age, Eden, not unnaturally, was anxious for a mandate in his own right and he decided upon an early election. The moment was propitious. In his April budget Butler had taken sixpence off the income tax and the economy looked buoyant. The campaign was correspondingly quiet, and on May 26 the Conservative Government was returned with its overall majority increased from seventeen to sixty. Macleod's own majority at Enfield was 11,518.

Eden's inheritance appeared to be a good one. Abroad there was a welcome thaw in East–West relations, and at home Butler had talked with confidence of doubling the standard of living in twenty-five years. In fact, as the year 1955 wore on, difficulties began to develop over the balance of payments and inflationary pressures increased. By July wages, prices and government expenditure were all rising too fast, and as early as August 30th Eden had become convinced that 'we must put the battle of inflation before anything else'.[1] In the autumn Butler introduced a deflationary second budget, much attacked by the Opposition after the tax reductions only seven months before.

1 Minute to R. A. Butler, quoted in *Full Circle* by Anthony Eden, Cassells, 1960.

On December 22, 1955, Eden announced a Christmas reshuffle of his Administration. Butler became Lord Privy Seal and Leader of the House of Commons, Macmillan succeeded him at the Treasury, and Selwyn Lloyd was made Foreign Secretary. Patrick Buchan-Hepburn joined the Cabinet as Minister of Works and his deputy, Edward Heath, became Chief Whip. Iain Macleod entered the Cabinet as Minister of Labour in succession to Walter Monckton, who had held this post since the formation of Churchill's second Government in 1951.

Just as he had been the first of the 1950 vintage to take charge of a department of his own, so now Macleod became the first Cabinet Minister of his political generation. It is not without interest that, in moving from Health to Labour, he made the same transition as Aneurin Bevan had done five years earlier, although the circumstances were of course different, as Bevan's had been a move across the board, whereas for Macleod this was an important promotion. His feet were now firmly on the ladder, and the *Economist* went so far as to comment that he had reached the Cabinet with an unmitigated reputation for success. He had won golden opinions for his performance at the despatch box and he was already acknowledged as an able administrator.

His promotion had been widely forecast. As early as August Henry Fairlie had predicted in the *Spectator* that he would succeed Monckton at the Ministry of Labour. I remember that Gwilym Lloyd-George (later Viscount Tenby) then Home Secretary, for whom I was working as Parliamentary Private Secretary, told me in confidence of the probability of Macleod's appointment and invited my opinion as one of the younger Members. I endorsed Iain's claims with enthusiasm. Anthony Eden wrote later that he regarded the Ministry of Labour as 'a useful training ground for a possible future Prime Minister'.[2]

Walter Monckton, acting under a general directive from Churchill to gain the confidence and co-operation of organised labour, had established a reputation as an impartial and conciliatory arbitrator between employers and the unions. But to some Conservatives his policy appeared to be little short of appeasement in the face of union pressure. It certainly contributed to wage-cost inflation, and his settlements with the railway workers in 1953 and 1955 would have forced any private enterprise company out of business. His approach was to conciliate between the two sides of industry without attempting to impose any overall Government strategy. In practice, the broad impression he created was that of halving

2 *Full Circle*, p. 318.

the difference between the union claim and the employer's offer. He was a man of great ability and infinite charm, and I cannot remember any senior member of the Government who was personally more liked and respected. He had carried through Churchill's 1951 policy with skill and success; but times had changed and the political world watched to see whether Macleod would follow the Monckton path or turn his Ministry into a more positive arm of Government policy.

The most non-political of Churchill's Ministers had been succeeded by one of the most professional politicians of the postwar period, but at first there was no apparent change of direction. Indeed in many respects Macleod would instinctively have liked the diplomatic role which Monckton had played with such natural finesse, but he was a much tougher character than Walter Monckton and he understood the importance of the growing economic problems to which his predecessor's policies had contributed. Within weeks of his arrival at the Ministry he had impressed upon his staff that one of his main objectives was to bring wage inflation under closer control.

The major responsibility for this policy rested of course with the Chancellor of the Exchequer, but in the first half of 1956 Macleod helped Macmillan with a series of unofficial meetings of industrialists and trade union leaders, urging upon both sides the need for restraint. The Government were anxious about inflation, but the scale of this issue was far smaller then than it was to become in the late 1960s and early 1970s, and there was no question of the wage freezes and incomes policies which became so predominant a feature of the economic debate a decade or more later.

Much depended on the 1956 budget. The Federation of British Industries was critical of government expenditure, which in their view entailed 'a correspondingly high level of taxation and the resultant distortion of the economy.' They argued that a reduction in public expenditure would be 'the biggest single contribution' the Government could make to curb inflation. The Trades Union Congress, on the other hand, considered that the rise in prices made wage restraint impossible and recommended that the budget 'should make its contribution towards lowering the price of necessities wherever possible.'

The Chancellor of the Exchequer promised a reduction of £100 million in government spending, and persuaded the boards of the nationalised industries to hold the prices of their goods and services steady. On July 12th the FBI urged its members to exercise restraint in price policy. But there was no corresponding response from the unions. In early September the TUC rejected wage restraint by an overwhelming majority and wage rates continued to rise rapidly.

Macleod had supported Macmillan in his attempts to achieve the co-operation of both sides of industry; but he had also embarked on an initiative of his own to improve industrial relations. The Conservative Party's Industrial Charter of 1947 had incorporated a 'Workers' Charter', an important section of which dealt with the concept of a contract of service. Macleod believed that a wider acceptance of this idea would help to resolve 'the conflict between a man's natural desire for security in his job and the national need for mobility of labour.'

In a speech to the Industrial Co-partnership Association which he was invited to address by my stepfather, Sir Geoffrey Shakespeare, he said: 'I do not believe that people are going to behave responsibly unless they are treated as responsible, mature individuals . . . it is madness to think that we can draw up a line of industrial battle in this country and hope that one side or another may at the end of a bitter struggle prove the more powerful.'

At a Ministry of Labour meeting of the National Joint Advisory Council, in which Government, management and unions discussed their mutual problems, Macleod suggested that he should draw up a code of practice which would set out the rights of workers; this would then receive non-statutory parliamentary endorsement through a resolution of both Houses. It seems a modest proposal today, but in the 1950s there were many people on both sides of industry who distrusted any interference by the Government in matters of this kind, and the reaction to his suggestion was hostile.

Macleod did not allow this lack of response to kill his proposals for more positive employment policies, and in a speech to the Conservative Party Conference at Llandudno on October 12, 1956, he reverted to the same theme:

We have not abandoned the ideals of the Workers' Charter. I think a man should be told in plain terms when he starts a new job what his rights are and the terms on which he is engaged. I think in principle that the period of notice should be related to a man's length of service. This would be recognition that a firm owes a greater loyalty to its old and faithful servants than to those who have come lately to its payroll. . . . Many firms have made admirable agreements embodying these principles but we want a general recognition that the period of notice should be an important part of a firm's management policy both because of its impact on human relations and because it is part of the orderly management of the labour market.

Later Macleod followed up this speech with the publication of a booklet[3] bringing to the notice of industry the best and latest employment practices, with examples from large firms and small, which he hoped would be more widely adopted. In a foreword he wrote: 'Individuals are naturally concerned about the security of their jobs and incomes, and change is feared as a step into the unknown.' He emphasised that industrial efficiency depended as much upon human as upon technical factors and that one of the answers lay 'in encouraging a sense of mutual responsibility; responsibility of the employer towards the worker and of the worker towards the employer.'

Macleod was ahead of his time. Fifteen years ago neither industry nor the public were ready for legislation on matters of this kind. But his idea of a code of industrial relations has since been introduced, following the Industrial Relations Act of 1971, by Robert Carr, who was Macleod's Parliamentary Secretary at the Ministry of Labour in 1956.

One of Macleod's main concerns arose from the problem of redundancy. In July 1956 the British Motor Corporation declared redundant 6,000 of their workers in factories in Oxford, Coventry and South Wales. The company gave the men very little notice and a partial strike ensued. Speaking in the House of Commons on June 28th Macleod was neutral but, following strong private negotiations, he secured agreement that employees who had been with the company for more than ten years should receive compensation for dismissal, and that the Ministry should be consulted before future dismissals of this kind. This agreement was at least a partial success for Macleod's policy of fairer and more imaginative management practices. As a result of the dispute he commissioned a special study on large scale redundancy. Later in the year[4] he observed that 'We do not know whether the jobs which are found for those concerned create housing problems for them and education problems for their

3 *Positive Employment Policies*, HMSO, 1958. This covered, *inter alia*, redundancy, length of notice, joint consultation, training, promotion and ways of presenting financial information to employees.

4 House of Commons, December 20, 1956.

children and whether they are able to meet hire purchase and other commitments on which they have embarked.' In fact, by November 1956, only seventy-five of the 6,000 BMC workers declared redundant in July were still unemployed.

Macleod's anxiety was heightened during the year by a series of alarmist articles in the press dealing with automation, some of which depicted the work force of whole factories being reduced to a handful of men. People feared that skill and experience would be devalued as men became mere minders of machines. In a speech to the International Labour Organisation at Geneva in July 1957, Macleod said: 'Overnight, almost, automation became news . . . and a flood of questions in the House of Commons urged the Government to set up a Ministry of Automation to pass special legislation for the robot age.' But public interest had later subsided, and Macleod added: 'It is a month since I was asked a question in Parliament on this subject.'

He did not himself think that automation would cause large-scale unemployment, but he realised that the acceptance of technological progress produced its own difficulties and he called on management and men to 'look at modern problems with modern eyes' and to plan for change in consultation and partnership with each other.

In all these ways Macleod's employment policies reflected the postwar evolution of the Tory Party. As early as 1956 his approach to these issues was the background to the Contracts of Employment Act of 1963, the Redundancies Act of 1965 and the Industrial Relations Act of 1971.

One of the major problems facing any Minister of Labour in any government is that of strikes. In his speech to the Conservative Party Conference in the autumn of 1956 Macleod had pointed out that 'We can afford strikes less than any other country in the world. We have got a knife-edge economy and the world is not going to wait for us while we squabble, and the orders that we must have may be lost to us because of industrial disturbance.' But he had studied the experience of other countries, which at that time gave little support to the view that a ballot imposed by law before a strike would reduce the number of strikes. 'I believe firmly,' he went on, 'that the British system of free voluntary negotiation in industry, with the minimum of government interference, is the best, and I believe firmly in the trade union system. These views are fundamental to my political beliefs and I have not altered them in any way. Nor will I.' The number, duration and scale of strikes in the middle

1950s were very different from the situation in Britain twelve or fifteen years later.

Within a few months of this speech, Macleod was faced with another difficult strike situation. As in the previous July, the trouble arose in the motor car industry. In February 1957 a dispute developed at Briggs Motors, a part of the Ford group, at Dagenham. This company had an unfortunate history of labour stoppages and unofficial strikes. The management suspended a shop steward and, despite union demands, refused to reinstate him. Macleod pressed the union leaders hard to agree to a Court of Inquiry and it was a personal victory when he was able to announce on February 25th that the Court would be set up under the chairmanship of Lord Cameron. The next day the strike was called off and the company agreed to pay the shop steward's wages until the report of the Court was received. This was published on March 30, 1957.[5] The company's right to dismiss the shop steward was upheld and the unions were urged to give immediate consideration to the amount of power exercised by shop stewards at the factory. Both sides were criticised for the bad labour relations which had been revealed as a result of the inquiry, and the outcome was widely regarded as a personal success for Iain Macleod.

During the early part of Macleod's tenure of the Ministry of Labour, one of the subjects which caused him the greatest personal anxiety was National Service. During Eden's premiership there had been much discussion on the run-down of the Services as a contribution to the reduction of government expenditure. The military arguments against it were as strong as the economic arguments. Two years is too short a period in which both to train and use manpower. In the guerrilla-type warfare of Malaya or Cyprus, a young man just out from England had insufficient time in which to make an effective contribution before he was due to return to civilian life.

There was a third factor with which Macleod was particularly concerned – the human aspect of many of the individual cases. It was his invidious responsibility to consider the pleas for deferment which poured into him in letters from Members of Parliament. His dislike of this task was intense. When he thought a young man had a genuine case for deferment, Macleod would leave no doubt in the minds of his officials as to where his personal sympathies lay. If such a case was frustrated by the

5 Cmd. 151.

departmental rules, a brusque note on the file from the Minister would lead to a rapid change in the official interpretation. He always referred scathingly to National Service as 'conscription'.

In his wish to be rid of National Service as soon as possible, Macleod was much assisted by the Prime Minister and by Duncan Sandys, the new Minister of Defence, who at the end of March 1957 published an important Defence White Paper, which proposed a substantial reduction in the manpower of the armed services. The Government's policy was to rely in future mainly upon the nuclear deterrent.

With this in view Macleod had announced in February 1957, the extension of the period of postponement of the call-up from six months to two years. He laid particular emphasis on domestic hardship:

> I have sent special instructions to all my officers to say that all those cases are to be considered with the fullest sympathy. . . . I think and hope that these changes will get rid of many of the cases which have caused all of us such anxiety and will reduce the amount of correspondence between Hon. Members and myself, which is something we can all bear with fortitude.

On April 17, 1957, Macleod announced in the House of Commons the beginning of the end of National Service and that there would be no call up of the 1940 class. He dealt with George Brown, the Shadow Minister of Defence, in a scornful comment: 'I am sorry. The Rt. Hon. Gentleman really cannot ask for the sight screen to be moved after his middle stump has been knocked away.'

The abolition of National Service met with widespread approval, and on the day after his speech the *Manchester Guardian*, long a critic of the policy, observed, 'The Prime Minister can thank his lucky stars that he has a Minister of Labour of Mr Macleod's calibre.'

Macleod's problems at the Ministry of Labour, and indeed the whole domestic scene in British politics, were overshadowed throughout the summer and autumn of 1956 by Colonel Nasser's seizure of the Suez Canal and the events which flowed from it.

In the spring of 1964 Macleod wrote a review for the *New York Herald Tribune* of a book on Foster Dulles by Professor Herman Finer.[6] By chance Anthony Eden saw this review and wrote to Iain to compliment him on its clarity and cogency. Macleod's article is of exceptional interest.

6 *Dulles over Suez. The theory and practice of his diplomacy.* Quadrangle Books.

'The Suez crisis,' he wrote, 'marked the lowest ebb of Anglo-American relations in modern times . . . the alliance was shaken to its foundations. . . . Having brusquely withdrawn his offer of a loan for the Aswan Dam he (Dulles) failed to put his weight behind the allies when Nasser seized the canal as a direct tit-for-tat.'

The British Cabinet was led up the garden path by Dulles, and Macleod thought Finer's book would 'make plain to American readers just why and where we British differed from this gifted but maddening statesman.'

Dulles was often unfairly critical of British colonialism, of which he appeared to think our intervention at Suez was a form. But, as Eden pointed out in his memoirs, the dispute was one between sovereign nations about the violation of a treaty: 'If the United States had to defend their treaty rights in the Panama Canal, they would not regard such action as colonialism, neither would I.' Macleod added in his article, 'And neither would I.' He agreed with Finer that Dulles was pursuing 'that obsession of his, to vie with the Soviet Union on every possible occasion', this time for the support of the Afro-Asian bloc. Macleod commented: 'I have no doubt that this was the principal motive and equally no doubt that it was ill-judged . . . we knew that any intervention would be disapproved of by several of our Commonwealth partners. What we found difficult to credit was that the United States should not recognise its identity of interest with ourselves in maintaining the peace and stability of the Middle East . . . an open flank which the Communists were trying to turn.'

At first the Cabinet had the support of the Opposition front bench in reacting strongly against the seizure of the canal, but approval in July turned to growing hostility when the House re-assembled in October and as our support for the Israeli attack on Egypt grew obvious, the anger of the Labour Party became more and more apparent, the scenes in the House of Commons more bitter and more violent. On one occasion the Speaker had to suspend the sitting for tempers to cool. There was to be nothing comparable in Parliament until the debates on the Industrial Relations Bill in 1971, but with this difference: in 1971 the indignation of the official Opposition appeared synthetic. In 1956 Hugh Gaitskell, as well as his supporters 'below the gangway', was genuinely furious. As events developed and Cabinet meetings became more and more frequent, the Government sometimes appeared to be only an hour or two ahead of the House of Commons.

The hostility of the United Nations, the United States and the Commonwealth to the Anglo/French enterprise was considerable. Some people feared a pro-Egyptian intervention by Russia in retaliation, but Rab Butler recollects[7] that 'speculation against sterling . . . had an even profounder effect on the Chancellor of the Exchequer, Harold Macmillan, who switched almost overnight from being the foremost protagonist of intervention to being the leading influence for disengagement.' As Randolph Churchill wrote at the time: 'What was the difference between Rab Butler who never wanted to go in and Harold Macmillan who took the Cabinet out?' The difference was to be one of the factors in the party's choice of a successor to Anthony Eden when the Prime Minister was forced to retire through ill-health two months later.

I remember the excited, flag-waving meeting of the 1922 Committee when the patriotic line taken by Macmillan was so much more in tune with the mood of the Parliamentary Party than the more moderate and more equivocal attitude of Rab Butler. 'I held the Tory Party for the weekend. It was all I intended to do,' said Macmillan to Gil Lloyd George and myself immediately after this meeting. It sounded to me, in my back-bench innocence, a somewhat cynical remark. Disarmingly, in the fourth volume of his autobiography[8] Macmillan wrote:

> I have often been reproached for having been at the same time one of the most keen supporters of strong action in the Middle East and one of the most rapid to withdraw when that policy met a serious check. 'First in, first out' was to be the elegant criticism of one of my chief Labour critics on many subsequent occasions.

This criticism was not confined to members of the Labour Party.

Iain Macleod played little part in these events. He was not a member of the Defence and Overseas Policy Committee of the Cabinet, and in any case the effective decisions on this occasion were made by a very small group of Ministers, to which the Cabinet as a whole were subsequently invited to agree. Nevertheless, Macleod had misgivings which he expressed privately to his friends. At one Cabinet meeting when some Ministers complained about the speed with which they were being asked to endorse decisions, the Prime Minister pointed out that they had never served in a War Cabinet. Macleod commented tartly 'we did not know we were at war'.[9] He had many reservations, but despite Randolph

7 *The Art of the Possible*, Hamish Hamilton, 1971.
8 *Riding the Storm*, Macmillan, 1971.
9 Quoted in *The Suez Affair*, by Hugh Thomas. Page 316 of Penguin edition.

Churchill's assertion that on November 4th he 'seriously considered resignation',[10] this was not in fact the case.

He knew well that, as the youngest and newest member of the Cabinet, with experience only of home affairs, he could not have altered the basic policy, which stemmed from the Prime Minister's own determination to settle with Nasser. And there was no clear lead in a different direction by any senior member of the Government. If Rab Butler had come out strongly against Eden's policy, he would have received support from Macleod, who shared his anxieties. He might even have resigned if Butler had done so, but he was not directly involved and would never have gone on his own. Nor had he been concerned in the secret discussions with the French and the Israelis and he knew little, if anything, about them.

In fact, the Cabinet was divided throughout the whole Suez affair into two main groups. Both groups supported the Prime Minister's policy but with different aims. One section agreed with Eden's 'anti-dictator' line against Nasser and wanted to invade Egypt through Alexandria. The other section wanted to save the Suez Canal and to internationalise it. There is no doubt that Iain Macleod was in the second group in support of Rab Butler. As matters turned out, the only resignations from the Government were those of two junior Ministers, Anthony Nutting and Edward Boyle.

The strain of the Suez crisis took a heavy toll of Eden's health and his doctors recommended a holiday for recuperation in Jamaica. Rab Butler was left in charge of the Government during the Prime Minister's absence. Eden returned to England on December 14th and said he would continue as Prime Minister. But his illness was more serious than he had thought and on January 9th he was forced to resign on the advice of his doctors. At the end of his last Cabinet he said goodbye to each of his colleagues individually. As the most junior, Macleod was the last to leave. He shook hands with the Prime Minister and said, 'Thank you for all your kindness to us younger ones.' Eden was touched and wrote later, 'I have never forgotten that.'[11]

The succession lay between Rab Butler and Harold Macmillan. There were no other contenders. The following day the Lord Chancellor, Lord Kilmuir, and Lord Salisbury took soundings among their Cabinet colleagues. Salisbury found it difficult to pronounce the letter 'r' and he

10 *The Rise and Fall of Sir Anthony Eden*, Randolph Churchill, MacGibbon and Kee, 1959, p. 287.
11 Lord Avon to the author, September 1, 1970.

asked each Minister in turn, 'Well, which is it to be, Wab or Hawold?' His own verdict was for Macmillan. And Churchill, who was consulted by the Queen, gave her the same advice. Macmillan 'emerged' with a clear Cabinet majority, which reflected the opinion of the Parliamentary Party, and on January 10, 1957, he kissed hands as Prime Minister.

'Fortunately,' as Macleod recalled in his review of Finer's book, 'the after-effects of Suez were neither as serious nor as permanent as was prophesied. Our intervention, though cut short, forestalled the development of a general war throughout the Middle East. . . . American and British policy in this area soon moved closer together, as could be seen in . . . the later United States landings in the Lebanon. The alliance survived the shocks of 1956, thanks to the good relations built up between Eisenhower and Macmillan.'

The new Prime Minister not only mended Britain's fences with the United States. His unruffled calm and aristocratic, almost Edwardian style did much to soothe the nerves and encourage the efforts of his colleagues, and every Conservative Member of Parliament was soon talking enthusiastically in almost every constituency speech about his exceptional leadership.

Eden, despite his many qualities, had tended to fuss his ministers with telephone calls and messages enquiring how their particular problems were progressing. Macmillan left them to mind their own departments. It was typical of him that at the height of the Dagenham dispute he telephoned Macleod with the suggestion: 'Iain, there's a very good film on to night. Dorothy and I would like you to come.' Few Prime Ministers can have taken office at such a low ebb in their Party's fortunes. Yet twenty-one months later, in the general election of 1959, the reputation of few peace-time Prime Ministers of Britain has stood higher. It was a remarkable achievement.

As part of the Suez legacy, sterling was still under severe pressure and the new Prime Minister was naturally anxious to avoid industrial disputes at home. But within two months of the formation of Macmillan's Government Macleod was facing one of the most serious strike threats since 1926. He was confronted with the possibility of a battle on three fronts in the vital railway, engineering and ship-building industries. Strikes over such a wide and important area would have amounted almost to a general strike and would have been disastrous for the economy. It was essential to separate the issues and avoid fighting on all three at once. Happily the threatened railway strike did not materialise and, when this was settled, the Prime Minister cabled Macleod from Bermuda congratulating him on having handled the matter with calmness and courage. The engineering and ship-building disputes remained.

In the autumn of 1956 the leaders of the ship-building and engineering unions had submitted separate claims for wage increases, both of which were rejected by the employers. On March 7, 1957, the Confederation of Shipbuilding and Engineering Unions called a national strike of shipbuilding workers from March 16th and a few days later the engineering unions associated their members with this decision. On March 12th Macleod proposed arbitration and announced that Lord Evershed, the Master of the Rolls, had agreed to act as arbitrator. The employers accepted this invitation but it was rejected by the union leaders who wanted direct negotiations and a cash offer. The strike, the first in the industry since 1926, began in all shipyards on March 16th and was followed on March 23rd by engineering strikes in selected areas, with the threat that, failing a settlement, there would be a complete stoppage on April 6th. The shipyard workers tried to prevent large liners using the port of Southampton and Admiralty tugs had to be provided to help the 'Queen Mary' sail on March 21st. On her return voyage from the United States she docked at Cherbourg instead of Southampton.

On March 25th Macleod decided to appoint a Court of Inquiry and asked the unions to call off the strike pending its report. The leaders of the shipbuilding and engineering unions then offered to end the strikes if their members were given an immediate and unconditional five per cent pay increase. If not, the engineering unions threatened to intensify the strike by calling out half a million workers in the Greater London area. Negotiations between the engineering employers and unions broke down on March 29th, and Macleod announced the appointment of a Court of Inquiry with the same members and under the same chairman, Professor D. T. Jack, as for the shipbuilding dispute. By Monday, April 1st, more than 780,000 men were idle. It was the largest stoppage in Britain since the general strike over thirty years before. But on April 4th, the union president, William Carron, gave his casting vote in favour of a return to work and acceptance of the findings of the Court, which had held its first meeting the day before.

The reports of the Courts of Inquiry were published on May 2nd, and the recommendation eventually accepted by both sides was for an 11s per week increase with the proviso of a wage claim standstill for at least a year. The engineering unions tried to evade the standstill by lodging, within a month of the settlement, a claim for a forty-hour week, which was rejected by the employers.

It was clear that the Courts of Inquiry would make concessions to the union demands and therefore that, in appointing them, Macleod had in effect promoted a settlement at the cost of a further round of inflationary wage increases and at a time when the employers were in a mood to fight. A leading article in the *Economist* on May 23rd commented that 'It would have been better for the economy to stand an engineering strike this year than . . . another blow to everybody's standard of life.'

The employers were angry over what they considered a lamentable lack of support from the Government. 'Twice in four years,' they complained, 'the Federation has been prepared to fight it out with the unions. Such a course involving, as it would have done, the virtual closing down of the industry, might have been a worthwhile calculated risk. It was no occasion for the kind of compromise which would inevitably emerge from a Court of Inquiry. The Federation can hardly be blamed for heeding Government warnings calling attention to the economic dangers of further wage increases . . . they were not allowed to resist after they had received every encouragement to have a firm purpose and to dare to make it known to the unions.'[12]

It was true that in the spring of 1957 the Government was not prepared to have a trial of strength with the unions in a key sector of the economy. But the Cabinet and the Parliamentary Party were well satisfied with Macleod's handling of a difficult situation.

One of the suggestions made by the Court of Inquiry had a wider application to industry as a whole. The Court recommended that 'an authoritative and impartial body should be appointed to consider wages, costs and prices as they affect the economy'. Peter Thorneycroft, the new Chancellor of the Exchequer, took up this idea and in August set up his Council on Prices, Productivity and Incomes, which quickly became known as 'the three wise men'.[13]

As the year 1957 wore on and inflationary wage rises continued, the Government became more and more concerned and in September Peter Thorneycroft decided on a severe credit squeeze including a sharp rise in bank rate. Speaking in an economic debate when Parliament re-assembled,

12 From a pamphlet entitled *Looking at Industrial Relations* published by the Engineering and Allied Employers' National Federation.
13 The members of it were Lord Cohen, Sir Harold Howitt and Sir Dennis Robertson.

he said: 'Wage increases, unrelated to and going far beyond the general growth of real wealth within the country, are by far the greatest danger we have to face . . . those who ask for wage increases, those who grant increases and those who adjudicate about wages should have this fact first, in the forefront of their minds.' On the following day Macleod went even further and talked of the Government's determination 'not to finance inflationary awards, however those awards are secured, whether through negotiation or through arbitration'. This was strong meat for the Opposition, and Gaitskell launched an immediate attack against the implication that the Government would not provide the money to implement an arbitration award in the public sector. Macleod, unusually for him, ducked a straight answer and it was left to the Prime Minister in a speech in the House on November 5th to make it clear that, while the Government would accept arbitral awards to public employees, the extra money would have to be found from existing Government expenditure. In private industry, too, he hoped that the credit squeeze would 'exert a healthy check on unreasonable wage demands . . . increases of wages must come from greater productivity, but not from increased supplies of money.'[14]

An important aspect of inflation was of course the Government's own expenditure, which Thorneycroft was determined to hold down. He had asked spending departments for cuts of £150 million but, in Cabinet discussion, the gap was narrowed to a difference of £50 million as between Thorneycroft's demands and the concessions made by his colleagues. Macmillan commented in his diary: 'The Chancellor wants some swingeing cuts in Welfare State expenditure – more, I fear, than are feasible politically.'[15]

The Prime Minister invited Macleod to prepare a paper on possible social service economies. Macleod concluded that there were only four sources of saving in this field: a hospital boarding charge, which was administratively difficult (it would require the recruitment of 1,000 extra clerks for a saving of £9 million in a full year); a cut in the ophthalmic service, which would only save about £3½ million; a cut in welfare milk which could produce £10 million at a charge of 6d as against the full cost of 8d a pint; and a further increase in the weekly insurance stamp. The last two were possible though politically difficult. Macleod thought a cut in defence expenditure of £7 million, which Thorneycroft had asked for,

14 *Riding the Storm*, p. 362.
15 *Ibid.*, p. 363.

was possible and desirable, but there was still a gap of about £50 million, one per cent of a year's expenditure.

On the evening of January 5th Macmillan invited Butler, Heath, Macleod and Sandys to dinner to discuss the problem and Macleod expressed the view that Thorneycroft 'was obsessed and dominated by Powell'.[16] He thought it absurd for the Cabinet to quarrel over Treasury figures which often turned out to be inaccurate, and that it was silly to fight a major battle over £50 million. The margin of error alone overwhelmed such calculations.

Next day Thorneycroft, Powell and Birch, the entire team of Treasury Ministers, resigned and Macmillan, about to set off on his tour of the Commonwealth, referred to the matter as 'a little local difficulty'. It was typical of his style, and amused rather than annoyed the British public. Derick Heathcoat Amory, formerly Minister of Agriculture, was appointed Chancellor of the Exchequer. And Randolph Churchill sent Macleod a telegram from America:

> You and Harold would be gratified by total lack of interest in Washington about recent resignations. Stop. My secretary does not know who Thorneycroft is or was or will be. Regards. Randolph.

16 *Riding the Storm*, p. 368.

CHAPTER 7

Minister of Labour and National Service (11) 1958-1959

∽∾∽∾∽

IN October 1957 the Transport and General Workers' Union, led by Frank Cousins, made a claim for an increase of 25s per week for all bus workers in the London area. In November this demand was rejected by the London Transport Executive, who made no counter-offer, and in December the union refused to go to arbitration. Union leaders were convinced that, but for Government instructions, the LTE would have made an offer of some kind and they may well have been right. The Cabinet had decided that, in an effort to avoid further wage escalation, a stand must be taken in the public sector.

An exception was, however, to be made for the railways. Macmillan was well aware that a national rail strike would cause serious dislocation in industry, whereas a London bus strike would not. With the support of Butler and Macleod he pressed a somewhat reluctant Cabinet to agree to a three per cent rise for the railwaymen, which was accepted by the railway unions after difficult negotiations. 'This was an immense relief,' Macmillan wrote later.[1] 'I was now prepared to face the bus strike.' He sent a personal minute to Macleod in May 1958, 'to express my admiration for the way you have handled the whole of this, as well as other troubles. It is a very great comfort to me to have this most difficult of all portfolios in your safe hands.'

Long before the railwaymen's claim was settled the talks with the London busmen had run into serious difficulties. In January 1958 a request was made by the London Transport Executive and the Transport and General Workers' Union to the Ministry of Labour for the department's assistance in conciliation. In normal circumstances this was the accepted procedure, but it quickly became clear that this dispute was being handled in a different way. The Chief Industrial Commissioner, Sir Wilfred

1 *Riding the Storm*, pp. 714, 715.

123

Neden, was given advice by 'a Cabinet Minister' that he was not to offer 'a penny more'. Remarkably, this instruction was conveyed without Macleod's knowledge.

The Minister of Labour's position was anomalous. He had to reconcile his responsibility as a member of the Cabinet for implementing the Government's policy of wage restraint, with the traditional role of his department to act as an impartial conciliator in industrial disputes. In these exceptional circumstances normal conciliation was impossible, but it would have been equally unusual and undesirable to refuse the good offices of the Ministry, when both sides in the dispute had asked for assistance.

After consulting Macleod, Sir Wilfred Neden suggested the formation of an ad hoc 'outside' committee to help in arriving at a settlement. This was to be a Committee of Investigation which would enquire into the dispute and make recommendations direct to the parties. It would consist of a representative from each side of the industry and an impartial chairman nominated by Macleod, whose name was acceptable both to the LTE and to the T & GW. Both sides agreed to this proposal and made a formal request to the Minister to implement it. But after a delay of fourteen days Macleod decided against this course. To the union and the Opposition in the House of Commons it appeared that the department's good offices were being deliberately withheld.

Macleod wrote to Cousins on January 24th saying that it would be inappropriate to consider the wages situation in London in isolation from that in the rest of the country, but a general enquiry would be a possibility. In the meantime, he reminded Cousins, 'the normal process of arbitration remains available. . . .' This letter infuriated Cousins, who believed that Macleod's decision was so unlike him that he must be acting on a Cabinet directive rather than on his own initiative, still less on departmental advice. This was true. Macleod's instinct was for conciliation, but once the Government's decision, with which he concurred, had been taken, he fought the issue with tenacity and brilliance.

On January 28th Cousins and Harry Nicholas, then Assistant General Secretary of the Union, spent two hours with the Minister, who again declined to set up the committee and repeated his offer of an investigation into the wages structure of the industry as a whole. The union leaders pointed out that Macleod had given no indication till January 24th that he would not accept the request put forward on January 10th; that his action was without precedent; that the suggestion of a wider enquiry did not deal with the immediate matter of the busmen's claim and that the men had already said they were not interested in arbitration.

On January 29th, Alfred Robens, the Shadow Minister of Labour, asked for an explanation in a private notice question in the House of Commons. Macleod replied: 'This was my own decision and my own responsibility. But naturally in an issue like this one consults one's colleagues.' In the original talks with the union, Neden had of course made it clear that the proposal would require the Minister's sanction, but Cousins and Nicholas no doubt genuinely regarded this as a formality and on the strength of this view they had, not without difficulty, persuaded the London busmen to agree to ask for the Committee.

Macleod knew that the Committee would probably recommend a compromise pay concession for the busmen and that this would open the way to further inflationary wage settlements prejudicial to the gradually improving economic situation. He did not, however, refuse to appoint the committee only for this reason. In his letter to Cousins he had suggested arbitration which carried the same risk of a pay settlement. This was not as inconsistent as it may seem because no government had ever interfered with arbitration machinery and Macleod was willing for the matter to be resolved within the framework set up for the purpose.

Macleod's position was a difficult one. He knew that in a curious way the trade unions did not think of the Ministry of Labour as part of the Government. They felt they could always go to St James's Square for advice and that the Minister would hold the ring impartially between them and the employers. Macleod appreciated the special relationship and wished to preserve it. He had therefore authorised Neden's approach to Cousins, which represented his personal policy at that stage. But the inflationary pressures were growing and, between January 10th and 24th, a unanimous decision of the Cabinet instructed the Minister of Labour to resist the busmen's claim. Macleod had no option but to implement this directive or resign. He decided reluctantly that the battle against inflation was of greater importance than the Ministry of Labour's traditional role as mediator and he therefore, sadly but deliberately, let Frank Cousins down. He much disliked having to do so and regretted that he could not even explain his reasons to the union leaders. He did, however, discuss his predicament with Alfred Robens on a Privy Councillor basis. Robens understood his position, respected his confidence and urged him not to resign. Robens is a man of warmth and generosity and Macleod, who felt a personal affection and respect for him, much valued and never forgot his understanding attitude on this occasion.

Press comment criticised the concept of a wider enquiry on the grounds that the municipal and privately employed provincial busmen had not yet lodged any formal claim. But this in itself indicated the real nature of the problem. Busmen in the provinces and in London had long been involved in a wage claim cycle. When one group secured an increase, the other would put in a leap-frogging claim for an even larger amount and this spiral could continue indefinitely. Indeed, this well-known device was one of the weakest links in Cousins' armour.

From the point of view of public presentation by the Government, Cousins was the ideal opponent. As a trenchant left-wing critic of the Administration he was already anathema to most Conservative supporters. The issue itself was also a good one on which to confront the unions. A busmen's strike does not harm production but it does much to annoy and inconvenience the public who, for this reason, tend to support the Government. This is not to say that the Cabinet was looking for a fight, but the battle which now developed was certainly one in which they were not reluctant to engage. The only real danger was that a strike might spread to the railways and the docks. Hence the Prime Minister's relief when the railway dispute was settled.

Cousins was in a difficult position, squeezed between a militant union membership and a Minister in no mood to compromise. Only two courses were open to him – to declare a strike or to try and persuade the men to accept arbitration. In the event both sides agreed that the issue should be referred to the Industrial Court, a form of voluntary arbitration. The union accepted this procedure on the normal condition that it was not bound to accept the Court's award.

On February 6th there was a debate in Parliament on an Opposition motion moved by Alfred Robens, who accused Macleod of humiliating the union leaders by rejecting a course of action which they had in any case had great difficulty in persuading their men to accept. 'This was political interference,' he declared, 'with the free negotiating machinery that has been painfully built up.'

There was much truth in the charge. The London bus dispute marked a turning point in the Ministry's attitude to industrial disputes. It also brought into sharp relief the difference in the position of employees in the public and private sectors. In the former they were subject, directly or indirectly, to government control. In the latter they were not.

The Court reported on March 11th. Its award was for an increase of 8s 6d per week for drivers and conductors in the central London area only. This was rejected by the union, which asked that the total amount of the award should be increased and spread over all the busmen to whom the wage claim related. The LTE declared this impracticable, but offered a further review in the autumn for all the grades not covered by the award.

In answer to a question in the House on April 16th, Macleod said: 'I cannot take any action which would have as its object a variation of the Industrial Court award. To do so would be, in effect, to question the award of the Industrial Court and this I am not prepared to do. . . .' On May 2nd Macleod was attacked in the House for failing to intervene. He re-stated the argument that he could not set aside the decision of the Court and that this was a matter of principle. On the same day a mass meeting of the London busmen took place at the Empress Hall, Earls Court. The strike began on the evening of Sunday, May 4th.

Gaitskell had made a strong attack on the Government in Glasgow at the weekend and there was a stormy scene in the House on Monday, culminating in the announcement by the Leader of the Opposition that he would table a censure motion against Macleod. It was the first motion of censure involving a Minister of Labour since before the war.

The Labour Party had made a political blunder. In the public mind its leaders were now identified with Cousins and the militants in support of an unpopular strike. The Tory ranks closed solidly behind Macleod and on the evening before the debate he received strong backing from a crowded meeting of the Party's labour committee.

On the same day, May 7th, the TUC issued a statement:

This strike has been made unavoidable by the Government's determination to hold down wages in publicly owned industries and services which, in times of rising prices, can only be done by cutting the living standards of the workers concerned.

This was also the view of the Labour Party and was reflected in Robens' opening speech for the Opposition in the censure debate next day. He further alleged that confidence in the impartiality of arbitration had been impaired by the speeches made in the House the previous October by the then Chancellor of the Exchequer and the Minister of Labour.

Macleod opened for the Government. He pointed out that 'although the awards (of Industrial Courts) are not legally binding, they have almost invariably been accepted . . . this is the first time that a major strike has followed the rejection of an Industrial Court award.' He went on to deplore the growing tendency of the Opposition to speak only for organised labour and never, in industrial disputes, for the public as a whole. He concluded his speech with these words[2]:

> I have deliberately not launched an attack on the Rt. Hon. Gentleman [Alfred Robens] or on the Labour Party; nor have I commented . . . on the TUC statement that was issued yesterday.
>
> The House may, however, remember a saying of Mr Marx, of whom I am a devoted follower – Groucho, not Karl – who said, 'Sir, I never forget a face, but I will make an exception of yours.' So the House may perhaps allow me quite briefly one exception to this.

He stopped speaking, though he was still standing at the despatch box. The House was completely silent. Everyone was watching Macleod except one person, Hugh Gaitskell, who was sitting doodling on a piece of paper. At last the silence became so oppressive that Gaitskell looked up – and saw Macleod glaring angrily straight at him. 'Yes,' Iain continued, 'however carefully I try to frame my words about the criticism which has been made against me by the Rt. Hon. Gentleman [Alfred Robens], I am bound to say that I cannot conceal my scorn and contempt for the part that the Leader of the Opposition has played in this . . . it is bound to be a debate which will make industrial affairs and their settlement a good deal more difficult. We are having this debate because the Leader of the Opposition, in a parliamentary scene on Monday, could not control himself. Because of his refusal on Friday to say a single word that would uphold the authority of an arbitration award; because of his mischievous speech over the weekend; because of his lack of authority on Monday. If we are to vote (on the censure motion) then let the censure of the House be on the Rt. Hon. Gentleman tonight and from the country tomorrow.'

Later that evening Robens went up to Macleod and said, 'Iain, that was a bloody fine speech.'

It is perhaps not generally realised how friendly most Members of Parliament are, outside the Chamber itself, with their political adversaries. The battles 'on the floor' are seldom carried into the smoking room. I remember well a comparable occasion in 1951 when Aneurin Bevan was Minister of Labour. He had made a superb winding-up speech for the then Labour Government which, from the Conservative point of view,

2 *Hansard*, Vol. 587, Cols. 1460/61, May 8, 1958.

As Minister of Labour, 1959. Macleod with the Rt. Hon. Reginald Maudling (then Paymaster General) after the announcement of the general election

As Colonial Secretary, 1960. Sir Richard Turnbull, Governor of Tanganyika, Macleod, and a Chief

As Colonial Secretary, 1960. Macleod in Uganda reviewing a Guard of Honour

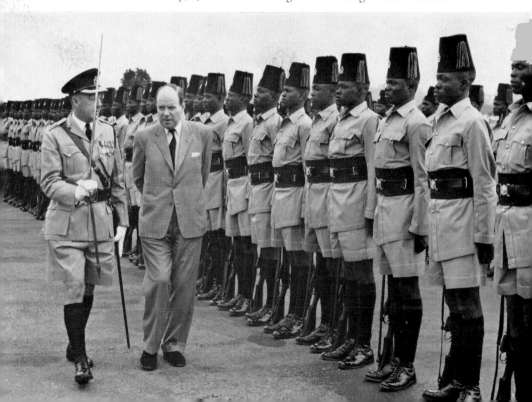

had been spoilt in the last five minutes by a personal attack on Winston Churchill, then Leader of the Opposition, which we thought was unnecessarily vitriolic. A few minutes after the debate finished, I chanced to be walking down a corridor behind Winston and noticed that Nye Bevan was advancing towards us from the opposite direction. There was no one else in sight. I wondered, in view of Bevan's attack only ten minutes earlier, if the two men would angrily ignore each other. But, with typical magnanimity, Churchill stopped and said: 'Congratulations – that was a magnificent speech', to which Bevan, almost coming to attention like a schoolboy before the headmaster, replied: 'Thank you, sir, thank you very much, sir.' Nothing further was said and each went his own way.

Iain Macleod's speech was enthusiastically praised in the press and he received shoals of congratulatory letters from his colleagues. Lord Reading, who had been in the peers' gallery, wrote of his admiration for 'one of the great Parliamentary performers of our time' and added: 'It was a tremendous feat to make a speech of that kind on such a motion without a note. . . . I particularly enjoyed your onslaught on Gaitskell. . . . It would be a pity if the art of Parliamentary invective were allowed to perish and you have now given it a powerful inoculation.'

In answer to a private notice question by Robens on May 16th Macleod declined to intervene in the dispute until there was 'a chink of light'. On May 20th the parallel problem of the London underground workers was settled with the same three per cent increase as had been accepted by the railwaymen. The LTE were the employers both of the busmen and the tube men.

Four days later Cousins asked the railway unions to support the busmen and on May 27th he threatened to extend the strike by bringing out the drivers of petrol lorries in London and south-east England and power workers in the generating stations. These attempts to widen the area of the dispute were unsuccessful and on May 28th the railway unions declined to take any further steps to help the London bus workers, who were now isolated.

Representatives of the TUC saw the Prime Minister on May 30th, and again on June 4th, and afterwards issued a warning to the TGWU not to spread the strike. They urged the union to resume negotiations. At this point Macleod saw Frank Cousins.

The Minister's room was on the corner of St James's Square and Duke of York Street with windows looking out on to both. When Iain's PPS, Reggie Bennett, entered the room that morning he noticed that the blinds were drawn down on the windows facing the side street and asked why. 'Oh, it's nothing,' replied Iain, 'I've got Frank Cousins coming here in a few minutes and just in case the *Daily Express* or anyone are in the rooms opposite I thought I'd draw the blinds so that they won't see Cousins on his knees.' Macleod knew that he had the union on the run and that victory was now in sight.

On June 8th Sir Vincent Tewson, the General Secretary of the TUC, issued a statement, making it clear that Congress did not wish to be involved. . . . 'This is not the time when the General Council would, from choice, desire to enter into full public controversy.' The statement stressed that when this decision was taken 'there were no dissenting voices amongst those not directly involved.'

The attitude of the TUC was a severe disappointment for Cousins; but he now courageously opposed a majority recommendation of the bus-men's negotiating council that the strike should be extended, and on June 13th he persuaded his strike committee and the delegates at an all-garage conference to resume talks with the LTE, during the course of which a basis for settlement gradually emerged.

It was finally agreed that central London drivers and conductors should receive an increase of 8s 6d a week with effect from the date of resumption of work; that Green Line drivers should receive an agreed increase from the same date, and that a joint review of the wages of the excluded staff should be carried out and any agreed increase would be payable from July 2nd. On June 19th a delegate conference of the union decided to recommend a return to work on this formula. A majority of the garages voted in favour and the strike ended on June 21st.[3] It had lasted for seven weeks.

One of the minor irritations made inevitable by the bus strike was the glare of publicity in which Macleod lived throughout its duration. He could not move without being photographed or invited to comment. In self-defence he discovered a back way out of the ministry which he often used when he did not want to be interviewed as he left St James's Square. One evening he escaped by this exit and returned to Enfield in time to hear the television commentator saying, 'The Minister of Labour is in his office and in the closest touch with the latest developments.'

So many press reporters besieged his house at weekends that Iain could

3 In subsequent negotiations the LTE offered increases of 7s 6d a week for the Green Line drivers and 5s for the other grades. The union accepted this offer reluctantly and under protest on July 17th.

not open the front door himself and, when Eve had to go out to do the weekend shopping, she was obliged to arrange for a 'Minister sitter' to answer the door bell.

As soon as the strike was over an ill-timed and somewhat maladroit statement was issued by Sir John Elliot, the Chairman of the London Transport Executive, stating that he would apply to the Transport Tribunal for unlimited charging powers. The implication that the strike had been settled at the expense of further inflation annoyed Ministers and alarmed the Parliamentary Party. On June 25th Macleod addressed a large meeting of the Conservative Party labour committee and assured members that there was no intention of increasing fares.

The outcome of the strike was regarded by all Conservatives and probably by the public as a whole as a major victory over militant trade unionism. The bus strike had been a relatively easy ball to hit, but Macleod had clouted it to the boundary and his reputation stood high. He was the man who had defeated Frank Cousins and who was not afraid to stand up to the unions.

At the Conservative Party Conference in October Macleod said that the Government was determined to maintain its anti-inflation policy. He pointed out that the rise in both wages and prices had been halved in 1958 and, in a reference to the London bus strike, he asked the conference not to concentrate their criticism on one man (Cousins), 'however arrogant or irresponsible you may have thought he was'. He paid a compliment to the realism and responsibility of the TUC in not seeking a confrontation with the Government. The conference carried unanimously a resolution applauding the handling of industrial disputes and Lord Hailsham, as Party Chairman, paid a long and elaborate tribute to the Minister of Labour.

Many people felt that the defeat of the strike was responsible for a more favourable political climate for the Government. Undoubtedly a stand against organised labour was popular with most Conservatives. To Socialists, however, it seemed that the Ministry of Labour had lost its traditional impartiality and that new ways of handling industrial relations would have to be devised. A logical outcome was the creation in the 1960s of the Prices and Incomes Board under the chairmanship of Aubrey Jones, a liberal-minded Conservative ex-Minister. Macmillan summed up the problem when he wrote later, '. . . the position of the Minister of Labour is extremely difficult. He acts nominally as an impartial conciliator to bring the parties together. This is something of a farce when one of the parties is a nationalised industry in which the Government is both equity holder and banker.'[4]

The victory over the left wing leadership of the Transport and General Workers' Union coincided with an upswing in the economy. Bank rate was falling, production was rising and the balance of payments was strong. If there was a fly in the pre-election Conservative ointment it was in the unemployment figures, which were higher than for many years past.

The Conservative Party was always sensitive to the socialist charge of being 'the Party of unemployment'. At the party conference in the autumn Macleod had acknowledged that unemployment would rise above the existing level of 2.2% during the winter months, but he was scornful of the 'crude calculations that are already being put around by the Socialists'. He stressed that the policies of the past year were the guardian not the assassin of full employment.

The unemployment figures for January 1959 were 621,000, the highest since 1947. There was widespread criticism and the Labour Party demanded a debate in the House of Commons. This took place on March 18th and provided the opportunity for one of Macleod's greatest Parliamentary triumphs.

Opening for the Government, he started quietly by teasing Douglas Jay, who had launched the Opposition attack and who had recently produced a pamphlet on the subject which was divided into two sections, the first called 'The Facts' and the second 'Action needed Now'. Macleod began: 'Using as polite words as I can, I would say that the facts are pretty selective.' Although Jay knew the February figures he had used the January figures except where those for February were higher.

In the second section, Macleod pointed out, 'Jay has twelve points, which are two less than those of President Woodrow Wilson and two more, as M. Clemenceau remarked on a similar occasion, than the Almighty needed. . . . He of course proceeds from a different diagnosis . . . but when we come to the general prescription, which is what matters, we are in a similar position. There is nothing new in this.' Jay had indeed suggested that the Government were following his lead; but, as Macleod remarked, his pamphlet was published on March 11th and the Government circular went to local authorities on the 12th. 'If he thinks, with his knowledge of Government, that we can get the departments together, get Ministerial approval and Treasury approval and the Chancellor of the

4 *Riding the Storm*, p. 715.

Exchequer's approval, draft the circular and get it printed by the stationery office in twenty-four hours, I am grateful to him for the compliment.' The *Financial Times* commented: 'Mr Jay presents his proposals with a flourish. But in fact they differ only marginally from what the Government is already doing.'

Macleod added that, as Jay had had experience in the two key Ministries in this matter, the Board of Trade and the Treasury, 'it is not wholly surprising that . . . he should reach somewhat similar answers to those which the Government are putting forward. . . . If I may mangle one metaphor and two sayings, Mahomet has been to the mountain and he has brought back a mouse.'

All this was good parliamentary fun; but with his classic sense of timing Macleod was leaving the best till the end. After explaining the variations in the monthly unemployment figures between November and February, he gave the figures for March which had just come in. He revealed, to the obvious chagrin of the Opposition, a decrease of more than 58,000, with the percentage down from 2.8% to 2.5%. In every region of England, Scotland, Wales and Northern Ireland there was a substantial improvement, the largest being in Scotland, where it was most needed, from 5.4% to 4.8%. With the exception of the 1947 fuel crisis year, it was the biggest March decrease since the war and the biggest decrease in any month since 1947. In the same month the vacancies figure had climbed by 25,000.

Macleod dryly drove the point home: 'To some extent, at least, this seems to me to put one side of the House in a little difficulty.' He read out the first two lines of the Opposition Motion which stated: 'That this House deplores the failure of Her Majesty's Government to prevent the recent substantial and widespread rise in unemployment. . . .'

Macleod continued: 'Frankly, I do not see how the Opposition can call on the House to vote on the motion because it is simply one hundred per cent away from the truth. There has in fact been a "recent substantial and widespread" *fall* in unemployment. . . . I have no doubt that the Opposition will improve. The first seven years in Opposition are always the most difficult. Nor indeed is there any point in the Labour Party getting cross with me. I did not put this motion on the Order Paper, and I cannot help it if every time the Opposition are asked to name their weapons they pick boomerangs.'

Macleod pointed out that under Socialism from 1945 to 1951 the average monthly unemployment figure was 334,000. Under the Tories the average monthly figure was also 334,000 – 'precisely to one thousand the figures are the same'. William Ross, the MP for Kilmarnock, tried to salvage something from the flames: 'The Rt. Hon. Gentleman has given the House a lot of figures. Will he give us one more? Will he tell us how many unemployed there are at the moment?'

Macleod: 'Almost exactly 550,000. . . It is a fairly simple calculation. From 608,000 one takes 58,000.'

By this time the Opposition were in total disarray. The faces of Labour Members were a study in gloom. But there was more to come. The Minister listed the comparable unemployment figures for ten other Western countries. Britain's were the lowest in the 'league table' and, except for Norway and the Netherlands, substantially so.

Macleod reached his peroration:

'We are used . . . to enduring vicious and vehement attacks from Hon. Members opposite and then, after a decent interval, for those attacks to whimper away into silence. . . . As they hear the ring of these unemployment figures this afternoon, I can only offer them the chilly comfort of those words . . . "never send to ask for whom the bell tolls; it tolls for thee".' He sat down to a crescendo of Conservative cheers.

The speech had again been delivered without a note of any kind and again many friends and colleagues sent messages of congratulation, including the Prime Minister who had not heard the speech but had read it in *Hansard*. The Permanent Secretary, Sir Harold Emmerson, said he had not enjoyed the House of Commons so much for a long time and Sir Harry Hylton-Foster wrote: 'What a magnificent speech: perhaps even *your* very best. No answer: enthusiasm compels.'

In November 1958 Macleod made his first visit to the United States. He went to New York, Chicago, Milwaukee and Washington, with the object of seeing for himself whether any of the policies adopted in America were relevant to his own departmental problems in Britain. But there was a lighter moment when, clad in a kilt, he spoke at the annual dinner of the American St Andrew's Day Society.

He also took part in the NBC programme *Meet the Press*, most of which on this occasion was devoted to foreign affairs. Macleod kept firmly to orthodox British policy and made the curt comment that, in dealing with the Soviet Union, he would in no circumstances give way to threats, 'and that goes for everything from Berlin to Quemoy and in between'. When he was questioned on economic policy, he rejected any suggestion of the statutory control of wages and profits and maintained that if government, as the largest employers of labour, set an example, some success could be achieved in controlling the rate of inflation.

Harold Macmillan's first Government, formed in January 1957, began to think about its manifesto for the next general election in December 1958, although the election was not due till the spring of 1960. A policy study group was set up, with Iain Macleod as chairman and Michael Fraser as secretary. The other members of it were Reggie Maudling, David Ormsby Gore (now Lord Harlech), Jack Simon, Enoch Powell and Peter Goldman. They were later joined by Toby Low (now Lord Aldington), Evelyn Emmet, and Geoffrey Rippon.

At a later stage the study group acted as a sub-committee doing detailed work for Harold Macmillan's Steering Committee, which produced the party manifesto before the 1959 election. The Steering Committee consisted of the Prime Minister, who took the chair, Rab Butler, Iain Macleod, Lord Hailsham as Chairman of the Party, Lord Home to represent the House of Lords and Scottish points of view and in his capacity as Secretary of State for Commonwealth Relations, and Edward Heath as Chief Whip. Michael Fraser acted as Secretary. The Steering Committee met seventeen times, and other Ministers were called in from time to time for their advice on departmental subjects. Oliver Poole[5] and Peter Goldman[6] joined the committee about half-way through.

The main problem, as Macleod remarked in a letter to the Prime Minister in May 1959, was 'to find new positive proposals – partly because of the astonishing energy of this Government. Here we are after eight and a half years in office already virtually through a vast programme of social reform in our last year, and instead of calling for their pipes and slippers everyone is bubbling with ideas. . . . A course of tranquillisers seems indicated, otherwise they will leave nothing for a manifesto. . . . But I daresay we can still pull out some plums.'

After the end of the bus strike in the summer of 1958 the Party's fortune took an upward turn. The economic outlook was brighter, hire purchase controls were removed in the autumn of 1958, and in the 1959 budget the Chancellor was able to take 9d off the income tax and 2d off the beer tax. Taxation was reduced by £350 million in a full year.

Macleod caught the prevailing mood in a speech at Reading in March

5 Lord Poole, MP for Oswestry, 1945/50. Chairman of the Conservative Party Organisation, 1955/57. Joint Chairman (with Macleod) 1963.
6 Director of the Conservative Political Centre, 1955–64.

1959 when he appealed for the support of the new middle class of property owners: 'They are as surely men of property,' he said, 'as if they held broad acres or led great firms. Perhaps they own a house or, more probably, they are buying one through a building society. They have a car and a television set – perhaps a refrigerator and a washing machine. They are beginning to invest in stocks and shares, either directly or through unit trusts. At this time of year you will find them looking at gaily coloured travel brochures and planning their summer holiday. But now they do not only think of the English seaside resorts – the pamphlets that they study are of the Costa Brava, the Rhineland, the Italian cities. They are for the most part employees drawing high wages in a prosperous and expanding economy. . . . We can give them the opportunity they long for instead of the equality they despise.'

This speech, which was later printed as a Conservative Party pamphlet, reflected the atmosphere of the election campaign and was the fore-runner of the famous slogan: 'Life is better with the Conservatives. Don't let Labour ruin it.' Macleod dubbed Gaitskell, 'Mr Rising Price himself.'

Macleod's handling of the bus strike was a contributory factor in the Conservatives' election success, but the main reason for it was the reflation of the economy between the autumn of 1958 and the autumn of 1959. Although it is, misleadingly, always quoted out of context, Macmillan's remark 'You have never had it so good' was true. Macleod often said 'You can't have full employment, stable prices and a strong balance of payments.' In fact all three coincided at the time of the 1959 election. The balance of payments was strong, prices were steady and unemployment was low. The Conservatives won the election with an overall majority of one hundred and Macleod's own majority rose again at Enfield to 13,803.

'Don't under-rate Mr Iain Macleod, the Tory Minister of Labour,' wrote Michael Foot in the Daily Herald, 'he is much the most intelligent member of the Stupid Party.' Macleod had certainly brought a new style to the department and made it a much more positive arm of government policy than it had ever been before.

It was noticeable that, as at the Ministry of Health, his departmental information was the best in the House of Commons. He often re-wrote whole sections of speeches prepared for him. He disliked officialese and on one occasion returned a draft to his private secretary with the sug-gestion, 'Try reading that into your shaving mirror.'

He attached great importance to the Ministry's relations with Members of Parliament, irrespective of Party, and commended the official responsible if a Member had written appreciatively to thank him for the information received or the way in which a difficult case had been handled. He seldom praised or blamed his staff, but he awarded his private secretary, Dudley Turner, a good mark for amending a departmental letter to Jo Grimond in such a way as to show that the Minister was aware of the special difficulties of people living in the Orkneys.

Macleod's manner was often abrupt, impatient, or cold almost to the point of discourtesy, and leaders of industry sometimes left a meeting feeling they had been brusquely treated, but his attitude concealed a sensitive concern for the feelings and problems of ordinary people and any instance of bureaucratic inhumanity made him angry.

He was a good Minister to work for because he knew his own mind, gave clear instructions, kept reasonable office hours and did not make excessive demands on the department for advice. He disliked having his time wasted and became restive if discussion was verbose or wandered off the point. He would listen in a withdrawn way to the arguments presented to him and then make his decision quickly and firmly. Acceptance or rejection of advice differed little in the manner of delivery. In weighing up the advantages of different courses, he always considered the likelihood of success: 'I never fight battles I can't win,' he said, and he would describe the options as a five-to-four on or six-to-four against chance. Some civil servants had to brush up their bookmaking!

Although he sometimes disagreed with them, Macleod was always conscious of the debt he owed to his officials. He liked to illustrate this by an apocryphal story which he sometimes introduced into after-dinner speeches:

> There was once a Minister who expected full speaking notes for every occasion. His demands for briefs were endless and sorely tried his patient staff. One day an official could stand it no longer. The Minister was on his feet reading his speech and was reaching his climax with the words, 'And these, my friends, are the answers to the questions an anxious world is asking.' He turned the page and was staggered to find a blank sheet of paper except for the words, 'You tell 'em. I quit'!

His own formal speeches as Minister of Labour were moderate and restrained and he tried to hold the balance fairly between the two sides of industry. He liked a bi-partisan approach to industrial problems where this was possible. He was quick to give praise to responsible employers and trade union leaders and reserved his scorn for the backwoodsmen whom he described as 'those caelocanths who have somehow survived to the twentieth century but do not know how to respond to its needs.' Nor did he spare members of his own party if they expressed reactionary ideas about the relations between 'masters and men'.

During train journeys to meetings all over the country Macleod would often sit in total silence, thinking out a speech or his line of approach to the problem he was about to deal with. He enjoyed doing the *Times* crossword puzzle and would sometimes devour a whole detective novel between London and Birmingham.

Important sporting events always captured his interest and on one occasion when his brother Rhoddy was in London, they planned to go to an international rugger match at Twickenham. There was a strike on at the time and he had attended a Ministerial meeting at Downing Street the evening before and left his hat in the hall. In fact he seldom wore a hat, but the next day was cold and wet and he decided to retrieve it before they left for the match. When he got to Downing Street there was such a large crowd outside that Iain didn't feel he could just walk in, collect his hat and walk out again, so he sat down inside and read the newspapers for twenty minutes before re-emerging. Meanwhile the story had spread that he was at Number 10 and when he re-appeared (with the hat) he was greeted by reporters with questions about the strike. He hurried to his car, murmuring 'No comment', but the evening papers carried headlines saying, 'Strike moves imminent. Minister of Labour at Number 10.'

Macleod enjoyed talking informally to journalists, many of whom became personal friends. Hugh Massingham was a regular visitor and others who came to see him included Henry Fairlie, James Margach, Trevor Evans – and of course Randolph Churchill. The time spent in discussion with them produced a useful dividend of articles and leaders. It was a two-way traffic valuable to the Minister and the newspapers. Most journalists admired Macleod. One who knew him well in Ministry of Labour days, thought he had 'unique ability and total integrity'; that he was very professional and understood the machine; and that he had 'a universal view of politics'. Macleod's relations with his officials were good, and he had a special affection and respect for the Permanent Secretary, Sir Harold Emmerson, whose experience, common sense and always imperturbable manner were a great help to him in the department.

A senior civil servant, now retired, once told me that there were three attributes he always hoped to find in a Minister: he should be strong in Cabinet and effective in Parliament; he should have ideas of his own and be a good critic of official advice; and he should have the quality of leadership. All these characteristics were combined in Iain Macleod.

Robert Carr, his Parliamentary Secretary for most of his time at the Ministry of Labour, found him an excellent Minister to work for. Macleod made it clear to Harold Emmerson that Carr was to be given real responsibility. This was more significant in 1955 than it would be today because at that time junior Ministers were regarded in some departments as of little importance.

Carr was made responsible for certain clearly defined areas, such as training, health, welfare, industrial safety, and local employment offices. He was expected not only to answer for these in Parliament but to take decisions without reference to the Minister unless they were unusually important or difficult. He was also made chairman of a committee investigating training which produced what became known as the Carr Report.'[7]

Robert Carr was impressed by the speed with which Macleod worked: 'He absorbed detail – he never skimped it – in an amazing manner. I always seem to be working hard. So often, when I came into his room, he had finished his work and was doing *The Times* crossword . . . or listening to the commentary on a test match!'[8]

When Carr retired temporarily from the Government at his own request in April 1958 to return to his family business, he was succeeded as Parliamentary Secretary by Richard Wood (Minister for Overseas Development in the present Government) who took over the responsibility of discussions on the Carr Report at meetings all over the country. Wood was also invited to take a special interest in the problems of the disabled, and was entrusted with much Parliamentary business. 'Under his (Macleod's) guidance . . . I can honestly say that I loved every minute of the job. It is impossible to over-estimate all that I learned from Iain – his consummate skill in the handling of industrial disputes; his blend of firmness and conciliation; his human sympathy; his willingness to listen.'

Wood recalled an occasion, soon after the failure of the London bus strike, when Macleod was dissuaded by strong civil service advice from a course he had favoured. After arguing bravely for half an hour, he smiled broadly and said: 'All right. You win. Unlike Frank Cousins, I know when I'm beaten.'[9]

7 *Training for Skill*, 1958.
8 Robert Carr to the author, September 13, 1971.
9 Richard Wood to the author, September, 1971.

As Macleod's tenure of the Ministry of Labour drew to its close and it was apparent that he would soon be moved to another department, there was speculation as to his next appointment. In those days a game was sometimes played in the Conservative Whips' office in which each of the Government Whips predicted the future of Ministers. One of them suggested that, with his Highland background, Macleod would make a popular and successful Secretary of State for Scotland. Had this in fact been his next assignment, it is interesting to consider its probable effect on his future career. Two years in the Scottish Office would have meant slower progress up the path to the top but would have avoided the pitfalls of the Colonial Office which, in some Conservative circles, prejudiced his popularity in the Party. In fact, however, he was about to make his greatest contribution in public life.

CHAPTER 8

Secretary of State for the Colonies (1) East and Central Africa 1959-1960

IAIN MACLEOD was appointed Secretary of State for the Colonies immediately after the general election in October 1959. He had been Minister of Labour for four years and was still the youngest member of the Cabinet. He expected a change of department and, in view of Alan Lennox Boyd's decision to retire, the Colonial Office was clearly a possibility, but until the moment of his appointment he did not know he was to be sent there.

Harold Macmillan prefaced the offer by saying: 'Iain, I've got the worst job of all for you.' In fact, it was the one he wanted. It was a slightly higher level in the Cabinet than the position he had occupied as Minister of Labour and to that extent it was a promotion in political terms, but not a dramatic one. Its career significance lay in the fact that, hitherto, Macleod's interest had been centred in home affairs. The new appointment widened his experience and qualified him for further promotion in the years ahead. But he did not look upon it as a vehicle for his own political advancement. He saw it as an opportunity to do something important which he believed to be right.

Until his appointment as Secretary of State Macleod had taken little interest in colonial affairs. He was not a member of the Defence and Overseas Policy Committee of the Cabinet, he had never set foot in a British colony and he had met scarcely any of the political leaders in the colonial territories. He had no experience of the men or problems he was now to encounter. There was, therefore, a complete break with the recent past.

Macleod's immediate predecessor, Alan Lennox Boyd, had been Secretary of State for five years and Minister of State at an earlier period. He had no ambition for higher office and his whole interest in public life had become centred in colonial affairs. He was an immensely able, popular and knowledgeable Secretary of State; but he had, perhaps, been too long in the office to appreciate fully the need to speed up political advance.

By a combination of personal charm and considerable wealth, Lennox Boyd had sat on the safety valve of African nationalism for five years. He was able to entertain the colonial political leaders in his beautiful house in Chapel Street, and most of them had become his personal friends. His relations with them were close and informal which was invaluable in negotiation. They trusted him completely. But the nationalist wind was beginning to blow and the warm personality, wide experience and complete dedication of one man could no longer divert it.

Once independence had been granted to the Indian sub-continent, Africa was bound to follow. Ghana, which became independent in 1957, had begun the process in West Africa, which was certain, soon, to be followed in East and Central Africa.

After two world wars Britain no longer had the military or economic strength to hold down its African colonies by force, even if a British Government had wished to do so. If de Gaulle could not contain one country, Algeria, we could not hope to impose our will upon a third of the continent. But this was not in any case our intention. Britain's policy had always been to lead her dependent territories to self-government within the Commonwealth.

In appointing Macleod as Colonial Secretary, Harold Macmillan was, in effect, issuing a general directive to 'get a move on' in Africa. Theoretically Government policy remained unaltered, but the change of timing was so radical that it amounted in practice to a change of policy.

In an article in the *Spectator* some years later, Macleod wrote:

It has been said that after I became Colonial Secretary there was a deliberate speeding-up of the movement towards independence. I agree. There was. And in my view any other policy would have led to terrible bloodshed in Africa. This is the heart of the argument.

In January 1959 Alan Lennox Boyd had presided over a conference at Chequers attended by the three Governors of the East African territories. It was tentatively decided that Tanganyika might achieve independence by 1970 and Kenya by 1975, with Uganda somewhere between the two. In fact, Tanganyika became independent in 1961, Uganda in 1962 and Kenya in 1963.

There can be no doubt that we could have made a better job of the transfer of power if the extra decade envisaged by Lennox Boyd had been adhered to. We could have trained more African magistrates, more technicians, more agricultural experts and more local administrators to succeed our own overseas civil servants. But in a conflict between politics and economics or administration, the political considerations tend to prevail, and in Africa in the 1960s delay would probably have proved fatal. We could have postponed independence, but only by the rule of the gun and at the risk of bloodshed. As it was, we devolved power too quickly but with goodwill.

Macleod took the view that, although it was dangerous to go too fast, it would be still more dangerous to go too slow. It was the doctrine of the lesser risk. In this belief he was responding to general political factors, not to strategic or defence considerations. There had been no special review of colonial policy in strategic terms. Nor was he reacting to a threat of force. It was often said at that time that the quickest way to independence was to organise riots and violence, but in fact Tanganyika, then the most peaceful country in Africa, moved faster to independence than any of the more turbulent colonies.

Just before his appointment as Secretary of State, Iain Macleod's interest in colonial affairs had been stimulated by the Hola Camp episode in which eleven Africans had been killed owing to a combination of ignorance and brutality on the part of their guards. Enoch Powell denounced this in a fine speech in the House of Commons, which deeply impressed us all; and the Cabinet, as well as Parliament, were shocked by the incident. No blame attached personally to Lennox Boyd, whose Ministerial responsibility for what had happened was remote; but it was clear that the old methods of government in Africa could not continue. And this view was reinforced by the Report of the Devlin Commission on conditions in Nyasaland which appeared at the same time. No doubt the Report was somewhat overwritten and did less than justice to the difficulties of the Governor and his small staff in trying to cope with a planned uprising: but the description of a British colony as a 'police state' was a further shock to public opinion.

Following these two reverses, Alan Lennox Boyd felt he ought to resign and wished to do so, but he was dissuaded by Macmillan who thought such a course would be politically disadvantageous to the party on the eve of a general election and personally unfair to Lennox Boyd, whose tenure of office had been a most successful and distinguished one until these events occurred. The Cabinet unanimously endorsed Macmillan's view.

If Iain Macleod and Quintin Hailsham had been especially outraged by Hola, the Prime Minister and Rab Butler felt almost equally strongly and they sympathised with and supported the new radical approach to colonial problems which was quickly to become evident. This was probably true of most if not all Macleod's Cabinet colleagues.

The attention of the new Secretary of State was bound to focus at first upon East and Central Africa, where the position of the entrenched European minority posed special problems. Macleod recognised that independence could not be withheld simply on the grounds that a white settler community had become established there. He took the view that the transfer of power must come swiftly in East Africa and steadily in Central Africa. He believed passionately in his policy and became emotionally as well as intellectually involved in carrying it out.

He turned his attention, first, to Kenya which he judged to be the most urgent of his problems. There were a number of liberal-minded Europeans in the colony who saw that the Africans were bound to rule Kenya and who regarded this prospect without despair. They were in a minority.

Until the late 1950s, Kenya had been a white man's country. Europeans had developed it by their capital and their skills and they expected it to be governed in their interests more or less indefinitely. This may have been myopic, but it was understandable. There was still a paternalistic assumption by some of the officials as well as by the majority of settlers that Kenya could continue under white and alien rule for a long time to come.

The nationalist wind, which was beginning to sweep across the African continent, went unrecognised by this privileged, anachronistic European society. Their way of life was threatened and they resented bitterly the man whose policies seemed to them a betrayal of all they had created and worked for in Kenya. As Macleod's intentions became clearer, their hostility became more pronounced. In a sense they were right, but their interests could only have been defended by force of arms and no British Government would have been prepared to start a repressive, colonial, race war in Africa in the second half of the twentieth century. It would have been better to be generous and to have given the smaller mixed-farming settlers adequate financial compensation at the outset to enable them to leave.

Many people were shocked by the 'wind of change' speech in February 1960. They reacted as though Harold Macmillan had invented nationalism in Africa, whereas he was merely stating a fact. It was already happening and there was nothing, short of force, which could have stopped it.

In an interview some months later, Macleod said: 'I fear stagnant thinking and I fear wishful thinking. When we talk about changing an Empire into a family, we do not see the future as a series of Dunkirks, of gallant, prolonged, bitter, rearguard actions. I believe it is our high destiny to help change and to sustain it.'

Macleod looked to the moderate Europeans for support. His younger brother, Rhoddy, had been in East Africa as a soldier in the war and had returned to Kenya as a farmer in 1946. He had done police intelligence work during the Mau Mau rebellion and in 1959 had joined Michael Blundell as political organiser of the New Kenya Party. He was later to enter the legislature and to become a Minister in Ronald Ngala's government. The other leading members of Blundell's party were Wilfred Havelock, Peter Marrion and Bruce Mackenzie, who subsequently became Minister of Agriculture in Kenyatta's Government.

The Mau Mau rebellion had split the country, and Rhoddy was able to explain to Iain the mistrust felt by the loyalist Kikuyu and the other tribes for the Mau Mau Kikuyu, and the anxieties felt by most Europeans about African advance. The settlers had genuine fears for the future, and those who had hitherto treated Africans as their servants saw the red light for the first time and disliked it. They had become conditioned to a system of government which suited them well and they did not see, because they did not wish to see, that it was already out of date. They expected Rhoddy to influence his brother in their interests, and he lost many of his friends when he did not do so. In fact, he supported Iain's policies.

Owing no doubt to the state of European opinion, the Kenya officials, including the Governor, Sir Patrick Renison, were much less enthusiastic than many other colonial governments about the speed of constitutional advance proposed by the new Secretary of State. But although they had doubts about the wisdom of his policies, they were entirely loyal.

In November 1959 Macleod lifted the emergency powers in Kenya which had lasted since 1952, and by the end of the year three-quarters of the detainees had been released. He was taking a risk, but there was no trouble.

The Kenya conference began in January 1960 with Macleod in the chair. It was his first colonial conference and was to last for five weeks. In his opening speech he said that the time had come to recognise that majority rule would come in Kenya and that the Africans were the majority race. This definitive statement created, curiously, less impression upon the Europeans than upon the Africans.

The first African demand was for the release of Kenyatta and for his presence at the conference. Macleod judged that to have released Kenyatta at that stage would have been to release a flood of violence in Kenya, so he refused to discuss it.

The second demand was that Peter Mbui Koinange, who had been exiled from Kenya and was then in London, should be admitted to the conference as an adviser to the African delegates. When this, too, was refused, the Africans boycotted the conference, and the impasse lasted for several days. After many meetings in Macleod's London flat, the matter was resolved by a compromise. A blank card was issued on which the Africans could fill in Koinange's name. It did not admit the bearer to the conference room, but it admitted him to Lancaster House. Koinange was at that time employed as a milkman in Watford, and Sir Hilton Poynton, the Permanent Secretary, who had a talent for light verse, composed this quatrain:

'Mau Mau milkman, have you any pass?'
'Yes sir, yes sir, but only second class.
Good for the cloakroom and good for the loo,
But not for the Music Room among the chosen few.'

The compromise, which followed the same sort of pattern as Macleod had often devised at the Ministry of Labour, was in a sense meaningless, but nevertheless important because it enabled the conference to continue with the Africans present. A Kenya conference without the African delegation would have been a waste of time.

Before the conference began Macleod had put in a Paper to the Cabinet giving in outline what he proposed and had obtained Cabinet authority for it, with wide limits of discretion. This method was not always followed by his successors. For instance, Duncan Sandys, a very strong and experienced Minister, often preferred to present his colleagues with a *fait accompli*.

In the conference itself Macleod adopted a standard method. After the opening speeches, he allowed a Second Reading debate, in which every delegate who wished to do so could make a prepared speech. After this it was possible to get down to serious negotiations without anyone feeling frustrated. At the Kenya conference one Somali delegate, who made the last and shortest speech, commented that all his colleagues had asked for independence. His own demand was not for independence, but for water for his goats! It seemed a most sensible request.

The constitution which the conference eventually accepted was on the Westminster model because the Africans – not the Europeans – insisted upon this. Macleod realized that they would later adapt it to their own circumstances, but thought it best to let them start with a type of government to which they were already accustomed.

In the end, as often happened at these constitutional conferences, Macleod produced a document and said, in effect: 'This is my plan which you must accept or reject.' He judged that the moment had come to force agreement, however reluctant, by a display of firmness. It was his own decision to handle the final phase in this way and it came off. His first conference had been a long and difficult one, but it had been successful. It was evidence at the outset of the practical application of the new Secretary of State's policies for Africa.

The land problem had been left unresolved, and the right-wing Europeans had not accepted the new constitution. Indeed, Group Captain Briggs, the leader of the United Party, declared that it was 'the greatest setback the European settlement has had since its inauguration'. He denied that Michael Blundell represented the views of the European community and this was true. But Macleod had achieved his main objective, which was to reach agreement between Blundell's group and the Africans. He wanted to persuade the 'moderates' of both races to work together, because he realised that this was the only possible pattern for peace in Kenya in the years ahead. 'I very much want to see moderate policies developed,' he said in a television interview. 'You can't compel people to be moderate. But you can so draft the constitutions that the moderate is encouraged.' Blundell was the bridge between white rule and black, and without his help in the transition period African advance might have been dangerously delayed.

Tom Mboya, the ablest of the African leaders, later described the Secretary of State's handling of the conference as masterly, and said it was a pleasure to watch his skill. Michael Blundell was less complimentary. He found Macleod difficult to understand and commented that in any discussion, however friendly, he was often conscious that Macleod's mind was 'ticking away, speculating on various courses of action quite remote from anything immediately before us'. Blundell added that Macleod was 'quite impervious to popularity and prepared to change the details of his approach overnight to secure his objective'.

Lady Violet Bonham Carter, who barely knew Iain, wrote to him in April: 'For weeks I have restrained myself with difficulty from writing to you to try and express my admiration and gratitude for what you have done and are doing in Africa. At last there is light – and your hands have lit it.'

In fact, much of the credit for the success of the Kenya Conference was due to Michael Blundell and his colleagues. Their signature of the final document was an act of courage, for which they were much abused on their return to Africa. They were regarded as traitors and renegades and ostracised by their friends. When Blundell arrived at Nairobi airport, a settler threw thirty pieces of silver at his feet and for years many Europeans would not speak to him. In his book, *So Rough a Wind*,[1] he tried to justify himself to his fellow settlers. He might have done better to claim more credit, to which he was fully entitled, for the results of the conference.

Blundell wrote generously to Iain Macleod a year later:

> I see you may be in for difficulties over Northern Rhodesia. I thought therefore that I would write and tell you that, although our agreement at Lancaster House practically killed me politically, nevertheless we were right.
>
> I have now spoken to more than 20,000 Africans at public meetings and many hundreds privately, and I have been left with an impression of great friendliness – all the jealous racial questions have gone . . . but their bitterness against the reactionary settler is most marked.
>
> What I want to impress on you is that the alternative to Lancaster House for Kenya was an explosion. The result of it is friendliness and a real chance of success here. Exactly the same applies to Northern Rhodesia. I am certain Welensky is wrong. . .

The Kenya coalition leader, Sir Ferdinand Cavendish-Bentinck, did not agree. When Macleod left the Colonial Office in October 1961, he commented tersely: 'Any change is for the better.'

The most important negotiations at Lancaster House conferences were always conducted in small groups outside the conference itself. Like all Colonial Office Ministers before and since, Iain Macleod found it necessary to discuss the difficult issues privately and seek compromises first with one group, then another, which could be ratified later at the conference table. The need to work in this way altered his ordinary life.

Until then he had lived in his constituency at Enfield; now he had to

---

1 Weidenfeld and Nicolson, 1964. In a review in the *Spectator* in March 1964 Macleod wrote, 'This is a magnificent book . . . it is also a story of courage; of the political journey of a very brave man.'

move to London. At first he took a temporary flat in Hans Crescent, then a larger one in Sloane Court West. From breakfast time until the early hours of the following morning there was often an endless flow of visitors, individually or in groups, and agreements were hammered out in the drawing room or dining room (and sometimes over bacon and eggs in the kitchen) which could never have been reached in the formal atmosphere of Lancaster House. In the summer of 1961 there were five constitutional conferences in progress at the same time.

The Macleods had no servants and Eve, still crippled after her polio, had to work hard providing drinks, coffee and impromptu meals without warning and for any number of people at any hour of the day or night. She remembers her despair when Michael Blundell left dirty shoe marks all over a new carpet which had only been laid that day.

On one occasion she was away with the children for the weekend, having left enough cold food in the flat to feed Iain in her absence. But on the Sunday at lunch time he telephoned her in the country to ask how to turn the gas on as he and Dr Banda, who had been at the flat for two hours, were hungry and wanted to cook themselves some bacon and eggs and sausages.

Hospitality was often more formal. Eve remembers a large lunch party for the Chief Minister of Sierra Leone which was to take place immediately after his arrival at London Airport. At 12.45 p.m. the Colonial Office telephoned to say that the Chief Minister was on his way but was not very well and could only eat a little steamed fish. By then she had cooked the meal, which did not include steamed fish, so there was nothing she could do. Fortunately the Chief Minister ate more than anyone else and appeared to suffer no ill-effects afterwards! For official entertaining of this sort government hospitality helped by providing a waiter and a small *per capita* reimbursement for the guests, which covered about a third of the actual cost, but Eve bought and cooked the food herself, laid the table, and cleaned the silver.

Macleod's predecessors, Oliver Lyttelton and Alan Lennox Boyd, had had space, staff and money, so for them the mechanics of entertaining were relatively easy. It is strange that, although the work of the Colonial Secretary at that time involved far more private hospitality than that of the Foreign Secretary, no official residence was provided. For the Macleods a flat at Marlborough House or Admiralty House would have been an immense asset, and would have relieved much of the strain and worry. In fact, the Colonial Secretaryship cost Iain a considerable sum of money, which he could ill afford, and he was obliged to cash in his £1,500 life insurance policy to defray the expenses. We did not treat our political leaders with much generosity in those days.

The Kenya Conference had foreshadowed not only advance for the Africans but the release of Jomo Kenyatta. It was therefore surprising that, soon afterwards, Sir Patrick Renison made a speech describing Kenyatta as 'the leader to darkness and death'. Macleod had strongly advised him against the use of this phrase, because it was already clear that sooner or later the British Government would have to deal with Kenyatta and Renison's speech did not seem a promising introduction. But the Governor threatened to resign if he was not allowed to describe the Kikuyu leader in this way. There were enough troubles in Kenya without adding Renison's resignation, and Macleod did not therefore formally veto the speech, although he deplored its wording and timing.

He did seriously consider the position of the Governor, whom he thought lacking in imagination and unsuitable for Kenya at that time. But Renison had a distinguished record of service, he had done well in the Caribbean and was a man of complete integrity. To have replaced him then would have intensified European antagonism. Two years later Duncan Sandys was able to take this step under easier circumstances when he made the brilliant and successful appointment of Malcolm MacDonald as Governor of Kenya.

In the early months of 1960 few people foresaw the part Kenyatta would play in Kenya. He was already an old man, who had spent some time in confinement. Yet within three years the Europeans, who had feared and condemned him, were describing their President as 'the great stabilising influence in East Africa'. He had proved a strong and unifying national leader, and by 1964 Duncan Sandys was saying to me privately, 'If every Commonwealth statesman was as wise, as co-operative and as helpful as Jomo Kenyatta, there would be no problems in the Commonwealth.'

Macleod decided, wisely, to deal with the release of Kenyatta in two stages. The first was to move him from complete inaccessibility to a place where people could see and consult him. If this was successful, his final release would follow, but there was no rigid time-table. It did not in fact take place until the summer of 1961, when it was announced simul-taneously in the House of Commons and in Kenya. Although by then the idea of Kenyatta's release had become accepted, it was still a blow to many Europeans and had to be clearly seen as a joint decision by the governments in Nairobi and at Westminster.

Meanwhile, a minority KADU Government, supported by the New Kenya Party, had taken office in Kenya as a result of the 1961 election. In fact, the election had produced a KANU majority, and some Government nominations had to be made to sustain Ronald Ngala's position in the legislature. Macleod realised that this state of affairs could not last for long, but it was a necessary transition and a temperate grouping which helped to allay European anxieties. A year later this interim administration was replaced by a KANU/KADU coalition and ultimately by a KANU Government led by Kenyatta, in which Ngala was a Minister. The last steps to independence in Colonial territories have usually been short and soon forgotten, but they are important and necessary stages which it is unwise to by-pass.

One individual matter should be mentioned because of its effect upon European and African opinion. On October 12, 1959, a man named Peter Poole shot and killed an African during the course of an argument. He was arrested, tried by jury and convicted of murder on December 10th. He appealed against the death sentence, first to the Court of Appeal for East Africa, then to the Judicial Committee of the Privy Council. Both appeals were dismissed and the sentence was confirmed by the Governor on August 12, 1960. A petition for mercy was submitted to the Queen and referred to the Secretary of State. He declined to advise Her Majesty to intervene. Although no doubt a painful one for a convinced abolitionist, the decision was clearly correct on the merits, and its impact in Kenya was considerable.

Poole was the first white man to be hanged for murdering an African, and many Europeans believed he should have been reprieved. The Africans, on the other hand, saw it as a test case for Macleod. That he put justice before race seemed to them evidence of his sincerity of purpose in implementing a non-racial policy in Kenya.

It is a fair criticism and one which is made in W. P. Kirkman's balanced and well-informed book, *Unscrambling an Empire*,[2] that the speed of political advance in Africa overwhelmed the administrative preparations. Africanisation was proceeding, but slowly. It was lagging far behind the constitutional developments. Macleod's problem was that he dare not lose the political momentum. He knew that he was doing in two years what, ideally, should have spread over ten. With hindsight, the real criticism of British policy may be that the previous decade had not been used to train more Africans to run their own countries.

2 Chatto and Windus, 1966.

If this was true of Kenya, it was still more evident in Nyasaland, where there were almost no qualified African magistrates and no civil servants above the most junior level. When I was staying with Sir Glyn Jones at Government House in the autumn of 1960, he invited a young man to meet me at dinner who was one of the only six African graduates in the whole country at that time. Dr Banda surmounted the difficulty by retaining the services of the British expatriates until Africans could be trained to replace them. It was a sensible policy, but not an easy one to follow in face of African aspirations.

One of the first African leaders Macleod met after his appointment as Secretary of State was Julius Nyerere. He is an intellectual and a man of great charm and sensitivity, with a peculiarly English sense of humour. Macleod liked him at once.

Nyerere and the Governor, Sir Richard Turnbull, had a very good relationship, and had already discussed the constitutional advance to full internal self-government for Tanganyika which would lead to independence. In the spring of 1960 Nyerere came to England and had two or three long talks with Macleod at his London flat. They were able to agree without difficulty on all the main points, which they jotted down on the back of a postcard. Nyerere then suggested that a conference should take place, not at Lancaster House but in Dar-es-Salaam. This was unusual and would certainly not have been possible if the issues for the conference had been at all controversial, but Macleod saw no objection in the case of Tanganyika and the preparations went forward smoothly and easily. The only problem, as in other colonies, was the inevitable administrative weakness, inseparable from an accelerated pace to independence. This became apparent in 1964, when we had to send troops to assist the East African governments.

Early in 1961 Macleod visited Dar-es-Salaam to preside over the conference. It was a happy occasion and he was greeted by cheering crowds waving palm branches.

The conference itself was brief and unremarkable and there were very few points of dispute. One arose from Nyerere's wish to be called Prime Minister in the pre-independence period. Macleod did not feel strongly about this, but the Colonial Office were against it because officials did not want to extend a practice which had already led to embarrassment in other colonies where it had been conceded. Indeed, I remember resisting the same demand made by George Price of British Honduras three years later when I was myself a Minister in the Colonial Office.

A long argument developed and finally, in the closing stages of the conference, Macleod faced Nyerere's entire Cabinet to settle the matter. With a stern expression, he announced solemnly that he had come to a decision, that there was no question whatever of changing his mind and that if the Cabinet did not accept it, the conference would have to end at once. There was consternation round the table, until he added quietly that the Premier's title would be 'Prime Minister'. Everyone roared with laughter and threw their papers in the air in their delight. Nyerere promptly responded by giving way on the only other point of disagreement and the conference ended happily with the announcement of the date for independence. Julius Nyerere thought Macleod had chaired the conference 'in a masterly fashion'. 'You have met us at every point with frankness and honesty and with willingness to help.'

The next day was spent celebrating; but, in contrast to the ecstatic exuberance of the African population, the expatriate civil servants were despondent because of the Treasury ruling, conveyed to them by the Secretary of State, that – in an effort to avoid a wholesale exodus – compensation would be paid to them over a period of six years.

It so happened that Macleod was attending a Government House garden party and, as he walked round in the heat, he asked the young Assistant-Superintendent of Police for a glass of water. No waiter was available, so the Assistant-Superintendent asked the expatriate Commissioner of Police for permission to go and fetch the water. 'No,' said the Commissioner, 'tell him he can have it in six annual instalments.'

In fact, Macleod took considerable trouble to get fair treatment for overseas civil servants. He appointed the Ramage Commission to consider expatriate officers' salaries and when the Commission recommended a thirty per cent increase he fought this through the Treasury with resolution and success. It was vital to the restoration of morale in the Overseas Service at that time. He also introduced an important Bill in Parliament under which the British Government undertook to top up the local salaries of expatriate officers; to pay for home passages for wives and children; to help towards the cost of education; and to provide for fifty per cent of the compensation for loss of office on independence to be paid for by Britain. This, too, was the occasion of a Treasury battle which Macleod fought and won, though he had to take it to Cabinet before the Chancellor gave way. It was an essential measure to avoid the collapse of the Service.

Macleod was always meticulous in keeping his word. When Tanganyika was on the eve of independence, he promised that Britain would be generous with grants and loans to the new state; but this undertaking was prejudiced by Selwyn Lloyd's 1961 economy measures, and Macleod had to fight very hard to keep it. He succeeded in obtaining nearly £20 million for Tanzania against the whole trend of Treasury policy. I know from personal experience how hard it is to wring money from the Chancellor for colonies which have no votes in Britain!

Occasionally there was an unexpected bonus. On a single afternoon in June 1961 the Treasury agreed to find £5 million for the compensation of the small European farmers in Kenya; but this unusual generosity was due partly to an attempt by the farmers to stone Macleod's Under-Secretary, Hugh Fraser, when he had had the unenviable task of explaining to them the very limited financial provision the British Government was prepared to make to help them.

Nyerere was a firm believer in an East African federation for Kenya, Uganda and Tanganyika and was prepared to delay his own country's independence to achieve this. Although the three countries have close links, the federation has not materialised, but Macleod shared Nyerere's hopes that it might develop in course of time. He recognised the danger of appearing too eager and, with Central Africa in mind, was anxious to avoid giving the impression that Britain was trying to impose a federation upon unwilling partners. The newspapers were helpful in describing our position as one of 'cool interest'. The wider setting of a federation would have eased the racial and tribal problems in East Africa and made Macleod's task lighter. In June 1961 he held joint talks with the three territories, with a view to turning the East African High Commission into the East African Common Services Organisation. The purpose of this change was a constitutional one – to enable the organisation to accommodate an independent nation in the same structure as two still-dependent territories. It was also seen as a bridge towards their possible federation at a later date.

It is true that every federation devised during the Colonial period has failed[3] – Central Africa, the West Indies, Aden and South Arabia, and Malaysia and Singapore. But, as Macleod pointed out in a lecture at Melbourne University in 1967, the federations created by the people themselves in Australia, Canada and the United States have succeeded; and perhaps this may yet happen in East Africa and the Caribbean.

Macleod was a strong advocate of overseas aid to under-developed

3 With the exception of Nigeria, which very nearly failed.

countries. He thought it should be given as between equals and without political or military strings. He did not believe that Communism was likely to make serious inroads in Africa, despite Chinese influence in Zanzibar, because the mind of the African is naturally unsympathetic to Communist doctrine. But he conceded that the West would have to show generosity and imagination to hold its position in Africa.

On October 13, 1960, Macleod made a speech to the Conservative Political Centre at the party conference. Its theme was 'One World'. He appealed for a spirit of generosity and referred to:

> the challenge of the Two Nations, rich and poor, white and coloured, in the wider world. . . . We are succeeding in creating One Nation at home. Now we must carry this policy into the Commonwealth and beyond; for there the gap between the industrialised and the under-developed nations confronts accusingly both our conscience and our plain self-interest. . . . We should aid the aspirations of less fortunate peoples for a better and more equal life. . . If we can succeed in this, if we can begin to create One World abroad to match One Nation at home, Communism will seem irrelevant to the problems of the world. . . With this great hope in our hearts, let us now respond, as we always have done, to the clear call of duty.

Linked to Tanganyika was the future of Zanzibar. It is the only example since South Africa – and, like South Africa, an unhappy one – of a British colony achieving legal independence under minority rule.

Owing to a freak election result in 1961, in which the seats did not correspond with the votes, the Arab party was in control at the time of independence. The Sultan was an old man, much revered, and had he lived the transition might have been easier. But the Africans were the majority race and the existence of racial tensions between the Arabs and the Africans was well known in London.

Under these circumstances, it is a possible criticism of Iain Macleod that he took no action to bring about majority rule peacefully before the Africans did so, violently, in the revolution of 1964. He hoped that the change to an African government, which he realised was inevitable, would come about by the normal constitutional process of another election. Meanwhile it was difficult to see how it could be managed, except by a deliberately imposed constitution to produce an African majority. With hindsight, this might have been wise, as it turned out to be in British Guiana some years later, but it did not seem to Macleod, or to anyone else, to be feasible or necessary at the time.

Many people criticise the governments of Commonwealth Africa, and no doubt there is much to censure. Zanzibar is certainly a case in point. But it is only ten years or less since these countries became independent, and we should be patient. The Westminster type of democracy suits us but is not necessarily an exportable commodity to the African continent.

In the past, Africa has known only a tribal society and a colonial society. In the first, opposition to authority usually meant a violent death. In the second, it usually resulted in the imprisonment of the critic as a seditious agitator. So the relatively sophisticated Western concept of a loyal Opposition is unknown in Africa and may take many decades to develop. In the meantime we should not censure these countries too severely if they experiment with forms of government, different from ours, which may seem to them more suitable to their own circumstances than the Westminster model. This was certainly the view held by Iain Macleod. He did not regard strong central powers as a sign of tyranny. He thought them essential to government in modern Africa.

On the other hand, it would be a mistake to criticise Britain for exporting our own system. In fact, the demand for written constitutions based on the British practice always came, not from the Colonial Office but from the opposition parties and minority groups in the Colony concerned. When British protection was being withdrawn, they wanted safeguards against oppression by the majority party in their own country and their fears were sometimes justified. As one wise African civil servant has remarked: 'When some African politicians talk of "one man, one vote" they really mean "one man, one vote, one election".'

The only other colony in this part of the world which the Secretary of State visited in 1960 was the island of Mauritius. It had just suffered a severe cyclone disaster and, as Macleod was in East Africa soon after this happened, it seemed right to show his interest and concern by flying to Port Louis. This was much appreciated in the island. There was no political motive for his visit, but there was a personal one. It so happened that his great-uncle had retired to Mauritius many years before, and Macleod had no less than sixty-three relations living on the island. With his strong sense of family, it was an additional reason for his visit.

Almost from the moment of his appointment as Secretary of State, Iain Macleod decided to move quickly in Nyasaland. He regarded Dr Banda, whom he had never met, as the key to this problem.

In March 1959 the Governor of Nyasaland had proclaimed a state of emergency. Four hours before his announcement a hundred arrests had been made, including that of Dr Banda, and altogether 1,346 Africans were detained. By December 1959, 532 of these were still in custody and another 500 were under restriction. Banda was in detention at Gwelo prison in Southern Rhodesia. He was the acknowledged leader of a country of four million people, of whom only seven or eight thousand were Europeans, and Macleod decided that he must be released. It was very much his own decision, taken against all official advice in the Colonial Office and in Africa. The Governor, Sir Robert Armitage, thought it unwise; so did the Governor-General of the Central African Federation. Sir Roy Welensky and his Cabinet were strongly opposed to it, and it was against the feeling of a number of Macleod's own Cabinet colleagues at home, including the Prime Minister himself.

It may be wondered why Macleod felt it necessary to release Banda much more quickly than Kenyatta. I think the explanation may lie in the fact that in Nyasaland there was no alternative African leader or party. In Kenya there was. So, if he was to deal with the majority race at all in Nyasaland, Macleod had to do so through Dr Banda. He took the view that, as long as Banda was in gaol, he was a myth, but that as soon as he came out he would be a man and that the man would be easier to deal with than the myth.

In retrospect, his decision was clearly the right one, but to many people it did not seem so at the time. Macleod persisted in his resolve, and even decided the date of Banda's release – April 1, 1960. As a matter of courtesy Sir Roy Welensky was informed, and later the Secretary of State visited Salisbury and met the Federal Cabinet in full session to discuss the matter. Sir Malcolm Barrow, a leading authority on Nyasaland, asserted that 10,000 Africans would be killed in riots if Banda was released. The other warnings Macleod received were almost as dramatic, and Welensky sent a request to London to defer the decision till after the Monckton Commission had reported.[4] This suggestion appealed to Harold Macmillan, who asked Macleod to agree to it. His refusal to do so led to almost their only serious disagreement. Macleod was prepared to push his judgement on the issue to the point of resignation, if necessary; but once they had

---

4 The Advisory Commission on Central Africa was appointed under the chairmanship of Viscount Monckton of Brenchley, in 1960, to enquire into the future of the Central African Federation.

talked it out and Macmillan had accepted the decision, he gave Macleod his full support.

Meanwhile Dingle Foot, who was acting as legal adviser to Dr Banda, had been to see the Secretary of State and had derived some encouragement from their talk. This led to a difficulty later when Foot had an interview with Banda in Gwelo prison. Unknown to either of them, the cell had been wired for sound, so Sir Roy Welensky received a report of their conversation, in which Macleod's attitude had been discussed. This cannot have improved Welensky's opinion of Macleod, which he expressed in his book *4,000 Days*:[5]

> The Colonial Secretary arrived in Salisbury on the evening of Thursday, March 24, 1960. From our first meeting on the tarmac at the airport until the moment he left the Colonial Office eighteen months later, I found Iain Macleod a very difficult man to get on terms with and to understand. I doubt if we ever talked the same language. He seemed to believe that he had a great and challenging mission, which he was ruthless in carrying out. . . To me his mixture of cold calculation, sudden gushes of undisciplined emotion and ignorance of Africa was perplexing and discouraging.

On another occasion he observed caustically that Macleod 'ought to have a fairly good understanding of the problems of Africa because to a large extent he created them'. But he acknowledged Macleod's capacity: 'We had acquired a new and disconcerting opponent. . . . For good or ill he was probably the most powerful holder of this office since Joseph Chamberlain.'

Welensky had cause for alarm. The whole future of the Central African Federation and his own position as its Prime Minister were threatened by the development of Macleod's policies.

It was not only Macleod who incurred Welensky's censure. As far back as April 1959 he had recorded the receipt of a personal letter from Mr Macmillan 'as soothing as cream and as sharp as a razor'. On the other hand, he liked and trusted Alan Lennox Boyd and Lord Home (later Sir Alec Douglas-Home). And although I did not agree with him at the time, I always liked Roy Welensky. Macleod thought his talk of partnership between European and African was disingenuous – that it was only the partnership between the rider and the horse. This may have been true, but Welensky was fighting his own corner and no one can be blamed for

5 Welensky's *4,000 Days*, Collins, 1964.

doing that. In retrospect, I think that Macleod was unfair to Welensky and Welensky was unfair to Macleod.

During his visit to Salisbury, the Secretary of State could not move without the press, who had become convinced that he would visit Dr Banda at Gwelo. In fact, he had no such intention. One morning he set out from his hotel in a southerly direction, pursued by a *Daily Express* correspondent, whose car broke down en route. When the reporter caught up with him, he was leaning over a fence discussing artificial insemination with a local farmer. After this the press lost interest and when Macleod left Salisbury for Nyasaland they did not follow him.

Randolph Churchill had insisted on travelling to Salisbury on the same aeroplane as the Secretary of State, much to the latter's concern because, in Macleod's words, Randolph had 'a genius for uncovering secrets'.[6] He was late and only boarded the plane as it was about to take off. 'Ho!' he said, as he sat down next to Macleod, 'I suppose you thought I'd missed it?' 'No,' replied Iain, 'I just hoped.' But like the other journalists, Randolph became bored and left for South Africa before Banda was freed. So that although he caught the plane, he too missed the story.

Early in the morning of April 1st, Banda was released, unobserved, from Gwelo gaol and flown to Blantyre. He was taken by car straight to Government House at Zomba (at that time the capital of Nyasaland) and no one was aware that he had left prison.

The two men met quite alone in the Governor's study and talked for an hour. They got on well. Macleod was soon sure that they understood each other and could do business together. From the moment of this first encounter, he decided to hold a constitutional conference. At the end of their conversation, he suggested that Dr Banda should broadcast to the people of Nyasaland and tell them of his release. He should say that the future of the country could safely be entrusted to the Secretary of State and that there was to be no rioting and no demonstrations of any kind. All this worked like a charm. It was as though a boil had been lanced and the release of tension throughout the land was immediate and universal. Despite all the sombre warnings, no security problems arose.

Even in Britain there were no repercussions, perhaps because a sun-spot broke all communications between the two countries, so no messages could be transmitted to London on the day of Banda's release. By the time the news got through, it was good news.

6 As quoted in *Randolph Churchill, the Young Unpretender* compiled by Kay Halle, Heinemann, 1971.

Macleod's judgement had been vindicated. But the strain had been intense. He knew that his own future and the success of his policies depended on the outcome. He had shown no sign of anxiety while he awaited news of the people's reaction to Dr Banda's broadcast; but as soon as it was clear that this was favourable those who were with him noticed that he became both highly excited and completely relaxed. The first and most difficult hurdle had been cleared, and from then on the Nyasaland problem was soluble.

Dr Banda's own magnanimity contributed to the new atmosphere. I remember him saying to me some time afterwards: 'I never resented Alan Lennox-Boyd, who put me inside; in a way it was rather helpful to me. But I have always loved Iain who let me out.' Soon after his release he visited London. He was given a tremendous send-off at Blantyre Airport and addressed the crowd from a lorry: 'I am here because we have a great man at the Colonial Office. Macleod is a great man. (Cheers.) It took courage to do what he did – to bring me back to you.' (Loud applause.) He told the National Press Club in Washington that Macleod was 'a good man, a great man and a Christian gentleman. He is a man with whom I can deal.'

Many children in Malawi (and in Uganda) are still named after Iain Macleod to this day, and, when he died, a letter to the British High Commissioner arrived from the Kawale school at Lilongwe. It read:

I am shocked of the death of Iain Macleod. Being the least boy of Malawi, I have not seen him. As I am enjoying some of his fruits, which are of course visible to every citizen of Malawi, this makes us sad. Sir, convey our deepest sorrow to his family and Government.

He enclosed a postal order for 2s 6d without any explanation, which was sent to Eve Macleod as it was apparently intended for her.

Dr Hastings Kamuzu Banda was a man of complete sincerity, but in presenting his point of view to the British public he was often his own worst enemy. He enjoyed giving press interviews and appearing on television, but he was easily provoked by any question he considered critical or unfriendly. With his eyes flashing and arms waving, his speech sometimes became almost unintelligible with passion and excitement.

One day he came to lunch with me at my London house. It was an unexpected visit and only my wife and children were present. For two hours his resentment and hatred of Sir Roy Welensky and the Federation poured out in a torrent of words and emotion.[7] I said nothing. It seemed better to let him get it all out of his system. At last his invective was exhausted and he turned to me and said: 'What do you think I should do to get my views across to your people?' I replied: 'Do nothing. Say nothing. The British people do not like extremism in any form. You appear to them an extreme nationalist and a dangerous man. Stop giving press interviews and let Roy Welensky hog the television screen. If you behave quietly and moderately and leave all the wild talk to him, he will soon appear more unreasonable than you.'

He thought for some time. At last he said: 'Perhaps that is good advice; but I have a press conference at London Airport this afternoon before I leave for Nyasaland.' I begged him to cancel it. 'I must talk to the Secretary of State,' he replied. 'I must see what he thinks. Can we see him now?' Banda had a touching faith in Macleod and regarded him as a friend, on whose advice he could rely. It was a Saturday afternoon and I telephoned Iain at his flat. He was always accessible and immediately invited us round. Banda walked in in his shapeless raincoat. 'Nigel Fisher has given me some surprising advice,' he said, 'I would like your opinion.' Macleod listened. 'It is very good advice,' he said. 'Follow it.' And there and then Banda telephoned to cancel the press conference.

For the next eighteen months he gave no television or newspaper interviews in England. People soon forgot about him and gradually came to regard him, if not as a 'moderate', at least as less tiresome than Welensky, who continued to denounce the British Government on every possible occasion and to antagonise the British public in the process.

Dr Banda always had the highest opinion of Iain Macleod, whom he described as 'tough, very incisive, a very sharp, quick intellect – but not pig-headed – that was how I found him and that was why I grew to like him.'

It was at about this time that Eve Macleod, on being told by a reporter that Dr Banda was to make another of his then frequent visits to London, commented: 'Oh, dear Dr Banda.' Unfortunately the newspaper transposed the position of the comma, so her remark read: 'Oh dear, Dr Banda. . . .'

An important factor in the constitutional development of Nyasaland was the appointment of Sir Glyn Jones as Governor. He and Dr Banda

---

7 It is agreeable to be able to record that after Welensky left office he and Banda became friends and many years later, when Welensky had suffered a serious illness, President Banda invited him to recuperate in Malawi and spend a holiday there.

quickly established a firm friendship which smoothed every problem. Glyn Jones had been Chief Secretary in Northern Rhodesia and had an instinctive sympathy with African aspirations. He got on well with Africans and this was essential for the evolution of Macleod's policies. But the appointment was a normal Colonial Office promotion. The Secretary of State did not pick him out personally, although he quickly realised that he had the right man in the right place, and they soon became friends as well as collaborators.

In Glyn Jones's view Macleod, and later Butler, 'were the only two British statesmen who had the feel of Africa and could converse with Banda and others easily and naturally . . . and wi   ut showing patronage or fear.'8 He found Macleod 'an honourable, wise and courageous Secretary of State . . . who was always ready to listen to advice and to follow it when it was reasonably presented.'

In June 1960 the state of emergency was ended, and in July the constitutional conference opened in London. The constitution proposed for Nyasaland was devised in the Colonial Office. It was based on four principles: an African majority in the Legislative Council, a qualitative franchise and an advisory Executive Council at the first stage, with its unofficial members drawn from the elected members of the Legislative Council. Surprisingly, in view of the situation in the country a few months earlier, the Europeans signed the conference document, which was accepted unanimously.

Macleod was content with the result: 'We have shown that men of different races, African, European and Asian, can come together round the table and reach agreement, even though they started from widely differing points of view.'

Sir Roy Welensky wrote that 'Mr Macleod sailed a skilful course into and through the dangerous shoals of the Nyasaland Conference . . . I want to make it clear that by letter and telegram he kept me fully posted throughout.' Banda stated that Macleod had won his complete confidence. It was remarkable to receive tributes about the same conference from two men so fiercely opposed to each other.

Dr Banda was pledged to leave the Federation as soon as his country became independent, and as Mr Blackwood, the European leader, had presumably secured Welensky's agreement before signing the conference report, the inference was that Welensky did not regard the retention of Nyasaland as essential to the future of the Federation. Indeed, many Europeans would be quite glad to see Nyasaland go because, with its over-

8 Sir Glyn Jones to the author, January 1972.

whelmingly black population, it reduced the relative strength of whites to blacks in the Federation as a whole. They preferred the 'line of rail' policy for Northern and Southern Rhodesia. Macleod was a believer in Federation but not as it was then constituted under Welensky. He knew that his own plans for the two northern territories would, in the end, lead to its dissolution. The fact that others did not understand this so clearly enabled him to work towards the independence of Malawi without much opposition from Salisbury. Dr Banda became, in effect, Chief Minister of Nyasaland after the general election of August 1961, and he at once began to demolish its links with the Federation.[9]

With his usual clarity of thought Macleod could see that the white-dominated multi-racial approach of Roy Welensky's Federation, well intentioned though it undoubtedly was, could not satisfy either the determination of the European settlers to retain power, or the ambitions of the Africans to acquire it. The compromise had achieved something, but it was a stepping stone to African rule, not a lasting solution for the future of Central Africa.

Political power was the prize. It could be held by a black majority, or by a white minority by force, as in South Africa. It could not be shared for long. So Welensky's Federation was an ephemeral concept, based on a chimera which could not endure. Most people understand this today. It was clear to Macleod twelve years ago.

The Monckton Commission had been appointed in the summer of 1959, before Macleod became Secretary of State and before any decision to increase the speed of African political advance had been taken. Its influence upon policy was therefore less than had been envisaged at the time it was set up. This was not of course the fault of Walter Monckton and his colleagues, who produced a wise and forward-looking report, which did not in any way cut across Macleod's policies; rather the reverse. The two men were friends and had discussed the contents of the report before it was published. In particular, Monckton recommended an African majority in the Northern Rhodesia Legislative Council and an unofficial majority in its Executive Council and, although Macleod had not sought to influence Monckton, this was the sort of pattern he hoped would emerge.

9 Malawi became independent in 1966, and Iain and Eve attended the independence cele-brations. Although by then Macleod was no longer Secretary of State, Dr Banda insisted on his presence because he felt that the country owed its independence to him. The main street in Blantyre is called Macleod Street to this day.

The Federal Review conference assembled at Lancaster House in December 1960. Harold Macmillan was surprised to find that Welensky was meeting Banda and Kaunda for the first time in London. Welensky had not thought it necessary to meet them in Africa, although they were the acknowledged leaders of majority opinion in two out of the three countries comprising the Federation of which he was Prime Minister.

The short-lived conference, which achieved nothing and was adjourned *sine die*, was of more concern to Duncan Sandys as Commonwealth Secretary than to Macleod as Colonial Secretary. Sandys wished, in-stinctively, to move more slowly towards African advance than Macleod, but he always acknowledged that it was bound to come, and his 1961 Constitution for Southern Rhodesia was designed to lead, ultimately, to an African majority. The differences between the two Ministers were of timing and emphasis, not of principle. But they were never friends. This was not surprising; their personalities were very different. I had the greatest admiration and affection for them both and each had exceptional qualities, but they were not the same qualities. Almost their only common charac-teristics were courage and determination. Their relations have been aptly described by Hugh Fraser as being as cold and bleak and silent as between the Matterhorn and Mont Blanc.

This is in no sense a criticism of Duncan Sandys, who was one of the strongest and most experienced Ministers in Macmillan's Government. He worked extremely hard and his thoroughness and attention to detail were remarkable. When he had been in a department for a few months he knew more about the main areas of its responsibilities than most of the civil servants who had worked there for twenty years. He is essentially a doer rather than a thinker, concerned to resolve practical problems, not to evolve theories or philosophies. His contribution to the public life of this country in innumerable departments of state has been second to none, and those who think that Britain is ruled by the civil servants can never have worked for Duncan Sandys.

Despite the failure of the Federal Review conference, much had been achieved in the difficult year of 1960: a major advance had been made in Kenya; the Nyasaland conference had been a success; Tanganyika was firmly on the road to self-government; Nigeria had reached independence, and Sierra Leone was well on the way to it; Macleod's Under-Secretary of State, Julian Amery, had done well in the long and difficult Cyprus negotiations, and the island was now independent. For the first time for nearly twenty years there was no emergency in any of the remaining thirty-eight territories of the colonial Empire.

Not the least of the Government's achievements in the first year of Macleod's Colonial Secretaryship was to have persuaded the Conservative Party to accept the wind of change. This owed something to the successful speech he delivered to the annual party conference in October. It crystallised his own hopes for Africa, but it also soothed the fears of those who spoke for the white people who had made their homes there. It was a brilliant, warm speech and it temporarily disarmed the diehards in his own party.

Macleod was a fine platform speaker, and his annual conference performances were always outstanding. At Scarborough he defined British policy as resting on four principles: all citizens should have full rights without regard to race, religion or tribe; responsibilities for those of our own blood should be accepted, so that they would play their role in the future, and our special duty to colonial servants should be remembered; an expensive technical aid programme should be undertaken; and protection for native minorities should be assured.

He quoted with pride the words of Sir Abubakar Balewa at Nigeria's independence celebrations about Britain's colonial contribution 'first as masters, then as leaders, finally as partners and always as friends.' He laid before the conference 'a simple and ancient call – the call to duty in this field':

> I cannot promise you a popular colonial policy. There will be toil and sweat and tears; but I hope not blood and I hope not bitterness – although in the turmoil that is Africa today, of even that one cannot be certain. But this is the road we must walk and we can walk no other.
>
> The Socialists can scheme their schemes and the Liberals can dream their dreams, but we, at least, have work to do. I make you one pledge only; nothing more than this and nothing less – that we will at all times, to all peoples, in all these territories, carry out our duty faithfully, steadfastly and without fear.

He sat down to thunderous applause, conscious that he had carried the Tory faithful in support of his progressive African policies.

He was now being talked of as a possible future Prime Minister. But there were storms ahead.

CHAPTER 9

Secretary of State for the Colonies (11)
Africa 1960-1961

WITH Kenya, Tanganyika and Nyasaland well set on the road to independence, Macleod turned his attention to Northern Rhodesia. The Constitutional Conference, which had met formally before Christmas and had then been adjourned, resumed its business sessions in February 1961.

Macleod wanted to get agreement between the Africans and as many Europeans as possible, ideally with them all; but John Roberts, the leader of the United Federal Party in Northern Rhodesia, decided – no doubt on the instructions of Sir Roy Welensky – to boycott the conference. Welensky may have thought that this would put an end to a conference of which he disapproved; but, if so, he was wrong and the decision to boycott was a major error of judgement, as it almost always is. One cannot influence the outcome of a conference of which one is not a member. Sir John Moffatt[1] and other independent Europeans were prepared to attend, and, although it would have been absurd to hold a Northern Rhodesia Conference without Kaunda, it was a pity, but not absurd, to hold one without John Roberts.

Whatever the European view about Nyasaland, there could be no doubt in anyone's mind that Northern Rhodesia was crucial to the future of the Federation. Macleod's ultimate objective of independence would mean the dissolution of the Federation, and was therefore bitterly opposed by Sir Roy Welensky. The negotiations which followed were complicated, almost continuous, and usually acrimonious.

Macleod's aim for Northern Rhodesia was approximate parity for one Parliament, to be followed by an African majority and independence in the next. Welensky might not have opposed parity in perpetuity; he

1 Member of the Legislative Council, Northern Rhodesia 1961/64. Leader of the Liberal Party of Northern Rhodesia until November 1962.

could not tolerate the prospect of an African majority. This was understandable. He was fighting, not merely for political gain in Northern Rhodesia, but for the survival of the Central African Federation.

He exerted great pressure upon the British Government and was supported throughout by the right wing of the Conservative party in Parliament. This tended to weaken the resolve of the Cabinet, whose attempts to mollify Welensky created distrust among the Africans. It was a vicious circle.

The Northern Rhodesia negotiations were of course conducted by the Colonial Secretary, but as they affected the Federation, Welensky claimed and was accorded the right to be consulted. The word 'consult' is always ambiguous. It was interpreted in Salisbury almost as a right of veto and as meaning that Macleod's proposals required Federal acquiescence. The British Government denied this and, in fact, under the preamble to the Federal Constitution, the Colonial Office was expressly made responsible for the political advancement of the people of Northern Rhodesia. But the consultation process led to concessions which not only aroused African suspicions but also misled Welensky, who imagined he could alter basic policy, which he could not.

The result was what Macleod described as 'parity of abuse'. He did not mind this; in fact he considered it helpful. If both Welensky and Kaunda criticised his proposals, neither could claim he had sold out to the other. His aim was to get both sides to take part in a general election. In this he was successful, but he had to tack and turn to get there.

The Northern Rhodesia constitution, as it finally emerged after the long, intricate and often tortuous negotiations, could be shot full of holes. It met the commitment to maintain the non-racial principle by creating fifteen 'national' roll seats elected by a complex system of percentages. It was far too complicated, and the technical criticisms made of it at the time were certainly valid – but in the end it worked.

The British Government could have argued that John Roberts and his colleagues were entitled to attend the conference, but as they had chosen not to do so, the United Federal Party had lost the right to influence its conclusions. This would have been the simple and straightforward way to handle the matter, but its danger lay in the possibility of disillusionment, leading to desperate and drastic action by the Europeans – perhaps to a 'coup' involving disorder and bloodshed.

Macleod's task was not made easier by the Cabinet's compromise decision to allow Welensky's representative, Julius Greenfield, to conduct

CENTRAL AND SOUTHERN AFRICA

NIGERIA

CAMEROONS

CENTRAL AFRICAN REPUBLIC

SUDAN

ETHIOPIA

SOMALI REP.

EQUAT. GUINEA

PEOPLES REP. OF THE CONGO

GABON

KABINDA

Congo

ZAIRE
(Republic of the Congo)

RWANDA

BURUNDI

Masindi

UGANDA

KAMPALA

Kisumu

KENYA

NAIROBI

Lake Victoria

Mwanza

Tabora

TANZANIA

Mombasa

Zanzibar

DAR ES SALAAM

Lake Tanganyika

Mbeya

Lake Malawi

Lindi

Kasama

ANGOLA

Ndola

Fort Jameson

MALAWI

ZAMBIA

LUSAKA

Zambesi

ZOMBA

Livingstone

SALISBURY

MOÇAMBIQUE

SOUTHERN

Gwelo

Bulawayo

RHODESIA

SOUTH WEST AFRICA

BOTSWANA

SWAZILAND

Limpopo

MALAGASY REP.
(Madagascar)

REPUBLIC

Orange

LESOTHO

OF

SOUTH AFRICA

KEY

Formerly The Federation of Rhodesia and Nyasaland

International Boundaries

SCALE 1:38,500,000

Map of Central and Southern Africa showing the former colonies of Tanganyika and Zanzibar (Tanzania), Northern Rhodesia (Zambia), and Nyasaland (Malawi).

parallel talks with the Commonwealth Relations Office, despite the fact that the Federal Government had no responsibility for the internal affairs of Northern Rhodesia. This caused many misunderstandings. It alarmed the Africans in Northern Rhodesia and misled the Europeans in Southern Rhodesia.

In an attempt to reconcile the two separate sets of negotiations now in progress, the Prime Minister set up a Cabinet committee, over which he himself presided, to co-ordinate the activities of the Colonial and Commonwealth Ministers. This became necessary because there was often a conflict of view between Sandys and Macleod. But it was a cumbersome procedure, involving the discussion of endless formulae and long hours of often abortive work.

The disagreements between the two Secretaries of State took up too much time and energy, and became a nuisance to Macmillan. He wanted to get the Central African Federation off the Cabinet agenda, and eventually he grew impatient with Macleod's persistent arguments. A rift developed in their hitherto close relationship. Reggie Bennett recalls that when there was a division in the House of Commons at ten o'clock, Macmillan and Macleod would often come swinging into the lobby together, the Prime Minister's arm round Iain's shoulder and the two of them clearly in the closest harmony. But one evening, early in the year 1961, as Macleod entered the lobby with Bennett, Macmillan was sitting on the bench opposite. He caught Iain's gaze and his eyes flickered away. At that moment it was clear to Bennett that Macleod no longer had the Prime Minister's full confidence and that he considered his Secretary of State expendable.

In the end the problem was resolved by the establishment of the Central Africa Office under Rab Butler, who conducted the prolonged negotiations for the dissolution of the Federation in 1963 with great tact and skill. The experience of divided control must also have influenced Macmillan to combine the direction of the Commonwealth and Colonial Offices under one Minister in 1962.

The absence of the United Federal Party delegation had enabled Macleod to conclude more liberal arrangements at the February conference than would have been possible if John Roberts had attended it. But to get the UFP to take part in elections, the Secretary of State knew that he would have to give some ground to Welensky's objections, which had by this time also generated disquiet in the Conservative Parliamentary Party. When he was in London the Federal Prime Minister used to be

invited to address the Party's Commonwealth Affairs Committee and he
never lost the opportunity to attack the policy of the British Government.

Reggie Bennett was able, assiduous and loyal. He had excellent
relations with Members of Parliament and with the lobby correspondents
and kept Iain fully informed of feeling in the party. He worked hard to
interpret Iain's views as favourably as possible to his parliamentary
colleagues, but despite his efforts and those of many other friends and
supporters, a back-bench revolt against Macleod's proposals found
expression in a motion on the Order Paper of the House of Commons,
signed by ninety Conservative members. The actual wording of the
motion was unexceptionable – indeed some of the signatories believed
they were helping Macleod by signing it – but the list included many
others who wished to see Welensky triumphant in a trial of strength with
African nationalism, and the general impression created by the motion
was one of strong back-bench opposition to Macleod's policy. Its importance lay in the fact that it attracted support from the centre of the
party as well as from known right-wingers.

Macleod was himself anxious about the effect of this upon opinion in
the Cabinet and feared there might be pressure from his colleagues to
water down his proposals. I therefore took the unusual step of writing
personally to the Prime Minister on February 14th, expressing my support
for the policy, and that of my friends who shared this view, and sent a
copy of my letter to Macleod. I know, as his biographer, how few letters
or documents he kept, and I was therefore surprised to find this copy still
filed among his papers when he died.

On February 21st the Secretary of State made a factual statement to the
House of Commons, outlining his proposals. His reception by his own
side was conspicuously cool. *The Times* reported that 'he was concise,
lucid and determined . . . he had the look and sound of a man in a corner,
but a man willing to fight for what he believes in'. Many Conservative
back-benchers were still critical and dissatisfied. The wounds of Suez were
healing, the 1959 election had been won, and a large section of the
Parliamentary Party was in a state of post-operative euphoria and against
concessions of any kind.

There were corresponding anxieties in the House of Lords, which
culminated in Lord Salisbury's denunciation of Macleod as 'too clever by
half'. Salisbury spoke of a crisis of confidence between the British and
Federal Governments. It was not just a matter of wide divergences of
view, but 'a miasma of mistrust which had arisen to cloud the issue and

embitter the controversy'. He went on to argue that the responsibility for this must be ascribed to Mr Macleod. He was a man of remarkable qualities, of unusual intellect, brave and resolute. But he had adopted, in his relationship to the white communities in Africa, an entirely wrong approach. He had been too clever by half. He was a very fine bridge player; bridge was a game in which two players were matched against two other players. The aim was to outwit the opponent and the more one out-witted him within the rules of the game, the better player one was. It was Macleod's object to outwit the white people of East and Central Africa and he had done it successfully, first at the Lancaster House Conference on Kenya, then subsequently in relation to Central Africa.

Lord Salisbury said he spoke for the white communities, who felt that they could not trust Macleod – hence the crisis of confidence. In reply to a question from Lord Listowel, a former Secretary of State for the Colonies, Salisbury said he thought Macleod had ignored his duty to the Europeans in Central Africa. He told Lady Summerskill that he had not described Macleod as 'disingenuous': 'I thought he was rather unscrupulous. I am not going to withdraw that.'

This was a direct and vicious attack upon the man as well as upon his policies. It was a calculated attempt at character assassination, which did lasting damage to Macleod's reputation, partly because it received wide publicity in the press, but mainly because many people thought there was an element of truth in it.

Macleod played his cards close to his chest. He thought ahead and calculated his next move and the move after. This was essential at chess, a game he played well, and it had much value in politics; but it sometimes gave an appearance of a certain lack of candour, and it was this impression which made Salisbury's jibe credible. The fact that it was totally un-justified and, in the words of the Lord Chancellor, Lord Kilmuir, that there was 'no jot or scintilla of evidence to support' the contention that Macleod desired to outwit his opponents, was irrelevant. The harm had been done.

In fact, Lord Salisbury scarcely knew Macleod personally. Iain and Eve had once spent a weekend at Hatfield, but this was the only private contact the two men had had and they differed so deeply over colonial policy that they hardly ever met after Lord Salisbury resigned from the Government.

The debate was resumed the next day. It was enlivened by Lord Hemingford's comment that he would 'rather have a statesman who has mastered bridge than one who is content with nap or snap'; and there was a further attack on the Secretary of State by the Duke of Montrose² who considered Macleod 'a fast worker in pursuing his aims'. Lord Perth, the Minister of State at the Colonial Office and one of Iain Macleod's most loyal friends and supporters, had opened the debate on the first day, so he could not speak again; but Lord Hailsham wound up with a strong attack on Lord Salisbury; perhaps too strong, as it alienated some peers who shared Salisbury's views but had deplored his slurs on Macleod. Hailsham referred to 'the series of insults which I thought were utterly unworthy of the noble Marquess and indeed of the conduct of public life in this House':

'We cannot all have great possessions, but we can all be proud of our personal honour. We can all be glad of our reputation as honest men. It was that which I thought the noble Marquess was seeking to take away from my Right Honourable friend.'

Lord Perth made a personal statement in the House of Lords the next day, to the effect that the criticisms which had been made of Macleod applied equally to him. This was helpful in the Lords where Perth was a respected and popular Minister.

Macleod was shocked and hurt by Lord Salisbury's words, which were a reflection on his integrity (as indeed they must have been intended)³ and he felt his motives had been misunderstood. He believed sincerely that his policies were as much in the long-term interests of the whites as of the blacks. Only by pursuing a non-racial policy would Europeans be able to remain in Africa and play their part in its future development.

Dr Banda had supported this claim in a speech in Dar-es-Salaam the previous year. Macleod was not selling out the Europeans, he said. He was their best friend in Africa: 'There can be no peace between Africans and Europeans other than by coming to terms with African nationalism. He is coming to terms.'

This was not the view of the diehards, who in any case did not wish to remain under a black government, but it gave good prospects for those like Lord Delamere in Kenya, who were prepared to work with African leaders.

2 Resident in Rhodesia, where he was known as Lord Graham and was a member of the Federal Assembly, and later a minister in Mr Ian Smith's Rhodesia Government.

3 Sir Colin Coote wrote of Lord Salisbury in an obituary (*Daily Telegraph*, February 24, 1972) that 'he embodied the definition of a gentleman as one who is never unintentionally offensive'.

Macleod never replied to Lord Salisbury's bitter attack. Indeed, he understood and shared Salisbury's anxieties. In a television interview shortly after the Lords debate, he speculated: 'Salisbury might say "the pace in Africa is dangerously fast. It would be better if we went more slowly." And I might say "the pace in Africa is dangerously fast but it might be more dangerous still if we went more slowly." So the anxieties of the people who live there are very close to me, just as they are to Lord Salisbury, and I do not wish to attack him.' It was a mild riposte, but perhaps the more effective for its moderation. Despite Macleod's restraint feeling continued to run deep. When Hugh Fraser loyally counter-attacked in Iain's defence, he found himself cut publicly by members of the Cecil family.

With the publication of the February White Paper on Northern Rhodesia, the five UFP Ministers resigned their offices and withdrew from the Executive Council. This enabled Sir John Moffat, who had played a helpful and important part at the February conference, to head the transitional government. He filled, selflessly, the same thankless but essential role that Michael Blundell was undertaking in Kenya.

Welensky's fierce condemnation of the White Paper had the effect of making it more acceptable to the Africans, and the Governor, Sir Evelyn Hone, worked hard and successfully to obtain Kaunda's agreement to it. But it had left many important points undecided, and this gave Welensky the opportunity to re-open the battle. The Commonwealth Prime Ministers' Conference in March, which, as Prime Minister of the Federa-tion, he traditionally attended, provided the occasion for further dis-cussions in London and various new Federal variations on the White Paper were put forward.

Subsequently, Duncan Sandys visited Salisbury, ostensibly to tie up the details of the Southern Rhodesia Constitution, but in fact to discuss Northern Rhodesia. Macleod did not object to this. Sandys was a strong, tough negotiator and at the same time a calming influence, and Macleod much preferred that he should hold discussions with Welensky in Salisbury to the alternative of having to talk to Welensky himself in London.

The pressure exerted by the Federal Government was now considerable. As a result, many modifications were made to the earlier White Paper. The principle of racial parity, with the Governor and his nominated officials holding the balance for the first Parliament, was maintained, but Macleod gave way on several points of detail.

Even before these concessions became known, the manoeuvres between

February and June had aroused the suspicions of the Africans. It was only with difficulty that they had been persuaded to accept the February plan, and when the June White Paper appeared, eroding some of the earlier proposals, they felt badly let down. There was considerable doubt as to whether Kaunda would agree to recommend it to his own people.

Kenneth Kaunda is a man of high character and strong Christian faith. I had met him on a visit to Northern Rhodesia the previous year and had got on well with him. Macleod thought I might be able to influence him to accept the White Paper, and he asked Charles Longbottom[4] to bring him round to my house for a talk. I knew nothing of the detailed proposals; my brief was simply to reassure Kaunda of Macleod's good faith and sincerity. I was myself so convinced of this that it was not difficult to convey my confidence to the UNIP leader.

Macleod himself saw Kaunda at Sloane Court before making his statement in the House of Commons, and was able to satisfy him that the principle of an African majority was still preserved. Kaunda agreed to try and sell it to his people when he got home. In this he was partly, though not completely, successful. There was some violence and sabotage in Northern Rhodesia during the summer, which Sir Evelyn Hone did well to contain.

Soon afterwards Macleod was succeeded as Secretary of State by Reggie Maudling, who made a number of concessions to the Africans and finally, though not without difficulty, brought the matter to a conclusion in February 1962 on very much the same basis as Macleod had recommended a year before.

The delay had achieved nothing for anyone. It had alienated the Africans without pacifying Welensky. The Federation was now doomed, and the often ambivalent attitude of the British Government had given substance to Welensky's charge of equivocation. At home the critics of Macleod's African policies had publicly questioned his good faith, and it was to be many years before he lived down this slander upon his political integrity. He had ensured the independence of Zambia, but at some cost to his own reputation in the Conservative Party.

Reginald Maudling, his successor as Colonial Secretary, had the same liberal outlook as Macleod and he pursued the same policies, but without the same passion. He was always agreeable and friendly and he always listened, apparently with sympathy and certainly with patience, to anyone who wished to see him. Everyone liked him.

4 MP for York 1959/66. Parliamentary Private Secretary to Macleod 1961/63.

Macleod's initiative and determination were needed to launch and sustain the new momentum in Africa, but Maudling's firm but milder technique smoothed many ruffled feathers. Macmillan's judgement was no doubt good in making the change at the Colonial Office when he did.

During the course of this long-drawn-out Rhodesian saga, South Africa had left the Commonwealth, following the Prime Ministers' conference in March 1961. Though not of direct departmental concern to Macleod, this event saddened him and we talked of it at the time.

Our generation had been taught history and geography when the power of the British Navy and the red of the British Empire in every school atlas inspired and focused our patriotism. With his strong sense of continuity and his Scottish pride in the imperial achievement, Iain Macleod was instinctively against South Africa leaving the Commonwealth and he always thought it need never have happened.

Almost all the prime ministers wanted South Africa to remain in. Diefenbaker of Canada was opposed to it, but even Nehru and Nkrumah would have agreed if Verwoerd had been able to accept the presence of coloured Commonwealth High Commissioners in Pretoria. He declined flatly to do so and this was the end of the road. He was prepared to meet with his fellow prime ministers of the new Commonwealth at Marlborough House, but he would not receive their representatives in his own country. Despite the strong feeling in black Africa (and especially Tanzania) against the apartheid policy, if Verwoerd had felt able to make this one concession, South Africa could have remained a member of the Commonwealth. Macleod would have welcomed this. He thought it might have eased the lot of the Africans in the Union, and that Britain and the Commonwealth would have retained greater influence with the South African government.

Tanganyika had been the easiest of the East African countries to set on the road to independence. Kenya, with its European problem, had presented greater difficulties. In some ways Uganda was the hardest of the three.

Progress depended on how soon a working relationship could be established between the kings, especially the Kabaka, and the politicians. Feeling between the two factions was bitter, and the unification of the country was made more difficult by the fact that its centre, the Kingdom of Buganda, was ruled by the Kabaka. Kampala, the capital, and Entebbe, the only other large town, are both in Buganda, so it was as though

Macleod playing the cards of his colonial policy.

"ALWAYS SCHEME AND PLAY TO GI[
CHANCES OF GUESSING WRONG A[
— MR. IAIN[

VICKY

"... ᴴᴱ DEFENDERS AS MANY
ᴼU CAN CONTRIVE "

ᴱOD , IN HIS BOOK "BRIDGE IS AN EASY GAME"

London and the home counties were under one government and the rest of England under another. The position was further complicated by the existence of three other kingdoms, Bunyoro, Toro and Ankole.

Macleod had visited Uganda in September 1960, and at the end of the year he appointed a commission, under the chairmanship of Lord Munster, a former Under-Secretary of State for the Colonies, to advise on this problem. Its report, in June 1961, recommended a federal relationship between Buganda and the rest of the country and rejected Buganda's demand for secession.

The Uganda Constitutional Conference opened in London in September 1961. It was to be the last colonial conference under Macleod's chairmanship, as he was made Leader of the House of Commons and Chairman of the Conservative Party on the day it ended. Until a few hours before the formal opening session, it was uncertain whether it would even begin.

The Buganda delegation were very reluctant to attend, and it was in fact the first occasion on which representatives of Buganda had taken part in constitutional discussions with those from the rest of the country; but an Uganda Conference without them would have been meaningless.

The discussions with the Kabaka were long and stubborn. His eventual agreement to take part was due to the diplomacy of Iain Macleod and the political and tactical skill of Dr Obote, the leader of the Opposition, who was in temporary alliance with the Kabaka and did much to persuade him to cooperate. Eventually Macleod bluffed his way to success. He told the Kabaka that the conference would in any event begin the following day, with or without the Buganda delegation, and that major decisions affecting the future of his country would be taken in their absence if his ministers did not appear. The Kabaka himself never attended the conference; it would have been beneath his dignity to do so, but his ministers reported to him each day.

Macleod found the Kabaka obstinate and almost impossible to deal with. He seemed really to regard himself as a king who should be negotiating not with one of the Queen's political underlings, but with the Sovereign herself. His preoccupation with minor points of precedence, gun salutes and other trivialities was irritating and absurd, and the two men never established a good relationship. But Oliver Lyttelton and Alan Lennox-Boyd had both been on friendly terms with the Kabaka, so the fault may have been at least partly Macleod's.

The Secretary of State's personal contacts with the Uganda political leaders were also less close than in other African countries, so he relied greatly upon the Governor, Sir Frederick Crawford. Fortunately there was a close accord between them, and Macleod always acknowledged that much of the credit for the success of the conference was due to Crawford.

Macleod did not attend all the sessions, but he had a meeting in his room at Lancaster House every day to consider the run of play. During the course of the conference, Mr Kiwanuka, the Chief Minister, put forward three papers on behalf of his government and, when invited by the Secretary of State to speak in support of them, he opposed them all – to the horror of his advisers. After many crises, which included a walk-out by Mr Kiwanuka and long negotiations with the Baganda outside the conference, it was at length agreed that Buganda should have a federal relationship with the rest of Uganda, retaining some autonomy in certain legislative and judicial matters.

The important matter of the 'lost counties' was left over for later decision. Macleod's only contribution was to appoint a Privy Councillor's Commission, consisting of Lords Molson, Listowel and Ward to advise on its solution. The issue is not strictly a part of this story, except in so far as Macleod can be criticised for not having settled it at the conference. It is always regrettable, if sometimes unavoidable, when difficult matters are left for inexperienced and newly independent governments to deal with; but Dr Obote, by then Prime Minister, resolved the 'lost counties' dispute fairly and firmly, and in so doing added to his growing authority in Uganda.

Until the last day of the conference it was by no means certain that agreement would be reached. The final session consisted almost entirely of a speech by Iain Macleod. There was an atmosphere of tension in the gilt music room at Lancaster House as he rose to speak. He explained the complex arrangements he had made with the Baganda, and announced that elections would be held before the introduction of the new constitution. This was a bitter pill for Kiwanuka to swallow; but with the next sentence the ground was cut from under his feet – the date of independence was to be a year from that day, on October 9, 1962. Although, traditionally, Kiwanuka had demanded independence, he had certainly not expected to get it so soon. Indeed, the time-table was unreasonably tight for the Colonial Office lawyers and officials. It involved the preparation of the internal self-government constitution, the enactment of the Uganda Independence Act, and the drafting of the Independence Order in Council, which was only completed a week before the independence date. Further negotiations with the four kingdoms had to be concluded, and the general election in Uganda had to be held. It was an exacting schedule and meant much hard work for many people. Macleod set high targets for his officials, but they were always attained.

As a result of the conference, the Baganda got the rather hollow formal guarantees on which they had set their hearts and Obote got the election which would give him the premiership. Kiwanuka got nothing – but no democratic colonial leader could protest against new elections and independence a year earlier than anyone had thought possible.

The final settlement was a significant achievement, which set the course for Uganda's development as an independent and united country. Macleod had correctly identified Obote as the leader who could win power and had the capacity to use it. Those who were present at Lancaster House felt that they had heard something of importance, done superbly well.

One of the Colonial Office officials said to me later: 'There were two good things about working for Iain Macleod. You were working on the right side and you were likely to win.'

When Macleod died an Ugandan admirer wrote to the *Daily Telegraph*:

> Before independence it used to be an unwritten law for us in the colonies compulsively to regard a Colonial Secretary as a declared enemy. . . . To a very great extent Mr Macleod effectively reversed the 'enemy' attitude and I believe that, owing to that reversal, friendship and not bitterness prevailed at independence. In that sense Commonwealth Africa owes him a great debt.

There is a personal postscript to the Uganda story.

The Independence Bill did not come before the House of Commons till July 1962. Just before its introduction, Macmillan had reconstructed his Government in the 'night of the long knives', which saw the departure of a third of his Cabinet. Reggie Maudling, who had followed Macleod at the Colonial Office, became Chancellor of the Exchequer and was succeeded as Colonial Secretary by Duncan Sandys. I was made Under-Secretary of State for the Colonies.

I went to the office next morning to take over from my predecessor, Hugh Fraser, who had become Secretary of State for Air. No one mentioned the Uganda Independence Bill until late in the afternoon, when I was told that I would have to introduce it in the House of Commons that evening. At that time I had never been to Uganda and had no know-

ledge of the independence negotiations. There was no time for a background briefing and I was simply handed a short and rather perfunctory
speech prepared by the department, with no additional information on
which to base a reply to points which might be raised in the debate.
Optimistically, I hoped there wouldn't be any. In fact I was at once
pressed from both sides of the House about the referendum arrangements
for the 'lost counties' of which I had barely heard. It was an awkward
debut at the despatch box and I should have been hard put to it to defend
the Government but for the presence of Iain Macleod, now Leader of the
House of Commons, who had deliberately come into the Chamber in
case I needed his help. I did – and he gave it, dealing with the situation
with his usual skill, without in any way making it appear that I could not
have coped equally well myself. It was typical of his kindness and of the
trouble he would always take to help a friend.

Macleod's time and attention had been devoted mainly to East and
Central Africa. During the two years of his Colonial Secretaryship this
area presented the most urgent and intractable problems and he concentrated, rightly, upon their solution.

By the time I went to the Colonial Office, less than a year after he had
left it, Malaysia, Aden and South Arabia, and the West Indies, especially
British Guiana, were in the forefront, and Malta was also taking up much
Colonial Office time. But, apart from the Kenya Independence Conference in 1963, East African advance had been charted and virtually
completed by Iain Macleod, and Rab Butler was presiding over the
funeral rites of the Central African Federation.

Macleod was much less concerned with West Africa. Ghana had
reached independence in 1957, two years before he went to the Colonial
Office, and although Nigeria did not become independent till October
1960, the important work there had been done by Oliver Lyttelton and
Alan Lennox-Boyd.

Climatically, West Africa had never been thought suitable for white
settlement, and the traders and administrators who worked there did not
regard it as a permanent home; so there was no European problem.
Constitutional advance had been more gradual and developments which
were telescoped into two years in Tanganyika were spread over twenty in
Sierra Leone.

By the time Macleod became Secretary of State, Sierra Leone had
already attained full internal self-government, and Britain was responsible

only for foreign affairs and defence, with a residual right to suspend the constitution.

In the spring of 1960 a conference was held in London to bring the country to full independence. The Opposition leader, Mr Siaka Stevens,[5] refused to sign, but this was almost a routine feature of colonial conferences and occasioned Macleod no particular anxiety. The Chief Minister, Sir Milton Margai, was a saintly man, who had been educated in England and was well known there. When Macleod asked him on what date he would like his country to become independent, he burst into tears and said he had never expected to live to be asked that question.

There was one setback, just before independence, when the situation in Sierra Leone suddenly became critical and for a short time a state of emergency had to be imposed. This was a great disappointment to the Secretary of State, who had taken much pride in eliminating all the five states of emergency he had inherited when he took office.

The only other Commonwealth territory in West Africa was the Gambia. It was our oldest and smallest African colony, 300 miles long and 30 miles wide, with a population of 300,000. It was dependent on British grant-in-aid and groundnuts, with no prospect of economic viability in the foreseeable future. Apart from its coast line, it was completely surrounded by the larger French-speaking state of Senegal.

The Colonial Office favoured a form of association between the two countries, and a United Nations Survey recommended this in 1964, but in practice its realisation has been limited and the Gambia became independent as a separate country in 1965.

Because of its geographical peculiarity, Macleod regarded the problem of the Gambia as *sui generis*, but its small size and economic weakness focused his mind on the future of the less important colonial territories, which seemed unlikely to be able to sustain independence in isolation in the modern world.

He thought they should be given full internal self-government and that Britain or some neighbouring Commonwealth country should be responsible for their defence and foreign relations. He put these ideas to the Commonwealth Prime Ministers' Conference in 1961 and they were partially implemented by the next Labour Government's creation of the Associated States in the West Indies. This status has obvious disadvantages, as became clear later in St Kitts/Anguilla, but no alternative solution has yet been devised.

5 Later Prime Minister and now President of Sierra Leone.

It was a weakness in Colonial Office administration that officials tended to regard each territory as a separate entity and to overlook the interaction of events in one part of Africa upon another. This was no doubt due to the expertise of most colonial governors, and to the fact that they had far greater local authority than, for instance, their French counterparts. Macleod took a much wider, more global view of colonial politics than most of his advisers. He was conscious of the effects of increasingly rapid communications, and he was acutely aware of events elsewhere – at Sharpeville, in the Congo and in France's African colonies, now moving very fast towards independence – which inevitably influenced opinion, both white and black, in Commonwealth Africa.

CHAPTER 10

Secretary of State for the Colonies (111). The other Colonial Territories 1959-1961

DESPITE his African preoccupation, Macleod had not neglected the other colonial territories. The first colony he ever visited, on his way to East Africa in December 1959, was Malta.

Governor's rule had been in operation on the island since the suspension of the Constitution following the 1958 riots, and was much resented by the Malta Labour Party. Its leader, Dom Mintoff, organised demonstrations to greet Macleod when he arrived and refused to meet him during his visit; but on the eve of his departure Mintoff sent him a letter which Macleod interpreted as meaning that Mintoff would be glad to be rescued from his limb of non-cooperation.

Colonial rule was an unsatisfactory system for a people with as long a history of representative government as the Maltese, and Macleod felt that we should return to a more democratic regime. He realised that the deadlock, which arose mainly because of the inconsistency between the local demand for independence and our own defence requirements in the island, had gone on too long; but he did not feel ready to give any indication of his thoughts, beyond re-affirming that economic support for Malta would continue. Macleod was not much involved in the Malta defence problem. His interest was to try and maintain the income of the colony in the face of reduced expenditure by the navy, and to get the island back on to the right constitutional road. He therefore bided his time. In 1961 Sir Hilary Blood devised a constitution, on which an election was fought and won by Dr Borg Olivier, who remained Prime Minister of Malta for the next ten years. He was defeated in the general election of June 1971 by the narrow majority of five votes in one seat, and Mintoff became Prime Minister.

Macleod felt that there was some difficulty in the traditional appointment of a senior military officer as Governor, and that this was a post which should in future be held by a Colonial Office career man or a politician. Sir Maurice Dorman, formerly Governor-General of Sierra Leone, became Governor of Malta in 1962, and stayed on as a most successful and popular Governor General when the island became independent in 1964.

Macleod was prepared to look outside his own immediate field of recruitment for governors, and one of his appointments was from the Foreign Office. Sir Charles Johnston, previously Ambassador to Jordan, had known Macleod for many years as a fellow-member of White's Club, but it surprised him when, in 1960, the Secretary of State invited him to become Governor of Aden.

Macleod asked him to make recommendations for the future development of the colony and the South Arabian Protectorate. At this time Aden had made little constitutional progress, and Johnston's proposals combined political advance for the colony with its entry into the South Arabian Federation, as a preliminary to subsequent independence for the whole area.

The success of this policy depended upon a scale of financial assistance from the British Government which was perhaps unrealistic and was certainly never achieved; but Macleod accepted the Governor's suggestions and invited the Aden and Federal Ministers to talks in London in July 1961, to discuss closer links between the colony and the Protectorate States. These were continued in Aden under Johnston's Chairmanship, and a year later a Government White Paper foreshadowed the accession of Aden to the Federation. The merger came into effect in January 1963.

We thought we had provided a framework for orderly progress leading to independence. But its weakness lay in the attempted marriage – against considerable nationalist opposition in Aden – between relatively progressive Ministers in the colony and loyal but largely feudal rulers in the Protectorate States.

The policy, adopted by Macleod, followed by Maudling and implemented by Sandys, might or might not have worked, and perhaps we were over-optimistic in thinking it could last in the face of Arab nationalism and Egyptian hostility; but in the event the British Labour Government, which was elected in 1964, overturned the table, let down the Protectorate rulers who had relied upon the good faith of a British Government, and had to scramble out of the area as best they could. It was a sad end to an association with Britain which had lasted for over 120 years.

Outside the African continent, the Caribbean was the most important remaining area of Colonial Office responsibility. The West Indian territories, though poor, were relatively sophisticated and much more ready for political advance than the African colonies. But most of them were too small for independence as separate units. The best prospect seemed to lie in the creation of a united nation, and much work had been done to lay its foundations.

The idea of a Federation of the West Indies was first suggested officially in a despatch from the then Colonial Secretary, Oliver Stanley, in March 1945, and was accepted in principle at the Montego Bay Conference in 1947. During the next two years the Standing Closer Association Committee, under the chairmanship of Sir Hubert Rance, a former Governor of Trinidad and Tobago, made detailed recommendations, and final agreement was reached at a conference in London in 1956. After elections had been held in 1958 Princess Margaret went out to the Caribbean to open the first, and last, Federal Parliament.

Macleod's handling of the West Indies Federation cannot be described as one of his successes; indeed he always regarded the Caribbean as his main area of failure. He established good personal relations with the West Indian leaders, he made a successful visit to Jamaica and Trinidad in the summer of 1960, and he presided over a Federal conference in London in 1961, which fixed the date for independence. Although he worked hopefully and hard to sustain and encourage the new Federation, it collapsed during his period as Secretary of State. It was never a lusty child.

There was much local goodwill for a united and independent West Indian nation. The concept had been fostered by Britain, but not imposed, and had been ten years in the making, so that it was certainly not rushed or ill-considered. There was at that time no colour issue in this genuinely multi-racial society. But the problems were formidable.

Federations consisting of a solid land mass are difficult enough; a nation, every unit of which was separated by sea, was correspondingly less cohesive. It is a thousand miles from Kingston in Jamaica to Port-of-Spain in Trinidad. There was very little inter-island travel and the people in the different territories did not know each other. Even the leading politicians were more accustomed to meeting in London than in the Caribbean. There was a strong island patriotism, but no real sense of West Indian nationhood. Cricket was almost the only unifying influence.

As soon as the Federation was formed, discord began to develop between the Federal Government and the individual units, and between the large islands and the small. Their interests were often in conflict. Jamaica and Trinidad did not wish to carry the small islands economically; the Eastern Caribbean was afraid of being dominated politically by Jamaica.

The Federal Government had too little power and too little money. Under these circumstances it was essential that it should have the best political leadership, to sell Federation as an idea to the people of the West Indies and to guide and direct the central government in its infancy. In fact, the two most able men, who were also the leaders of the two most important islands – Norman Manley of Jamaica and Eric Williams of Trinidad – chose to remain in their own territories. The Federation was run by a second eleven from the small islands.

The Prime Minister, Sir Grantley Adams, had been a wise and respected Premier of Barbados, who had served his country well. Robert Bradshaw of St Kitts was an able and hard-working Finance Minister. But these men and their colleagues in the Federal Government lacked the authority and acceptability in the larger countries which might have made the difference between success and failure for the Federation as a whole.

I remember pleading with Norman Manley to go to Port-of-Spain, but he was always reluctant to do so, perhaps because he was afraid of what his cousin, Sir Alexander Bustamante, a skilful and formidable political opponent, might do in Jamaica in his absence.

Manley and Eric Williams were declared and enthusiastic supporters of Federation, but by the summer of 1960 strong opposition was building up against it in Jamaica and tensions had developed between Trinidad and Britain which needed attention. A ministerial visit was clearly overdue.

The Parliamentary Under-Secretary, Julian Amery, had been planning to go, but when the protracted Cyprus negotiations made this impossible Macleod decided to take his place. The Governor-General, Lord Hailes, had been urging this for some time. Macleod wanted to talk to him and to the territorial governors; to get the 'feel' of the West Indies and to make contact with its leading politicians. He had just made the imaginative appointment of Sir Solomon Hochoi, a West Indian career civil servant of Chinese descent, to succeed Sir Edward Beetham as Governor of Trinidad, and he was anxious, if possible, to iron out the differences which had arisen between Eric Williams and the Colonial Office.

The timing of the visit was excellent, but it began badly. Eve Macleod was accompanying Iain for the first time on a tour of this kind, and on the day after their arrival at King's House, Jamaica, she slipped and broke her leg while going round a hospital. It was a sad disappointment, and meant that she had to miss the rest of the trip and remain in Kingston to recover. The Jamaican people were concerned that she would have a bad impression of their island and sent her many messages of sympathy and good wishes. As always, Eve was brave and patient in adversity.

During the Jamaica visit Iain had an official engagement on the other side of the island and, as time was short, he and the Governor, Sir Kenneth Blackburne, travelled in a three-seater Cesna aircraft. A bad tropical storm blew up just before take-off, but Iain insisted on keeping to his schedule. As he climbed into the Cesna he saw a notice opposite the pilot's seat which read 'God is my co-pilot'. The storm grew worse, and they returned very late from the expedition in pitch darkness and pouring rain.

After talks with Manley and Bustamante, Iain Macleod flew on to Trinidad, where his stay was an unqualified success. The Governor, Sir Edward Beetham, described it as a personal triumph. Patrick Hailes wrote to me to say: 'Iain has done magnificently and never put a foot wrong,' and the local press were enthusiastic. The *Trinidad Guardian* reported that his visit had been 'a tonic for the Federation'; it had 'brightened the outlook and improved the whole atmosphere'. And the *Nation*, the PNM's party newspaper, paid tribute to his 'ability, political awareness and generosity, which has impressed us all'.

He concluded an awkward procedural agreement on the Chaguaramas base, and in the course of long private conversations with Eric Williams, with no advisers or secretaries present, established an excellent relationship with the Trinidadian leader. Dr Williams is a man of rare intellectual quality and great ability, but officials found him enigmatic and sometimes difficult to get on with. The personal friendship which he and Macleod formed seemed a good augury for future negotiations.

On his return from the West Indies the Secretary of State was still optimistic about the prospects for the Federation. He told the House of Commons that 'it has much to teach the world, not least the way in which people of many varying racials origins can live together in friendship and co-operation'. This was true; but he had under-estimated the gulf between the large islands and the small, and he acknowledged later that, in the year which followed, he was building on sand. It did not seem so at the time, and although doubts were developing in his mind the conference which assembled in London in June 1961 agreed upon May 31, 1962, as the date for the independence of the Federation. Ironically, it was the day of its dissolution

It was a difficult conference, at which tensions between the island leaders soon became apparent. A fundamental difference had developed between the supporters of a strong central government and those who preferred the real power to remain in the units. Jamaica was in the second category. She did not want her growing industrial development controlled by the Federal Government, and Manley insisted on a right of veto for this and for the imposition of a Federal income tax. Trinidad felt equally strongly that freedom of movement should be left in unit hands.

The real problem of power was not resolved, and the Federal Government was left too weak to be effective. Perhaps Macleod should have brought greater pressure to bear to strengthen the finances of the central government, but to have done so would have made more certain the adverse vote in Jamaica which led directly to her withdrawal and to the end of the Federation.

It has always puzzled me that Manley, himself a convinced Federalist, chose to put the issue to the people of Jamaica in the form of a referendum. Had he held a general election, he could at least have counted upon the support of his own party. As it was, some of his leading ministers worked actively against Federation, and this was too heavy a handicap in the face of Bustamante's rip-roaring campaign which united his own party against Jamaica's continued participation.

The trouble lay as much in the months and years before it as in the referendum itself. None of the political leaders had made any serious attempt to sell the advantages of Federation to the Jamaican people. I remember, on a visit to Kingston in January 1960, being met by the local press reporters who all asked me what Jamaica would gain from Federation. I told them that it was not for itinerant politicians from Britain, but for their own leaders, to make the federal case, and it alarmed me at the time that they had not done so. Nevertheless, most people expected Manley to win his referendum and, had he done so, Macleod thought the other issues would have proved negotiable.

The result of the referendum held on September 19th, 1961 was a shock, which took everyone, including the British Government, by surprise. There had been no contingency planning. It has been argued that Macleod should have reconvened the Federal Conference in order to see what could be salvaged; and this was the policy advocated by Dr Eric Williams when he remarked that, in this kind of arithmetic, the Secretary of State should remember that one from 10 doesn't leave nine, it leaves 0. But no one could have prevented Jamaica's defection, and the outcome would therefore have been the same. The discovery of bauxite had made Jamaica self-confident and self-reliant. She knew she could sustain independence on her own and would have resented any attempt by Britain to delay it. Trinidad, viable owing to her oil, had already made it clear that she would not stay in the Federation if Jamaica left it. As a result the Leeward and Windward Islands were abandoned, and the Federation, which had been their hope of independence, had disintegrated. We were all left to pick up the pieces as best we could, and an abortive attempt was made to form a Federation of the 'Little Eight' under the leadership of Barbados. But this, too, failed.

It may be that the rapid advance elsewhere was, paradoxically, an indirect cause of the failure in the Caribbean. As long as Federation seemed the only way to independence, the West Indies favoured it. But when it became apparent that quite small territories, Malta and Cyprus and even the Gambia, were moving towards independence on their own, it was not surprising that larger and more viable colonies like Jamaica and Trinidad should realise that their political aspirations could be achieved without the economic liabilities of supporting a Federation of weaker units which would nevertheless limit their control of their own destiny. From their point of view they were right and, as things turned out, Jamaica and Trinidad became independent members of the Commonwealth in 1962 and Guyana and Barbados in 1966.

Although the West Indies were within the American sphere of influence, the United States Government never sought to influence British policy in our attempt to establish a workable island Federation. But, in the aftermath of the Bay of Pigs, the Americans were naturally interested in British Guiana and did not care for the prospect of an independent, Jagan-led, Castro-type government on the South American mainland.

President Kennedy told Macleod of his anxieties during a long talk in the Oval Room at the White House. He said he understood our policy but he hoped we would not move too quickly towards independence. Macleod replied: 'Do I understand, Mr President, that you want us to decolonise as fast as possible all over the world except on your own doorstep?' President Kennedy laughed and said: 'Well, that's probably just about it.' Macleod answered that he appreciated the President's point of view, but that our policy to bring Guiana to independence would continue. The American attitude did not slow down his own approach, although the serious racial strife between the African and Indian communities in the colony a year or two later, and the difficulty of getting any agreement on

an Independence Constitution between Cheddi Jagan and Forbes Burn-
ham, did impose an inevitable delay.

At a British Guiana conference in March 1960, Macleod had taken an
unfortunate decision to allow Jagan's government to assume responsibility for internal security, including control of the police. The Governor,
Sir Ralph Grey, was left with no reserve powers, although he was still
responsible for the armed forces. This caused much trouble later. Macleod
was never afraid to use power. He had the courage to take controversial
decisions against official advice but they were not always the right
ones.

Sometimes the official advice differed, and the Secretary of State had to
decide between conflicting views. One decision concerned the United
Nations, which had long been pressing us to supply information on
political and constitutional matters to the UN Colonial Committee of
Twenty-four. The suggestion had been rejected at the San Francisco Conference as an infringement of sovereignty, and successive Secretaries of
State had adhered to this view. The Colonial Office felt strongly that the
evolution of the Empire into a free Commonwealth concerned only
Britain and her colonies, and that our bilateral negotiations with them
should not be made into an international football to be kicked round the
corridors of New York. Sir Hilton Poynton, who was not a UN
enthusiast, advised Macleod to stand firm against the pressures to change
this policy. Sir Hugh Foot, (later Lord Caradon) an able and progressive
ex-Governor who was at that time our spokesman in New York on
Colonial affairs, disagreed with this view. He argued that our 'image' in
the United Nations was bad and would be worse if we refused to co-
operate. Macleod did not like foreign meddling any more than Poynton,
but he felt that the need to damp down adverse criticism in New York
was of overriding importance at that time. He therefore, somewhat reluctantly, accepted Foot's advice. The new policy did not yield any apparent
dividends, and Macleod's decision may have been mistaken.

Iain and Eve Macleod paid a visit to New York in 1961 when Sir
Andrew Cohen, a civil servant of exceptional ability, was representing us
at the United Nations. They stayed with the Cohens at their tall, narrow
brownstone house in Manhattan, and Helen Cohen kindly converted the
ground floor dining room into a bedroom for Eve, who found steep stairs
a hazard after breaking her leg in Jamaica shortly before. The Cohens
awaited the Secretary of State's arrival with some trepidation. If the
weather held, they could have meals in the paved garden behind the house;

if there was rain, there would also have been chaos. Luckily the sun shone and the visit was a success. Andrew Cohen arranged for Macleod to meet many of the African representatives at the United Nations, who were impressed by his understanding of their problems.

During the West Indies Conference of 1961, Macleod was lent Chequers for a weekend and he invited my wife and me to stay to help him entertain Sir Grantley Adams, who was an old friend of mine, and Eric Williams and his daughter Erica, who came down for the day on the Sunday, as did Hugh and Antonia Fraser.

This weekend provided the occasion for an extraordinary example of Iain Macleod's photographic memory. At lunch time on Saturday my wife commented casually on a book she had bought recently and asked Iain if he had read it. He said he had, on holiday a year before. He remarked that the most interesting passage was on page 137 and he proceeded to quote from it. My wife could not believe that he could remember so exactly something he had not read for so long. To prove it, he asked one of the staff to try and find the book in the Chequers library. It took some time to trace, but by tea time it had been produced and Iain opened it at page 137. He had quoted it almost verbatim.

On the same occasion someone mentioned the name of a Derby winner, but got the year of its victory wrong. Iain corrected him and then listed the name of the winner, owner, trainer and jockey of every Derby, backwards from 1960 to 1920.

At his first meeting with Norman Manley, who had mentioned a Jamaican victory in the Helsinki Olympics, Iain was able to give, immediately, the names of all the runners and their individual lap times. He was fascinated by all forms of sport and had a fantastic knowledge of every result he had seen or read about.

On one occasion, in reply to a supplementary question in the House of Commons, he gave a wrong figure in connection with the complicated Northern Rhodesia voting provisions. Afterwards he asked the department to check the information with which he had been supplied. It was found that the background note for the original question had contained three paragraphs, to each of which a footnote had been added, but the typist had inadvertently transposed two of the footnotes, so the answer was wrong. Macleod's memory was, literally, visual and he had correctly remembered the piece of paper he had read. Knowledge of his phenomenal memory alerted his advisers to the danger of giving him any information which was not completely accurate. They knew that any detail fed into the computer would be retained and might bring nemesis later if it was incorrect.

At that time the Colonial Office used to have two House of Commons question days a week, averaging fifty oral questions each, but the Secretary of State was always calm, methodical and unhurried. He had invariably been through all the supplementary material and had everything ready by lunch time – in marked contrast to some Ministers.

There was not much time in those days for long-term thinking about future policy, but Macleod and David Perth both gave some attention to this and, although the Africa departments were overworked, there were other areas of Colonial Office responsibility in the Pacific and Indian oceans and the Far East where the pressures were less and the senior officials in charge of these had time to 'stand and stare'.

During Macleod's period as Secretary of State and increasingly there-after, the Colonial Office areas of responsibility were shrinking, and as early as 1960 Sir Hilton Poynton had suggested the amalgamation of the department with the Commonwealth Relations Office. He thought it important to preserve the expertise which the Colonial Office had built up for handling financial aid and that many of the newly independent countries would wish to go on using this advice. Macleod agreed with him. The Select Committee on Estimates had also been studying this subject and had reached the same conclusion. But the Commonwealth Office felt that independent countries would not wish their diplomatic relations to be handled by a department which was also administering dependent territories, and when the matter was discussed in Cabinet this view prevailed.

The compromise solution decided upon was the creation of the Depart-ment of Technical Co-operation, which worked as an aid agency for the Colonial Office, the Commonwealth Office and the Foreign Office. Under the Labour government which came to power in 1964, this department became the Ministry of Overseas Development, but it has now been absorbed, like the old Colonial Office, into the Foreign and Common-wealth Office, so that the original proposal put forward by Macleod and Poynton a decade earlier has at length been implemented.

Iain Macleod's relations with the department were excellent. I came to know well most of those with whom he had worked and found that they all admired and respected him. Some became his personal friends. But he never encouraged familiarity and was less relaxed than Reggie Maudling, who succeeded him. He expected a high standard of efficiency, and his immense intelligence and sometimes rather chilling manner discouraged small talk. He was workmanlike, clear-minded and articulate, and his professional judgements commanded respect and confidence. As under Duncan Sandys, policy was coming from the top, not from the officials. Sir Hilton Poynton told me that Macleod was ready to change his mind if he saw that there was a good argument for doing so, but that the civil servants always felt that the Secretary of State was leading the policy. I have met no one who did not describe him as a good administrator and a good Minister to work for. Many thought him the best they had served.

In his conduct of business he was economical with time and never wasted words. He gave his officials a hearing, sometimes asking searching questions, sometimes making no comment, which could be disconcerting. When he had absorbed their views, he would make up his mind quickly and give his decisions without any unnecessary summary of the various courses of action which could be followed. He seemed to conserve his strength and energy.

Officials like Ministers who think quickly and decide quickly, and even a mistaken decision is, from their point of view, usually better than no decision at all. Charles Longbottom remembers him saying one day in the Colonial Office: 'My job here is to take decisions. Some of them may, with the benefit of hindsight, be wrong; but the worst thing I could do would be to postpone them till tomorrow. In a constantly moving job like this, the worst crime is indecision.'

Macleod's opinion of those who worked for him varied. Of all the departments he presided over, he thought the Colonial Office the most uneven. It had, in his view, the best people and the worst. He considered the average official at the Ministry of Labour was of higher quality than the average in the Colonial Office, but that the 'flyers' at the Colonial Office were better than their opposite numbers in the Ministry of Labour. He thought the Permanent Secretary, Sir Hilton Poynton, had a first class brain, and he had a high opinion of Sir John Martin and Sir Arthur Galsworthy, who were men of exceptional calibre and entirely attuned to what he was trying to do.

Macleod was always accessible to his junior Ministers and kept them fully informed. His relations with his Minister of State, David Perth, and his Under-Secretary of State, Hugh Fraser, were close and cordial. Fraser's predecessor, Julian Amery, did not share Macleod's approach to colonial problems and thought he was going too fast in Africa. They did relatively little work together because, out of the ten months of their joint service, Amery was in Cyprus for five months, in the Pacific for two, and on holiday for one; but they liked and respected each other personally and, when Iain died, Julian said: 'He had a staunch heart and a subtle brain. I grieve and mourn his loss.'

Macleod was an exceptionally good delegator. He held regular meetings, known as 'morning prayers', with his junior Ministers and senior officials, at which the problems of the day were identified and allocated for action in the office. Delegation was thereafter absolute, and this enabled Macleod to concentrate on the essentials. But his support for his subordinates was always assured and complete in the event of criticism.

On a visit to Kenya Hugh Fraser caused a storm by stating at a press conference that independence would be a matter of several years and several conferences. When this was raised in the House of Commons Macleod disarmed the critics with the suave explanation that 'several' meant 'more than one' – and within this definition Fraser was proved right. He was a good Under-Secretary of State, devoted to Iain and a loyal adherent of his policies.

The Minister of State, Lord Perth, was – like Fraser – a close personal friend of Macleod's and a firm supporter of his new approach to colonial problems. As he had been second in command to Alan Lennox-Boyd for nearly four years, he had already visited most of the territories and knew their leaders.

The attitude of the press was helpful to Macleod throughout the Colonial Secretaryship, and he was grateful for the support he received. Of course there were exceptions. In view of the policy of the Beaverbrook newspapers, it was not surprising that they were usually hostile and sometimes unfair; but, generally, there was a real and sympathetic understanding of what he was trying to do, which conditioned the climate of public opinion and had an important effect on Parliament and even upon the Cabinet. In some cases this may have been decisive, since it gave him greater freedom to negotiate than he might otherwise have had. He thought the press support for his approach to the problem of Nyasaland had an especially favourable influence.

In his dealings with the press he was completely honest, and his relations with journalists, particularly with the Commonwealth correspondents of the 'quality' newspapers, were very good. He could not always be as frank with them as he would have liked, but many people, including

Michael Blundell, have acknowledged that he handled the press very well.

He enjoyed the company of journalists and regarded his contacts with them as more than formal. At the end of the trying summer of 1961, he and Eve Macleod gave a party for all those who had covered the Northern Rhodesian story, and their wives. He had nothing to gain politically by this gesture, since by then the crisis was over.

'Leaks' to the newspapers are usually deliberate and usually from a Minister. Sometimes they are designed merely to gain personal publicity, and these are quite easily identifiable. Macleod was not interested in publicity or popularity. He never kept press reports about himself and often didn't even read them. Any information he gave to the papers was shrewder and less attributable. Its object was to help the Government and to further his own policies.

If Macleod was accorded sympathetic treatment by the press, the same was certainly true of the attitude of the Opposition in Parliament. He had taken colonial affairs out of party politics and had succeeded in making Britain's policy bi-partisan. This is always best in overseas departments if it can be achieved, and it was an advantage to him both in the colonies and in the House of Commons. It was a remarkable achievement against the bitter background of Hola and the Devlin Report of less than two years before.

No Socialist Secretary of State could have moved with the same speed as Macleod in the rapid devolution of power in Africa between 1959 and 1961. Jim Callaghan, then Shadow Colonial Secretary, was especially helpful. He knew what Macleod was trying to do, and he supported it. The two men got on well personally, and although they differed some-times on individual issues – such as the release of Kenyatta, which Calla-ghan thought should have come sooner – there was no real opposition from the Labour Party to the main lines of policy. This was a source of strength to Macleod, who was always grateful for it. He had sufficient trouble from the back benches of his own party.

Many Conservatives, in Parliament and outside, thought the security and interests of the white communities in Africa could best be protected by maintaining the status quo for as long as possible; and it is true that independence could have been delayed, but only by resorting to emer-gency powers and the use of force. Macleod thought this a short-term policy. He was as interested as his critics in safeguarding the position of the Europeans, but he was convinced that this could only be done by settling the constitutional future of East and Central Africa quickly and with goodwill. In this way the Europeans who wished to stay would be able to do so. Some did not; they left to go to South Africa or perhaps to Australia. But many remained and accepted the changes that were inevitable. They were no longer the masters, but they were still the friends of the Africans, and their future was better and surer and happier than it would have been in an explosive atmosphere, which denied to the majority race the right to run its own affairs. Many Europeans in East Africa who questioned and fought this policy at the time would acknowledge today that it was long-sighted and wise.

Macleod believed so sincerely that he was doing what was best for both races in Africa that he found his two years at the Colonial Office the most constructive and rewarding of his whole twenty years in public life. The opportunities were greater for him than in any appointment he had held before and perhaps (as he was denied even one budget as Chancellor) since. It was a satisfying time, and he looked back on it with much pride and few regrets. Referring to the Colonial Secretaryship in a television interview with John Freeman in the summer of 1961, he said that the Ministry of Labour 'took the whole of my mind, but this job takes the whole of my heart as well'.

He drove himself hard. He would see anyone at any time, and work till any hour of the night. It was certainly the most arduous period of his life, and sometimes he would sleep all day on Sunday to restore his strength and energy for the next week.

Once his mind was made up he was very determined and nothing would deflect him from his policy. His strength lay in his conviction that he was doing something of importance and that it was right. He believed deeply in majority rule and in the right of men to guide their own destinies – on the principle that, from their point of view, self-government was better than good government by an alien power. He believed in the dignity of man and thought British paternalism, though it had done much for Africa in the previous sixty years, had outlived its role and its acceptability in the second half of the twentieth century. He believed that it was Britain's duty, as it had always been Britain's policy, not to rule subject peoples but to enable them to rule themselves.

In Whitehall, no single statesman did more to evolve the New Commonwealth out of the Old Empire. Overseas, in numerous posts under successive governments over a period of thirty years, Malcolm MacDonald has at least an equal claim. Thanks to men like these, our record was creditable. Despite all the earlier criticisms of 'Colonialism', despite the strictures of the United Nations 'Committee of 24', we did not leave behind us in Africa either a Congo or an Algeria.

It is as difficult to dissolve an Empire as to create one, and in my judgement Macleod saved Africa for the Commonwealth. He transferred power just in time, without bloodshed, and so retained the friendship of the now independent African countries. None of them left the Commonwealth. I believe that his Colonial Secretaryship at a crucial period will be assessed by history as the most significant contribution of his career and indeed of the whole Macmillan Administration. Alan Watkins wrote: 'He was certainly a great Colonial Secretary, probably the greatest since Joe Chamberlain; perhaps the greatest ever.'[1]

In terms of personal ambition Macleod paid a heavy price. His policy irreparably offended the white settler lobby in Kenya and Rhodesia and, therefore, the right wing of the Tory Party in Parliament. And this, as much perhaps as any other single factor, was later to cost him the Conservative leadership. To lead a great political party, one must be acceptable to all sections of it. During and after the Colonial Secretaryship Iain Macleod was anathema to many of his Parliamentary colleagues.

In April 1970 a television interviewer observed that Macleod had probably lost the future leadership of the party because of his African policies. The interviewer then asked him: 'If you could choose, in 1970, between doing what you did in Africa or becoming Prime Minister, which would you choose?'

Macleod replied: 'I would do what I did in Africa. I could not have done anything else and stayed in politics. You must just take the consequences of the actions you believe to be right.'

That is a good political philosophy. Macleod was not a trimmer. He was one of the most ambitious men in public life, but he was also one of the bravest and one of the most honest. It is the measure of his courage and integrity that he put what he believed to be right before what he knew would be to his personal advantage.

1 *Sunday Telegraph*, July 26, 1970.

CHAPTER II

Chancellor of the
Duchy of Lancaster (1)
Leader of the House of Commons
1961-1963

ON October 9, 1961, the Prime Minister announced his second Cabinet reshuffle since the 1959 election. Iain Macleod was appointed Chancellor of the Duchy of Lancaster, Leader of the House of Commons and Chairman of the Conservative Party organisation.

He had been offered and had accepted these positions on October 2nd, and went round to Hugh Fraser's house in Campden Hill Square that evening to tell him the news. Antonia Fraser returned from a television debate to find them drinking champagne in the drawing room. She recorded in her diary:

'Hugh: Iain has something to tell you.

Iain: Yes . . . I'm to be Leader of the House. And Chairman of the Party. And Chancellor of the Duchy. I've got the lot.'

Tears of emotion sprang into my eyes and the first thing that sprang into my head (which I said) was: 'Oh, I'd give a thousand pounds, I'd give my Marks and Spencer shares, to see Lord Salisbury's face when he hears the news.'

This seemed to please Iain.'

The next evening Iain and Eve arrived unexpectedly at my own house in Lord North Street to tell my wife and me of his new appointments. Another bottle of champagne was opened and later we went out to dinner together at Quaglino's. I suggested tentatively that the two jobs might be difficult to combine, but Iain, who had asked the Prime Minister for them both, brushed the idea aside. He was in a state of euphoria and asked the band to play all his favourite tunes. I shall always remember him singing 'Don't fence me in' in his croaky voice, with a beaker of brandy in one hand and a large cigar in the other. I had never seen him happier or more relaxed.

A few days later Malcolm Muggeridge interviewed him for a Granada television programme:

Muggeridge: Do you want to be Prime Minister?

Macleod: I suppose the honest answer to that would be 'Yes'.

Muggeridge: Do you think you will be?

Macleod: No.

He added that, so far, every change had been to 'precisely the job that I hoped in my heart I would be given'. The answer to the second question was probably rather less than honest. At that moment the sky seemed the limit. But Lord Altrincham showed prescience when he wrote in *The Guardian* on October 19th: 'Macleod has been handed what may prove to be a poisoned chalice.'

When the Government changes were announced, the newspapers were almost unanimous in their comments on Macleod's prospects. The *Daily Mirror* described him as 'favourite to succeed Macmillan' and the *Daily Express*, which was not usually enthusiastic about him, as 'the potential new heir'. Walter Terry wrote of him in the *Daily Mail* as 'the Tories' man of the future'. The *Daily Herald* carried a cartoon of him with the caption 'Supermac Mk II'.

The more serious weekly papers took the same view. Anthony Howard's 'Spotlight on Politics' article in the *New Statesman* was headed 'Mr Macleod's coronation' and the *Economist*, more guardedly, forecast a bright political future with a reference to 'the best next Prime Minister we've got. . . . This is still a precarious prophesy to make but, at the very least, Mr Macleod has been given his chance.'

James Margach wrote in the *Sunday Times* of October 15th that Macleod 'must be seen as a commanding figure, controlling the levers of power both at Westminster and in the country. For a man of his intellectual capacity and genius for political organisation, the impact he could make over the next year must be profound. And as the leader of the new forces that make up modern Toryism, especially among the younger generation, he will have a persuasive appeal to the uncommitted and middle-class voters.'

The Times leader of October 10th considered that 'Mr Iain Macleod emerges as one of the strongest men in the Government' and its political correspondent wrote: 'One important effect of Mr Macmillan's recon- struction of his Ministry is to leave Mr Butler with one hat instead of three and to give Mr Macleod three hats instead of one[1]. . . . It is not only a mark of Mr Macmillan's confidence in him and a significant recognition of his standing in the Party's highest counsels; it must also give Mr Macleod, a self-styled Tory radical, an opportunity to impress his personal stamp on party policy at a crucial time.'

A public opinion poll published on October 11th was less enthusiastic: In answer to the question 'Who should be the next Prime Minister?', 36% of those polled said Rab Butler, 19% Selwyn Lloyd, 18% Peter Thorneycroft, 11% each Iain Macleod and Duncan Sandys and 3% Edward Heath. Even so, Macleod's rating was higher in 1961 than it proved to be two years later when a *Daily Express* poll on October 16, 1963 gave him only 1% of the public opinion vote.

There is no doubt that the Prime Minister intended the new appoint- ments as promotion. He liked Macleod as a man, admired him as a poli- tician and wanted to show his confidence in him and in his policies. But Macmillan thought two years at the Colonial Office were long enough. He had become irritated and a little worried over Macleod's handling of the problems of Central Africa and he thought that Maudling would carry through the same policies in a more amiable way and without becoming so emotionally involved. Especially in the last six months of the Colonial Secretaryship, the Prime Minister had found Macleod too abrupt and abrasive and too intolerant of those whose views differed from his own.

By this time Macmillan's attention was focused mainly on Europe. Our application to join the European Economic Community had been made on July 31, 1961, and the Prime Minister knew that Party cohesion would be important for this major policy. He was anxious to lower the tempera- ture on other divisive issues like Central Africa, and he considered that the appointment of Reggie Maudling would achieve this. He was right in this assessment. In Lord Boyle's words, Maudling 'got the ball out of the hole' in Northern Rhodesia and had a short but successful period as Colonial Secretary from October 1961 until July 1962, when Duncan Sandys – by dint of determination, strength of character and sheer hard work – contrived to combine the office with that of Commonwealth Secretary at a very hectic period of decolonisation.

The Prime Minister realised that, by promoting Macleod to the Chair-

1 R. A. Butler had been Home Secretary, Leader of the House of Commons and Chairman of the Party. Macleod now took over the last two positions from him.

manship of the Party, there was a risk that 'a lot of colonels will resign' from it[2], and he did not mind this; but he was bored with the bickering between Macleod and Sandys in Cabinet, and with Iain's tendency to become worried over what seemed to Macmillan relatively minor points in the Northern Rhodesia Constitution. Nevertheless, he much admired Macleod's courage and his imagination: 'He had ideas and knew how to express them, and he didn't make too many jokes. Iain was the last of the orators in the Tory Party.'

Macleod had been anxious that a change of Ministers might mean a change of policy; but Macmillan assured him that this would not be so and Iain was relieved and pleased when he was told that Maudling was to succeed him.

Lord Woolton wrote to him:

> This peculiar and undefined office of Chairman is one that can be made of tremendous importance . . . because he has an influence with the constituency members that is really second to none. Happily you are blessed with the qualities that will appeal to them – the power of speech and the even greater power of sincerity and political integrity. I watch with nostalgic envy and admiration and wanted to write and wish you well.

Iain valued this encouragement from the most successful Chairman the Party had ever had and he kept Lord Woolton's letter.

On October 11th my wife and I travelled to Brighton with the Macleods for the party conference. Iain was to make his last speech as Colonial Secretary that afternoon. He spoke movingly of the principles on which his colonial policy had been based. He believed, he said, in the rights and duties of men, which meant of all men; he believed in the British Imperial mission; and he quoted Robert Burns:

> 'That man to man the world o'er
> Shall brothers be for a' that'

– men of all races, colours and creeds – 'I believe quite simply,' he said, 'in the brotherhood of man.'

When he declared that at the end of the last war 'something like 630 million people lived in the dependent countries of the Crown . . .', a woman Empire Loyalist shouted from the gallery: 'and you betrayed them all'; but her charge was out of tune with the mood of the conference and the delegates gave their new chairman a great ovation both at the beginning and at the end of his speech.

2 Harold Macmillan to Iain Macleod, as recorded in Lady Antonia Fraser's diary.

Lady Antonia Fraser noted in her diary:

His physical appearance is so statesmanlike, with that enormous domed forehead. Another asset is his charming smile. A man, particularly a public man, can be as ugly as you please, provided his features light up from time to time with a really sweet and sincere smile. After lunch we listened to the debate on immigration which depressed me personally, although perhaps unreasonably. It seemed so odd to be discussing a resolution to keep West Indians out an hour after Iain's moving speech for the brotherhood of man.

I agreed with Antonia and said so in the conference debate and subsequently in the House of Commons.

Two days later Macleod made his second conference speech and his first as Chairman of the Party. He said that his task was not just the creation of a theme for the next election, but a pattern for the 1960s. He promised that the policies would be 'decisive and relevant'.

David Wood, the political correspondent of *The Times*, commented that this promise should be interpreted in the light of the increasing number of younger conference delegates 'contemporary in attitude, whose stake is not in the past or in privilege, but in the future and in opportunity'. It was from these that Macleod drew his strength. He had the gifts to use the Chairmanship to bring nearer his vision of One Nation, 'but he ought not to ignore or underestimate some of the powerful, instinctive tides that surge within the party'. A week later David Wood added the wise warning that over the next few years Macleod's main worry would be the electorate's feeling that it was time for a change after ten years in power and when the party's stock of ideas had run down.

When Macleod took over two of Butler's former posts, Rab had been generous and uncomplaining in the face of newspaper headlines such as 'Macleod up, Butler down', and he made a fine speech at the conference. Mollie Butler recalls that there were tears in Iain's eyes when he congratulated Rab with the words 'Rab up again' after this speech. But an extraordinary squabble arose between the two men when Parliament re-assembled a few days later. The room traditionally allocated to the Leader of the House is conveniently close to the chamber, and not unnaturally Macleod expected to move into this, but Butler refused to vacate it and, after an embarrassing interval of several days, another room had to be found for the new Leader.

*

The Government's position when Iain Macleod took over his new responsibilities was not encouraging. After a decade of increasing prosperity doubts were again developing about the economy. The balance of payments was becoming a problem and with imports rising faster than exports sterling looked vulnerable. Real growth was slow and wage increases were outpacing productivity. Selwyn Lloyd's corrective measures in July had included the unpopular pay pause and the use of the regulator, which increased purchase tax by 10%. Bank rate, at 7%, was two points up.

In the House of Commons the Government had encountered rough water and the Opposition was becoming more united. In the country Labour was moving ahead of the Conservatives in the public opinion polls. Macleod had become Leader of the House and Chairman of the Party at an inauspicious time.

By December 1961 industrial production was back to the 1960 level and wage restraint for the nurses, teachers, railwaymen and postmen was being enforced in the public sector. The momentum of rising prosperity had checked at the very time when a more affluent society was becoming increasingly conscious of material benefits and more expectant of improved living standards.

The long series of by-election reverses, beginning in November 1961, reflected these adverse factors. They were coincidental with Macleod's appointment as Chairman of the Party and not in any way his fault, but his popularity was bound to fall with that of the Government and he would inevitably carry much of the blame.

During a visit to the United States in June 1963, Macleod remarked – in answer to questions at a meeting of the Washington Press Club – that the post of Chancellor of the Duchy of Lancaster had been created in 1499, and that his predecessors had included Churchill and Attlee. He added that the office had also been held by 'Sir Thomas More, who was a saint, and by Sir Oswald Mosley, who was not.' The work consisted of appointing JPs on the recommendation of advisory committees, and of occasional meetings with the Council of the Duchy. 'The duties attached to this office take me half an hour in a tough week. I do not get a penny piece for either of my full-time jobs. I receive the whole of my salary for doing this work as Chancellor of the Duchy.'

The transition from a major Ministry was a difficult one. Macleod had been accustomed to a large private office and all the professional advice he needed. But as his new post was virtually a sinecure, it carried the correspondingly small staff of a private secretary, an assistant private secretary and a shorthand typist. At the Conservative Central Office his personal staff was even smaller. It consisted of his loyal and efficient personal assistant, Felicity Yonge, and one shorthand typist. The help he received was of course supplemented for his parliamentary work by the officials of the House of Commons, but he always felt rather under-serviced for the immense amount of paperwork which the Leadership of the House involved.

It was essential to keep closely in touch with backbench opinion in Parliament, and Macleod's first step was to invite Charles Longbottom to work with Reggie Bennett as an additional Parliamentary Private Secretary. It was a good appointment, and the new Leader was kept fully informed of the views of his parliamentary colleagues and of the political commentators in Fleet Street.

The Government's relationship with the lobby was important, and Macleod arranged to hold regular weekly meetings with a small 'inner circle' of senior lobby correspondents, which included David Wood of *The Times*, Harry Boyne of the *Daily Telegraph* and Walter Terry of the *Daily Mail*. These sessions took place informally on Wednesday evenings at about six o'clock over a glass of whisky. The two-way traffic of thought and information was of mutual value. Macleod supplied the political correspondents with useful background material on the normal lobby terms, while they kept him in touch with Fleet Street and public reaction to Government policies.

The work of the Leader of the House of Commons, although of great importance in the management of parliamentary business, is a day to day job which has no continuing theme and from which few lasting initiatives are likely to develop. It is rightly regarded by Members of Parliament as a key position in the Palace of Westminster, but it is necessarily introspective and makes little impact on the public.

The House of Commons reassembled on October 30th with the usual debate on the Queen's Speech, outlining the Government's legislative programme for the new session. Macleod made his first speech as Leader of the House when he wound up the debate on November 7th. Replying to Harold Wilson, he commented: 'the speech which the Rt Hon Gentleman the Member for Huyton has just delivered was, as always, witty, cogent and polished (pause) and polished (pause) and polished (laughter). He paid me the great compliment of saying that to this situation and to this debate I had brought a fresh mind. I wish that he would bring a fresh speech.' Harold Wilson, a most agreeable and courteous man in his personal relationships, who did not know Iain at all well, told me later that he considered this one of the wittiest comments of its kind made against him on the floor of the House. At about this time Wilson, who had just given a television performance, had this private exchange, which I paraphrase, with the interviewer:

> Interviewer: 'Mr Wilson, as a possible future Leader of the Opposition, is there anyone whom you would fear as a Conservative Prime Minister in succession to Harold Macmillan?'
> Wilson: 'Only one man and they'll never have the sense to choose him – Macleod.'

In more serious vein Macleod went on to compare the differing political philosophies of the two parties – 'Socialism is about equality, Conservatism is about opportunity' – and refuted the suggestion that Selwyn Lloyd had introduced a rich man's budget in raising the surtax starting level from £2,000 to £5,000 a year, by pointing out that £2,000 in 1961 was worth no more than £700 before the war.

On October 11th Rab Butler had announced that he was preparing proposals to limit the entry of immigrants into Britain, and the Commonwealth Immigrants Bill was published on November 1st. Speaking earlier in the debate on the Address, Hugh Gaitskell enquired caustically how Macleod could reconcile his conference speech about the brotherhood of man with his support for the Bill. Macleod replied to this challenge:

'I detest the necessity for it . . . I said almost a year ago that administrative methods alone were no good because this country, with its prosperity, was a magnet. . . . I believe that the choice is only between doing it now or in a year's time when the pressure will have become extremely acutute. . . . I have seen this, when I was Minister of Labour, grow from something about which no figures and no problem existed into a problem that flared into the headlines with race riots in this country of all countries, and I have seen it when I was Colonial Secretary. I came to the conclusion in the spring of this year that it was no longer possible to avoid such legislation.'

Two days later Macleod announced that the Second Reading debate on the Bill would occupy only one day on the floor and that, as he was advised that it was not a Constitutional Bill, the committee stage would be taken 'upstairs'. Sir Kenneth Pickthorn, MP for Carlton, questioned

Macleod's understanding of what a Constitutional Bill was, and Iain recalled that he had been a pupil of Pickthorn's at Cambridge a quarter of a century earlier. 'And you were pretty hopeless,' Pickthorn interjected.

Many Labour members, including Gaitskell, argued that the committee stage should be debated on the floor of the House and Macleod, after undertaking to re-check his advice, agreed to this procedure. The decision was praised in *The Times* leading article next day on the grounds that, whether the Bill was strictly a constitutional one or not, it certainly was in spirit for it struck 'at the very roots of British tradition and Commonwealth ties'.

The Bill was debated on Second Reading on November 16th and was vigorously opposed by Gaitskell, who described it as a 'miserable, shameful and shabby Bill'. He thought that Macleod and Butler, with their known liberal attitudes, had been a disappointment to the House. I spoke against the Bill and Robin Balniel (a Minister of State in the present Government) and I abstained, in the face of a three-line whip, when the vote was taken. After arguing the case as I saw it then, I concluded my speech with the words: 'I believe my Rt Hon friend was absolutely sincere in his Brighton speech when he talked of the brotherhood of man. I believe in it too, and it is because I believe in it that I cannot vote for this Bill tonight.' These were hard words from a friend and I regretted them in restrospect. But Iain was always generous to anyone he was fond of and when I met him at a party the following evening he congratulated me on the speech, with much of which he had agreed, and only remonstrated gently about my peroration which, he pointed out, had added strength to Gaitskell's criticism.

It was the first major issue on which we had disagreed and of course he was right, as I acknowledged in the House three years later. I had been thinking mainly of the Caribbean, which I knew well, and had not fully foreseen the flood of applications for entry which poured in from the Asian countries of the Commonwealth and which our small island could not have absorbed.

In December Macleod announced that he would invite the House to consider an allocation of time motion for the Commonwealth Immigrants Bill and the Army Reserve Bill. This decision led, predictably, to furious complaints from the Opposition. George Brown described Macleod as a contemptuous Leader of the House, and said that in sixteen years he had known no Leader treat Parliament so badly. The right-wing press were equally critical for opposite reasons. Crossbencher complained in the

Sunday Express that the Tories regarded his leadership as feeble, and two weeks later alleged that 'few reputations have plunged so swiftly as that of Macleod.' *The Times* did not mention him by name, but a leading article on December 21st considered that the first months of the session had gone badly for the Government, which had given the impression of a weakening of judgement and assurance. But writing in *Time and Tide* a week later, Jo Grimond commented: 'No Leader of the House could have made sense of what the Government has been doing in the last few weeks. It is quite unfair to blame him for all that has gone wrong.'

Parliament reassembled after the Christmas recess on January 23rd, and two days later Macleod moved the time-table motion. He did not justify its general use, but claimed that it was occasionally essential, as in this case. *The Times* Parliamentary correspondent wrote: 'It was a day notable mainly for Mr Macleod's deft handling of the presentation of the guillotine[3]. . . . He scored gently, but well, on one occasion and later deserved some appreciative laughter as he recalled his own reasons for rejecting a course which would have seemed 'too clever by half'. Mr Macleod was observed at one point to be laughing – a rare sight which may signify a new relaxation in the Leader of the House.'

Members were beginning to enjoy his dry, self-deprecating wit and his genuine attempts to respond to the wishes of the House. He was learning to get his way by politeness, and by April the *Daily Mirror* reported that his stature was increasing: 'This term he has moved nearer the top of the Parliamentary class.'

In March Macleod announced that the Transport Bill and the Housing (Scotland) Bill were to be subject to the guillotine, due to the slow progress they had been making; and in early July a time-table was also introduced for the Pipelines Bill. Five guillotined Bills was a large number in one session, and a *Times* leader headline described Macleod as the 'Robespierre of debate'. At this stage of the session it was necessary if the Pipelines Bill was not to be lost, but the Government had underestimated the time it would take and had brought it in too late and with too many contentious provisions.

Either by good management or over-application of the guillotine, or a combination of both, the Government's heavy legislative programme had in fact been carried through with unusual expedition, and Macleod was able to announce at the end of May that the Whitsun Recess would be for

---

3 A method of curtailing debate in order to get Government business through in a reasonable time. It is used by every Government and disliked by every Opposition.

nineteen days, as compared with eleven the year before, and that there would not be any need for the usual extra week in the autumn to complete the consideration of Bills left over from the summer. It was only the second time in ten years that no overspill had been left for October. The *Statist* described this as 'a remarkable achievement' and the *Yorkshire Post* reported that less of the time of the House had been devoted to Government legislation and more of it to general debates than in any session since the war. This was no doubt a conscious reaction by the new Leader to the perennial back-bench demand for fewer Government Bills and more parliamentary time for debates on important issues of interest to the public.

Macleod sympathised with the claims of private members, but in reply to Dame Irene Ward, he pointed out that about a third of the time of the House was already used on the direct initiative of back-benchers. He acknowledged that a number of useful Private Members' Bills stood little chance of reaching the statute book and suggested that these could be given quicker progress if both sides agreed in advance that they would be unopposed.

This procedure could clearly not apply to controversial measures, and he refused to provide special facilities for the discussion of Fenner Brockway's Racial Discrimination and Incitement Bill. This measure was widely supported in the Labour and Liberal parties and by a few Conservatives including myself. I went to see Macleod about it, but he took the tenable view that it was impossible to change human nature by legislation, and that any attempt to deal with prejudice by Act of Parliament would be counterproductive. The public reason he gave for refusing Parliamentary time was that it would be a dangerous practice for a Government to start selecting Private Member's Bills to which precedence should be given. The Labour Government of 1964/70 reversed this judgement and facilitated the progress of a number of measures of social reform which could not otherwise have become law.

By the time the House rose for the summer recess of 1962 it was possible for his parliamentary colleagues to make an assessment of Macleod's Leadership of the House of Commons during his first session in that capacity. Whatever the criticisms of him as Chairman of the Party, it was generally acknowledged that he was a tough and effective Leader. He was also subtle. His outstanding ability as a debater was an important asset, and he knew how to handle the House. He never minded staying up late at night, and he spent more time sitting in the Chamber and listening to other people's speeches than most Leaders before or since. Owing to his physical disability he was unable to turn his head, and this made more difficult the whispered consultations on the Front Bench about the conduct of business which were often necessary between the Leader of the House and the Chief Whip.

Outside the Chamber his relationship with the Whips' Office was not as close as it should have been, but the blame for this should not be attributed only to him. He sometimes felt that he did not receive the full support and confidence to which he was entitled.

In a warm letter of encouragement during a difficult period, Lord Woolton wondered if Macleod was putting too great a strain on his health in attempting to combine the leadership of both the House and the party organisation. No doubt he was overworked, but this never worried him. The hours were long, and night after night he sat late at Westminster, with little respite at weekends because he never spared himself in addressing party workers or public meetings up and down the country. But he worked best under pressure and had remarkable reserves of spirit and resilience, which enabled him to respond to the challenge of a difficult task.

Despite this – and although he never acknowledged it – I believe he came to realise, as time went on, that the two responsibilities he had undertaken were incompatible. As Chairman of the Party he had to be the most partisan of Ministers, as Leader of the House, the least. It has been said that 'the trouble with being Leader of the House is that you are the spokesman in Cabinet for no one but the Opposition'. Even Rab Butler had been unable to make a complete success of both positions at the same time, and it is probably a mistake to combine the chairmanship of the Party with any Cabinet office other than a sinecure.

There is little doubt that Macleod enjoyed his duties in Parliament more than his work at Smith Square, and he was certainly more successful as Leader of the House of Commons than as Chairman of the Party organisation.

In November 1961 Muller published Macleod's biography of Neville Chamberlain. He had begun work on the book in 1958 but had underestimated the scale of the undertaking and found it difficult to spare sufficient time for it during his exacting period as Colonial Secretary. He worked fast, but he was appalled when he visited an aged aunt of Chamberlain's to be handed seven large boxes of papers, and wondered a little naively whether it was necessary to read them all. He did most of the work at week-ends: 'Other men garden. I prefer to write.' But he could not spare more than three or four hours a week, which included time spent on research.

He turned for help to Peter Goldman, with whom he had worked in the Conservative Research Department ten years earlier, and the book was a joint effort. Macleod wrote the first half of it up to 1931 and Goldman the last half. This distribution enabled Iain to cover Chamberlain's work on social reform which was the ground he found most interesting. Goldman was responsible for the later years as Chancellor of the Exchequer and Prime Minister. Their judgement on Munich was not preconceived; it emerged as the work progressed. No doubt the press comment that Macleod was 'a man of Munich' was inevitable, but it probably did him little harm politically.

The preface to the book lists the Conservative Research Department and the National Service organisation among the interests which Macleod and Chamberlain shared in their different generations, but the genesis of the book was Iain's admiration for Chamberlain as Minister of Health and as a Tory who, like himself, had radical views on social policy. He had never met Chamberlain, and it was this concept rather than the man himself which appealed to him.

Macleod intended to portray Chamberlain more kindly than Feiling had done in an earlier biography[4], but in this he failed. Chamberlain was perhaps too unsympathetic a personality; efficient but not attractive; and Feiling's book, which omitted evidence of his harshness and severity was a narrower but a kinder picture. Feiling had shortened some of the documents and omitted sections from Chamberlain's diary. It was a pity that Macleod did not use his opportunity to quote from and amplify these records.

The bibliography of A. J. P. Taylor's volume in the Oxford History 1914/45 states that 'the recent life by Iain Macleod adds nothing' to Feiling's and this is no doubt true to the historian, but to the politician the information about Cabinet changes and appointments, much of which had not appeared before, is of considerable interest. Lord Woolton wrote to Macleod: 'Fielding (sic) could not do him justice – I think because he was an historian and couldn't assess the importance of Party and political forces on Chamberlain's judgements. You have done this and have done justice to a man who strove so hard for the right thing at a time when he was foredoomed to fail'. Macleod wrote with an instinctive understanding of the political calculations Chamberlain had to make and his analysis of the events after the 1923 general election is admirable.

4 *The life of Neville Chamberlain*, Macmillan, 1970 (new edition).

Some interesting minor points emerged in the course of the research work. For instance, Chamberlain was said to like poetry and music, but Macleod discovered that this simply meant that he liked Shakespeare and Beethoven.

The book was not a very good one and was never properly reviewed;[5] it did not sell well and did nothing to enhance Macleod's reputation as a writer or as a politician.

Iain told me, half-seriously, that it was written as a pot-boiler to raise money for his daughter Diana's 'season'. He shared the expense of a dance for her with my wife, whose younger daughter came out the same year. The dance was given in the summer of 1962 at the home in Sussex of Sir Geoffrey Kitchen, who kindly lent it to us for the occasion. But Iain's packing was careless and his dinner jacket had been left behind, so that he had to be driven back to London to retrieve it. This prevented his joining the 'receiving line' for the first half hour and put him in a thoroughly bad temper for the next.

Apart from his articles and poems, Macleod's only other literary efforts consisted of a play called *The False Men* and three chapters of an uncompleted book which was to be entitled *The Last Rung*.

The play was set in the Western Isles and much of the dialogue is in Scottish dialect. It is a rather whimsical 'Whodunit' and would no doubt have been unsuitable for a London audience, though it might have been performed on Scottish television.

The Last Rung, again in collaboration with Peter Goldman, was to consist of a number of essays on individual statesmen who had just failed to reach the premiership. The chapters on Austen Chamberlain, Curzon and Halifax had been drafted and make uninspiring reading. Macleod had not considered including himself, but he told me that the last chapter might be an appreciation of Rab Butler.

5 In *The Times* of 27 November, 1961, the book was reviewed in the form of a reappraisal of Chamberlain on the leader page.

CHAPTER 12

Chancellor of the Duchy of Lancaster (11) Chairman of the Conservative Party Organisation 1961-1963

THE management of the legislative programme and the Government's business in the House of Commons, liaison with the back benches, and the maintenance of the morale of the Parliamentary Party were important tactical responsibilities for the Leader of the House. At the Conservative Central Office Macleod was also answerable to the Prime Minister for the organisation and enthusiasm of the party in the country and for keeping him informed of movements of opinion and constituency reactions to government policies. But he went much further than this in his letters and memoranda to Macmillan. A stream of suggestions and advice, including draft passages for major speeches, was constantly coming forward from Smith Square. New ideas and policy initiatives were submitted and often adopted. Macleod thought of the Chairmanship as a power base. This was a quite different and a much wider, more strategic approach to his duties than that adopted by other holders of the office.

Throughout his time as Chairman, Macleod was handicapped by – and often blamed for – the growing unpopularity of the Government. An Administration which senses that it is losing public support watches by-elections with care and some anxiety. There were sixteen during Macleod's Chairmanship, the first three within a month of his appointment, and the trend throughout the whole two year period was unfavourable.

The Conservative poll fell consistently, often by 20% or more, but initially it was the Liberals, not the official Opposition, who were the beneficiaries. Bad Government results at Moss Side, Oswestry, East Fife, Bridgetown (Glasgow) and Lincoln followed each other in swift succession, with the Liberal often running second, and became serious at Blackpool North where the Conservative majority fell from nearly 16,000 to 973. At East Middlesbrough the Tory vote was down by 23.7%.

Even these reverses were eclipsed at Orpington on March 14, 1962. In this traditionally Conservative stronghold, the former Member[1] had had a 1959 majority of over 14,000, which was now transformed into a Liberal majority of 7,855. Eric Lubbock increased the Liberal vote by 32%, and by ability and sheer hard work, held the seat until 1970. The Labour candidate, whose vote was nearly halved, lost his deposit. It was a sensational result and Macleod immediately set in train a professional appraisal of the factors responsible for the landslide. He had realised that the campaign was not going well, but he was shattered by the extent of the Liberal revival and the enormous swing Lubbock had achieved. He was also deeply sorry for the Conservative candidate, Peter Goldman, who had to bear the blame for a much deeper malaise.

As Macleod commented later to the Prime Minister, it seemed to make no difference whether the candidate was young or old, a local man or a carpet-bagger, an intellectual or a lawyer or a businessman. In some seats like Orpington the decision of the electorate was shown in positive votes for the Liberal. In others like Blackpool it was due to massive Conservative abstentions. A national opinion poll on March 28, 1962, reflected the Orpington result, It gave the Liberals 33.7% of the national vote, Labour 33.5% and the Conservatives 32.8%.

The Government was paying the penalty for the economic situation. Against a background of mounting inflation, the balance of payments difficulties had forced the Chancellor to adopt a policy of restraint which, however necessary, was not a recipe for electoral success.

In the face of the by-election reverses, Macleod strove hard to rally the party in the country in a series of fighting speeches. On the day after Orpington he gave the Conservative Central Council what he called the centuries-old motto of the clan Macleod, 'Hold Fast':

'Fear not because you have lost a skirmish here or a battle there. . . . Do not trim your sails at all in the face of the gales that may blow upon you.'

Ten days later in Manchester he was describing the Liberals as 'faceless men – the pedlars of politics with a solution for every problem.' And on

1 Donald Sumner, QC, MP for Orpington 1955/61. A County Court judge since 1961.

April 5th he spoke to one of the Conservative area councils on the need for a new vision:

> We are not as a nation confident of our future. We have not as a nation been ready to face the reappraisal that must follow the closing of the chapter of imperial power. . . . One road for us is clearly marked 'No Thoroughfare' – the road back. That way lies defeat. The modern Tory Party, largely fashioned after the war by Butler and Woolton . . . has no future as a party of reaction.

He was especially anxious to retain the faith of the young, and a speech to the Young Conservative National Conference in February 1962 was notable for its idealism. His theme was opportunity and service – opportunity to prosper and opportunity to serve. He liked to see the signs of prosperity – the cars outside small houses, the television aerials on the roof tops, the labour-saving devices in the kitchens. But service should march with citizenship, and duties with rights: 'It is your duty to put back into the national pool more than you take out. You must sow as well as reap because you are not only the heirs of the past but the trustees of the future. . . . You are lucky to have been born into a generation which can reach towards the stars.' He stressed the bleak contrast between Britain and the underdeveloped countries of the world and underlined the contribution of Voluntary Service Overseas. It was a task as exciting, as inspiring and as noble as the creation of the Empire itself. He urged young men and women to give a part of their working lives to this ideal, if not overseas, then at home in the voluntary services – in church or chapel, in youth organisations or in the League of Hospital Friends, in local government or in the territorial regiments; in help to old people, not just spasmodically at Christmas time but continuously throughout the year. He had in mind the sort of service which 'the state is sometimes too large or too blind or too mean to do. . . . So I call you to service, not because you are Tories but because you are citizens – service which will give you pride and satisfaction and honour. . . . The object of service and its sufficient reward is service itself. You serve because you love your fellowmen and no other test suffices.'

In the same month he spoke to the Oxford University Conservative Association and two days later the *Sunday Telegraph* commented:

> Why did Mr Macleod succeed in moving his Oxford undergraduate audience . . . only a week after the Prime Minister had so singularly

failed to do so? Partly because, more than any other British politician, he has evolved a style of political speaking strikingly akin to that of President Kennedy, which somehow matches the mood and manner of young people today – a certain bare, tense, unrhetorical intensity . . . practical without being unprincipled, gripping without being inspirational.

Iain Macleod always thought it worthwhile encouraging the young. Robert Godber was secretary of the Manchester University Conservative Association when an entire term's list of speakers, including a Minister, was cancelled.[2] He was full of righteous indignation and 'did everything calculated to annoy the establishment; the press were told and the area office imperiously ignored; a letter of adolescent insolence was dispatched to Mr Macleod. . . . Instead of a dusty answer I received a letter as courteous as mine had been rude; as understanding as mine had been intolerant. Within days he came to Manchester and found room for a big meeting in the university Union. Three days later I received a letter from him thanking *me* for assembling a large audience: "It was worth while for me," he wrote, "I hope it was for you. . . ." Last June I was totally convinced that the life of politics was for me; now I am less sure; one of the great lights has gone out.'[3]

Iain Macleod was always prepared to champion any cause he believed in. While he was Party Chairman, the elimination of the small county of Rutland was under consideration. Keith Joseph was the Minister responsible, and he put forward his department's view that Rutland should go. A Cabinet committee endorsed the proposal, but when the matter went to Cabinet, Macleod defended Rutland and pressed for its retention. Kenneth Lewis records: 'He won. Rutland stayed. It was Keith Joseph who told me this story. Iain would always stand up for the little fellow when odds were against him.'[4]

Macleod was well aware that the Government's economic policy was the main cause of its unpopularity. The National Economic Development Council, itself a concession to the problems of the economy, had just been established and in a speech in London on February 21, 1962, he underlined its importance as the first formal experiment in joint consultation between representatives of the Government, private employers, the

2 By the Conservative Central Office, due mainly to whips in the House of Commons.
3 Robert Godber to the author, April 19, 1971.
4 Kenneth Lewis, MP for Rutland and Stamford since 1959, to the author, August 12, 1970.

nationalised industries and the trade unions. He recognised that the pay pause and the need for restraint in incomes had caught all the limelight, and stressed that 'restraint is not a policy in itself unless it is the springboard for growth'.

The NEDC was not 'just another committee'. It was a compact team, backed by a first-class staff, working together to overcome the obstacles that stood in the way of economic expansion. It held its first meeting on March 7th.

During the spring of 1962 Selwyn Lloyd, Iain Macleod and Michael Fraser were summoned to Chequers for a meeting with the Prime Minister. After dinner, in a pause in the conversation, Selwyn said suddenly 'Floreat Fettesia'. When the Prime Minister looked a little puzzled, Selwyn pointed out that he was at that moment in the undiluted company of three Old Fettesians.

The pay pause came to an end officially in April, but its replacement by Selwyn Lloyd's 'guiding light' of $2\frac{1}{2}$% to 3% a year for wage increases did not give people much encouragement; and in the April by-elections the Socialists began to improve their position at the expense of both the other parties. Pontefract, Stockton-on-Tees – despite the personal intervention of the Prime Minister – and North Derby all followed this pattern.

Meanwhile Macleod had received the special Orpington survey, and on April 27th he analysed the by-election results in a ten-page paper to the Prime Minister. He pointed out that both Orpington and North Derby revealed the emergence of people who were prepared to vote Liberal, although they had little affinity with the Liberal Party. But it was more than a protest vote. He underlined his view that economic policy was the key. People felt that the Government's emphasis was upon restraint when, rightly or wrongly, they were in a mood for expansion; and he stressed that for some people, especially the nurses, the pay pause was plainly unfair. He thought this issue had done great harm and that it was difficult, in the face of it, to project the image that 'Conservatives care'.

'The electorate are bored with us as a Government,' he wrote, 'this springs mainly from the fact that we have been in office so long, but also because so many issues like the Common Market cannot yet be shown to be the success that we believe they will be in fact. It follows that an air of indecision is attributed unfairly to what we do.' He warned that the press were turning against the Conservatives, largely on the idea of 'time for a change'. 'The most dangerous of all slogans against a party that has been in power for a decade or more'.

He thought it was becoming fashionable to be Liberal and 'in some strange way it is almost non-political. This has a particular appeal to those who are disenchanted with the Tories but can never bring themselves to vote Socialist. It is from these people that our defections have come. Orpington has been described as a revolt of the unorganised against the organised and I believe there is truth in this. We must aim our policies consciously at these people.'

He predicted 'very heavy losses indeed' in the local elections the following month and hoped to avoid further by-elections with a period of convalescence 'while we await the great events that will follow the conclusion of the discussions on the Common Market'.

He advised that the Government should 'get off the hook as far as nurses and perhaps university teachers are concerned'; that we should begin to reflate; and that we should proclaim our belief that entry into the Common Market 'is the right future for this country'.

In this document Macleod not only analysed the causes of past reverses. He looked ahead to the strategy the Government should follow for a revival of its fortunes. This advice was in tune with the Prime Minister's own thinking, and on the eve of his departure for the United States, Macmillan requested Rab Butler to arrange for a Cabinet on May 3rd, the day of his return, to be continued on the 4th, in order to discuss 'any reflation that may be required'. He asked Butler to 'have a talk with the Chancellor of the Exchequer and the Chairman of the Party, so that we can make these discussions as fruitful as possible'.

Following these meetings of the Cabinet, the Prime Minister drafted a paper, setting out ways in which the Government's economic policies could be more effectively presented to the country. He urged Ministers to forget their preoccupations with particular issues and concentrate on claiming success for the handling of the economy: 'It will be of no avail to have kept our eyes on the distant horizon if we lose the ground beneath our feet.' But no specific proposals for reflation emerged. The 'sweets and ice-cream' budget – dubbed by Jo Grimond 'a mouse of a budget' – had been deliberately neutral, and Treasury advice was very cautious. It was hoped that an investment boom would follow our entry into the European Economic Community and in the meantime premature reflationary measures were considered dangerous.

The local elections in May resulted, as Macleod had forecast, in heavy

Conservative losses, and on June 6th Labour recorded their first by-election gain in the Parliament by winning Middlesbrough. A sense of frustration was becoming evident on the Tory back-benches, and there was growing criticism in the press and in the constituencies of the Chairman of the Party. Macleod was the whipping boy for the general discontent and the *Daily Express* demanded his replacement by Lord Hailsham. But he bore these attacks with stoic reserve and usually showed a good-humoured restraint even to his sternest critics. When John Junor, the editor of the *Sunday Express*, returned from a holiday with his leg in plaster, Macleod greeted him cheerfully: 'Ah, John,' he commented, 'I see you've stubbed your toe against me once too often.'

Lord Woolton wrote sympathetically in May, deploring the weak faith of some members of the party:

'In days of success these people cheer you, sharing in a manner quite unjustified in the praise you earn. When things don't go well they are stricken with the palsy. I have left them in no doubt about my confidence in you.'

Through the spring and early summer of 1962 the Government was in a hiatus with, as Macleod had observed, 'an absence of positive policies'. Against a background of change in Britain's world role, which he had himself done much to accelerate, the public mood was introspective and satirical. *Beyond the Fringe* played to full houses, *Private Eye* began its stormy and often libellous career, the television series *That Was the Week That Was* commanded huge audiences every Saturday night. An economist, Michael Shanks, sold 60,000 copies of his book *The Stagnant Society*, which was typical of the prevalent self-critical vein. At the same time, and even more dangerous for the Government, the affluent society was developing its own logic – a general expectancy of a continually rising standard of living.

Many Conservative Members of Parliament were now demanding economic expansion as the only way of restoring the popularity of the Government. Selwyn Lloyd was in a dilemma. He was trying to lay the foundations for sustained growth, but the deterioration in the balance of payments prejudiced his policies and delayed the reflation which he knew to be necessary. His period as Chancellor was therefore a difficult one and he has been given insufficient credit for the many reforms he introduced. He initiated the long-term planning of Government expenditure; developed a new approach to the nationalised industries, which much improved their morale and internal organisation; introduced the regulators which made it possible to vary indirect taxation between budgets; and made the concept of an incomes policy more acceptable in Government circles. His National Economic Development Council was a major contribution in focusing attention on the problems of economic growth.

In spite of these achievements, Macmillan was becoming increasingly impatient with Lloyd's reluctance to reflate. He considered the Chancellor's approach politically unacceptable and far too cautious. The Prime Minister was also concerned about the form the next phase of the incomes policy should take and, after disagreements in Cabinet, he bypassed the Chancellor and instructed senior civil servants to work out a system by which priorities could be established for the pay claims of different categories of workers. The outcome of this initiative was the National Incomes Commission, established in July 1962.

Conservative morale continued to decline and the Prime Minister became aware of the formation of anti-Macmillan factions within the Parliamentary Party. He began to think in terms of a Government reshuffle to restore confidence in his Administration.

On July 10th Butler and Macleod went to see Macmillan. They argued strongly for reflation and although they made no specific attack on Selwyn Lloyd, it was clear that he was the target and that their demand for a more positive direction of the economy could only be met if the Treasury was placed in different hands. Macmillan had already reached the same conclusion.

Macleod reported constituency criticism that the Government appeared to be tired and he appealed for a 'new look'. The following day he sent a note to the Prime Minister, warning him that the result of the North-East Leicester by-election would be bad, with a drop in the Conservative vote which would put them in third place.[5] 'I recognise,' he went on, 'that we are in a period in which it is extremely difficult to produce positive policies, but I feel I should urge upon you that if you are contemplating making changes in the Government, these should be made before we rise for the recess.'

Macleod had helped to sow the seed, but he was unprepared for the whirlwind. On Thursday, July 12th, Walter Terry forecast a major Government reshuffle. Macmillan, by now convinced of the need for a change, decided to act at once – perhaps in order to avoid further specula-

5 The Conservative vote fell from nearly 18,000 in 1959 to 6,500 and the Liberals, who had not contested the seat since 1950, came second. Macleod had said publicly only a week before that it was a two-horse race between Conservative and Labour.

tion in the Sunday newspapers. That evening Selwyn Lloyd was summoned to Admiralty House[6] and relieved of his appointment. At seven p.m. on Friday, July 13th, the Cabinet changes were announced. No less than seven senior Ministers[7] – a third of the Cabinet – had been requested to resign at a few hours' notice. Only Butler, Macleod and the Chief Whip, Martin Redmayne, seem to have known in advance about the 'July massacre' and even they were probably unaware of its extent. It was a display of ruthlessness, or panic, which disturbed rather than reassured the Parliamentary party. Macleod thought it too drastic, and this was the general view in the country. It was followed early the next week by an almost equally draconian purge of junior Ministers, as a side result of which I became a member of the Government.

It was freely rumoured that Macmillan had dismissed his colleagues to save himself, and Jeremy Thorpe commented wittily, if unkindly: 'Greater love hath no man than this – that he lay down his friends for his life.' In fact, Kilmuir, Maclay, Watkinson and Mills had all intimated earlier to the Prime Minister that they were willing to go at the next convenient opportunity. Nevertheless, the whole episode did little to enhance Macmillan's reputation; and it failed to produce either a settling effect upon the Parliamentary party or a look of renewed vitality for the public.

Macmillan had now presented power to the younger political generation – Macleod, Maudling, Powell, Heath, Joseph and Boyle – but many people felt that Lloyd and Kilmuir had been harshly treated. Both had given long, loyal and distinguished service to the party and the country; and Selwyn Lloyd's pay pause policy, although inevitably unpopular, had had some success. He had focused attention on slow economic growth and had introduced new methods for dealing with it.

Macleod wrote to the Prime Minister on July 18th to advise on the main lines of the latter's speech in the forthcoming debate, and again on July 20th to suggest a draft of the passage in it paying tribute to Selwyn Lloyd. Many of his suggestions and some of his phrases were adopted by Macmillan in his speech in the House of Commons on July 26th.

It was perhaps surprising that Macleod should have chosen this politi-

6 10 Downing Street was under repair and the Prime Minister was living at Admiralty House.

7 In addition to Selwyn Lloyd and the Lord Chancellor, Lord Kilmuir, the following Ministers left the Government: Harold Watkinson (Minister of Defence), Jack Maclay (Secretary of State for Scotland), Charles Hill (Minister of Housing), Sir David Eccles (Minister of Education), and Lord Mills (Minister without Portfolio).

cally sensitive moment to write to all constituency chairmen urging them to replace association and ward officers if they had held their positions for too long. He suggested three years as in most cases a suitable period in any one office. The *Sunday Express*, never friendly to Macleod, described this circular letter as 'an extraordinary piece of ineptitude' and Roy Wise, then MP for Rugby, complained at a meeting of the 1922 Committee that it was tactless and likely to cause offence. But other Members supported Macleod and argued that young people would lose their interest and enthusiasm if they saw the same faces in influential local positions year after year. In fact, the letter was a reminder, not an innovation, because the model rules for constituency associations, dating from 1945, had laid down that no one should hold the same office for more than three consecutive years. This rule has been much more generally observed in most associations since Macleod's letter than it was before.

Speaking at the Annual General Meeting of his own association at Enfield in April 1962, Macleod said that although the by-elections had been making the headlines, they were only 'the small change of politics. . . . From now on more important matters' were going to occupy the centre of the stage, of which by far the most important was the issue of Britain's entry into the Common Market: 'The Socialists think they can afford the luxury of indecision,' he declared. 'I think they will be proved wrong. We welcome the opportunity to join with the countries of Western Europe. We believe that Britain ought to play her full part in the great movement towards European unity. We are convinced that it is right for ourselves and for the Commonwealth, which needs a strong, prosperous Britain with money to invest overseas. It will not prove an easy road to prosperity. It will be hard but rewarding. Out of date practices will have to go. But as a nation we should thrill to the challenge. I believe we have nothing to fear and much to gain. Our people are inventive and skilful; our agriculture is efficient and competitive. Our industry will respond to the challenge of competition and to high rewards for success.'

Entry into Europe was to be the great psychological fillip for the British people. Britain's role of broker between the super powers was no longer an effective one. The Tory leadership, especially perhaps Macmillan and Macleod, sensed and expressed the need to look towards new areas of vitality, political and economic; to a wider sweep of ideas and events; and to the exciting prospects which seemed to be opening in Europe.

In July a guidance document was prepared for Ministers, setting out the reasons for our application, the method of negotiation and the answers to the criticisms which opponents of entry were already voicing. This was revised and reissued early in September.

On September 18th Macleod circulated to members of the Cabinet, though not as a Cabinet paper, a memorandum on public opinion. He reported that the country was evenly divided and that opinion on Europe was volatile, with swings of up to 10% occurring within a month or two. There was a hard nucleus of enthusiastic supporters and another of equally convinced opponents, with a large section of floating opinion between the two, the balance of which seemed slightly inclined against entry, though this could easily be reversed. The issue cut right across party lines. There was a Conservative majority in favour of entry and a Labour majority against, with the pro-European Socialists balancing the anti-European Conservatives. Many people were bewildered by the complexities of the arguments, but when the local MP had made up his mind 'he was usually followed by his supporters'. There were complaints about lack of information and indications that the country would welcome a clear lead. Young people, the professional classes, and white-collar workers were in favour of joining; many of the middle-aged and elderly and the majority of manual workers were against. Opponents of entry usually gave emotional or political reasons for their view. Many were anxious 'not to let the Commonwealth down', by which they clearly meant the 'white Commonwealth'. The main reason for opposition appeared to be a sort of xenophobia about our own sovereignty and our links with the old Commonwealth. Some people imagined we were likely to be outvoted in Europe or to 'surrender our independence to Frogs and Wogs'. Macleod concluded that the country's head was convinced but its heart was not. He thought there was a real need for an idealistic approach; that the support of the young people and the opinion formers was the key and that the issue should be presented 'with trumpets' as the next great adventure in our country's history.

In a covering note to his colleagues, the Chairman of the Party reported a loss of ground while Ministers hesitated, and he argued strongly for an unequivocal lead by the Government and by individual Members of Parliament.[8] Throughout September and October he urged Ministers to

8 The state of public opinion as recorded in this minute was remarkably similar in the summer of 1962 to the situation in the summer of 1971. In 1962, as nine years later, the Government Chief Whip expected a hard core of about thirty Conservative MPs who would vote against entry on principle, whatever the terms.

make major pro-Market speeches. In response to one of these requests, Freddie Erroll (then President of the Board of Trade) wrote him a letter on October 3rd, setting out the economic arguments for joining and the difficulties British industry would face if we stayed out. It was accompanied by supporting Board of Trade papers which were virtually speakers' notes for Ministers.

By September the Prime Minister had cleared the hurdle of the Commonwealth Prime Ministers' conference and was able to issue a pamphlet entitled *Britain, the Commonwealth and Europe*, which ranks with the 'wind of change' speech as a major policy pronouncement. It was based on his speech to his fellow Prime Ministers and set out the arguments for British entry with such cogency that Macleod urged its publication as a booklet. It received a wide circulation within the party and the main points made in it are just as relevant and conclusive today as they were ten years ago. It laid special stress on the political arguments for joining the EEC. The Common Market was at last being put forward by Ministers as a major policy of over-riding importance. The Government had a positive goal in sight which they believed to be in the best interests of the nation.

The Conservative conference in 1962 was held at Llandudno. In his speech as Chairman of the Party Organisation Macleod took as his theme what he believed the people were seeking – a society that was more tolerant, more efficient and more just: If the Tory Party represented the votes of fourteen million people, it was because it was a coalition 'accepting under one great sky of policy a score of divergent views. It would be disastrous for the Party to leave behind it those who hold what are called right-wing or traditionalist views.' There was no inconsistency in standing at the same time for a radical policy of social reform and for a robust approach to foreign affairs. He drew attention to the disparity between the limited bargaining power of public employees like teachers and nurses and the much stronger negotiating position of those in private industry who were supported by the large unions. His idea of a just society was one in which people can make their own way in the world because no reasonable opportunity is denied to them: 'You cannot ask men to stand on their own feet if you give them no ground to stand on. . . . We do not know where men may find equality. . . . We do know that men can be taught to seek and to love justice. We are not very good at defining freedom, but we do know how to preserve a society in which freedom is a habit. . . . We do not preach tolerance as much as the Socialists may do, but we practice it a good deal more.'

Iain with his son-in-law, David Heimann, Diana, and Eve

At Chequers, 1961. A picture taken by Lady Antonia Fraser

Editor of the *Spectator*, 1964. With John Freeman, then editor of the *New Statesman*, and his successor, Paul Johnson

In discussing the efficiency of the party, Macleod commended the Maxwell Fyfe Report of 1948 which 'had a profound effect in helping to shape the more modern appeal' of the party, and he remarked that it was only because of its financial recommendations 'that very many people now Members of Parliament were able to stand for election'. He thought there should be much closer liaison between MPs, the National Union and the Central Office, and announced that a new investigation into this aspect of party organisation would be carried out by Selwyn Lloyd who had agreed to undertake it.[9]

Macleod barely mentioned the Common Market. He wished to leave this great issue to the Prime Minister, who was to make it the main theme of his own speech the following day. At the Labour Party Conference the previous week Hugh Gaitskell had come out against joining the EEC and this helped the collective Tory mind to focus and ensured that the Conservative conference would give a resounding vote in favour of entry.[10] Butler replied effectively to Gaitskell's reference to a thousand years of history: 'For them (the Labour Party) a thousand years of history books. For us, the future.' But Macmillan's speech was the outstanding performance at Llandudno. He made those who opposed the Market seem atavistic and absurdly out of tune with their time: 'Now is the opportunity and we must seize it,' he declared. It was his last great triumph, and *The Times* commented next day: 'In Cabinet, in the Parliamentary Party and in Conference, Mr Macmillan's victory, for the time being, has been complete.'

This Great Design, had in fact been launched the previous year, on July 31, 1961, when the Prime Minister announced that he had lodged Britain's application to join the European Economic Community. It was a political and economic watershed; a considered and deliberate attempt to change the whole framework within which Britain had hitherto operated. A small minority of Conservative MPs opposed the project from the outset, and some others felt doubtful and uneasy; but as the fortunes of the party declined throughout 1961 and 1962, most Members, and certainly most Ministers, looked increasingly to the Common Market to relieve the Administration of some of its more intractable problems. It was hoped that the vitality of the Six would help Britain's sagging performance,

9 On September 24th Macleod had sent a minute to the Prime Minister suggesting that Selwyn Lloyd should carry out a survey on these lines. Macmillan had accepted this recommendation.

10 History was to repeat itself at Brighton nine years later.

and that the immense amount of legislation which would be entailed in joining the Community would provide the Parliamentary Party with a sense of purpose and do much to improve morale.

Macmillan thought that membership of the EEC would produce more forward-looking long term prospects and that it would have a dynamic effect on our economy. Against the sombre background of the 'night of the long knives' and the continuing by-election reverses, the Prime Minister believed he had an ace up his sleeve. He was himself mainly interested in the more influential political role which membership would enable Britain to play in Europe and in the world. He made clear his personal commitment to our entry at the Stockton by-election in May 1962, when the *Daily Mail* applauded his speech with the words: 'Last night we saw a statesman rise to the level of his own statesmanship.' Macmillan regarded our accession to the Market as his last major contribution in public life and hoped it would ensure his place as one of the great peace-time Prime Ministers in the history of Britain.

After the Llandudno conference the party's prospects looked better than for some time past. Macmillan had achieved his objective of securing support for the European policy at constituency level and although there might be some trouble with the Parliamentary Party,[11] it would not be on such a scale as to threaten the future of the Government. The Prime Minister was poised to lead Britain into Europe, and he hoped that this great enterprise would arouse the enthusiasm of the nation.

In the same month the Cuban missile crisis brought the world to the brink of war. Perhaps for the first time men realised how close to the abyss a confrontation between the USA and the USSR could bring mankind. But President Kennedy and his advisers handled the crisis with courage, and the Russian leaders retracted in time to avert it. Lord Harlech, our Ambassador in Washington, played a helpful part, and Macmillan gave the President his fullest support throughout the ordeal.

At home Macleod wrote to party workers that 'we may well hope that a real corner in our affairs has been turned'. But it was a false dawn and, in the absence of any major reflationary measures, the by-election results on November 22nd showed a drop in the Tory percentage of the vote in every constituency. South Dorset, Chippenham, Central Norfolk, South Northants, and the Woodside division of Glasgow all went to the polls on the same day. Chippenham, Central Norfolk and the Northamptonshire seat were held precariously with much reduced majorities. Woodside and

11 In December, 47 Conservative back-benchers signed an anti-Market motion.

South Dorset were lost to Labour – though in the latter case the reverse was attributable to the intervention of Sir Piers Debenham, an anti-Common Market candidate, supported by the popular former Member, Lord Hinchingbrooke, who had just succeeded to the peerage on the death of his father. The independent candidate split the Conservative vote and presented the seat to Labour.

Macleod analysed these results in a long memorandum to the Prime Minister: he thought that all five seats would have been lost if contested in the summer. The unemployment figures were high, which was the principal reason for the loss of Woodside, and would rise still further in the winter. After eleven years in power 'we have no margin of error left and the smallest slip by any Minister becomes a liability out of all proportion to its worth. And we are awaiting events in Brussels. This means that many proposals by industrial firms are still in the pending tray and this in turn means that reflation does not move as swiftly as . . . in 1958/59. . . . We are upon a painted ocean until the end of these negotiations. . . . I think we should tell our people frankly that this winter is bound to be very difficult indeed.' He emphasised that the key mottoes should be 'Conservatives care' and 'Efficiency'. A successful conclusion to the negotiations in Brussels was of central importance.

Macleod's concern about unemployment was soon borne out by the figures, which rose in February to over 878,000, or nearly 4% of the working population. They were especially bad in Scotland and Wales, where 6% were unemployed and in the North-East they went as high as 7%. Macmillan gave Quintin Hailsham the responsibility for improving this depressing situation in the North East of England.

'Modernisation' was becoming fashionable and committees were set up to encourage it. Beeching was enquiring into the railways, Newsom into secondary education, Robbins into higher education, Buchanan into roads and traffic and Trend into the Civil Service. All this activity demonstrated the Government's interest in change but it did nothing to improve the political fortunes of the Administration. As Chairman of the Party Macleod was riding sheet anchor in a very choppy sea.

On January 14, 1963, came the cruellest blow of all. General de Gaulle vetoed Britain's application to join the Common Market. The key to future prosperity was curtly cast aside and the Government's best prospect for sustained growth was denied them. The French President explained his attitude in a private conversation: 'If Britain was in the Community, there would, at best, be two cocks in the hen run. At worst there would only be one and it would not be France. And that is not interesting to me.' To de Gaulle, who saw himself as the modern Louis XIV, this was an understandable point of view. To Macmillan it was a bitter end to all his hopes.

Macleod put the best face on it he could. In a letter to the Prime Minister he advised: 'The line I would suggest is that the European policy was the right one; that it remains the right one; that the course of history cannot be permanently frustrated . . . that we believe Britain's entry is delayed but not finally voted out. . . .'

The early months of 1963 were indeed 'The winter of the Tories' discontent.'[12]

12 Randolph Churchill in *The Fight for the Tory Leadership*, Heinemann, 1964.

CHAPTER 13

Chancellor of the Duchy of Lancaster (111) The Leadership Crisis in the Tory Party 1963

❧

THE New Year began sadly with the death of Hugh Gaitskell on January 18th. In a tribute to the Leader of the Opposition Macleod said: 'The word that came first to my mind was courage. He was a very courageous man and I remember what Sir James Barrie said forty years ago in his rectorial address to St Andrews: "Courage is the thing – if that goes all goes." . . . This is a tragic loss to the party of which he was the head, but it goes much wider than that: it is a great loss to the whole political and national life of this country.' The same quality of courage was singled out in every tribute to Iain Macleod himself when he died seven years later.

Within a few days the Vassal Tribunal began its public hearings. This affair, which Macmillan took too seriously, resulted in the unjust and unnecessary resignation of Tam Galbraith[1] and in two journalists being sent to prison for six months. Macleod observed to me that the press would not forgive or forget this unrewarding incident for some time to come, and he was right. Relations between Whitehall and Fleet Street were at a low ebb. But the episode was soon eclipsed by the Profumo scandal.

Rumours of Jack Profumo's involvement with Miss Christine Keeler began to circulate in February, and by March were the subject of general cocktail party gossip in London. Perhaps in reaction to press criticism of his handling of the Vassal incident, Macmillan did not take the Profumo story seriously enough. He left it to others to interview his War Minister, and at three-thirty a.m. on March 22nd Profumo was roused from sleep to attend a meeting in the House of Commons arranged by Martyn Redmayne at which the Leader of the House, the Minister without

1 Thomas Galbraith, MP for Hillhead since 1948. Parliamentary Secretary to Ministry of Transport 1962/63.

Portfolio and the Law Officers of the Crown were also present. They did not question the word of a colleague; they believed their duty was simply to help him draft his statement for the following day. Their assistance was needed because Profumo had taken a strong sleeping pill after midnight and when he was awoken two hours later he was still in a state of sedation.

It is arguable that if the statement was a purely personal one, the other Ministers ought not to have helped to prepare it; if, on the other hand, it was a Government statement, it should have been discussed in the Cabinet. But by now the matter had become urgent, because on March 21st George Wigg, supported by Richard Crossman and Barbara Castle, had publicly coupled Miss Keeler's name with 'a member of the Government front bench' and had called on the Home Secretary to 'deny the truth of these rumours'.

In fact, but for Profumo's inexcusable action in lying to the House of Commons, the whole incident was of minor importance. The association of Captain Ivanov, an attache at the Russian Embassy, with Miss Keeler was coincidental and no security risk was involved. It may be that Profumo had not told his wife about his relationship with Christine Keeler and could not bear that she should hear of it through a public statement in the House. He hoped he would get away with it and, but for the statement, he might have done. If, a month or two earlier, he had quietly resigned as Secretary of State for War, he need never have given up his membership of the House of Commons and could have continued in public life, perhaps even returning to ministerial office after a suitable interval. But the statement was a fatal mistake, and in June Profumo felt obliged to write to the Prime Minister, admitting he had lied to the House of Commons. He resigned his office, his Privy Councillorship and his seat and retired into private life.

He is an attractive and intelligent man, and had been a good Minister. It was a personal tragedy, and if ever a man paid dearly for a grave error of judgement, it was Jack Profumo. He has never attempted to excuse his mistake or to justify his conduct. But he has worked selflessly and with complete dedication and devotion for the unfortunate in the East End of London and has found solace and satisfaction not only in his work but in the loyalty and support of his wife and the understanding of his friends.

Iain Macleod, who had not been particularly close to him in the days of success, was a rock of support at this time of disaster. When Profumo's letter to the Prime Minister was published, Iain and Eve were in the United

States. Questioned at a meeting of the Washington Press Club, Macleod said simply: 'I was, and am, a friend of Jack and Valerie Profumo. I think it is a personal tragedy that this should have happened.' It was typical of Iain's unfailing loyalty. He had used almost the same words five years earlier about Ian Harvey, his old friend from Fettes days, who had been involved in a personal scandal and been forced to resign as a junior Minister.

In April 1963 Lord Poole was appointed Joint Chairman, with Macleod, of the Conservative Party. The two men did not like each other and under these circumstances it was surprising that the new arrangement worked as well as it did.

Macmillan had seriously considered relieving Macleod of the Chairmanship (though retaining him as Leader of the House of Commons) and replacing him by Poole. But Oliver Poole himself discouraged this as he thought it unfair to blame Macleod for the fall in the party's popularity.

At the same time Lord Aldington, who was devoted to Macleod and completely loyal to him resigned the Deputy Chairmanship of the Party which he had held since 1959. They had worked closely together and Aldington did not think that the Prime Minister and the Chief Whip were giving Macleod the support to which he was entitled.

One of his successors, Edward Du Cann, considered that, with his power of communication and his shrewd political instinct, Macleod could have been a great Party Chairman, but that his potential in this position was not fully realised because he held it at such a difficult time.

July was a better month for the Government, with the negotiation of the important Test Ban Treaty in Moscow and Butler's success at Victoria Falls in winding up the Central Africa Federation. In the same month the Peerage Act was passed, allowing hereditary peers to renounce their titles and, if they wished, to stand for election to the House of Commons. Following an amendment in the House of Lords, the Act was to come into operation not, as originally intended, after the next election but as soon as the Royal Assent was given.[2] The acceptance of this amendment was to have a profound effect upon the leadership issue in the Conservative Party three months later.

After the Vassall and Profumo reverses Harold Macmillan, who had been in poor health, thought of resigning as Prime Minister, but during the summer recess his spirits improved and he decided to continue in

2 The Peerage Act came into force on July 31, 1963.

office and to lead the party at the general election which was due to take place not later than November, 1964.

This resolve had the enthusiastic support of Iain Macleod who, in a notable speech at Horsham on July 13th, sought to distinguish the principles and policies of political parties from the personalisation of issues which was becoming fashionable in the press. He thought peace and safety in the nuclear age, consent and co-operation in the Commonwealth, and modern homes throughout Britain were the priorities which politics should be about; and if they had to be personalised, there was no doubt in his mind that it was the Prime Minister whose vision had inspired each one of them. The Moscow meeting stemmed from Macmillan's peace initiatives, the Commonwealth developments grew naturally from the philosophy of the wind of change and the housing policy was child and heir to those Macmillan had devised as Minister of Housing ten years before.

Macmillan's contribution to the party and the country had been considerable. He succeeded Anthony Eden in the aftermath of the Suez crisis and restored the morale and reputation of the party to such effect that the Conservatives achieved the remarkable feat of winning their third election in succession and by the much increased majority of one hundred. As Macleod wrote in an article in the *Spectator* in 1964, Macmillan had style and he had skill, especially in controlling and guiding the Cabinet.

He knew how to delegate and he left his Ministers to get on with their departmental work, in which he seldom interfered. His authority in Parliament was unquestioned, and few cared to take him on in debate. He was a superb speaker in a sophisticated, sometimes Edwardian vein; a philosophic statesman of wide range with a deep understanding of history; a mixture of idealism and good humoured cynicism; a brilliant con-versationalist and a man of outstanding intellect. He will be remembered in history as one of the great peace-time Prime Ministers of Britain.

In the summer and autumn of 1963 Iain Macleod 'held steadily to the view that the Tory Party would do better under Macmillan's leadership at the polls than they would under any of the possible alternatives.'[3] But the Prime Minister was already suffering from the prostate trouble which later became acute; and during September he discussed with the Chief Whip the procedure for choosing a successor in the event of his own resignation through ill-health.

When Eden had had to retire in 1957, Macmillan had been selected to

3 *Spectator* article on the Tory leadership, January 17, 1964.

succeed him by the Cabinet. Members of Parliament were free to write to the then Chief Whip, submitting their views on the succession, but there was no formal consultation with the Parliamentary Party, and the members of the Cabinet, sounded individually by the Lord Chancellor and Lord Salisbury, made the choice. There was much to be said for this method. Those who worked closely together in Cabinet had the best opportunity of assessing which of them would be the most acceptable to his colleagues and would make the best leader of the party and the best Prime Minister of the country. But Macmillan decided to change the system and greatly to increase the area of consultation. He arranged that the Lord Chancellor should sound the Cabinet; that the Chief Whip should invite the views of the junior Ministers in the House of Commons and the Conservative Members of Parliament; that the Chief Whip in the House of Lords should consult the Unionist peers; and that constituency chairmen, agents, candidates and Young Conservative leaders should be given an opportunity of expressing their opinions through the Conservative Central Office. In the event, so far as the last category was concerned, where soundings were taken at all they were indecisive and played no part in the final decision.

A routine meeting of the Cabinet was held on Tuesday, October 8th. Macmillan looked ill and left before it ended. He said nothing about his health and still intended to travel to Blackpool on the Friday to address the party conference on Saturday afternoon. But his appearance alarmed his colleagues and when he left the room there was speculation about the possibility of his resignation. Lord Dilhorne then told the Cabinet about the arrangements which had already been made for choosing a successor and said that he would be available to take the views of members of the Cabinet if this became necessary. Lord Home mentioned that as he, too, was not a candidate, he would be ready to help his colleagues in any way he could. He certainly had no thought at that time of being considered for the Premiership.

Some Ministers, including Macleod, left for Blackpool during the afternoon. Butler, Dilhorne and Home remained in London. That evening Macmillan sent for the Chief Whip, Martin Redmayne, and told him that he had to go into the King Edward VII Hospital for a serious operation and that the machinery for selecting a successor should therefore be prepared.

The news of the Prime Minister's illness was telephoned to Iain Macleod, as Chairman of the Party, at the Imperial Hotel at Blackpool, but he was attending an agents' dinner and the call had to be transferred. A waiter informed him that he was wanted on the telephone from London. 'What about?' he enquired, and the reply that Iain's sister was ill was a surprising one as his only sister, Rhodabel, had died over a year before. Macleod thought he had better find out what the mysterious message meant and he followed the waiter to the only telephone in the building, by which time the call had been cut off. Somehow contact with Downing Street was re-established and the news of Macmillan's operation conveyed. It meant that the Prime Minister would be unable to address the conference on Saturday and, after some discussion, it was agreed that the task should fall to Rab Butler, as Deputy Prime Minister, who was now in charge of the Government. At this point there was no indication of Macmillan's intention to resign; but on the following evening, the Wednesday, another telephone call to Macleod brought the news of Macmillan's retirement. The leadership crisis had begun.

The events which followed are inexplicable unless it is accepted that Macmillan had long since resolved that Butler should not succeed him as Prime Minister. In *The Fight for the Tory Leadership* Randolph Churchill wrote later:

It can be argued that Macmillan did all he could during his seven years as Prime Minister to advance the fortunes of Butler.

Iain Macleod commented coldly in his article in the *Spectator*:

Almost anything can no doubt be argued, but no one close to politics or to Harold Macmillan could seriously support this suggestion for a moment. Although incomparably the best qualified of the contenders, the truth is that at all times, from the first day of his premiership to the last, Macmillan was determined that Butler should not succeed him.[4]

Macleod was right. It was well known in the House of Commons that Macmillan was implacably opposed to Butler as the future leader of the party. There was nothing ignoble in this attitude. I am sure that Macmillan genuinely believed, in Macleod's words, that 'Butler had not in him the steel that makes a Prime Minister, nor the inspiration that a leader needs to pull his party through a fierce general election.' But Butler had one great asset. He could attract 'wide understanding support from many

4 Kenneth Young confirms this in his biography of Sir Alec Douglas-Home (Dent, 1971): 'It was widely known that Macmillan would never countenance Butler as his heir. . . . It was appropriate that the postal address of Chequers was Butler's Cross.'

people outside the Tory Party. And without such an appeal no general election can be won.' Macleod was always conscious of the need to win the central, uncommitted ground in politics and this, perhaps more than any other factor, made him a Butler supporter in the contest which was developing within the party. Macmillan's own view was, however, accepted by many who mattered, and in particular by those with whom the Prime Minister, from his sick-bed, consulted and conferred. Of these the Lord Chancellor and the Chief Whip were by far the most influential.

In order to avoid the possibility that Butler might be chosen, Macmillan had brought forward three younger men who were of sufficient experience and seniority to be considered. Reggie Maudling had been made Chancellor of the Exchequer, Iain Macleod was Leader of the House of Commons and Chairman of the Party, and Edward Heath had been responsible for the Common Market negotiations. Each of them had been given opportunities, but none of them had emerged decisively at that time as generally acceptable to the party. Macmillan did not consider that any other member of his Cabinet in the House of Commons was even a possibility. Given his determination to stop Butler at any price, the Prime Minister had to consider a candidate from the House of Lords, now made conceivable by the passing of the Peerage Act that summer.

Macmillan's first choice was Lord Hailsham, whom he had sent to Moscow to finalise the Test Ban Treaty and who, he thought, had 'a touch of genius'. But it was quickly apparent that many members of the Cabinet and of the Parliamentary Party would not accept Quintin Hailsham as Prime Minister. Most considered he would make an inspiring leader of the party at a general election but they questioned his judgement, should we win it, as the leader of the nation. He had been a splendid Chairman of the Party, uniquely capable of rousing the enthusiasm of the constituency associations; he has a brilliant mind and, at his best, his speeches can be moving and eloquent. But his performance was as uneven in Cabinet as it was in public and it is improbable that he could have formed a Government because some of his colleagues would not have served under him.

Macmillan's initial support for Hailsham's candidature can only be explained by his inflexible opposition to Butler. Nevertheless, the bandwagon was set in motion. The Prime Minister's son, Maurice, and his son-in-law, Julian Amery, arrived in Blackpool and at once began to canvass Quintin's claims. Their efforts were reinforced (or prejudiced) by the extraordinary performance of Randolph Churchill, hotfoot from the

United States, who peddled 'Q' lapel badges and buttons round Blackpool and did much to diminish Hailsham's chances by the Americanised antics which he thought suitable for the presidential type of public campaign now made inevitable by the timing of Macmillan's resignation.

It happened that Hailsham was already booked to address the Conservative Political Centre meeting arranged for the Thursday evening. Everyone expected him to throw his hat in the ring, and my wife and I went along to see him do it. To our surprise he made a long and dullish speech, in which the leadership of the party was never mentioned. His speech had already been issued to the press so he was obliged to adhere to the text of it. But in response to the more or less perfunctory applause, he added the sensational postscript that he had decided to renounce his peerage and stand as a candidate for the House of Commons. There was a great burst of cheering from his supporters and, flushed and excited, he rushed from the hall to a Young Conservative dance where he was received, as Kenneth Young records,[5] 'with the sort of rapture more often accorded by teenage girls to pop singers than to potential Prime Ministers.' In fact, the uninhibited and undignified canvassing on his behalf had reacted against him and had alienated more people than it had pleased. His erratic judgement seemed to be confirmed and his too-evident eagerness for the premiership ensured that he would never achieve it. The Hailsham bandwagon came to a halt almost as soon as it had started to roll.

Meanwhile the other candidates were also losing ground. In 1963 Edward Heath, despite his admirable and painstaking conduct of the abortive Common Market negotiations, was not seriously considered by anyone. At that time he had had too little departmental experience.

Iain Macleod had made his usual brilliant conference speech, which was received with great enthusiasm and a standing ovation (not so common in those days as they have since become), but the applause was for the speech, not the man, and the Colonial Secretaryship, which had so antagonised the right wing of the party, was still too fresh in people's minds to allow him more than an outside chance of breaking the deadlock between Butler and Hailsham. Macleod may have hoped he was the dark horse who might come up on the rails in the last furlong. Indeed, on Monday October 14th, this exchange took place between him and Randolph Churchill:

Macleod: 'Keep your eye on the back of the field.'

Churchill: 'You mean looking for a dark horse?'

5 *Sir Alec Douglas-Home*, p. 164.

Macleod: 'That's it.'

Churchill: 'Would the dark horse be called Macleod?'

Macleod: 'That's about it.'

But he must have known in his heart that the prospects of this were poor.

The only other possible contender was Reggie Maudling. His stock in the Parliamentary Party had been high when the House rose in July and of the younger men his chances were the most hopeful. His private pact with Macleod – that whichever's star was in the ascendant when the tapes went up would not be opposed by the other – now came into operation. Knowing Maudling's prospects were better than his own, Iain tried tactfully to help him with his conference speech. He begged Reggie to get his timing and his pauses right, to give the audience time to cheer and to think up a rousing peroration. It was all to no purpose. Maudling's performance was pedestrian, and his chances slipped away as the speech sagged heavily to its conclusion. No one felt that he could inspire the faithful to an electoral victory. Another candidate must be found, and to the uninformed Butler looked the obvious choice. But Macmillan still had a card to play.

On the Wednesday evening, October 9th, the Prime Minister summoned Lord Home to the King Edward VII Hospital and, to the latter's astonishment, indicated that he regarded the Foreign Secretary as a potential successor. Home remarked that he was a peer and that the idea was impossible. He dismissed it from his mind. But as that year's President of the National Union of Conservative and Unionist Associations, he was entrusted with the task of announcing to the conference on the next afternoon the news of Macmillan's resignation. And on the Friday morning he wound up the foreign affairs debate with a very good speech. He was, and is, immensely popular in the constituencies and, in direct contrast to Macleod, the prolonged applause was for the man as much as for the performance. But even before this there were rumours that Home might be 'drafted', and the previous evening Reggie Bennett, who was keeping his eyes and ears open, had reported to Macleod that there was a strong fancy for the Foreign Secretary to break the deadlock. Iain laughed in his face: 'Don't be so bloody ridiculous,' he said, 'that's absolutely cuckoo. Alec told us in Cabinet that he wasn't a runner.' When Bennett pointed out that Home might well have meant that at the time but might have come under considerable pressure since to allow his name to go forward, Iain was still adamant that the idea was out of the question, and there is no doubt that he believed this. In fact, Bennett was right.

Although in the foreign affairs debate Alec Home had actually said: 'I am offering a prize to any newspaper man who can find a clue in my speech that this is Lord Home's bid for the leadership', he was already being privately approached by colleagues to accept nomination. Among them were Dilhorne, Duncan Sandys and John Hare, supported by Selwyn Lloyd and other senior back-benchers like Bill Anstruther-Gray[6] and Charles Mott-Radclyffe, MP for Windsor. Home agreed to consult his doctor as to whether he would be fit enough to assume the burden of the premiership, but he gave no commitment that he would become a candidate. Indeed, he told Hailsham the same day that he thought Quintin still had a good chance of being chosen. But Macmillan, who was too skilled a tactician to run two candidates at the same time, had already decided to switch his bet to another horse from the same stable. His choice was the Earl of Home.

By this time the Imperial Hotel at Blackpool was a hothouse of gossip and intrigue. Little groups of supporters of one contender or another gathered in corners or in hotel bedrooms, discussing the best tactics for furthering the prospects of their respective nominees. There was a disagreeable atmosphere of back-stabbing and criticism of other candidates. To some this was a stimulating and exciting drama. I found it intensely distasteful and so did Iain. He took no part in it himself and spent his spare time in his own room. He heard little of the gossip at first hand and perhaps this was why he ignored Reggie Bennett's important information. He might have mingled more, and heard more, if Eve had been with him at Blackpool.[7] Just before the last conference session on Saturday, Home informed Butler that he was going to consult his doctor – a polite way of saying he was now in the race as a rival candidate.

That afternoon Butler made the Leader's conference speech. It was not a particularly impressive performance and did not enhance his claims. In the course of a short introduction of the Deputy Prime Minister, Home made an interesting observation: 'We choose a leader not for what he does or does not do at the party conference,' he said, 'but because the leader we choose is in every respect a whole man who in all circumstances is fit to lead the nation.' It was a curious and unlikely remark if, at that time, he considered himself a candidate.

That evening the conference broke up and we all returned to London.

6 Deputy Speaker of the House of Commons, 1962/66. Now Lord Kilmany.
7 Eve Macleod was unable to attend the conference because of the serious illness of her daughter, Diana.

My wife and I travelled back with Iain Macleod, the Maudlings and Hugh and Antonia Fraser. In the course of the journey I prepared my list of first, second and third preferences for the leadership, to be handed in to the Chief Whip on Monday. Iain Macleod was my first choice, although I recognised that he had virtually no chance of being selected, and Reggie Maudling my second. It was not a very helpful (or hopeful) selection. Maudling's prospects had fallen after his poor conference speech, Macleod's had not risen despite his brilliant one. It was clear to me by this time that the contest was effectively between Butler and Home. I admired and respected them both and was happy to serve under either. I said so in my note to the Whips.

On the Monday Alec's doctor declared him fit to undertake the responsibility. The detailed soundings took place early that week. Many members of Parliament who had put Home on their lists, but not very high, were asked if their order of preference would be different if they knew for certain that he would be prepared to renounce his peerage and was a firm candidate who alone could unite the party. I am sure Alec knew nothing of this 'second round'; but in the light of it several members elevated Home's name from third place to second or from second to first. Iain Macleod was correct when he wrote later in the *Spectator* that the Whips had been working hard for several days to influence the votes of the Parliamentary Party, including the junior Ministers, in favour of Lord Home. Many senior members on the back benches had been doing the same. This is in no sense a criticism. They were perfectly entitled to ensure, if they could, the selection of the man they thought best able to unite the party and best fitted to lead the country.

The Chief Whip gave weight 'to people on whose opinion one would more strongly rely than on others' and on this basis Home was 'marginally' the leader on first choices in the House of Commons and became 'outstandingly so as you took it further through the field'.[8] Lord St Aldwyn, the Chief Whip in the House of Lords, was able to report that 'the peers were overwhelmingly for Home'. As Macleod commented in the *Spectator* article, 'it would have been surprising if they were not'.

Much the most important of the soundings was that of the Cabinet. Only someone acceptable to his colleagues could be Prime Minister, and when Dilhorne reported an overwhelming Cabinet consensus for Home, that was no doubt decisive. But it is difficult to see how this large majority could have been composed. By this time at least nine members of the

8 Interview with Lord Redmayne in The *Listener*, December 19, 1963.

Cabinet (Boyd-Carpenter, Boyle, Brooke, Butler, Erroll, Hailsham, Macleod, Maudling and Powell) were for Butler. At least four (Dilhorne, Hare, Home and Sandys) were presumably for Home. This left seven whose views were not known. Macleod wrote in the *Spectator*: 'From my personal knowledge eleven were for candidates other than Lord Home.' Apart from Macmillan, there were twenty members of the Cabinet. If Macleod was correct and even if all the remaining members of the Cabinet were for Home, it is still impossible to reconcile the figures with Lord Dilhorne's report of an overwhelming consensus. Suggestions to Dilhorne that the Cabinet (or the Cabinet less the chief contenders) should meet to discuss the succession fell on stony ground. But Harold Macmillan saw most members of the Cabinet individually on Tuesday and Wednesday, October 15th and 16th, and inferred to many of them, where he did not actually state it, that Home was his choice as Prime Minister.

At breakfast on Thursday, October 17th, Eve Macleod was telephoned on another matter by Lady Monckton, who mentioned that she had heard from Lady Dorothy Macmillan that the leadership issue was to be resolved that day. Iain was surprised but not disturbed. It seemed to him that, if there was to be an early decision, it must be for Butler. But later in the day it became generally known that it was for Home. As soon as this information, which came from reliable press sources, was confirmed, Maudling and Powell met at Macleod's flat, where they were joined by Toby Aldington. Later that evening both Macleod and Powell spoke to Alec Home on the telephone and told him that they could not serve under him. Maudling, Erroll and Aldington joined them at Powell's house in South Eaton Place, after their dinner engagements, for what became known as 'the midnight meeting'. Hailsham kept in close touch by telephone and was by this time in agreement with the others that Butler should be Prime Minister. Maudling, Macleod and Powell spoke to Butler and told him what had been agreed, and that he could be assured of their support. The understanding thus reached between three out of the four principal contenders (Butler, Maudling and Hailsham) seemed of decisive importance, and they telephoned the Chief Whip, who then joined them at Powell's house. He undertook to inform the Prime Minister of their views.

On the Friday Edward Boyle told Macleod and Powell that he would join them in staying out of the Government. But by the next day he had changed his mind, partly as the result of a talk with Butler, and partly because there were crucial decisions pending at the Ministry of Education which he felt it important to take.

On the morning of Friday, October 18th, Macleod arranged and was present at a meeting between the acknowledged candidates, Butler, Maudling and Hailsham; but, forewarned by Redmayne, Macmillan was too quick for them. He sent his letter of resignation to the Palace, and the Queen visited him in hospital later in the morning to seek his advice as to whom she should send for to form an Administration. He received her in a wheel-chair and, as he was too ill to carry on a conversation of any length, simply handed her a memorandum incorporating the reports he had obtained from Dilhorne, Redmayne and St Aldwyn. These indicated Alec Home not merely as Macmillan's personal choice but as the collective recommendation of the Cabinet and the Conservative Parliamentary Party in both Houses. Given such a document, there could be no question of asking for a second opinion and the Queen had no option but to send for Lord Home. She did so immediately, and Alec Home drove to the Palace before lunch. He asked for time to see if he could form a Government, and a simple announcement was made that the Queen had invited him to do so.

Lord Home began his interviews with his Cabinet colleagues after lunch and at first Butler, Hailsham, Macleod, Maudling and Powell all declined to serve. There was nothing personal in Macleod's decision. He liked and admired Home and, as he wrote later in the *Spectator*, if Alec 'had been in the House of Commons he could perhaps have been the first choice'. Home is the most modest and generous of men and he regretfully accepted the decision in which Macleod and Powell persisted. 'Both were straightforward,' he told me, 'they simply felt that I could not win an election for the party and they said so. There was no ill-feeling.'

Hailsham took the view, no doubt rightly, that all should come in or none. Had such a pact materialised and all had declined, Alec Home could not have formed a government and Rab Butler would have become Prime Minister. But in the event it did not and Hailsham felt he must serve because, as a candidate himself, he would otherwise have been criticised for not doing so on grounds of personal pique. By that evening he had agreed to join. Rab Butler felt that this amounted to an erosion of support for his own candidature and, in order to unite the Party, he himself came in the following morning. Reggie Maudling followed on the general and not unreasonable proposition that it was pointless to be more royal than the King. Alec Home tried to persuade Macleod and

Powell to change their minds, but they felt unable to do so. Five resignations (and especially Butler's) would have made Home's task impossible. Two were a pity but could be accepted. By lunch time on Saturday Home was able to drive to the Palace and kiss hands on his appointment as First Lord of the Treasury. The leadership crisis was over.

Macleod's decision not to serve was gravely damaging to his reputation in the Conservative Party, and to his prospects of ever becoming its leader. The right wing of the Party had distrusted him for some time; now the solid centre questioned his loyalty and his motives. Many attributed his defection to self-interest, some even going as far as to say that he was hoping for a Conservative defeat in the forthcoming election, so that he could emerge thereafter as an alternative leader. In fact politics do not work that way. All Iain's friends knew (and he knew himself) that his action – and the *Spectator* article three months later – was the nail in the coffin, constructed during the Colonial Secretaryship, which put an end to his hopes of the leadership in the future.

Macleod's refusal to serve under Alec Home was a serious mistake of judgement, but it was certainly an honest mistake which did him no good, personally or politically, with the party. Why, then, did such an ambitious man fall into so grievous an error?

It was not his first blunder in the ten days of the leadership crisis. Although Reggie Bennett had warned him on the previous Thursday that Alec Home was a likely late entry in the race, and although several of us had underlined this to him by the Saturday, he refused to accept the possibility till the following Thursday. Normally Iain Macleod was very much a political animal with acute and sensitive political antennae, but on this occasion he was not. It was naive not to have realised that, as soon as Hailsham had fallen at the first fence, Macmillan had to find another runner to stop Butler. No one, usually, had a quicker grasp of the realities of politics than Macleod. What, then, clouded his judgement during this fateful period?

It is conceivable, though I believe unlikely, that family anxieties played an important part. His daughter, Diana, whom he adored, was desperately ill. She had had an operation for appendicitis, which was followed by severe complications, and it was uncertain from day to day whether she would live. Iain's decision not to take office under Alec was taken with this sword over his head. And this factor would itself have been sufficient to unbalance the judgement of most ordinary men. But it was unlike Macleod not to be able to discipline his mind. He would usually have been able to assess and compartmentalise the political priorities and separate them from the domestic strain.

No doubt the reasons which he listed later in the *Spectator* article influenced and rationalised his decision. He did, I know, find it unpalatable that, after twelve years in power, the Conservative Party was admitting that, out of a parliamentary membership of 363, it could not find anyone acceptable as Prime Minister in the House of Commons. It is true, too, that he thought it a mistake in the 1960s that the party should be led, for the first time for forty years, from the right of centre. And he did not think the 'grouse-moor image' of Lord Home would be helpful in the next election. These were factors, no doubt, in his mind. But I question whether, by themselves, they fully accounted for his decision. More important to him, I believe, was his personal view of his own political integrity – he had told Alec Home that he would not serve and he felt he was committed to this course.

Perhaps there was also another psychological explanation, never publicly acknowledged. He was intensely ambitious and he knew his own capacity. He was sure he could do the job better than anyone else and he may have hoped he had an outside chance of getting it. It was a bitter blow when he realised, not only that he had no prospect of emerging as the compromise candidate, but that he was not even going to be consulted about who the future leader should be. This was an oversight on Macmillan's part. Macleod was, after all, the Chairman of the Party and the Leader of the House of Commons. If he had been brought into the consultative process, he might conceivably have accepted Home as the interim leader.

When at last he understood where the choice lay, it was perhaps natural that he should prefer Butler to Home. He always attached great importance to the middle ground in politics, and he thought Rab's chances of retaining it at an election were greater than Alec Home's. But he only became a firm Butler protagonist when he realised, at length, that the race was between these two. If his usually shrewd political judgement had not been warped by his personal disappointment, he would have appreciated this far sooner and would therefore have organised Cabinet support for Rab far earlier. He was outmanoeuvred, as Butler was, by the skill of Macmillan's tactics. From his hospital bed, sick as he was, the Prime Minister controlled the situation through Dilhorne, Redmayne, St Aldwyn and Poole.

In the end Macmillan was presented with Butler's defeat by Butler himself, who was anxious not to split the party and who may also have lacked the ruthlessness to fight his own corner. Under these circumstances, Maudling was right to serve and Macleod should have done the same. His friends begged him to do so. We saw the damage he was inflicting on his own career and this became even clearer with the passage of time.

It is probable that, had he continued in Government in 1963, he would have become Shadow Chancellor when the Conservative Party went into Opposition in 1964. And if so, there can be little doubt that, with his great debating skill, he would have fought the 1965 Finance Bill with as much success as Edward Heath. This was the base from which Heath was able to take the leadership when Home retired in the summer of 1965. And from this base Macleod might well have captured the prize. If the Colonial Secretaryship had destroyed his first chance in 1963, his own decision to resign from the Government destroyed his second chance in 1965.

After nearly twelve years in office, Macleod missed the life he loved. One evening he talked to me gloomily about giving up politics altogether. I did not take it seriously because I knew that in the end he could not do it. Indeed, a fortnight later he came to dinner at my house in Lord North Street and, as he sat drinking a whisky and soda before the meal, I saw his eye fall on my red Government despatch box, lying open beside my chair. 'What you really want, Iain, is to get that bloody box back,' I suggested, and with a rueful smile he admitted it. 'Yes,' he said, 'you're right. I shall have to come back.' And he added, with a touch of defiance: 'And I don't run in a race to run second.' But even then, I think, he knew that his chances of ever becoming Prime Minister were now very small. From 1964, when he returned to the Front Bench after our defeat in the election, he had to work his passage back and it took him many long years to do so. He had succeeded, but only just, by the day he died.

CHAPTER 14

Editor of the *Spectator*

❧❧❧

THE autumn of 1963 was a depressing period for Iain Macleod. For seventeen years his whole interest had been centred in politics. Now he was out of office at a time when his party was still in power, and there was no contribution he could make. His political future was uncertain, he had too little to do, and his financial position was insecure. The first essential was to augment the back-bencher's salary to which he had so abruptly reverted. There were two ways of increasing his income and occupying his time – business, of which he had no experience, and journalism, for which he had a talent and which he enjoyed. There seemed no reason why he should not try both.

Opportunities in each sphere arose almost immediately. In November Macleod received an offer to join Lombard Banking as a non-executive director. It was a small board, consisting then of Eric Knight and Max Joseph, as joint chairmen, and Mrs Knight, Norman Osborne, Henry Alfrey and David Hawkins as the other members. Eric Knight had already decided that the time had come to increase the size and scope of the board by appointing an external director. Macleod liked Knight and the informal atmosphere of the organisation. He thought an appointment in the world of banking and finance, of which he knew little, would extend his experience. When I asked him why, out of the many approaches which must have been made to him, he had chosen Lombard's, he replied half seriously: 'They were the first company to offer me a car and a chauffeur.' By this time Iain's disability prevented him driving himself, and mobility was essential. He saw no reason to look further for the new business interest and the additional income he needed. He joined the company in November 1963 and remained a director until his appointment as Chancellor of the Exchequer after the 1970 election.

It was a happy, friendly board and one to which Macleod made a positive contribution. He would often remark that, although far from conversant with the problem under discussion, it seemed to him that 'this' or 'that' course might resolve the issue. Eric Knight observed later that Macleod's 'mind was so clear that nine times out of ten the proposal was the ideal compromise and provided the answer.'[1]

Just before this business opportunity presented itself, an even more interesting prospect arose in journalism. Ian Gilmour had been elected for Central Norfolk at the by-election there a year earlier and was an admirer of Iain Macleod. He was also owner of the *Spectator*. This weekly review, which had been founded in 1828, had a high reputation but a low circulation. It seemed to need an editorial transfusion to increase its importance and its readership, and as early as August 1963 Gilmour and two other full-time directors had decided in principle on a change of editor. In October Macleod unexpectedly became available. Gilmour telephoned to offer him the appointment.

Macleod was delighted. The proposal went far beyond his own tentative plans to enter journalism. The salary of £5,000 a year, which was later agreed upon, resolved his financial anxieties, and the paper would give him a platform for his political views. If his practical experience was slight, his self-confidence was considerable and he did not doubt his capacity for the task. As a Minister of the Crown he had directed government departments for the past decade, often with little prior knowledge of their problems, and he did not anticipate any greater difficulty in taking charge of a well-established journal, the contributors and staff of which would take the places of the civil servants upon whom he had hitherto relied. He lunched with Gilmour next day and accepted his offer. The negotiation had been brief and agreeable, and they both felt that the prospects were exhilarating. But within a few days the situation had changed.

The *Spectator* already had an editor, Iain Hamilton, who had been appointed by Gilmour and whose contract had several years to run. In September, when Macleod was still a member of the Government (and therefore ineligible) Gilmour and another director had tried tactfully to warn Hamilton of the decision to change the editorship. Unfortunately Hamilton had not understood these warnings and did not realise he was to be replaced. Gilmour invited his editor to meet him for a drink at White's later in the week, when he intended to break the news and to suggest that Hamilton should continue with the paper as Macleod's deputy. It would in any circumstances have been a painful interview. The events which followed made it more so.

1 Eric Knight to the author, November 23, 1971.

Macleod setting up shop as a director of Lombard Banking and editor of the **Spectator** *(Emwood of the* **Daily Mail,** *November 7, 1963).*

A few hours before he was due to meet Gilmour, Hamilton was tele-phoned at the *Spectator*'s office in Gower Street by an *Evening Standard* reporter, who had heard the news of Macleod's appointment. Hamilton did not believe the rumour but was disturbed by it; wisely, he declined to comment. Nevertheless the *Standard* was sure enough of its source to print the story that afternoon. Coming so soon after Iain Macleod's refusal to serve under Alec Douglas-Home, the news was electrifying and Fleet Street was agog for further information. In the midst of the hue and cry Hamilton had to meet his paper's proprietor to learn the truth.

The source of the 'leak' was hard to identify. Neither Gilmour nor Macleod had any intention of releasing the story prematurely; indeed, it was against their own interests to do so. But, unwisely, Macleod had mentioned the matter in confidence to a few senior political colleagues and the information had made its way with damaging speed from West-minster to Fleet Street. The person mainly and most immediately pre-judiced was Iain Hamilton, who could scarcely have been displaced in a more wounding or disagreeable manner; but Macleod, Gilmour and the *Spectator* itself were all harmed by the way in which the affair had been handled.

Gilmour apologised to Hamilton for the unfortunate turn of events and offered him the deputy-editorship, which was not accepted. Next morn-ing Gilmour telephoned Gower Street to renew the proposal, but was informed that Hamilton, accompanied by his solicitor, was at the moment holding a press conference. The newspapers had realised that, in addition to the surprising appointment of Macleod, there was also a background of drama and dissension, and they took up the story with professional enthusiasm. The *Spectator* press conference on November 1st was well-attended.

Hamilton read out a letter which he had written only a week or so earlier, in which, with an irony only now apparent, he had invited Macleod to write for the *Spectator*. Macleod's reply was characteristically brief: 'Dear Iain, Thank you, but not yet. And probably not for a fairly long time. It will then be good to see you again.' This was dated October 25th. The inference could be drawn – and was by some – that Macleod had been less than frank in replying in this way when he must already have been negotiating to take Hamilton's place. This was not in fact the case. Gilmour first offered Macleod the editorship on October 27th. But the proximity of the dates was unfortunate and contributed its extra draught of poison to the controversy.

The uproar and publicity crashed like a tidal wave through the doors of 99 Gower Street and continued for some time in the newspapers and on the radio and television. Journalists besieged the building and showed an almost morbid interest over the washing of the *Spectator*'s dirty linen. *Private Eye* offered a £5,000 post to Enoch Powell because they 'did not want him to feel left out'. There was a flurry of writs issued by Hamilton against Gilmour and the *Spectator* company.[2] Brian Inglis, a former editor, protested publicly against Macleod's appointment and resigned from the board of directors. The staff of the paper joined in by issuing a public statement 'vehemently protesting against the shabby treatment' of their editor. Without pause for reflection sides were taken, interviews given, and angry letters written to the press. There was an atmosphere of near-hysteria at Gower Street and a deep sense of shock and confusion among all those caught up in the storm. But many aggressive correspondents were disarmed by the polite and gentle replies they received from the proprietor, and regretted their hasty rudeness.

Macleod was unhappy about the tumult he had caused by accepting Gilmour's offer, but he remained silent. It was not, strictly speaking, his quarrel. But one theme of criticism directly concerned him. Many people felt it was wrong for a politician to edit a paper like the *Spectator*. They feared that the journal would lose its independence under an editor who retained political ambitions. Some contributors announced that they would not write for the paper as long as a politician was its editor. Others, more discerning, took a different view. One columnist wrote that she 'wasn't tearing any hair out about the appointment, because journalism is in dire need of an influx of first class brains from outside the profession'. In fact the criticism was ill-founded. No one could suggest that Macleod was a party conformist, and in any event there was nothing unique about a politician serving as an editor. C. P. Scott of the *Manchester Guardian* was often cited as the personification of journalistic independence, but combined for many years his editorial responsibilities with those of a Member of Parliament. John Freeman, himself a former Labour Minister, was at the time editing the rival weekly, the *New Statesman*, and sent Macleod a message of good wishes. Independence is better judged in practice than in prospect, and it would have been fairer if the critics had waited to see how the new editor interpreted his role before condemning him; but in the

2 This litigation was amicably settled the following year by an agreed statement in court and the payment of compensation to Hamilton for loss of office.

general pandemonium which followed the appointment, few observed such restraint.

Under these circumstances Macleod took over the editorship in an atmosphere of noisy acrimony, with the paper's staff depleted, some of its readers antagonised, and many of its best known contributors estranged. It was not at all the same as becoming a new Minister at the head of a great department of state. Indeed, he felt more like an inexperienced mariner taking over the command of a small sailing ship which was short of crew, already battered by storms, and heading into some more rough weather.

Correspondence was flowing into Macleod's flat in Sloane Court West as well as into 99 Gower Street, and before going to the office, he asked the editorial secretary to visit him at home. Joan Baylis, whose service to the *Spectator* went back to 1940, was efficient and experienced. She had worked for many editors and understood every facet of the organisation, or lack of it; but she did not assume that Macleod would wish her to continue to run his office and she made her way to Chelsea with trepidation, after swallowing two tranquillisers to calm her for the ordeal ahead. Her fears proved groundless. She was greeted with an outstretched hand, a charming, welcoming smile and the clear, high voice she knew well from the television programmes. The atmosphere was cheerful, calm, unhurried, and all tension dissolved in the serene climate which was to become the hallmark of Iain Macleod's editorship. He saw each of the senior staff separately and asked them to stay on. To some he seemed embarrassed by the office statement of sympathy for Hamilton, but in the end everyone except the deputy editor, Anthony Hartley, accepted his invitation to remain with the paper. He arrived in Gower Street a few days later in buoyant spirits.

Traditionally, the editor occupied an agreeable room adjoining the still more handsome board room in which the proprietor's desk had long been located. Macleod now changed this arrangement. He himself moved into the board room and Ian Gilmour took over the smaller room. It was a trivial alteration but it indicated at once how the new editor regarded his position. Gilmour was the owner of the paper and Macleod's employer, but he was also a newcomer to the House of Commons who treated the former Cabinet Minister with suitable deference.

On the first day of the new regime television cameras and journalists again gathered at Gower Street and attempted, unsuccessfully, to invade the board room for photographs and interviews. The telephone rang incessantly. At length, late that afternoon, Joan Baylis took an internal call; the voice of the Right Honourable Iain Macleod, MP, former Chairman of the Conservative Party and Leader of the House of Commons, asked: 'Can I go now?'

Macleod soon proved the most approachable of men. There was no formality and visitors to the board room were welcomed, with no need to knock on the door. The atmosphere was one of friendliness and consideration. Macleod was treated with the respect due to an editor but he was also called by his Christian name by even junior members of his staff. Everything was dealt with as it arose; the editor's in-tray was emptied as rapidly as it filled; correspondence was brief and to the point; delegation was practised as a fine art and the board room became, in the words of Joan Baylis, 'a haven of tranquillity and efficiency in which I could breathe'.

The first issue of the paper under Macleod's editorship was the Christmas number which was prepared by the staff in the strained period between Hamilton's departure and Macleod's arrival. By custom this production was festive and light-hearted, but the theme was out of tune with the mood in the office and was further overshadowed by the assassination of Jack Kennedy which dominated the news that week. I remember the ugly, garish cover across which had been affixed a black and white sticker starkly announcing 'Death of President Kennedy'. It might have been better to abandon the gaudy and tasteless binding, even at the cost of delaying publication. Macleod wrote his first leading article for this issue, in which he paid his tribute to Kennedy and reflected upon the dangers and difficulties for democratic politicians in a world of bigotry and violence.

The new editor grasped the nature of his responsibilities with a rapidity which surprised his staff, but he also appreciated the need for expert advice. He had a good political correspondent in David Watt; a good foreign editor in Malcolm Rutherford; able joint literary editors in David Rees and David Pryce-Jones, and Joan Baylis as his editorial secretary. But the departure of Anthony Hartley left him without a deputy, and there was no one with whom he could share the general direction of the paper. He needed someone with journalistic and editorial experience to match his own political expertise, and he invited J. W. M. Thompson to become deputy editor.

Thompson had never worked for the *Spectator* and had not met Ian Gilmour; he was a feature writer on the *Evening Standard* and had known

Macleod for some years. At first he hesitated lest, under the new regime, the *Spectator* should cease to be genuinely independent and its contributors be denied the freedom to express dissenting views. Macleod refuted this with vigour. He was appalled, he said, by the suggestion that he would be interested in running anything so dull as a conformist party publication. His concept of the *Spectator* was that the editorials should reflect his own kind of Tory radicalism – which was in any case almost indistinguishable from the political stance of the paper in the immediately preceding period – but that there should be scope in its pages for a wide diversity of opinion. That, he averred, was the whole point of the paper. He soon persuaded Thompson that the direction of the *Spectator* would be a worthwhile and stimulating professional enterprise, and throughout Macleod's editorship they worked well together. Macleod had abolished the conventional editorial conference as soon as he arrived, and the nearest approach to it became the frequent lunches with Thompson at one of Iain's favourite restaurants, the White Tower in Soho, where they talked over the affairs of the paper and discussed in depth the political scene.

Towards the end of 1964 the *Spectator* was further strengthened by the arrival of George Hutchinson, who joined the board as managing director. Hutchinson was a former political correspondent of the *Evening Standard*, and had subsequently been in charge of publicity at the Conservative Central Office when Macleod was Chairman of the Party. He had undertaken to remain at Smith Square until after the general election in October, or he would no doubt have joined the *Spectator* earlier, as he was a friend both of Macleod and Gilmour and was much in the former's confidence. He has since written a biography of Edward Heath.[3]

Soon after Macleod became editor, the possibility arose of an article about the leadership crisis in the Tory Party. Randolph Churchill had already written his own version, which was about to be published as a book. 'Why don't you review it?' suggested Thompson. 'I'm going to,' Iain replied with relish: 'Macleod speaks! – that sort of thing. There'll be a row.' For some time he had considered making a personal explanation of his refusal to serve under Alec Home, and Churchill's book seemed to provide the occasion for it. He found much to criticise in Randolph's one-sided account and felt he could not allow it to pass unchallenged. Its importance,' he wrote sardonically, 'comes from the fact that this is Mr Macmillan's trailer for the screenplay of his memoirs.' The more he thought about it the more determined he became to place the facts as he

3 *Edward Heath: A personal and political biography*, Longman's, 1970.

saw them on record, however embarrassing such frankness might be.

On January 17, 1964, Macleod's article occupied three pages of the *Spectator* and spelled out in biting detail the manoeuvres which had led to the exclusion of Butler and the emergence of Home as Prime Minister of Britain. There had never been so informed an exposure of the power of the 'magic circle' – the phrase, at once to become part of the political vocabulary, which Macleod used to label the few men close to Macmillan who, in his view, had engineered the outcome.

The article was written with pungency and zest. It was brilliant journalism. The national newspapers quoted from it at length, discerning not only political history, but also a political event in its own right; provincial and overseas papers sought permission to reprint; some showed scant courtesy by publishing pirated versions without payment. The press again besieged Gower Street for interviews and photographs. That week's sale of the *Spectator* was unprecedented, with orders for extra copies repeatedly transmitted to the printers at Aldershot, and the circulation shot up like the chart of a high fever. The publicity over the change of editors was now far eclipsed by the furore which Macleod's article created. Fleet Street and the public enjoyed every caustic phrase of it, but a very different reaction was at once evident within the Conservative Party.

Macleod had realised there would be a row; he had not foreseen its scale and duration. It was widely thought that he had heaped disloyalty upon disloyalty; that having first cooked his goose, he had now stuffed it with sour grapes. There were deep misgivings in his constituency where, on January 26th, one of the ward committees passed a vote of no confidence in their Member by 30 votes to 26. Two days later the Enfield Executive Council censured him for the article by 15 votes to 14, with 7 abstentions, but a no-confidence motion was defeated by 29 votes to 7. At Westminster many of his Parliamentary colleagues were shocked and angry, and when Humphry Berkeley persuaded him to go into the smoking room for a drink one evening, they were ostentatiously cut by every Tory in the room. For a time he was deeply depressed and talked of giving up politics altogether, but many of us pointed out that this would betray a large number of younger members of the party who only adhered to it because he was one of its leading figures.

A stream of abusive letters flooded into the *Spectator*, some of which Macleod printed in the next issue of the paper, including one which began, 'What a nasty little bit of work you are.' There were others which expressed appreciation for his courage in setting the record straight, but the torrent of denunciation was formidable and for many traditional Conservatives he had set the seal upon his reputation as the 'outsider' of the party.

Macleod bore all this with fortitude. He had underestimated the effect his article would have, but it was not in his character to complain. At Gower Street he remained cheerful and serene, and during the months that followed the office settled down to a normal flow of work with no headlines and no crises. But it was perhaps unfortunate that the new editorship had begun in such a glare of publicity because, thereafter, anticlimax was inevitable. Within the organisation harmony prevailed except in the literary department, where the approach of the joint editors was soon seen to be disparate and the dual role was therefore dissolved. In April David Rees was confirmed as sole literary editor.

The leadership article had been politically reckless, but it had at least confounded some of the earlier critics and the suggestion that Macleod the politician would manipulate the puppet figure of Macleod the editor had now been demolished. Indeed, the chief characteristic of his regime was the freedom he gave to the members of his staff to do their work in their own way and he was as good as his word in ensuring that a wide diversity of opinions was expressed.

David Watt wrote whatever he wished in his political articles, although Macleod often disagreed with him. The two men never became very close, and Macleod seldom gave guidance or suggested new initiatives. But the only argument between them arose from a piece Watt wrote on race, which he thought should not be made into a political issue. Macleod maintained that it *was* a political issue, at least in the Birmingham area, and must be treated as such.

When Watt left to work elsewhere, Macleod engaged Alan Watkins to replace him. Watkins was an able journalist who also happened to be a socialist. He wrote later that Macleod had given him 'that most valuable of journalistic gifts, freedom'. Every Wednesday morning the editor enacted a pantomime of horror as Watkins brought in his weekly article: 'Oh God,' he groaned, 'the moment I dread.' Then: 'Must you really say that about Ted? Well, if you must, I suppose you must.' The journalist in Macleod enjoyed the barbs which the politician winced to see inserted.

Another new recruit was Hilary Spurling, aged twenty-three and beginning her first job as a journalist. Macleod asked her to do a piece about all-in wrestling which, he informed her, was one of his passions; if he once started to watch it on television, he was caught for the whole afternoon; he wanted to know if the agonising struggles he saw on the screen were genuine or faked. As she had never been to a wrestling match, he acted one for her, heaving and grunting behind his desk in the most alarming way. 'It was a magnificently humorous performance,' she recalled later 'and, as I afterwards found out, completely realistic, besides being so frightening that I asked whether it was perhaps unwise to send a girl.' Macleod replied: 'If we sent a man, they'd screw his head off.'

Hilary Spurling's story illustrates a picture of Macleod which many people at Gower Street remember: 'He had a way of bringing his whole attention to bear, of making you feel that you were the one person he wanted to see, and of ending an interview so that you felt, however brisk it had been, that business had been done, witty things had been said on both sides (which on his side was certainly true) and the whole day somehow much improved. I liked him enormously and so, I think, did everyone else. Certainly the *Spectator* was often a very gay place in his day.' Time was never wasted, but the atmosphere was usually light-hearted and often hilarious. Macleod was not concerned about the hours his staff kept or the holidays they took as long as their work was effectively done. He assumed they enjoyed it as much as he did.

Visitors to the board room came and went: politicians, columnists, lobby correspondents, Americans such as Walter Lippmann, African leaders, or people like Leo Baron reporting what they had seen in South Africa or Rhodesia. The *Spectator*'s contributors were always welcome, including Nicholas Davenport and Jean Robertson, both avowed socialists, who derived much pleasure from their association with their Conservative editor. Randolph Churchill was another favourite contributor whose torrent of telegrams from all over the world must have consumed most of the profit he derived from his *Spectator* articles.

Macleod arrived late at the office, stayed there for the morning and usually went to the House of Commons in the afternoon. He cleared his desk quickly, and dealt with even the most difficult problems at once. Nothing was left for the next day. He saw his staff separately or occasionally in small groups. He worked fast and wrote fast, almost always in longhand. His letters were usually very short. In the early days he visited the printers, but he soon understood the lay-out requirements and thereafter ceased to concern himself with the technical and production aspects of the paper.

Macleod was a good journalist and a competent editor. He might even have become a great editor. His political experience and prestige gave added insight and authority to his editorials, but he did not display the intellectual pyrotechnics which some had expected. His articles were remarkable not so much for original thought as for their grasp of important issues. He did not regard political questions as subjects for enlivening journalistic debate; for him they were about the exercise of power. He was not an intellectual in the accepted sense of the word, and he did not produce the flow of ideas which many would consider the main purpose of a serious weekly newspaper. He was, more often, the knowledgeable man of affairs, concerned with the solution of practical problems.

As editor of the *Spectator*, Iain Macleod was not an innovator. He took the paper's format as he found it and was content to work within it. He made some minor changes, such as the introduction of a chess column and a crossword puzzle, and he enjoyed expressing his own irreverence and sense of fun, sometimes affectionately and sometimes impatiently, towards revered national institutions, but he did so within the framework he had inherited. He had little interest in the arts section of the paper, and although he sometimes reviewed books of political memoirs, he left everything else to his efficient literary editor, David Rees, and never interfered. In his own contributions there were occasional romantic outbursts, but for the most part Macleod was circumspect and realistic in his political attitudes. The period was useful to him in widening his outlook in areas with which he might not otherwise have bothered.

The Spectator's Notebook, which he wrote under the pseudonym of Quoodle, was Macleod's most characteristic and effective contribution to the paper. He chose the name with no thought of concealment and indeed the column was written in a style which proclaimed its authorship in every paragraph. It was very successful journalism – terse and pithy and readable. He liked to dive straight into each subject and polish it off in about a hundred words, which usually included some comic flashes or typically sardonic observations. He was never pompous or evasive, and his economy of language and directness of expression were models of the journalistic art. Quoodle was always crisp and to the point, and often endearingly boyish. He took the pen name from G. K. Chesterton's lines in 'The Song of Quoodle':

> *And Quoodle here discloses*
> *All things that Quoodle can.*

In fact he disclosed very little in the sense of revealing inside knowledge or confidential information, but he disclosed much about himself. Re-

THE WHITE COTTAGE

POTTERS BAR

HERTFORDSHIRE

POTTERS BAR 52381

25 . 10 .

My dear Nigel.

As you will see I have written to the Times. I have also written to Willy and said that if you go I go. And so I will.

Ever

Iain

Facsimile of a letter from Macleod to the author, 1969. ('Willy' refers to William Whitelaw, then Conservative Chief Whip)

A meeting of the Shadow Cabinet. Extreme left is Iain Macleod, in conversation with Edward Heath

reading the column brings back to my mind the style of his conversation, indeed of his personality, more vividly than almost anything else. It is as though he is in the room, talking, arguing, commenting, and I can almost see his smile, sometimes wry, sometimes mischievous, lighting his whole face.

He wrote: 'A columnist has a number of unfair advantages. He can inflict his enthusiasms and his prejudices on his readers.' And he did. The enthusiasms covered almost all forms of sport, with cricket in the first place and rugger a close second. How he would have enjoyed, John Arlott's well-written biography of that great Yorkshire fast bowler Fred Trueman[4], whom he so greatly admired. Joan Baylis recalls that during a test match all work in the board room was done to the continuous accompaniment of the commentaries from the small transistor radio on the editor's desk. No appointments were ever made on the afternoon of a Calcutta Cup match or on Derby Day.

Macleod's favourite targets included the BBC and its then Director-General, Sir Hugh Greene, and many of the political activities of Harold Wilson. But he also used the column to support any good cause in which he had become interested. In his Quoodle *vale* on December 31, 1965, he recorded: 'For me, the name stays as the symbol of two very happy years; of many friendships; of my attempt to prove the truth of something Lord Beaverbrook said in his last speech on his eighty-fifth birthday, that politics and journalism are closely allied.'

At least a third of the *Spectator*'s leading articles in Macleod's time were written by the editor, and he also contributed quite frequently in his own name. He wrote quickly and fluently, and enjoyed it, although his neat, clipped prose was often produced under conditions which would have defeated the concentration of most writers. Many of his articles were composed while he was watching a sporting programme on the television, and he wrote others in bed on Sunday mornings. Most were about politics, including his views on foreign policy and an analysis of the task of the Chairman of the Conservative Party. Occasionally there would be reminiscences like his vivid, personal account of the Normandy beaches, written for the twentieth anniversary of D-day.

Unlike many men who have mastered the art of public speaking, Macleod was instinctively aware of the difference in style required by the written word. He seldom confused the resounding phrases which would inspire an audience with those which would read well in print.

4 Published by Eyre and Spottiswoode, 1971.

Despite his competence as an editor and his skill as a writer, Macleod was never more than a visitor to journalism. His career had suffered a set-back, but his roots had remained at Westminster, his hopes were still fixed on Whitehall, and during the second year of his editorship he was increasingly concerned to reconstruct his life at the centre of politics. His duties on the front bench and his weekend speaking engagements and television appearances began to occupy more of his time after he rejoined the Shadow Cabinet in November 1964, and when he became Shadow Chancellor the following summer it was clear that he would have to give up the *Spectator* and concentrate on his new responsibilities. In October 1965 he announced that he would leave the paper at the end of the year: 'I feel the job I have now been given is of such importance,' he said, 'that it would be unfair to the *Spectator* to continue as its editor.'

The Christmas celebrations at Gower Street were combined with a farewell party. Speeches were made and Macleod was presented with a complete set of Edmund Burke in its original leather bindings, for which Quentin Blake had designed a book-plate showing a trail of galley proofs lying across the editorial chair. On December 30th Iain Macleod walked out of the board room and down the stairs to his waiting car. No one was about, for it was a Thursday, the quiet afternoon when the paper has gone to press. After the clamour of his arrival two years before, it was a curiously subdued departure.

Macleod had not achieved all that Gilmour had hoped for from his appointment. The circulation, when he left, was not much higher than when he arrived and it would be an exaggeration to claim that he had made the paper a new force in politics; but he had done well in an un-accustomed role and had made a refreshing and distinctive contribution to weekly journalism. Soon afterwards Gilmour sold the *Spectator* and, although Macleod continued to write for it from time to time, he was now swimming strongly again in the main stream of public life. He was back in the world he loved.

CHAPTER 15

In Opposition: Spokesman on Steel and Shadow Chancellor 1964-1966

~~~~~~~

In the general election of 1964, Alec Douglas-Home fought a gallant campaign in an atmosphere of heckling and sometimes near-hooliganism which must have been distasteful to him. He was often denied a hearing but he always behaved with dignity and courage. When every vote had been counted, the new Labour Government had a majority of thirteen over the Conservatives and of only four over all other parties combined.

There were some who blamed Home, unfairly I thought, for the Tory defeat; others attributed it to the defection of Macleod and Powell. In so narrow a result there were no doubt a number of contributory factors. But the main reason for the Labour victory was that Conservative governments had been in power for thirteen years and the electorate wanted a change This enabled Harold Wilson to capture at least part of the middle ground. Iain Macleod went to the heart of the matter when he said: 'I look to the centre – the centre which decides elections. . . . For the first time in five elections our grip on the centre has weakened. We must offer something better because we believe in something better.' He never blamed the voters for the defeat of his party, because he believed in the judgement and good sense of the British people.

With typical generosity, but also because the party needed Macleod's skill in debate, Alec Home invited Iain to resume his place on the Conservative Front Bench and to rejoin the Shadow Cabinet. He accepted the offer without hesitation. He knew there was a long haul ahead for the party and there was no point in sitting idle on the back benches. Once he had decided to remain in politics he realised that he had to work his passage back and prepare again for government when the opportunity came.

Macleod asked Home if he could be Opposition spokesman on steel because he thought the nationalisation of the industry would be the most controversial issue in the new Parliament and would give him the best chance of using his debating ability to rout the socialists in argument and, in the process, to restore his own reputation with the Tory rank and file. It seemed a good idea at the time, but as early as November 12th, he was writing to Home to say that Wilson would probably take a long time to bring the Steel Bill before the House 'if indeed he ever does. Certainly I don't expect it before, say, March. I do hope therefore that . . . you will regard me as available for general duties, whatever they may be. . . .' As things turned out the Government did not attempt to nationalise the industry on a majority of four and Macleod made only two speeches as spokesman on steel, one of which was almost the only bad speech he ever made in the House of Commons. The industry wanted to be free of state control, but at the same time to enjoy a state monopoly. Macleod did not think it could be denationalised, and he never established a good rapport with its leaders.

After over a decade in government a party does not take easily to Opposition. Shadow Ministers missed the day-to-day information and the machine which provided it. They were accustomed to being serviced by large departmental staffs and the abrupt transition to one private secretary, or the share of one, and the assistance of a small team at the Conservative Research Department, was not an easy one. Ex-Ministers were full of confidence for their first month or two in Opposition because they knew more about the problems of Government than their successors, but this situation was rapidly reversed as the new Ministers became more knowledgeable and the Conservative Front Bench became less up-to-date. Moreover the Conservative Party disliked opposition and was therefore not very good at it. By contrast, the Socialists were the party of protest and many of them were happier criticising than governing.

Alec Home's personal position was not an easy one. He had been a good Prime Minister and could have continued in that role for another Conservative Parliament, but he was less successful in Opposition. The state of the economy was the predominant issue of the day and he was no economist. His whole background and departmental experience had been confined, except for four years as Minister of State in the Scottish Office, to foreign and Commonwealth affairs. His endearing modesty in saying that he needed matchsticks to work out economic problems did not give people much confidence, and he was insufficiently combative in the House of Commons to restore the morale and arouse the enthusiasm of the Parliamentary Party.

The Tory pack wanted blood. They wanted their leaders to show them game and they hoped that Alec Home would take on Harold Wilson and beat him on the floor of the House of Commons. This was not Home's strong suit. He is a good speaker and is widely liked and respected on both sides of the Chamber, but he has never been an outstanding debater and Wilson was often too quick for him. Perhaps realising his own limitations in Opposition, he seldom went in to bat and, when he did, scarcely ever made many runs. Critical murmurs gradually gathered strength in the lobbies and corridors of Parliament and the press publicised the growing discontent and fanned the flames.

Alec Douglas-Home was sensitive to the criticism that his election as Leader of the Party had been undemocratic, and in February 1965 he announced a new method for choosing his successor.[1] It followed, broadly, the system already used in the Labour Party, by which the Leader is elected by the votes of the Parliamentary Party in the House of Commons.

Soon after the 1964 election Humphry Berkeley had suggested to Macleod that a serious attempt should be made to restore him to a central position in the party. Berkeley offered the services of David Rogers as a full-time personal assistant whose salary was to be paid by Berkeley's merchant bank. A small group of Conservative MPs met from time to time to plan the strategy. One of these sessions took place over dinner in my house in Lord North Street; one at the home of Barney Hayhoe (MP for Heston and Isleworth since 1970) and others in a flat Iain had taken off St James's Street.

At no time did any member of this group, least of all Macleod himself, contemplate the overthrow of Alec Home. Indeed, apart from considerations of loyalty to Home, it would have suited Iain far better if Alec's resignation had been delayed. The object of the operation was to put Macleod in a better position to gain the succession when, in course of time, Home decided to retire from public life. But the essence of the exercise was that there should be plenty of time. Macleod was not yet acceptable as a potential leader to the centre of the party, let alone to the right wing, and it took several sessions of Parliament and many attacking

1 Humphry Berkeley was one of the critics and had sent a memorandum to Sir Alec Douglas-Home which appears as an appendix in George Hutchinson's biography of Edward Heath, together with the new procedure laid down by Douglas-Home. But the resemblance between the two documents is in fact coincidental because consideration of a new method of selecting the Leader of the Party, on these lines, had been going on for some time.

speeches in Opposition before he was forgiven for declining to serve in Home's 1963 Cabinet and for the *Spectator* article three months later.

During the early summer of 1965 newspaper denigration of Home's leadership grew steadily more strident and even a less sensitive man would have found it hard to endure. To Alec Home, upon whom the leadership had been thrust by Macmillan, the game of power simply wasn't worth the candle of criticism. On Thursday, July 22nd, he announced his resignation as Leader of the Party to a crowded end-of-term meeting of the 1922 Committee. Few Members wanted him to go, but he had thought the matter over carefully and he made it clear that his decision was irrevocable. Many of us left Room 14 depressed and a little ashamed that a leader we loved and admired had been forced to retire owing to pressure from the press and perhaps from a few malcontents in the party, who did not include Heath, Maudling or Macleod.

Once again a leadership crisis had arisen in the Tory Party. But this time, owing to the changes made by Home in the method of election, the matter was much less painfully resolved. Macleod knew that he had no chance of being chosen and he issued an immediate statement saying he was not a candidate. Heath, Maudling and Powell put their names forward.

It was clear that the contest lay between Heath and Maudling. Heath had two advantages: As Shadow Chancellor he had just led the Opposition with spirit and success against the 1965 Finance Bill. His name was in the news and his Parliamentary standing had never been higher. By comparison Reggie Maudling had slipped back a little and he was not at that time much in the public eye. But the election was a close one and an important factor in Heath's favour was the brisker, more efficient and much more comprehensive campaign quickly mounted by his supporters, led by Peter Walker and Anthony Kershaw. Walker had been a leading member of the group working for Macleod, but when he realised that Iain had no chance, he went to see him in the most straightforward way and told him he was transferring his support to Heath. Macleod, who had already decided not to stand, fully endorsed Walker's decision and there was no hard feeling between them.

Despite their old friendship, Iain did not cast his own vote for Reggie Maudling when the ballot was taken. He voted for Heath because he thought he would make a stronger, tougher leader both in Opposition and in Government. Heath's biographer, George Hutchinson, believed that Macleod's decision not to stand for the leadership presented it to

Heath, 'for almost to a man his followers switched to Heath . . . the best estimate is that he [Macleod] would have received forty-five votes. But he would have deprived Heath of such vital support that victory would in all probability have gone to Maudling.'[2]

The new Leader of the Opposition announced the appointment of Iain Macleod as Shadow Chancellor of the Exchequer on August 4th. Macleod was not an economist and had never been interested in what he regarded as a somewhat arid science; but, as the *Economist* pointed out: 'Mr Macleod has something of the first importance to get his sharp little teeth into.' He worked hard that summer to master the subject, and enlisted the help of younger friends like Peter Walker, who spent many successive briefing weekends at Potters Bar. He wrote to David Howell: 'I have much to learn quickly, but then I learn quickly.' He knew he had been given the key position in the Shadow Cabinet and he appreciated the opportunity to prepare plans for the reform of the whole tax structure of Britain. He had long deplored a situation in which most men, however able and hard-working, could not build up out of income enough capital to retire on or to leave to their children. He believed that 'this was something that a radical Conservative Government, or indeed any Conservative Government, ought to put right'.

Macleod succeeded Heath as chairman of the Opposition's Economic Policy Group, which concentrated initially on the reform of the tax system and especially on the discouraging burden of personal taxation. The Group's first draft report was ready by September 23rd, and its broad conclusions were incorporated in the policy statement 'Putting Britain Right Ahead', which Edward Heath presented to the 1965 party conference. It included among others Terence Higgins (now Financial Secretary to the Treasury), Patrick Jenkin (now Chief Secretary to the Treasury) and Arthur Cockfield, who were joined later by Reginald Maudling, Keith Joseph and David Montagu, chairman of Samuel Montagu and Co. Ltd. Other Shadow Ministers, such as Robert Carr, attended meetings at which policy in their own areas of responsibility was being discussed.

Macleod believed that one of the major defects in the British tax system was the penalties it imposed on the pacemakers, the salaried managers and entrepreneurs, on whom economic growth depended, owing to the excessive levels of tax, up to a marginal rate of $91\frac{1}{4}\%$, levied on the higher

2 The *Spectator*, July 31, 1970.

income brackets. This could be remedied simply and quite inexpensively in course of time by providing that no one should pay more than an effective rate of 12s 6d in the pound in income and surtax combined. Macleod thought the two taxes should be merged and that both should be collected through PAYE. The small or would-be capitalist presented a more difficult problem. The differential against investment income was equivalent to a tax on capital of $\frac{1}{2}$% per annum at £20,000 and nearly 1% at £100,000. Yet it fell thereafter to $\frac{1}{4}$% on £1 million. So the system was heavily weighted against the small capitalist, as compared to the millionaire. At one stage some members of the Economic Policy Group were attracted by the idea of a wealth tax. They wanted to sweep away stamp duties and the capital gains tax, to halve estate duty and to introduce instead a single graduated tax on capital.

This suggestion had the merit of mitigating both the near-lottery effect of death duties and unduly severe penalities on changes in investment; but the proposal to tax capital provoked immediate criticism as being a dangerous innovation which could be exploited by a socialist government. The wealth tax rates required were moderate and ranged from $\frac{1}{2}$% on £25,000 to 2% on £1 million or more, with household chattels exempt, but the idea met with strong resistance from some members of the Economic Policy Group, which was reinforced when it was put to members of other policy groups at a Swinton[3] weekend. Another suggestion was to exempt from death duties estates up to £25,000 in value and to limit the duty to a maximum of 50% at the £1 million or higher level, with the addition of a small gifts tax to discourage evasion.

The policy was designed to encourage the acquisition of capital, to simplify and reduce direct taxation and partially to eliminate hardship due to inflation by removing, for the benefit of retired people, the differential against investment income. The Policy Group's report was based on the premise that economic growth depends upon human energy and ingenuity and that the tax system in Britain had discouraged these qualities and must therefore be changed: 'Too much has been taken and the dice has been too heavily loaded against initiative and enterprise. The proposals we put forward are designed to produce a fundamental change and to recreate in our economy the conditions in which growth will flourish.'

3 Swinton Conservative College was opened in 1948. The widely varied lecture courses and discussion weekends on all aspects of party policy are attended by about two thousand students each year.

The Shadow Cabinet considered carefully the package proposals Macleod's committee had formulated and in particular the controversial wealth tax, which was strongly opposed on the grounds enunciated by William Pitt, that it was better to tax the fruit than the tree and that it would be a mistake for the party which supports capitalism to introduce a new tax on capital. It was also argued that it would be difficult to apply the tax to agricultural property, but impossible to exempt it; and that the tax would have to include valuable chattels. These objections were sufficiently valid to arouse serious doubts on political grounds and in the end the wealth tax proposal was abandoned.

The 1965 Conservative Party conference at Brighton gave Macleod an opportunity to restate his political philosophy: 'It is our clear intention throughout this document,' he said, referring to 'Putting Britain Right Ahead', to provide for 'choice in the social services; choice for the customer; choice for the individual; choice for the family.' His call was for a nation-wide capital-owning democracy, a vain dream under Socialism or with the existing levels of personal taxation. There was a limit to the amount of the national product which could be taken in public expenditure and a limit to the amount which could be put on personal taxation without a drop in efficiency and enterprise, and Britain was already beyond the limit.

Macleod made no precise commitments. The careful management of the economy and the repayment of debt must come first; but the road he would travel as Chancellor was clearly marked: taxes would be brought down, companies would be encouraged to distribute profits not needed for the provision of new plant, and the tax arrangements made in the 1965 Finance Act for overseas companies would not be continued. Macleod did not go into detail. He painted with a broad brush: 'The key to the door of excellence lies in a modern taxation policy. . . . We stand for humanity as well as efficiency, for compassion as well as competition and even the pursuit of excellence is but part of the pursuit of happiness. It is because I believe that we can meet this double challenge, to heart as well as to head, that I long for confrontation at the polls.'

The Economist commented on this speech: 'In the economic debate the conference was swept off its feet by that great voice of Mr Iain Macleod' promising a decrease in taxation and lambasting Labour's policy. Here was one of Mr Heath's hard-headed pacemakers, but with an additional gift of being able to point out some promised land to the faithful. No wonder Mr Heath beamed on him and no wonder that he beamed back in sheer happiness at his reception by the conference. It was the hour of the prodigal son.'

Macleod's powerful platform oratory, his gift for the vivid phrase and his good judgement in not giving hostages to fortune were all assets in Opposition, but he believed that the point and purpose of politics is the exercise of power. He thought opposition was sterile and disliked it. He regarded it merely as a time for preparation and he longed for the years of achievement.

George Brown published his short-lived and soon forgotten 'National Plan' on September 16, 1965, and Macleod described it as 'an infinitely depressing document' which contained no proposals 'to increase incentives, boost exports or help savings'. It was based on over-optimistic estimates of the country's economic growth which were never realised. The Chancellor had put a sharp curb on the economy in July and had destroyed in the process the basis on which the Plan had been worked out. George Brown was made to resemble the apocryphal politician who relied upon statistics rather as a homeward bound alcoholic relies upon a lamp post – more for support than for illumination!

The National Plan purported to set out the Labour Government's economic strategy for the next five years, but its target of a 25% growth over six years was not only never attained, it was also well short of what Labour leaders in Opposition had said was necessary if their own programme was to be carried out. Macleod was scornful: 'Industry is given the question and told to work out the answers,' he declared on television. In fact, it was worse than that. Industry had also been given the answer in terms of a growth rate and had been told to base their arithmetic upon it. But even a computer cannot produce the right answer if it is given the wrong information. A number of glaring mistakes soon became apparent, not least the '400,000 manpower gap'. The Plan worked on paper except that it required an extra 400,000 men who did not exist. The productivity target could not therefore be achieved. It was a classic case of 'planning by wish fulfilment'.[4]

The re-assembly of Parliament in the autumn gave Macleod the opportunity to voice these doubts and point out the factors which were certain to kill the Plan. He described Jim Callaghan's speech the day before as 'a blunt attack' on George Brown and added that Callaghan 'does not seem to realise that it is also an indictment of himself. We know . . . that earnings are going up much faster than productivity and have soared up

4 Conservative Campaign Guide, 1970.

by 8% in the first eight months of this year.' He thought that the prices and incomes policy 'has proved a fiasco' and that Callaghan 'seemed to delight in rubbing this in'.

Two days later the National Plan itself was debated in the House. Macleod pointed out that it was already inaccurate; it was vague about 1966, yet firm and precise about 1970. This was the reverse of a business plan 'which would be precise about next year and get increasingly more vague as one goes further ahead. . . . The Government's action in some-times pulling against the facts will increasingly try to make the facts conform to the Plan instead of the other way round. . . . What the First Secretary is putting before the House is not a plan, but a Party political document.' He quoted Lord Robens who had said: 'You can count me out as one of the people who are trying to reach the objectives of the National Plan as far as my industry is concerned.'

On November 17, 1965, Macleod supported the Opposition amend-ment in the debate on the Address. He had some caustic comments to make about the omission of steel nationalisation from the Queen's speech and about Liberal support for the Government: 'I congratulate the Prime Minister on the cheapest piece of political horse-trading this century,' he said: 'he has not even had to pay the price of the electoral pottage that the Liberal Party hoped for. . . .'[5] But his real target was the Government's prices and incomes policy. After a reference to Callaghan as 'the first Chancellor who has no responsibility for the economy',[6] he attacked George Brown. 'The First Secretary is hard at it putting forward his policy . . . he has gone to meeting after meeting, coming away triumphant each time with a scrap of paper – and we are seeing how effective those have been. . . . Like Pyrrhus, the First Secretary might well say: "If we have another such victory we are undone." ' The Government's record had been one of stagnant production and rampant inflation – 'stagflation', as Macleod described it.

On November 3rd Macleod had pointed out that 'we have two Ministries . . . headed by two very different characters. We have a

5 During the Recess there had been speculation about a Lib-Lab pact and Gerald Kaufman had flown a kite in the *New Statesman* on August 6th for conceding the Liberals the alter-native vote. But at the Labour Party conference in October Wilson rejected the idea of a pact and later talked adroitly of 'parallel courses' to justify Liberal support for the government.

6 The creation of George Brown's Department of Economic Affairs had split the fiscal and economic functions of the Treasury and handed over much of the latter to the new Ministry, thus reducing Callaghan's control of the economy.

Minister of long-term "go" and a Minister of short-term "stop".' Under a Tory administration the Chancellor was Chairman of the NEDC 'whereas now he is not even a member of it. The First Secretary plans busily away and just when he gets to the stage of galley proofs the Chancellor makes a nonsense of it all with his July measures.'

Although opposed to a statutory incomes policy Macleod was not against the sort of policy Maudling had operated. When Enoch Powell described this as silly, transparent and dangerous nonsense which 'in any relevant and useful sense does not and cannot exist, except perhaps in a Communist dictatorship,' Macleod made it clear that he disagreed: 'Nor do I see any logical stopping point,' he went on, 'between such a belief and an abandonment of all collective bargaining and indeed association. We cannot travel the road back.'[7] But he did doubt the TUC's ability to co-operate effectively. The policy could only succeed if inflationary wage claims were not pressed or, if pressed, were not bought off either by the Government or the employers. And he was anxious to eliminate the restrictive practices which bedevilled some industries: 'Deeds not words will impress me,' he said, 'our prayers are a declaration of intent to live the good life. It is what we do, not what we say, that will be entered in the book.'

By September 1965 the entries in the book made depressing reading. Figures issued by the Ministry of Labour in the first week of September showed that average weekly earnings had risen by more than twice the 3.5% norm in the six months since Labour's victory in the general election. The Government's decision to strengthen the incomes policy reflected American anxiety and was the prelude to a massive short-term loan of $1000 million. Temporarily the pound was safe, but Britain was deeper in debt.

By November 1965 the continuing deficit on the balance of payments induced the Government, despite its promises to EFTA, to renew the 10% import surcharge for a further year. The proposal was debated on November 29th and Macleod listed the Government's misdeeds and mistakes: we had angered our EFTA partners; we had broken no less than nine treaties and were continuing to do so; we were the most vulnerable nation in the world to retaliation in this sphere; and we had more to gain than any other country by lowering trade barriers. He threw back at the Chancellor Callaghan's own earlier dictum that a protected economy in time becomes an uncompetitive economy. The Chancellor had said the

7 December 4, 1964.

surcharge would be temporary. 'How long is temporary?' Macleod demanded. 'The Rt Hon Gentleman invites us to accept Humpty Dumpty's definition: "When I use a word it means just what I choose it to mean – neither more nor less.' The surcharge had added to the pressure on wages, had damaged Britain's commercial integrity and had weakened her bargaining position. He advised the Opposition to divide against the motion.

Macleod was never entirely at home with the problems of the economy. He was neither an economist nor an academic and trying to manage a situation he was not managing or enunciating theories about it, seemed to him a waste of time. He would listen to a theoretical argument without showing much interest, but he would seize unerringly on the nugget of hard, new information from which it derived. He was not always constructive in discussing economic issues and the pundits, even some of his own friends in the City considered this a weakness. He did not agree. He preferred to concentrate on matters which could be dealt with in a practical way and which would not slip from his control. Tax reform was clearly the most important area in that category and he made it his main priority.

Macleod spent much time in the early months of 1966 on Conservative plans for the reform of company taxation. Callaghan had brought in the corporation tax in the 1965 budget and the arguments which Heath, who himself took over the chairmanship of the Economic Policy Group after the 1966 election, had used against it inevitably influenced the work of the Group. But they did not wish to revert to the position in which two different sets of taxes had been imposed on companies. They therefore advised that corporation tax should be retained but modified to remove the distinction it drew between distributed and undistributed profits. In principle Macleod could see no reason for discriminating between the two; but while distributed profits could be taxed at a rate set by the individual liabilities of the recipients, it was difficult to find a corresponding average rate for the undistributed profits of companies and almost impossible to conceive of differing rates for different companies. In the end the Group admitted frankly that the figure must be arbitrary and they set it, in relation to the Exchequer's needs, at 50%.

The genuine advantages of the new tax had been retained, but Macleod believed that the modifications the Policy Group recommended gave a more generous measure of relief for taxes paid overseas, a more equitable treatment of dividends and a boost to the value of investment allowances.

There was a further uncovenanted by-product. By quite independent reasoning the Group had arrived at the same sort of arrangement as the Neumark Report had just recommended for adoption by the European Economic Community. To a party committed to entry into the Common Market, this was a considerable advantage.

It was not enough to content Macleod and his colleagues. They shared the common Conservative belief that, however necessary it might be to tax profits, to do so was bound to penalise the efficient. They wanted to use the tax system to bring home costs, especially labour costs, to the producer and so induce him to use his resources in the most economical way. This line of thought tied in closely with the work that another policy group was doing on the financing of the social services.

Macleod had always disliked the socialist bias towards universalism in the structure of the Welfare State. It was thirteen years since, in collaboration with Enoch Powell he had written *The Social Services – Needs and Means*, but he had not lost his interest in the subject and the ideas he had put forward in 1952 were by now widely accepted in the Tory Party. The reasoning remained the same – the importance of concentrating scarce resources where they were most needed – but the development of the affluent society had altered the perspective and there was a growing realisation that what the Exchequer could afford was not the same as what the people could afford and that the dichotomy between welfare and earnings had no basis in reality.

The new approach was an attempt to transform the Welfare State into the 'welfare society' and even within the Labour Party there were some who were prepared to grasp this nettle. Indeed, Macleod had himself welcomed Labour's conversion to a wage related superannuation scheme: 'It is pleasant to see our opponents being converted to the capitalist system,' he observed, 'and to a proposal which in fact intends to carry into provision for retirement the inequalities of earnings in working life.'[8] The income guarantee proposed in Labour's official policy seemed to imply conversion to the case Macleod had argued for so long, but was quickly forgotten once Harold Wilson's Government was in office.

Macleod had been critical in his speech to the Conservative Conference in 1963 when he declared: 'The other parties may be content to put putty in any crack that may appear or perhaps to replace a brick. We must ask a much more fundamental question: Should the wall of social security be the same height for everyone? Does the Beveridge approach make sense

8 CPC publication: *The Future of the Welfare State*, p. 18.

twenty years on, when the whole of his plans were built on the assumption of an $8\frac{1}{2}$% unemployment rate in the postwar years whereas, in fact, it has averaged under 2%? Does it make sense when every year more and more of those retiring are covered by non-state pensions and other benefits? We must ask ourselves whether a new wall should not be built. . . . I sense a feeling in this Conference that we may be doing less than we ought to do for those with special needs and special problems because we insist on providing a flat level of benefits for everybody. It is on these lines that we are working. I am convinced that they will lead us to proposals more modern, more realistic and better attuned to our concept of society's care for the individual.'

Macleod wanted private shoulders to bear a larger share of the burden of social insurance. He realised that the state could not provide, for everyone, the middle-class standards which were now demanded and that, if it sought to do so, there would inevitably be 'a slow decline in standards, which is in fact what the National Plan forecasts, or inconceivable rates of taxation. . . .' He thought that too high a proportion of the cost of the social services was met out of general taxation and that social security for the employee should be regarded as part of the cost of labour and recovered as such rather than by a tax on profits.

As a director of a group of pharmaceutical companies, I pointed out to Iain Macleod the prejudicial effect of high rates of tax on innovating industries, upon which the future of Britain so largely depends. Patrick Jenkin took up the point when he spoke later at a Conservative economic seminar: 'The essence of innovation,' he said, 'is that the innovator will make a pioneer's profit – this is the incentive for him . . . but of course if you have a high rate of tax on profits, you are taxing the extra profit which he makes at a penalty rate. . . .' It was small wonder, Jenkin thought, that Britain failed to take advantage of her inventions. 'It may well be,' he added, 'that our tax system has more to blame for this than we generally acknowledge.'

As it was Conservative policy to reduce direct taxation,[9] the Economic Policy Group had to consider ways of increasing indirect taxation in order to sustain the revenue. It was clear that we should have to adopt a value added tax if Britain entered the Common Market, so the Group gave careful consideration to the arguments for and against this measure.

Initially Macleod and his colleagues could see little advantage in a retail

9 There was in fact a net reduction in taxation as a whole of £1400 million in the first full year of Conservative government.

sales tax as compared with an extension of the purchase tax. There would have to be many exemptions and purchase tax, combined with the existing duties on drink, tobacco and petrol, seemed easier to administer. There was, however, the major argument in favour of the value added tax that it could be rebated on exports. It was decided to leave the issue open for the time being.

In the meantime Macleod had been doing some organisational work for the party in an endeavour to increase the effectiveness of the Young Conservative Movement. Lord Blakenham set up a committee under Macleod's chairmanship in December 1964, which produced its report a year later. The appointment was a good one because there was no one in the party hierarchy more acceptable to the YCs. Macleod was an articulate idealist who could put into words what so many of them felt about injustice, compassion and the under-privileged in our society. He understood how they thought and they responded to his leadership.

At each meeting of his committee, he concentrated attention on only one or two items and dealt with these very thoroughly, extracting every ounce of information and experience from those who gave evidence and from the committee members themselves. Elizabeth Steel, National Vice Chairman of the YCs from 1965–67, was impressed by the way in which he drew out contributions from even the most junior members of his team, and then, after he had listened patiently to a long discussion, by his skill in drawing all the threads together and guiding and summarising the conclusions. He was very much a working chairman, and personally wrote the final draft of the report which appeared in December 1965.

He was president of the National Young Conservatives for the year 1965/66, during which he visited every area and undertook innumerable speaking engagements.

Until August 1965 the political tide had been running with the Opposition, but in mid-September both Gallup and the NOP recorded a lead for Labour. Macleod knew that Wilson would not miss the opportunity to increase his precarious majority in the House of Commons and publicly prophesied that the election would be held in March 1966.

The Conservative Party's prospects did not look encouraging. The work of the policy groups was beginning to come forward, the candidates list had been overhauled and Edward Du Cann, as Chairman of the Party, had begun a reform of its organisation. But Central Office was short of money and in any case did not feel that the electorate was yet in a mood to respond favourably to an intensive publicity campaign.

Outwardly Macleod was sceptical about the accuracy of public opinion polls and he was genuinely concerned about their long-term effect upon politics;[10] but he never completely ignored them and, although he placed greater reliance upon his own instinct and experience, he was perhaps more influenced by the polls than he admitted even to himself. And he was never opposed to the market research projects which Du Cann was organising at the Conservative Central Office.

Two by-elections took place in November 1965. Predictably, the Conservatives held Westminster and the Government Erith. In each constituency the Liberals fared badly[11] and Macleod commented: 'The most significant thing about Erith is the disastrous showing by the Liberals. Westminster and Erith, taken together, are a clear warning to Mr Grimond that votes cast in 1964 were not cast for Socialism and he is heading for suicide if he believes he can trade the Liberal Party to Mr Wilson.'

On the same day as the poll at Erith, Ian Smith made his unilateral declaration of independence in Rhodesia and that evening Harold Wilson retaliated with the best television broadcast he has ever made, condemning the illegal act of the government in Salisbury. As at any moment of crisis, there was an instinctive movement of public opinion in Britain in support of the Government. And the split in the Conservative Party on the Rhodesia issue over the next few months was to prove an embarrassing prelude to the 1966 general election.

The dissolution of the Central African Federation had left Britain with a difficult problem. Alec Douglas-Home and Duncan Sandys had laid down the five principles[12] before leaving office in October 1964 and the Conservative Opposition supported the incoming Government's warning to Smith about the consequences of an UDI which, they agreed, 'would have no legal validity'. At the Conservative Conference at Brighton in October 1965 Lord Salisbury tried to commit the party against sanctions. Alec Home argued that a rejection of sanctions at that time could only be

10 Macleod wrote a devastating review in *The Times* of Stoke's and Butler's book *Political Change in Britain*. (Macmillan, 1969).
11 In Westminster the Liberal share of the poll fell from 11% to 6.3%; and at Erith from 14.4% to 7.2%.
12 These were the principles on which successive British Governments of both parties agreed that Rhodesian independence could be based.

regarded as a direct encouragement to the white Rhodesians to declare their independence and the conference endorsed this view.

In a speech at Amherst, Massachusetts, Macleod had said bluntly that UDI would be an act of open rebellion and that 'there must be a clearer promise of an African majority than the 1961 Constitution affords.' But in a television interview with Robin Day on October 17th he refused to be drawn any further. He had no wish to put a gloss on what Home had said only two evenings earlier and he endorsed Heath's closing speech to the 1965 conference declining to give the Government a blank cheque: 'The handling of the negotiations is for them and all our experience tells us . . . that the thing to do is never to stop talking . . . in Churchill's famous phrase "jaw jaw is better than war war". . . . And so we have made our statements all the time with that in mind.'

Macleod did not wish to use force, which he thought impracticable, against the Rhodesian Government; and he explained his attitude to sanctions: 'If there be an illegal act, there may well be certain consequences that flow automatically from that fact. That is one thing. Those are what one might call automatic sanctions. But then there are the more penal sanctions . . . to use Lord Salisbury's words, and it was on this point that he and those who supported him put their point of view, with a good deal of support from the conference and indeed from the Conservative Party as a whole.'

Macleod had not committed himself, nor could he commit the party, against penal sanctions although he was doubtful of their wisdom; but he approved of Wilson's attempts to reach a settlement and contrasted them with the abortive Commonwealth Peace Mission to Vietnam: 'Harold Wilson's initiatives are right,' he told an audience at Greenock on October 22nd, 'and I hope very much in this Rhodesian mission that something . . . can be plucked out of the failures of the past.' But it was too late and on November 11th Smith declared Rhodesia independent.

In the House of Commons next day the Prime Minister gave notice of an immediate debate and made it clear that the Rhodesian Constitution would be suspended as soon as an enabling Act could be passed. Heath condemned the UDI and the Conservative Party did not dissent from his statement. But in a speech in Liverpool that evening Macleod again stressed the distinction between the measures which flowed automatically from an illegal act and those that did not. 'With the former I have no quarrel,' he reiterated, 'but the latter . . . will have to be probed very deeply before the Conservative Party commits itself.'

The tone was beginning to harden and in the debate in Parliament which followed, Heath expressed the view that sanctions should not be 'punitive'. He questioned the need to suspend the constitution and reserved his position on individual Orders made under the enabling Bill. Wilson gave an immediate assurance that force would not be used; but there were already signs of criticism from both sides of the Conservative Party. Its right wing members felt that Heath was going too far in his endorsement of the Prime Minister's policy and the left wing that he was not going far enough.

Those of us in the Tory Party who had liberal attitudes on Commonwealth issues had, ever since his Colonial Secretaryship, looked to Macleod as our natural leader. We were distressed and disturbed that he seemed to be out of sympathy with our anxiety to safeguard the rights of the majority race in Rhodesia and with our wish to bring about a change in the policy of Smith and his colleagues in Salisbury. We wanted to hear his arguments against the use of economic sanctions. We understood the damage which disunity could inflict on the party in a pre-election period and we were genuinely reluctant to oppose the leadership on this divisive matter. Many of us hoped he could persuade us that he was right. I therefore invited him to come to my house on December 8th to meet privately twenty or twenty-five of our colleagues who felt strongly on this subject and answer our questions. We were all friends and admirers of Iain's, but it was a painful evening. He dealt patiently, but to most of us unconvincingly, with every point we made. But we could not change his mind any more than he could change ours and I wished afterwards that I had not arranged the meeting. It did not alter our affection and admiration for him, but it shook temporarily our sense of sympathy and identity with his views.

On December 14th Macleod made the principal speech for the Opposition in a debate on two Government Orders which, in effect, froze the assets of the Reserve Bank of Rhodesia. In an earlier speech Julian Amery had pointed out that even at the time of Suez the Government had not frozen Egyptian assets. Macleod doubted whether the Orders were merely consequential; he thought they represented a change of policy. And he underlined the fact that this was 'the first time that there has been a default on British Commonwealth or Colonial Stock . . . I ask the Chief Secretary for a specific undertaking that the Government will meet the interest payments on Rhodesia loan stock.' He received no undertaking but he did not divide the House against the Orders. Indeed, he expressed the hope that 'we shall get through the whole of this Rhodesia crisis without a division.' Within a week the hope had proved vain.

On December 17th the Government imposed an oil embargo on Rhodesia, which split the Conservative Parliamentary Party three ways. To the right wing the oil Order was a penal sanction; to the left wing it seemed illogical to support minor sanctions and reject an important one which might prove effective. In an abortive attempt to hold the party together, Heath advised his followers to abstain; but at the end of the debate on December 21st, fifty Conservative back-benchers divided the House against the Order and another thirty-one of us voted in the Government lobby. We had told the Chief Whip beforehand that we hoped there would be no division, but that, if there was one, we must support the Order. Whitelaw did his best to persuade the right wing not to divide the House and he never reproached my friends and myself for our own action, although it was a desperate situation for him to see the Tory Party in such disarray. He was, on this as on every occasion, patient, understanding and tolerant and I have always considered him the best Chief Whip under whom I have served.

It was an unhappy period for the Conservative Party, and was not made easier by a public dispute on incomes policy between Maudling and Powell. Macleod did his best to put a good face on the situation by saying that the divisions in the party on the abolition of capital punishment and on Rhodesia were 'wholly to be welcomed . . .' as reflecting public opinion.

He sought to divert attention by criticism of the Liberals. Jo Grimond had just announced his decision to resign as their leader after the general election. Speaking at Chatham on January 4th Macleod claimed that this exposed 'the nakedness of the Liberal land . . . it has no more than a temporary relevance because of the paper-thin Socialist majority.'

In a television broadcast on January 19th he denounced the 'rising price of Socialism' for the housewives and concluded 'we simply can't afford it – can we?' *The Times* commented on his 'matey mastery of screen technique'. But whistling in the dark was an unprofitable pursuit and did nothing to reduce Labour's lead in the public opinion polls which was tempting Harold Wilson to go to the country.

In the House of Commons there were further instalments of Labour's economic planning, and on January 17th Callaghan announced that investment allowances would be replaced by investment grants. There was some disagreement between Reginald Maudling, the former Chancellor, and his shadow successor – Maudling favoured the allowance system while Macleod was sceptical of the whole concept of incentives to invest. But in Parliament Macleod could let himself go because no one on the Conservative side cared much for the new system. Not only were the grants less generous, but they discriminated against whole areas of industry, especially the service sector. In practice they justified Macleod's fears by subsidising the unprofitable and prompting capital intensive industries to move to development areas. They were an obvious target for Macleod's expenditure axe and have duly fallen to his successor.

There was no real thaw in the Government's economic policies. Indeed, Harold Wilson seemed almost to be making a virtue out of the prospect of a stern budget. Macleod reacted strongly: 'Mr Wilson has threatened the country with a tough budget,' he told the Young Conservatives at Eastbourne on February 5th, 'in fifteen months the Socialist Government has produced three tough budgets. Each one has failed in its objective of restraining demand, although vast burdens of extra taxation have been humped on our shoulders. . . . Production is stagnant, prices are soaring, competition and efficiency are impaired.'[13]

Two days later the Chancellor gave a further turn to the screw. Hire purchase controls were tightened, and in a speech in the House of Commons Jim Callaghan demanded restraint in private spending and forecast the indefinite continuation of the cuts in public expenditure announced in the previous July. Macleod described this as the Chancellor's fourth budget and added: 'The Rt Hon Gentleman justifies this and his other three budgets on the effect on the balance of payments. He has had the terms of trade very much in his favour. . . . Has he achieved his target of halving the 1964 deficit?'[14]

It was true that much of the improvement in the trade balance during 1965 had been due to an exceptionally rapid growth in world trade, which could not be expected to last. The economic situation was remarkable: the increase in unemployment which most economists had forecast as a result of the Government's earlier deflationary measures had not materialised and unemployment in fact dropped to below 1.2% in March. Nor was the voluntary incomes policy making any contribution to the solution of the immediate problems. The Bill embodying the early warning system was not introduced until February and there were signs

13 *The Times*, February 7, 1966.
14 *Hansard*, Cols. 215/216, February 8.

that the unions were moving quickly before any detailed scrutiny of their claims could begin. Average hourly earnings were running at a level more than 9% higher than in the previous year. Retail prices were rising more slowly at about 4% or 5%. Production was almost stagnant.

The failure of their measures to work on anything but production surprised Ministers, but they were not slow to see the electoral advantages. Very little of their legislation was yet in the pipeline for introduction in the House, although it could soon be displayed in the shop window of an electoral campaign. It seemed likely that there would be a long and unpopular Finance Bill to fill the second half of the Parliamentary calendar and it was not to be expected that Macleod would oppose it any less fiercely than Edward Heath had done the year before. Wilson's decision to go to the country did not therefore come as any surprise to the Shadow Cabinet, although they attempted to deter him by talk of running away from a difficult budget.

The last major move on the economic front was the creation of the Industrial Reorganisation Corporation, a statutory body financed by the State to help promote nationalisation, mergers and the re-structuring of industry. In a debate on February 15th, Macleod criticised the Government's measures: their new investment incentives were riddled with fallacies; while the IRC, dubbed 'Irc' – 'which is the proper name for this corporation' – by Iain Macleod, would lay the dead hand and distortions of Government control on some sectors of industry and would enable the Government to indulge in 'back-door nationalisation'. Macleod pointed out that the White Paper had promised that the corporation 'will not support ventures which have no prospect of achieving eventual viability'. 'With respect,' he commented, 'that is exactly like a newspaper announcing that in future its racing correspondents will only tip winners. . . .'[15]

Although Harold Wilson has since denied that Hull, North, affected his plans, the by-election there at the end of January was seen by both parties as a crucial indicator. The seat was the most marginal to fall vacant during the 1964 Parliament and needed little more than a 1% swing to result in a Conservative victory. Press reports up to the eve of the poll made it sound a possible Labour loss, and when Macleod went there on January 21st to speak for the Conservative candidate, Toby Jessel, he was in scornful vein and attacked with derision the bridge across the Humber as a 'political bribe' offered to the electors by Barbara Castle. Whether this promise made its contribution or not, there was in fact a 4.5% swing to

15 *Hansard*, Cols. 1228/1232, February 15, 1966. Vol.

Labour on January 27th. It was the largest swing obtained by any party in government since 1924 and, after it, Wilson could scarcely have avoided an appeal to the country to increase his precarious Parliamentary majority. Press speculation changed gear. It now became not whether but when.

The run-in to the 1966 election had not been propitious for the Tory Party, and it was difficult to devise the right tactics for the coming campaign. It was decided that Edward Heath should concentrate on projecting his new policies and should avoid attempts to destroy the Prime Minister's credibility. This could be left to other members of the Shadow Cabinet. It was hoped that this strategy would build Heath up as a man concerned about the nation's problems, while making Wilson seem more interested in the success of his party at the polls. This approach had unavoidable disadvantages. There was grumbling in the constituencies that the case against the Labour Government was being allowed to go by default; worse still, there was insufficient time before the election campaign began for the public to grasp and digest the wide range of new Conservative policies which were being presented for the first time.

On February 5th Heath produced what later became known as the Birmingham manifesto on the social services'. Five days later, at Hammersmith, he announced the Conservative housing programme. Macleod did not go beyond the broad outlines of the Conservative tax package already made public in *Putting Britain Right Ahead*. But on February 19th he gave notice of his intention to start an industrial guarantee corporation and a small business development bureau and he forecast a tax on gambling: 'I regard it as ludicrous,' he said, 'that our newest and most milkable industry, that of gambling, does not contribute much more to the national kitty and it will do so under a Conservative Chancellor.' But he believed in taxing the punter who bets off course more heavily than the man who has already spent money on going to the racecourse to see and support his selection. He understood that if attendances were to be improved on the horse and greyhound racecourses, in the face of the growing attraction of betting shops, it must be made less onerous to bet on the course.[16]

Conservative morale was still at a low ebb. The Shadow Cabinet had only just begun the task of converting the country to the new policies and their work was about to be tested before it was complete. Edward Heath outlined his plans for a positive campaign to the 1922 Committee on February 17th.

16 P. B. Lucas. Chairman of the GRA, to the author, August 27, 1970.

The avoidance of a threatened national railway strike cleared the stage for the poll, and on February 12th Emmanuel Shinwell, the Chairman of the Parliamentary Labour Party, publicly called for an early election. On the 16th Harold Wilson's staff let it be known that he had been presented with a case for going in the spring and it became apparent from the programme of House of Commons debates on the Welfare State and leasehold reform, announced for the remainder of the month, that an election was imminent.

Macleod was early in action. Two days before Wilson's announcement that polling day would be on March 31st, he highlighted the reasons for the Prime Minister's decision: 'We have not had an election in March in modern times. Mr Wilson only a few days ago was boasting about the success of his programme and warning us against a tough budget. Now suddenly he eats his words, runs away from the budget and ignores the convenience of the electorate. Why? There is only one reason: he hopes to snatch more power. . . . His sudden decision is a dramatic admission of the true weakness of our economic position. He dare not risk going on. He hopes that by a flood of new promises and by a daily bribe the old pledges will be forgotten. . . .'

It was to offset this sort of charge that the Prime Minister had already asked Callaghan to indicate to the House of Commons his broad budget judgement, and on Marsh 1st the Chancellor presented a reassuring picture of the improving balance of payments and said that the outstanding debt to the Federal Reserve Bank of New York had been repaid. He stated that he did not 'foresee the need for severe increases in taxation'. He made few specific commitments, but among them was his decision to tax betting and gaming and the long-deferred announcement of the mortage option scheme to help owner-occupiers.

Macleod replied with a savage attack, mainly directed against the Prime Minister:

'The more one studies and dissects the speech of the Chancellor, the more politically dishonest it is. . . . It is a classic example of the new sort of substitute government, in which if you are not able to do something, you say something. So we have White Papers instead of Bills, leaks instead of statements, and speeches instead of a budget. . . . I believe the Prime Minister is running away, because he hopes the running is good, just as the Socialists ran away in 1931 and 1951. So much for the gutsy purposive Government we hear so much about. . . . We are asked to congratulate the Government . . . they should not be congratulated, they should be certified. . . . The Chancellor has written himself a blank cheque and has undertaken to write in the figures later. . . . What we have had throughout this last sixteen months is a long, painful and costly education of the Chancellor. I deal with him; I do not deal with the First Secretary, because the First Secretary is a one-man national disaster area. I have some sympathy with the Chancellor, who has the Prime Minister on his shoulder all the time. No one knows what role the Prime Minister is playing at any given moment. The Prime Minister in his first one hundred days until Leyton[17] was a combination of J. F. Kennedy and Napoleon. . . . Then there was the Dunkirk spirit, the reincarnation of Sir Winston Churchill, and then for a time – and, Heaven help us, over Rhodesia – the Prime Minister was Abraham Lincoln, with malice towards none. He has emerged recently as the Duke of Wellington. J. F. Kennedy described himself in a brilliant phrase as an idealist without illusions. I would describe the Prime Minister as an illusionist without ideals. Abraham Lincoln said that you cannot fool all of the people all of the time . . . he wants to know if he can fool fifty per cent of the people for three weeks. . . . He was seen through at Westminster long ago; and it becomes the task of the Tory Party in this month to make sure he is seen through in the country.'

It was brilliant invective but it could not turn the Labour tide.

The Conservative manifesto was already in draft and Macleod's role in the campaign was largely confined to speeches and to the control of the party's television arrangements. There were plans for liaison between Heath, Maudling and Macleod but little positive co-ordination. The central direction of the campaign was entirely in Heath's hands.

Macleod began the election at Enfield; on March 14th he was in Manchester, where he took a moderate line on comprehensive education; and on the 15th he moved to the crucial marginals at Preston. Later that week he was in London and on March 19th he attacked the opinion polls which were showing a massive Labour lead: 'Take no notice of opinion polls,' he said, 'the public opinion poll in the 1948 Presidential election said that Truman had not the slightest chance of beating Dewey.'[18] In this as in other elections, Eve drove him everywhere by car and covered thousands of miles in the process.

17 Wilson's first Foreign Secretary Patrick Gordon-Walker, had lost Smethwick in the 1964 general election and was defeated in the Leyton by-election three months later.
18 Harry Truman, the Democratic candidate, won the election to become President of the United States in his own right. He had been Roosevelt's Vice-President.

It was a dull election. There were few if any rash statements and it was hard to convey to the public the real state of the economy. At Chelmsford, on March 25th, Macleod reverted to the central theme: 'If we pay ourselves nine times as much as we earn, there is no doubt where we are heading.' But if it was a recipe for economic disaster, it was also a recipe for electoral success. In addition the Conservatives had to rebut the charge that they were talking down sterling: 'I don't say there will be any dramatic collapse,' Macleod told his audiences, 'we are a strong country and there are . . . in the last resort, very considerable reserves. . . .'

The British electorate is very fair and it quickly became apparent that the most telling argument in favour of the Labour Government was that they had not yet had time to prove their worth or carry out their promises. When I was canvassing in my constituency, I encountered again and again the comment: 'You had thirteen years. Wilson has not had much more than thirteen months. We must give him a chance.' It is almost impossible to argue convincingly against a proposition of this kind. When the votes were counted, the Labour Party had increased their majority to ninety-six over all other parties in the House of Commons and the country faced another four years of Harold Wilson's Government.

CHAPTER 16

Shadow Chancellor and Chancellor of the Exchequer 1966-1970

WHEN the new Parliament assembled in April 1966, there was nothing in the Government's programme on which to base the debate on the Address. Much of the Prime Minister's opening speech had been devoted to the modernisation of Parliament, and Macleod made this the centrepiece of his attack: 'The Government,' he asserted, 'intend to use boredom as a political weapon. The Rt Hon Gentleman's only new proposal is that they should occupy themselves with some form of congressional committees. We know the motivation of the Prime Minister. He has dozens of new members; we are told they are all very clever. Perhaps they are too clever by half. So the Prime Minister has decided to keep them as busy as squirrels in a cage and give them the illusion of occupation and importance.'

The Labour Government had been returned with a majority of almost a hundred, and Macleod remembered wrily the problems this could present. He predicted that throughout the Parliament Wilson would be in difficulty with his own party: 'The National Plan targets are already in ruins and long before the end of this Parliament they will have to be abandoned with consequences for the party opposite which I do not find at all unattractive to contemplate.'

Edward Heath had fought a constructive, straightforward campaign and he emerged from it with an enhanced reputation; but he was in the difficult position of leading the party without ever having been Prime Minister, and in the aftermath of a crushing electoral defeat. He did not shine in his bi-weekly duels with Wilson in the House of Commons, and his leadership sometimes seemed touchy and hesitant. As his stock failed to rise, he became more tense. He lacked the relaxed affability of Alec Douglas-Home and there were no Baldwin touches to reassure the people and to win their hearts. But the Tory instinct for self-preservation is always strong, and a party which had edged one leader towards resignation was in no position to cashier another. With hindsight it is right to add that in my time in politics there has been no stronger or more determined Prime Minister of either party than Edward Heath.

Macleod might have tried to exploit the puzzled sense of dissatisfaction that most Conservatives felt over their leader's failure to make headway in Parliament or in the public opinion polls. He did not do so. He had opted for the role of a tax reforming Chancellor and he was content with it. He was always careful to confine his interventions in the House of Commons to points directly connected with his own Front Bench responsibilities, and because of this the party sometimes missed opportunities to score useful debating points at Question time.

Macleod's loyalty to his leader was meticulous; but their personal relationship was correct rather than close and he was not among Heath's most intimate colleagues. Home's position was a special one and Whitelaw, Carrington and Barber were all more in his confidence than Maudling or Macleod.

Heath kept a watchful eye on the economy and after the election he resumed the chairmanship of the Economic Policy Group. Maudling normally acted as his deputy and Macleod only occasionally took the chair. In practice this made little difference. Over the whole field of economic policy and particularly taxation, Heath and Macleod saw eye to eye and steered a middle course between the two lines of thought represented respectively by Maudling and Keith Joseph.

At first Macleod was doubtful about the style of Opposition. Heath ran the Shadow Cabinet on a tight rein and treated it almost like a real Cabinet, with the portfolios shared out and Shadow Ministers instructed not to trespass on each other's territory. This tidy allocation of duties contrasted with Macleod's memories of the earlier style of opposition practised by Sir Winston Churchill after the war. Churchill's informality, the blurred division of responsibility and the aggressive debating technique were all temperamentally attractive to Macleod and he was critical of the restrictions Heath seemed to be imposing on his colleagues. Nor was he happy about the tendency for the Opposition Front Bench to argue the case in detail. Perhaps he recalled how, as a young member of the Research Department, he had armed Churchill with a sheaf of notes for a debate on welfare policy and had heard him use one single statistic with devastating effect: 'Young man,' Churchill said afterwards, 'the first lesson you must learn is that when I call for statistics about the rate of infant mortality, what I want is proof that fewer babies died when I was Prime Minister than when anyone else was Prime Minister. That is a political statistic.'

Macleod's objection was not only one of style. He was reluctant to spell out too much. It offered clothes for stealing in opposition and hostages to fortune for a future government.

He expressed his thoughts in an article for the *Spectator* in August 1966:

The country thinks every Opposition in turn is ineffective . . . and electorates never, or hardly ever, vote for an Opposition. Sometimes they vote against governments. Certainly they did so in 1951 and again in 1964. . . . It presents the Tories with a most difficult problem of timing. They must prepare for office at any time and yet keep the details of their policies to themselves. In spite of the drama of the present political situation, the odds are still that Mr Wilson will run to 1970. And if that is so, 1966 is not too early to be hard at work, but it is much too soon for publication. . . . At the first Blackpool Conference after our 1945 election disaster, there was a sweeping demand from the floor for a policy – as if a policy was a pill to cure the ache of opposition. . . . The policies of 1966 are still valid. The backroom work on them is far advanced. The further unveiling ceremony can wait awhile. For the moment what is needed is opposition. Just that.

It was a shrewd and realistic summary of what politics in opposition is about.

About a month before each budget Macleod enlisted the help of the Conservative Research Department in making his assessment of what the Chancellor was likely to propose. 'I'm the QC, you're the solicitor,' he told Brendon Sewill, 'it's your job to mug up the brief.' He made full use of the department's estimates and statistics, but he never required speech notes or drafts. He preferred to use his own judgement, make up his own mind and prepare his own speeches.

As a general rule he left fiscal speculation and broad economic surveys to the financial journalists and when he felt obliged to comment on the state of the economy, he relied upon Patrick Jenkin, Terence Higgins, Tony Newton, the head of the Research Department's economic section and Brian Reading, who had been recruited to the Research Department from the Civil Service. On only one occasion – in an article for the *Financial Times* in April 1967 – did he venture to publish his budget judgement before the Chancellor had spoken.

He discussed the Chancellor's options with his Shadow Treasury team well in advance of every budget and by February he had set up sub-committees of the Party's Finance Committee – mainly, at that stage, to start work on amendments arising from the previous year's Finance Bill. He developed useful contacts with tax experts from industry and the professions, who were able to provide him with practical material for this purpose. Within the Research Department John Cope until the summer of 1967, and Charles Dumas thereafter, did much of the liaison with outside organisations.

Although Edward Heath's opposition to the 1965 Bill had been outstandingly successful, some members of the party's Finance Committee had felt inadequately briefed and Sir Henry d'Avigdor Goldsmid records in an unpublished memorandum that Macleod 'made it his responsibility to ensure that such a state of unpreparedness could not occur again. He achieved this by an almost continuous contact with outside experts of every kind. I think it is fair to say that from 1966 onwards the Conservative Opposition contrived to be as well briefed for economic debates as the Government itself . . . and much of this was due to Iain's skill.'

Macleod understood the importance of the City as a 'market place' and kept in close personal touch with opinion there through his friends. One of these was David Montagu, the head of Samuel Montagu, with whom he sometimes spent week-ends at Newmarket, combining a day's racing with an evening's discussion on market reactions. He was receptive, but he would usually put a political gloss on the information he received. He knew instinctively when an otherwise sound idea could not be adopted because it was politically unsellable, and he always considered what effect any proposal would have upon the party or in the country.

On budget day itself the first reaction to the Chancellor's proposals came traditionally from the leader of the Opposition in an impromptu speech as soon as the Chancellor had finished. This was always an able performance, for which Heath drew on the extensive preparatory work he and Macleod had already done. Although their sources were often different, their conclusions were in broad agreement. They sat side by side on the front bench, discussed in whispers the main points to attack and had a few minutes, while the budget resolutions were put, to confer together before Heath rose to reply. Macleod was impressed by his leader's speeches on these occasions and, as time went on, referred to him privately with growing admiration.

As soon as Heath sat down, the Party Finance Committee met upstairs under Macleod's chairmanship to discuss the main budget proposals. At about 6.30 there was a session with his Shadow Cabinet colleagues and by 8 o'clock the Opposition Treasury team would meet the Research Department officials to talk over the line of attack and decide who should deal with each aspect of it.

Macleod then watched the Chancellor's television broadcast before leaving with Barney Hayhoe (MP for Heston and Isleworth since 1970, then in the Conservative Research Department) to go over the script for his own television appearance the following night. He and Hayhoe had often worked together on this for as long as a fortnight and by budget day much of it would already be in draft. At 8 o'clock next morning they met again to complete the script, which was then typed and circulated for comment while Macleod worked on his speech for the House of Commons that afternoon. But there were inevitable last minute alterations to the broadcast, and the final decision on some of these would often only be made in the car on the way to the studio.

After checking the visual aids, Macleod invariably did a sustained piece straight to camera without any rehearsal and without a single mistake. It was always an able performance and even if a visual went wrong or a graph was misplaced, he never faltered or fluffed a line. Although the Chancellor sometimes used an interviewer, a much easier method, Macleod never did so. And nothing upset him. On one occasion he was told his tie would not look good on the screen, so he borrowed Hayhoe's, gave a flawless broadcast and returned the tie to its owner. Whereupon an apologetic deputation from the gallery reported a recording fault; the piece would have to be done again. Many people would have been angry, but Macleod merely asked for the tie back and did another take which was, if anything, even better than the first.

At this period Iain Macleod and Harold Wilson were, in the opinion of the experts, the most professional of the politicians in their use of the medium. John Grist, then the head of the BBC's Current Affairs department, thought Macleod was 'probably the first man in the Conservative hierarchy to appreciate and understand television'.[1] Wilson came to it later and found it more difficult, but both worked hard at it, and each acquired a mastery which none of their contemporaries achieved. This seemed to breed a slightly contemptuous attitude which Macleod disguised but which Wilson sometimes showed on the screen. The respect of the professionals was genuine and ungrudging, and John Grist sent me this appreciation of Macleod's television talent:

1 John Grist to the author, Jan. 5, 1971.

He was a communicator and he was interested in all forms of communication as a part of political life. He found out all he wanted to know in the late fifties . . . and he applied his very considerable intelligence to make himself into a first-rate performer. But there was no question of falling in love with television . . . the appreciation of his own ego was not bolstered in any way by his appearances. Television, to him, was there to be made use of by intelligent politicians. He had an incomparable sense of timing . . . a natural sense for the value of words and the weight of a sentence. He was interested in and knowledgeable about methods of explanation by chart and film. He was the only member of the Conservative Administration who had any idea at all of the imaginative use of television – for example, the use of music to enhance a point. In the studio he was always the same – slightly detached and somewhat wary, but totally in command.

Although Macleod attached much importance to the budget television appearance, he never neglected the House of Commons. Throughout the long debates on the Finance Bills, his attendance in the Chamber was constant though often silent. Roy Jenkins described him to me as sphinx-like.

'He seemed to like sitting through the night,' Jim Callaghan recalled. 'I used to say to him "For heaven's sake, Iain, can't we go home?" And he would say, "No, no, it's all right, I'm enjoying it." He would sit for hours at the end of the Front Bench, hunched up, perhaps because he was in pain, watchful, alert, but not interfering.'

'Most of us, when we become senior Ministers,' Callaghan acknowledged, 'like to hog the limelight if it's something that's going to take the headlines and leave it to our junior Ministers to do the rather dull stuff. Macleod wasn't like that.'

Patrick Jenkin, Terence Higgins, John Nott, Michael Alison and Kenneth Baker have all become Ministers in Heath's Government and they owe much to the encouragement and opportunities Macleod gave them in Opposition. He seldom commented on their speeches, either to praise or to criticise, but was always there to listen and to support them if necessary.

He was a good delegator and ran his team on a loose rein, but he was always in control. He was also a good 'floor manager', sensitive to back-bench feeling. His approach was to let the party vote if members wanted to and not to keep them waiting to do so if it could be avoided.

Gradually Macleod re-established himself as a hard campaigner and a good party man. Opposition gave full rein to his talent for destructive oratory and even those who had been out of sympathy with his policies in Government admired his killer instinct in debate.

His brooding presence compelled attention and Ministers took no risks with him which they could possibly avoid. They never knew what line he was going to take and, as Callaghan noted, 'he would see the weak point and constantly go for it and that was what you had to watch.' Roy Jenkins felt 'a little nervous . . . slightly apprehensive' when Macleod rose to attack him. The House respected his intellectual power and listened to him not only for what he had to say but because he always said it in an interesting way. Callaghan recalls his wit and 'a remarkable turn of phrase . . . he could really make you laugh at yourself.' And Robert Carr described him as 'a man of power in the House of Commons, I think more than any other member of my generation.'

Macleod never claimed to be an economist and Roy Jenkins thought he did not fully understand the complexities of demand management; but in the tax field, though he began as an amateur, Arthur Cockfield, who worked closely with him at this period, considered that he had made himself a professional by hard work and careful preparation. Cockfield was impressed by his determination and strength of mind and by his power of decision. Macleod understood the transitional difficulties of new policies, but he was confident he could overcome them and his long-term objectives were based on a clear philosophy which he never abandoned.

It was soon evident that, from the Government's point of view, the election had come just in time. Sterling, which had been under inter-mittent pressure since the end of February, weakened further in April when it became clear that Britain was running a current deficit. There would have to be at least an element of deflation in the May budget and this was provided by the new Selective Employment tax, devised in haste by Professor Kaldor. It was in effect a payroll tax on the service industries designed to attract labour from them into the manufacturing and export-ing industries.

Macleod disliked the tax, which he described as 'economically illiterate', and was critical of its timing. He feared that a budget which seemed too soft would create lack of confidence abroad and a new run on the reserves. Yet SET would only take effect in the autumn. On July 14th he developed the argument in the House of Commons: '. . . it was an extremely dangerous policy to do nothing until the autumn and then take out a vast interest-free loan which is the sole feature of the budget. . . .' Bank rate was raised the same day and the Prime Minister announced that further measures would soon follow. Not surprisingly there was a heavy run on sterling.

On July 20th the Government were forced to bring in the stiffest deflationary package since 1949. Domestic demand was reduced by £500 million and a statutory freeze of wages, salaries and dividends was introduced. The National Plan was now dead and the Government's entire economic strategy was in ruins. As Macleod said later:

> The truth about this Parliament is that it died three months after the last General Election, when it was clear that they were elected on a false prospectus. And four years is a terrible time to wait for a burial service, while the corpse lies cold in the lobbies at Westminster.

Some thought that Callaghan had not gone far enough and that sterling should have been devalued. Macleod did not yet share this view and, under the circumstances, he supported the July measures. But the contrast between them and the Government's election promises was more than any Opposition could disregard and the Tories tabled a censure motion. Macleod quoted Callaghan's earlier condemnation of the Conservative 1961 measures and his promise that the Labour Government 'would not tread that path again'. 'They are treading it now,' he asserted, 'and it is a rougher and harder road than any that the British people have ever previously been asked to walk.'

He made a caustic attack on the Prime Minister:

> As long as he sits in this House, on whichever side he sits, my Hon and Rt Hon friends do not feel that we will ever be able to trust him again.[2]

In a division on the Prices and Incomes Bill on July 29th, the Government's majority fell to 52 – little more than half its normal level.

> Agreements already signed . . . are to be broken by order of the Government (Macleod declared). Part of the law of contract is to be suspended, Arbitration is to be overruled. And against this massive breach of faith with the British electorate, not a ministerial mouse squeaks.

At the Conservative Party conference in the autumn Macleod made fun

2 Hansard, Cols. 1844/7, 27th July 1966.

of 'the architects of our present disaster. . . . The easiest to attack is Mr Brown; he is also the one I am most reluctant to attack. There is a national society for not being beastly to George Brown and I pay my dues like anyone else. And now that he is Foreign Secretary, I only hope [pause], I only hope! . . . Mr Callaghan suffers from what you may regard as a fatal defect in a Chancellor. He is always wrong. Not just sometimes. For Jim Callaghan the laws of averages have been suspended. . . .'

It was good conference dialectic and his audience loved it, but it was scarcely fair to the Chancellor of the Exchequer. Macleod was himself wrong about the betting tax which Callaghan had introduced in the 1966 Finance Bill. He argued strongly against it in Committee and sent Callaghan a copy of Edgar Wallace's book, *The Calendar*, to prove that the tax wouldn't work. In fact it did, as Macleod subsequently acknowledged.

In more serious vein, he observed: 'If there is cynicism about politics and about politicians – and there always has been – it is perhaps because they think we concern ourselves too much with ideas and too little with idealism.'

By the end of the year the position looked better. There was an overall surplus on the balance of payments, funds were flowing back into London and by March 1967 almost all the Central Bank loans had been repaid. Even the unemployment figures were lower than had been feared and Ministers seemed not to appreciate, as Macleod did, that the effects of deflation on employment do not reach their peak in the first but in the second winter which follows. The Cabinet were confident that the corner had been turned.

Under these circumstances the Opposition were forced for a time to turn their attention to other issues, and the Decimal Currency Bill came in for criticism. Callaghan had opted for the £ unit while Macleod was a convinced 'ten-bobber' and rightly predicted that the £ system would have the effect of forcing up prices. But other and more serious inflationary pressures were soon apparent. Private investment was falling while public expenditure was rising and there was virtually no economic growth. Despite these trends the Chancellor was still optimistic: 'We are back on course,' he proclaimed proudly, 'the ship is picking up speed . . . every seaman knows the command at such a moment – "Steady as she goes".'

Macleod thought Callaghan was wrong to do nothing. He forecast a figure of 650,000 unemployed by the end of the year, 'yet Mr Callaghan rests on his oars, burbling inept nautical metaphors. . . .' He recognised the Chancellor's reluctance to move too soon but commented with some justification. '. . . Some of them reflate too late, some reflate by too little and some by too much, but no Chancellor ever reflates too soon.' This truism was reflected in a turn in the political tide with a Conservative by-election victory at Pollok, increased majorities at Honiton and Brierley Hill and massive gains in the GLC and Borough elections.

During the debates on the Finance Bill Macleod hammered away at the level of unemployment and the need to reduce direct taxation. He was scornful about the Government's compulsory prices and incomes policy and insisted that price control 'is impossible to define and is the wrong target'. He had argued for reflation provided it was export-led and fuelled by a boost to investment. These conditions were unfulfilled, but bank rate was cut to $5\frac{1}{2}$% in June, some hire purchase restrictions were relaxed and better pensions and family allowances had been announced. It looked like 'stop-go' over again with another balance of payments crisis to follow.

As time went on Macleod became convinced (and said privately) that devaluation was inevitable; but it would certainly have been unwise to make such a suggestion in public since this would merely have increased the pressure on sterling. Nevertheless Macleod gave much latitude to the financial journalist, Samuel Brittan, who put the case for devaluation at a Conservative seminar in July.

The August unemployment figures were the highest for that month for thirty years and there were further hire purchase relaxations in the teeth of Treasury opposition. These did not prevent an 18.4% swing in Attlee's old seat at West Walthamstow which fell to the Conservatives in a by-election in September. Britain's current account had been in heavy deficit since April and the closure of the Suez Canal and the dock strike in October accentuated an already critical situation. By this time Callaghan must have known that devaluation would be necessary, but the Government were still talking with two voices, one story for home consumption and a different version for the foreign bankers. 'Double talk is Mr Wilson's mother tongue,' declared Macleod at the Tory Party conference. He promised that a Conservative Government would abolish the Selective Employment tax and reduce the burden of direct personal taxation. He did not think it necessary to increase indirect taxes by an equivalent amount because he relied on larger savings and a higher growth rate to fill the revenue gap under a Conservative Administration.

He was humorously scathing in his attack on the Labour Ministers: 'Secretaries of State come and go,' he told the conference. 'We started with George Brown. Happy days. Three per cent mortgages. The National Plan. Where have all the flowers gone? Gone to the graveyard, every one. Then you will remember Michael [pause] – No, of course you do not remember Michael Stewart. He was Secretary of State for Education and Science and he was moved. He was Secretary of State for Foreign Affairs and he was moved. He was Secretary of State for Economic Affairs and he was moved. He is now First Secretary of State. He has no discernible occupation whatever and he has a label round his neck which not only says "not to be moved" but "not to be resuscitated." In nominal charge we have the Prime Minister himself, a man whose vision is limited to tomorrow's headlines. . . . However, I am determined to pay somebody a compliment and I pay it to Mr Callaghan. He is by a long chalk the best of them although, as Shakespeare said, "there is small choice in rotten apples." '

He accused the Government of having invented the doctrine of the league tables and then of actually planning to come last in the international growth table. And he finished his speech with the words: 'We do not seek to destroy socialists. They are unimportant and incompetent men. The fight is against state socialism itself. If we go into that fight with relish . . . the battleground can become the killing-ground as well.'

Callaghan's main problem was the low growth rate which could not now average more than 2.2% up to 1970. The difference between this and the National Plan target was no less than £9,600 million: 'That is the cost of socialism in practice over these years,' Macleod commented, and he criticised public expenditure which was still running at the National Plan levels. But he was vague about any constructive proposals of his own. He thought devaluation was the only way in which the Government could regain control of its economic destinies; but if Callaghan would not face the harsh reality, Macleod could not precipitate the crisis. The Government was in trouble, but the Opposition was in a trap. They could not publicly advocate a devaluation of the currency.

In fact, the die was already cast. When the economic estimates became available at the beginning of November, it was clear that the basic deficit for 1967 would be £500 million, with little or no improvement in 1968. Late on November 13th, Wilson and Callaghan took the decision to devalue and the Cabinet ratified this on November 16th. The Chancellor's answer to a supplementary question in the House of Commons opened the floodgates to a run on sterling and devaluation was announced on November 18th. The maintenance of the value of the pound, for which everything else had been sacrificed, was now itself abandoned.

Macleod called for Callaghan's resignation, but his scorn was reserved for the Prime Minister: 'This country has only had three Socialist Prime Ministers,' he said, 'and each one of them has devalued the £. This is no coincidence except the coincidence of incompetence. There is only one man living who has sat in two Cabinets which have devalued the British £ and that is the present Prime Minister. . . . He now offers to the country as a new and exciting challenge a policy which he has denounced as lunatic, as a flight from reality and as a betrayal of trust. Yet of course he will cling like a limpet to the Treasury Bench. . . . He has not only devalued the £. He has devalued his own word, he has betrayed his high office and it is time for him to get out.'

Macleod's attacks on Wilson were becoming increasingly bitter. The explanation may lie in his view that the game of politics had to be played by the rules. To Macleod politics was a profession in which he took pride. He thought Wilson was lowering its standards.

James Callaghan resigned as Chancellor of the Exchequer and became Home Secretary. Roy Jenkins moved from the Home Office to the Treasury. Macleod had always liked Jim Callaghan; and he developed a warm regard for the very able Chief Secretary to the Treasury, Jack (now Lord) Diamond, whom he greatly respected as a parliamentary craftsman. But he did not establish as easy a personal relationship with Jenkins and he was soon attacking the new Chancellor for lack of candour.

The International Monetary Fund had granted Britain a stand-by credit and the arrangements for this were incorporated in a Letter of Intent which included a number of conditions. Jenkins maintained that these did not restrict his freedom of manoeuvre, but Macleod quoted the last paragraph of the letter which showed quite clearly, he claimed, that they did. He went on: 'You cannot go cap in hand to the central bankers of Europe . . . and maintain your freedom of action. . . . Those are not my words, but the words of the Prime Minister before the election and they are an accurate description of our present situation.'

There followed a period of 'government by instalment'. It was not until a month after devaluation that Wilson announced a public expenditure review in which 'nothing would be sacrosanct.' Despite unusually high pre-Christmas spending, there were no new restrictions on consumption and, as David Butler and Pinto-Duschinsky observed: 'The delay in taking action after November 18th, when its psychological impact would have been greatest, was one of the gravest failures of the

Labour Government and was substantially responsible for the catalogue of woe during the next two years.'[3]

Announcement of the Government economies was delayed until January 16, 1968. Even then the cuts did not go far enough or operate soon enough. Many of them were shadowy in the extreme and a quarter of the package was represented by a notional saving on investment grants: 'It is an estimate of the amount which would have been saved if an announcement which has not been made had been made,' Macleod commented. He would have used the regulator to curtail consumer demand. Jenkins preferred to wait and proved wrong to do so. The result was a 'beat the budget' spending spree which pushed imports to a record level.

In January 1968 Iain and Eve Macleod paid a short visit to Australia on a goodwill tour for Lombard's and to open the new Sydney offices of the bank. They travelled by air via San Francisco and Hawaii to Sydney, where Iain inspected the famous cricket ground but was disappointed to miss seeing a test match. The then Prime Minister, Harold Holt, was about to leave for New Zealand and would not be in Canberra when the Macleods visited the capital, so he flew to Sydney in order to give a large dinner party for them and enable them to meet some of the leading Australian politicians.

They went on to stay with the British High Commissioner, Sir Charles Johnston, and Iain spoke at Canberra University. After a short visit to Melbourne, where they lunched with the Governor-General, the Macleods left for New York and Iain wrote a letter of appreciation to Lady Johnston in the Australian idiom:

My dear Natasha,

I seem to have souveneered some of yer blow piper, so i'll use it for a thank-you letter. We had a beaut of a time in Canberra, my word we did. The weather in Melbourne was crook but everything else is apples especially my sheila who anyway reckons everything strine is extra grouse. Back to-day to New York and three feet of snow. Canberra was just bliss especially all those excursions we didn't go on. We were supremely happy with you.

Good on ya both.

My love – Iain.

3 *The British General Election of* 1970. Macmillan, 1971.

In February the new Home Secretary introduced the Commonwealth Immigrants' Bill to restrict Asian entry into Britain from East Africa. This arose from the Kenya Independence Act of 1963 which gave holders of British passports the right to return to the United Kingdom. Although Duncan Sandys' objective, as the Secretary of State who provided this loophole, had been to safeguard the white settlers who preferred not to remain under a black Government in their country of adoption, the Act had not excluded Indians in the same position. Indeed it could scarcely have done so without inviting a charge of colour discrimination. As time went on the 'Africanisation' policy of the Kenya Government proved prejudicial to the Kenya Asians, many of whom therefore opted to emigrate to Britain.

Enoch Powell and Duncan Sandys drew attention to this in the House of Commons and demanded restrictions on Asian immigration. Powell claimed that '200,000 Indians in Kenya alone have an absolute right of entry into this country.' The numbers were exaggerated but the speech caused much public concern. Callaghan succumbed to the pressure and introduced a panic measure on February 27th. Its Second Reading and Committee stages were rushed through the House of Commons in two days with the somewhat shamefaced acquiescence of the Opposition Front Bench.

Macleod was shocked by the racial character of the Bill and by the breach of a government undertaking on which people had relied. He had anticipated its introduction and a week before had written an article in the *Spectator* containing a strong attack upon Duncan Sandys: 'Your Kenya Constitution is devastatingly clear. So is Hansard. So are all the statutes. And so therefore is my position. I gave my word. I meant to give it. I wish to keep it.'

The *Spectator* article was shrewdly timed. It was written before the Shadow Cabinet's decision not to oppose the Bill. After committing himself publicly in such forthright terms, Macleod could not be forced to eat his own words a few days later. He was therefore given tacit permission to vote against the Bill despite the Shadow Cabinet decision to support it. Thirty-five Labour MPs, fourteen other Conservatives including myself, and the Liberals opposed the measure. Eighty peers voted against it when it went to the House of Lords.

During the first evening of the debate, Iain sent me a note of good wishes for my speech and added that he was dining out with the family but would return by 10 p.m., 'to vote against this shabby Bill'.

Maudling was never happy about having supported this legislation and later, as Home Secretary, he introduced modifications which mitigated its harshness. But the Shadow Cabinet's decision was widely regarded at the time as a victory for the right wing of the party, which now stepped up its pressure on the leadership to oppose the Government's Race Relations Bill, due to be introduced in April.

Macleod did not wish to be out of step with his colleagues so soon after his independent stand on the Kenya Asian Bill and he was always doubtful whether Parliament could legislate effectively to change people's attitudes on matters of this kind. He therefore supported the Opposition's reasoned amendment to the Bill. In a letter to *The Times* on April 22nd, he expressed his 'contempt for discrimination' but went on, 'I have always held it a mistake to believe that legislation has any significant part to play in a field where there is so much ignorance and prejudice. . . .' He was sure that members would make up their minds which course to follow and would do so 'without pressure or reproach'. This was so and when some of us felt unable to accept the Opposition amendment, our views were treated with respect and consideration.

Macleod used his influence in the Shadow Cabinet to ensure that the Party did not vote against the Third Reading of the Bill. One of his motives for doing so was his concern for the position of Edward Boyle and Robert Carr, both of whom had only voted for the Commonwealth Immigrants Bill on the understanding that the party would not oppose the Race Relations Bill. He felt that they had been let down over this and should now be supported.

Meanwhile Enoch Powell had made the intemperate and notorious speech at Birmingham which resulted in his instant dismissal from the Shadow Cabinet. Macleod shared the opinion of Powell's speech which was publicly expressed by Quintin Hogg and told me that, had Powell remained, he would himself have felt obliged to resign from the Shadow Cabinet. But the Leader of the Opposition needed no prompting. Although Powell's new-found prominence and the public support he received suggested the possibility of a serious division within the party, Heath did not waver and made no further concessions on policy. This was wise as well as right and by the summer of 1968 the danger of disunity had receded.

The 1968 budget was designed to create a balance of payments surplus of £500 million. It was the first budget since 1951 which had the avowed aim of reducing the standard of living, and the additional tax burden of

£923 million was the largest ever imposed on the British people in one budget.

It was also the first year in which the Government decided to send most of the Committee stage of the Finance Bill 'upstairs' without the 'usual channel' talks which normally precede changes of this sort in House of Commons procedure. Macleod resented this and fought the Bill remorselessly through endless late sittings and all-night sittings. Sir Henry d'Avigdor-Goldsmid recalls that on one occasion he encouraged the Opposition to vote even against adjourning for breakfast. The modest tax relief accorded to the thalidomide babies was the result of a concession Macleod obtained on their behalf during these long debates on the 1968 Bill.

Devaluation and such a severe budget took their toll of the Government's popularity, which plummeted to a level unparalleled in post-war politics. Meriden, Acton and even George Wigg's stronghold at Dudley were all lost in the next round of by-elections. The strange affair of the South African arms embargo caused tension and distrust in the Labour hierarchy and contributed to George Brown's resignation later in the summer.

In the months following the budget, exports improved but imports rose faster and Macleod believed that a flight from money was taking place which was keeping consumption high at the expense of savings. There was growing pressure for further restrictions by the Government, but at an eve of the poll meeting in the Bassetlaw by-election in October, Barbara Castle stated 'there is no economic freeze on the way'. The Government held the seat by 740 votes and announced more hire purchase restrictions two days later. Macleod made this the subject of a fierce attack, which Jenkins described as 'a storm in a cup of very weak tea' but within a fortnight the Chancellor announced a further £250 million of taxation and a severe tightening of the credit squeeze.

Macleod had no confidence that Jenkins would stick to a business arrangement with the Opposition and he resented what he considered the Chancellor's contempt for the House of Commons. He acknowledged that Jenkins made good speeches but 'he has no dialogue with the House. The reason is that his disdain for his political opponents is only matched by his contempt for his political friends.'[4]

Roy Jenkins was more generous in a tribute after Macleod's death: 'I am not tremendously convinced,' he said, 'by the picture of a man who

4 Hansard, Col. 149, 25 Nov. 1968.

delivers the most appalling thunderbolts across the floor of the House and then comes out and slaps you on the back. Iain Macleod never did that. . . . The differences between him and his opponents were not all that wide but he fought them very hard . . . he was absolutely straightforward, an honest man. You knew exactly where you were with him. And he presented the same face in public as in private.'[5]

The Times described 1968 as 'the year of the strike', but Macleod was more concerned with the inflationary wage settlements and thought that Barbara Castle's interventions in the railway and engineering disputes were undermining the Chancellor's whole strategy. He claimed that she was either 'inside the Trojan Horse and plotting the fall of the city from within the walls, or she has no idea where Troy is, does not know what the horse is doing there and does not know why she has been locked up inside it. In all chivalry, I appeal to the House to take the kindly view.'[6]

The year ended in an atmosphere of unrelieved gloom and with the approach of the 1969 budget, Macleod charged the Government with having 'failed to take the opportunity bought so dearly with devaluation'. He thought that long-term reforms should at once be put in hand and singled out industrial relations, the reduction and simplification of taxation and the encouragement of savings as the three most important matters to be dealt with. On the need for savings he clashed publicly with Enoch Powell, describing the latter's view that savings were not an alternative to higher taxation in an inflationary climate as 'a trifle bizarre'.

The budget speech on April 15th included the promise of immediate legislation on industrial relations and the announcement of a contractual savings scheme for which the Conservatives had been pressing. Roy Jenkins even borrowed the Macleod title 'Save as you earn' for this innovation. But the main feature of the budget was an increase in taxation of £340 million. SET went up by 28 %, the corporation and petrol taxes were raised and purchase tax extended. Macleod described it as 'the defeatist budget of a defeated Government'.

In a powerful television broadcast he pointed out that 'for every £1 raised in the last Conservative year, the Chancellor will be taking over £2 this year.' He was savagely critical of the SET increase, which brought this tax to 48/– per man per week and argued that it was bound to raise prices.

5 Twenty-four Hours programme, July 21, 1970.
6 Hansard, Col. 147, Nov. 25, 1968.

He sketched out the Conservative alternative as being a switch from 'the general subsidy, soup-kitchen world of Socialism' to selectivity, import levies instead of agricultural subsidies, a cut in public expenditure and the reduction of direct taxation.

Macleod declined to follow the Chancellor into the realm of a budget judgement on the ground that 'touches on the tiller are of little value if there is no rudder on the ship'. But during the discussions on the 1969 Finance Bill, he extracted six new clauses from the Government on the issue of the disallowance of interest, each of which had originated in Opposition amendments.

During the summer of 1969 there was a marked improvement in Britain's economic fortunes, which first became apparent on June 12th with the publication of the May trade figures. The experience of the previous three years and the advice he was receiving from the Conservative Research Department made Macleod cautious in his reaction; but when a large rise in exports in August reinforced a good overall trade surplus for the second quarter of the year, Conservative doubts began to appear captious in the face of good news and the Tory lead in the public opinion polls, which had been over 19% in July, fell to 4% in October.

During the economic debate at the party conference Enoch Powell advocated the abandonment of a fixed rate of exchange, citing the floating of the mark prior to its revaluation as a precedent. Macleod disagreed. It was one thing to float the mark from strength, he declared, 'quite another to contemplate this for sterling, buffeted by all the lack of confidence that we have had over recent years.'

The most important part of Macleod's conference speech dealt with the value added tax. He revealed the talks he had been having on this subject with the CBI, the Chambers of Commerce, the National Chamber of Trade and with foreign experts; and he announced that Professor Wheatcroft, Professor of Law at London University and a most distinguished expert on taxation problems, had been invited to prepare a draft of a possible VAT for this country. 'Work on this,' he told the conference, 'is far advanced.'

Macleod used the so-called Wheatcroft Report, which did not in fact exist as such, as a means of avoiding any specific public commitment to the tax; but he was by this time strongly in favour of it and would like to have made a more positive statement if his colleagues had agreed. He did not think it intellectually honest to pretend that the Conservative cuts in taxation could all be paid for through cuts in expenditure. The value added tax was not Macleod's baby, but he may fairly be regarded as its midwife. He worked closely and well with Wheatcroft, with whom he developed an easy personal relationship.

In a speech to the Institute of Directors in November 1969 Macleod outlined some of his thinking on future taxation policy. He showed sympathy with proposals to abolish the short-term capital gains tax, endorsed the reform of housing finance, rejected tax relief for private education and emphasised his dislike of the term 'unearned income'. On the principle that injustice cannot be condoned merely because it is done to only a few people, he declared his determination to abolish the aggregation of married women's incomes with those of their husbands; and he announced an intensive study of the United States system of self-assessment, whereby the same number of officials as in Britain collected twelve times as much tax from four times as many people. 'It must be possible to save out of taxed income,' he concluded, 'and . . . to keep a large proportion of what one saves. . . . We are going to discriminate all right – for the energetic against the idle, for the saver against the spendthrift, for the ambitious against the complaisant . . . that is what tomorrow's taxation will mean.'

By the turn of the year the Government appeared to have abandoned the attempt to slow down wage increases. Many of the largest pay settlements, averaging 12 %, were in the public sector and it looked as though the Prime Minister was trying to ride back to Downing Street on a tide of rising incomes before the price inflation which would follow could spoil his electoral prospects.

Edward Heath prepared for an election. At the end of January the Shadow Cabinet gathered for a working weekend at Selsdon Park. Macleod took a prominent part in the discussions, but the Tory tax package, unlike the industrial relations policy, was never published officially – although an observant reader could have detected the main lines of it in the March brief issued by the Conservative Political Centre.

Macleod kept no diaries or records and very few personal letters or papers of any kind from the departments in which he had served, but there was one exception – a copy of the 163 page report on the reform of taxation which he had presented in draft to the Leader of the party in November 1968. More work had been done on it later, especially on the value added tax, and a computer study had been carried out 'to determine the right mix'.

The document began with the words 'the present level of taxation is excessive', and it set out in detail the plans which have since been incorporated in Tony Barber's first two budgets. The tax emphasis was to be on spending rather than earning, with reductions in direct personal taxation as the centrepiece.

The proposals included the combination of income tax and surtax into a single tax and at a reduced rate; the substitution of a direct tax on income from investment for the previous system of an earned income allowance; a lower rate of corporation tax and a reform of its structure to remove the discrimination against distribution and to help small businesses; the abolition of SET and the purchase tax and their replacement by a 10% value added tax, from which food and the smallest firms would be exempt. Investment grants were to be replaced by tax allowances; regional employment premiums would go, although the principle of investment incentives for the regions would be retained; the betterment levy would be abolished – and perhaps the short-term gains tax – and death duties would be modified.

Macleod often talked of a capital owning democracy and he would have liked to go further towards this aim than Barber has yet felt able to do. But the only part of the tax package which has been modified is the section dealing with investment grants.

The general commitment was to reduce the level of taxation and to simplify the whole tax system. It was a programme which would fulfil Macleod's remaining ambition to be remembered as a great reforming Chancellor.

As the general election drew nearer, he identified the main issues as rising prices and industrial anarchy: 'A handful of trade union leaders,' he observed, 'warn the Chancellor that if he will not reflate the economy, they will force wage claims through without regard to productivity . . . "Militancy pays" is the new motto,' he added, and he traced this back to the 'humiliating surrender of Mr Wilson and Mrs Castle' in the previous year. It was true that the Government had by now adopted a policy of appeasement towards organised labour.

Macleod acknowledged that there was no magic formula for price stability, but he believed that reductions in public expenditure, the encouragement of savings and the use of the public sector as an example to private industry would all combine to achieve success: 'As the largest employer in the country,' he said, 'we as the Government will set the trend that the private sector will follow. We will use our influence to encourage non-inflationary settlements.' But although the tax reform policies had been worked out in such detail, the central problem of inflation had never been faced.

At this period – and indeed since – there was much concern in the Conservative Party about political bias in BBC broadcasts and Macleod's relations with the Corporation's current affairs department became very strained. In a reference to the Conservative victory in a by-election at Bridgwater, he had commented that 'anyone who saw the result on the BBC would have been hard put to it to decide who had won.'

The pressures, some of them respectable, for a 'give-away' budget were considerable. In fact it was neutral and the Chancellor's remission of nearly £200 million did little more than offset the effects of inflation. 'One shouldn't shoot even a one-legged Santa Claus,' Macleod conceded, and he did not divide the House against the budget proposals. He welcomed many of the minor reforms Jenkins had introduced but was critical of the omission of any relief 'directly aimed at child poverty'. He reminded the country of the Prime Minister's promises in 1964 and he coined 'Wilson's law – the more definite the promise, the more certain the breach.'

On television he endorsed Jenkins' warning that the current level of wage settlements must lead to intolerable price increases, and at Cheltenham on April 18th he asserted that 'Britain is in the grip of the worst cost-push inflation since 1951.'

Macleod's concern was not shared by the public. The budget proved popular and a swing to Labour in the municipal elections heralded an appeal to the country. The Gallup Poll on May 12th showed a 7% lead for the Government and on May 18th the Prime Minister announced the date of the general election.

During the previous few weeks Macleod had become unusually depressed. He did not believe the opinion poll figures 'but they do tell the trend' and he feared a Labour victory. 'You'll be all right,' he told Patrick Jenkin, 'you'll still be young enough. But my generation will be finished.' He seemed more concerned about Heath's future than about his own: 'We'll go out and have a bloody good fight,' he said, 'but I am worried about Ted.'

Immediately after the Prime Minister's announcement, the Macleods took a quick holiday on the Costa Brava, returning on May 28th to open the campaign at Enfield. Iain's spirits were fully restored and, dining with Lord and Lady Rothermere, he made the confident prediction that the Conservatives would win by 31 or 32 seats. After touring Lancashire and

Yorkshire, he telephoned me to say we were winning and would win and he repeated this to a press conference in Glasgow on the day after the publication of a poll which showed a 12% lead for the Labour Party. A week before polling day he predicted a Tory majority of 35 seats.

He thought this election was the most important he had ever fought. To him it was a crusade. He was greatly helped in the campaign not only by Eve but by his personal assistant, Gerry Wade, the Chairman of the Greater London Young Conservatives.

In contrast to some of us, like Edward Boyle, who normally shared his views, he was strongly critical of the cancellation of the South African cricket tour which he described as 'contemptible, miserable weakness, a surrender to the mob'; and he wrote to Nick Scott: 'I am so sad that on a subject that combines cricket and race we take different views. . . . For you I have the highest hopes for the future. For myself I sniff the breeze like an old war horse and I love it.'

Fully committed as he was to the principle of our entry into the European Economic Community, he thought the decision on the terms, when they had been negotiated, should be made by a free vote of the House of Commons.

Leonard Beaton described him in action during the campaign: '. . . a speech such as few men in public life now put on; ordered and economical to the intelligent and brilliantly rousing to the faithful.'[7]

On June 1st Iain's mother died in Yorkshire and he went north for the funeral. He was deeply devoted to her and cancelled all his speaking engagements for a week. On his return he appeared in a television broadcast which was so effective that many people considered it a landmark in election television.

Macleod was furious about the part played by Powell in the closing stages of the campaign. We talked about it on the telephone and he was outspoken in his condemnation of what he regarded as a dangerous distraction and of Powell's disloyalty to the party and its leader; but he thought it wise to avoid any public comment which would only have added fuel to the fire and made the party look divided at a crucial time.

On June 18th, Iain did not feel at all well and he stayed in bed for election day while Eve toured the constituency committee rooms, but he got up in time for the count and listened to the early results on a transistor radio while he waited for his own. He realised at once that the party had won and that the outcome would be within a few seats of his own con-

7 *The Times*, June 1, 1970.

sistent prediction. When the Enfield figures were announced he was returned with a personal majority of 11,962.

At 11 a.m. on June 20th, he saw the Prime Minister at Downing Street and was appointed Chancellor of the Exchequer. He was delighted to hear that Reggie Maudling was to be Home Secretary and Robert Carr Secretary of State for Employment. After he had seen Sir Douglas Allen, the Permanent Secretary at the Treasury, Iain went to Lords to watch England play the Rest of the World, but he felt ill and soon had to be driven home to Potters Bar.

For the rest of that week he was at his office in Great George Street. 'Like Sidney Smith,' he told his private secretary, 'I arrive late and leave early.' But he was already hard at work on the reduction of public expenditure, which he regarded as the essential prerequisite for lower levels of taxation and higher levels of savings. At his first meeting with his senior officials he reassured them with the words: 'Whatever I may have said in Opposition, I am not interested in opposition. I am interested in administration.' On June 29th, he and Eve moved into 11 Downing Street.

Macleod knew that he was the key figure in the new government. If his policies were unsuccessful, those of almost every other Minister would be prejudiced. He hoped to change the whole emphasis of taxation from income to consumption and in so doing to provide his own version of an old socialist dream – the transformation of society by means of the tax system.

When he reached the Treasury he was faced at once with a difficult situation. He inherited a combination of stagnant production and cost inflation, of relatively high unemployment and strongly rising wages and prices. He had always been genuinely concerned for the unemployed, and given a longer period as Chancellor, he might have expanded the economy rather more quickly than his successor in order to increase employment opportunities.

By July 7th he was sufficiently unwell to call the doctor, who thought an operation for appendicitis might be necessary. But he insisted on going to the House of Commons to answer Treasury questions and to make his first (and only) speech as Chancellor of the Exchequer. In it he expressly rejected the idea of an autumn Budget though no doubt, like Tony Barber, he would have found it necessary when the time came. He acknowledged that he was more likely to wish to stimulate demand than to restrain it, but he took the view that to do so at that moment would be premature. He undertook to lay the conclusions of his review of public expenditure before the House in the autumn.

He concluded in lighter vein by referring to Harold Wilson's speech when opening the debate on the Address a few days earlier. The Leader of the Opposition had lectured Ministers on the need to keep their election promises. 'Look who is talking,' Macleod counter-attacked, 'the walking wastepaper basket himself, filled with lightly-given promises and pledges.' He took up the challenge. He was ready to be judged by results. And he read out the relevant undertakings from the Conservative manifesto, which his successor has since redeemed.

He was in pain throughout the speech and the doctors confirmed that he would have to undergo an immediate operation. Later that evening Eve took him into St George's Hospital. His daughter, Diana, underwent a major spinal operation the same day at University College Hospital and Eve spent her time going from one to the other. Both patients were slowly recovering and there seemed no cause for anxiety; but she could not cope with the additional task of settling in at No. 11 and supervising the changes there, and on July 15th Iain's cousin, Catherine Ross, arrived to stay and to help. Owing to her habitual unpunctuality she was known in the family as 'the late Miss Ross', but she was a tower of strength to Eve at this difficult time.

My wife and I visited Iain in St George's on July 12th. He looked tired but said that the enforced rest had done him good and that he could hardly wait to get down to serious work in the department. He outlined to me in some detail his future plans and hopes for tax reform. It was an uncanny experience nine months later to hear Tony Barber introduce the budget in the House of Commons and I mentally ticked off the changes Iain had forecast. They were almost identical except that the tax allowance for bank interest against overdrafts was omitted. When I congratulated Tony Barber on 'Iain's budget' and recalled this solitary deviation, he regretted he had felt unable to include it but assured me it would be in the following year – which it was.

Towards the end of his speech, Tony Barber correctly claimed that it constituted the most comprehensive and far-reaching reform of the tax system of this country in this century. In strategy and tactics, in essence and in detail, this radical Tory budget was the product – during the years of Opposition – of the brains and the imagination, the philosophy and the research work of Iain Macleod and Edward Heath.

This is in no way to detract from Barber's performance. He deserves much credit not only for his speech, which was a personal triumph, but for his strength and resolution in forcing Iain's reforms through the Treasury almost unaltered. Macleod's tax strategy was virtually completed in the 1972 budget. Thanks to Tony Barber, these two budgets were, in effect, Iain Macleod's memorial, and his posthumous contribution to the public life of the nation.

He told me before he died that, owing to his health, he did not expect to introduce more than two, or at the most three, budgets and hoped then to retire to the House of Lords. He had even selected his title, Lord Macleod of Borve, which was the one Eve herself took when she became a life peeress in 1971.

Although he was still in hospital on July 18th, Iain insisted that the annual Enfield cricket match, which had been planned for that day, should go on. On the 19th, he was well enough to return to No. 11, where he remained in bed for the rest of the day reading Cabinet and departmental papers. Several people called to see him on the 20th, including the Financial Secretary, Patrick Jenkin, his Parliamentary Private Secretary, Nick Scott, and Bill Ryrie, his private secretary at the Treasury.

Before he went into hospital Macleod had been determined to get a grip on wages and to hold prices by setting an example in the nationalised industries. But on his return to Downing Street, he was told by Patrick Jenkin that approval had been given to increase electricity prices: 'It's all slipping away,' he said bleakly.

He was anxious to attend the Cabinet next day but was clearly not strong enough to do so. That evening Charles Johnston telephoned to discuss a visit to Australia, New Zealand and Singapore which they were planning for the autumn. He was the last person outside the immediate family to whom Iain spoke.

Soon afterwards he put on his dressing gown and walked across the hall to the small television room to watch an athletics programme. On the way back to bed at about 10.30 p.m. he had a heart attack. Catherine Ross ran to help him and Eve telephoned for a doctor, who was delayed in getting to Downing Street, so that by the time he arrived it was too late.

Iain Macleod died at 11.35 p.m. on July 20, 1970. He was 56 years old. He had been a senior minister for longer than anyone in the new Government and had barely embarked upon his most important assignment, for which he had prepared himself assiduously for nearly five years.

Edward Heath and Willy Whitelaw called to see Eve within half an hour. Iain's own doctor at Potters Bar, Dr Matthew Forster, arrived soon afterwards and was a great help to her. Next morning the letters and messages of sympathy began to pour in. She received nearly 4,000, one of the first being from Dr Hastings Banda, the President of Malawi. Her son, Torquil, coped with them while Nick Scott and her son-in-law, David Heimann, dealt with the press and helped her with the arrangements for the funeral and for services of thanksgiving in London and at Enfield.

On the evening of July 22nd, Eve packed their belongings and early next morning she left for Potters Bar with Torquil and his wife, Mel, and Catherine Ross. She had lived at 11 Downing Street for just over three weeks.

CHAPTER 17

Iain Macleod – the Man and the Statesman

⦿⦿⦿⦿⦿

IAIN MACLEOD had a strong sense of continuity and of family, which extended beyond his own immediate relations to the Macleod clan generally, and to his Highland ancestry: 'I married a Sassenach,' he used to say. 'My children regard themselves as Scots, I sign a register always as Scottish and I regard the English in a curious sort of way with tremendous affection and liking, as people not quite foreign but in some way rather different from me. I am a Yorkshireman in the cricket season.' His daughter, Diana, shared his feeling for the Highlands and Islands and this love of their common heritage made a bond between them.

Iain and Diana were very close to each other. He adored her and in his eyes everything she did was right. She is an intelligent girl with a quick mind and a spontaneous gaiety and sense of fun. She was usually successful in anything she undertook and Iain liked this. He believed people, including young girls and including Diana, should work hard and if she was out of a job for a few months, he was displeased and said so. But he did not mind about school reports. He had made his own assessment of his daughter and he did not think a schoolmistress's would be more valuable.

When Torquil and Diana were children he often asked them general knowledge questions and he made them learn a poem every week which they had to recite to him on Sunday. One of the first he taught them was Robert Louis Stevenson's 'Requiem'. He read poetry to them, especially Shakespeare's sonnets and G. K. Chesterton. The epitaph inscribed on the cross above his grave is Chesterton's:

> *The men that worked for England*
> *They have their graves at home.*

Iain was in high office for more than a decade as the children were growing up and he had insufficient time to spend with them. He was often not there when they asked questions or wanted information and this may have affected his relationship, especially with Torquil who did not consider it an unmixed advantage to have a famous father. Diana, a more extrovert character, thought it was.

'I have a ten year old son,' Iain said in an interview at the London Press Club in 1952, 'he's a lot like I was at that age. I'd like to take him out and play cricket, but there isn't any time.'

After Diana left school, she and Iain had lunch or dinner alone together at least once a week, usually at the Aperitif or the Ritz, and he often asked her views on political issues; he seldom expressed his own opinions but was always ready to listen to hers. It was the same with his son. If Torquil showed an interest in any major political event, Iain was prepared to discuss it, but he did not often raise political subjects himself and there were no arguments about politics at home or with the children's friends.

Iain had not met Diana's fiancé, David Heimann, until they became engaged and he and David did not get on particularly well until the annual cricket match which Iain organised every summer at Enfield. Somewhat pessimistically, he put David in at No. 8, but the young man made 39 not out, which was the top score, and from that day their relationship changed. David is almost as keen a cricket enthusiast as Iain was. And he was able and successful, which Iain liked. He and Diana were married on March 14, 1968. I made the traditional speech proposing their health at the wedding reception at Grosvenor House afterwards.

Iain was devoted to Torquil's wife, Meriol Trevor, who came from an old family in North Wales, and had been trained as a nurse at St Thomas's Hospital. She was almost as close to him as if she had been another daughter, and he was overjoyed when he heard he was going to be a grandfather. He had taken Eve, Torquil and Mel to the White Tower one evening to celebrate Eve's birthday and Torquil's the next day and they told him the news at dinner. He was convinced the new arrival would be a boy, and was so happy that he openly wept for joy in the restaurant. When the baby was born on September 3, 1970, six weeks after his grandfather died, Torquil decided to call him Iain, and at his christening in the crypt of the House of Commons I noticed the uncanny resemblance between them; their faces and the distinctive shape of the head were almost identical.

In September 1968, Iain Macleod took the whole family – Eve, Torquil and Mel, Diana and David – on a visit to the Isle of Lewis. They went to

Scaliscro, now a hotel, and to Lab Macleod's old home at Borve. The children had not been there for twenty years. It was a sentimental and a very successful pilgrimage.

Iain liked the family to be together for holidays. In the early years they rented houses in England and in 1957 they took the car to Normandy to see the D-day beaches and the war graves at Caen. After that they always went to Spain and stayed at the Hostel de la Gavina at S'Agaro on the Costa Brava at the kind invitation of its owner, Don Jose Ensesa.

Christmas was always spent at home at Enfield until the Macleods moved to London after Iain became Colonial Secretary. Then for some years they stayed with Geoffrey and Joan Kitchen at Rusper in Sussex. From 1964, when they leased the White Cottage at Potters Bar from the National Trust, all non-summer holidays were spent there until January 1970, when Iain and Eve went to Cyprus for a fortnight. They loved it and wanted to go back.

Occasionally Iain took an extra week or two on his own, as it was difficult for Eve to get away from her duties on the local Bench. He came to our house in Northern Ireland in September 1964 and again in 1965. It is well sited on a point of land jutting out into the sea, with lovely views across to the Copeland Islands and the coast of Scotland beyond. Iain said it reminded him of his boyhood holidays on the Isle of Lewis. He spent most of the time reading in the garden in the sunshine, but one day he came with us on a rough country walk with the dogs and almost got stuck on the top of a difficult gate that he was determined to climb. Until then I had not quite realised the extent of his disability. He never forgot the incident and never risked that sort of walk again. He sometimes seemed to have second sight and when my eldest stepdaughter, Sally, had just broken off her engagement to Michael Grylls (now M.P. for Chertsey), he confidently predicted that she would end up happily married to him, which in fact happened.

Iain and Torquil shared a common love of sport. If cricket and rugger were Iain's main interests, racing and athletics came very close behind. Indeed, he was fascinated by the best in any form of sport. It was the pursuit of excellence which attracted him. He took Torquil to the Olympic Games at Rome in 1960. They were there for a fortnight and watched every event from the first day to the last. The highlight was an afternoon when they saw two record-breaking track events and dined with Roger Bannister afterwards.

At home, Iain used to play tennis and cricket himself as long as his health allowed and he kept wicket for the Cockfosters Cricket Club until about 1954. Thereafter he got together a boys' cricket team every year, which included Torquil and Ian Orr-Ewing's son, Colin, to play against another boys' side recruited by a neighbour. The matches took place at Cockfosters ground near Barnet. There were four or five of them in successive seasons and later, as the boys grew up, they were replaced by a corresponding fixture against the local Myddleton Cricket Club, of which Iain was president. He fielded a president's team on the third Saturday in July from 1966 until he died, and always umpired the game himself. For these matches he supplemented Torquil's friends with two or three older players to strengthen the side. Nick Scott often played and Aidan Crawley, a former Harrow, Oxford and county cricketer, was usually the captain. Play was from 2.30 p.m. to 7.30, with lunch at Iain's house before and supper there afterwards. Iain loved the day.

He also enjoyed an afternoon at Lord's whenever he had time, especially the Lord's test match and the games between Middlesex and Yorkshire. I was almost as keen a supporter of Middlesex as he was of Yorkshire and we sometimes sat in the pavilion together, each cheering the successes of our respective sides. He loved the peace and leisure of watching cricket with his friends, and during the 1970 general election he took a box at Lord's for a match between England and the Rest of the World. Mr S. C. Griffith, secretary of the MCC, wrote of him: 'I have seldom known anyone more devoted to the game, nor anyone who had a wider knowledge of cricket records.'[1] When my wife and I went to see him at St George's hospital just before he died we were struck that the only photograph beside his bed was a large one of Gary Sobers, perhaps the greatest all-rounder in the game. It was evidence of Iain's love of cricket and of his passion for excellence in everything.

Rugger was an almost equal enthusiasm. He hardly ever missed a Calcutta Cup match and often made the after-dinner speech which followed the game. At the height of the shipyard and engineering strike, when he was Minister of Labour, he wrote to an old friend Dr Michael Mungavin: 'Shipyards permitting, I'll be at Twickenham. In fact I think I'll be there anyway.'

He had loved racing since Cambridge days and the prowess and achievements of a really good horse excited his imagination almost as much as those of a human being. In November 1965 he was to make the opening speech at a Conservative candidates' weekend conference in

1 Letter to the author, August 28, 1970.

Derbyshire. Somewhat to the surprise of the Chairman, Ann Spokes, he mentioned at lunch beforehand that he would like a television set available at the meeting 'so that we can see Arkle race'. It was known that this race would be in the middle of his speech. In the event, no television set could be found but half-way through the speech Geoffrey Johnson-Smith walked unobtrusively into the room holding a small radio. Abruptly Macleod stopped speaking and sat down, the set was tuned to full volume and everyone had to listen to the race commentator instead of to him. As soon as Arkle had won, Macleod continued his address without comment, as though it was the most natural thing in the world for Shadow Cabinet Ministers to interrupt their speeches to listen to horse races.

His other interests outside politics were chess, which he was fond of and played well, and reading, especially poetry. Almost every night he played a game of chess against himself in bed just before he went to sleep. He read Shakespeare over and over again for hours on end, political biography and detective stories if they were good ones. He was not interested in music or the arts. On one occasion, when he was Minister of Labour, the German Ambassador invited him to Glyndebourne. He declined politely. He regarded the opera as a penance. But he liked going to the theatre whenever he could spare the time and never minded what sort of play provided it was good of its kind. He was indifferent to beautiful scenery, and when he was abroad would prefer to stay in his hotel than motor any distance to look at a view.

In small personal things Iain was incapable of keeping a secret. If he had bought a birthday present for Eve, he always gave her guesses and hints as to what it was and when, in the end, she guessed right, he accused Diana or Torquil of having told her. He loved Christmas and took it seriously. He always lit the candles himself and enjoyed buying presents and wrapping them up. His Christmas present purchasing routine was always the same. The car dropped him at the top of the Burlington arcade and met him an hour later at the Piccadilly end, from which he emerged carrying innumerable parcels of every shape and size, his Christmas shopping completed.

He enjoyed recounting silly stories if he thought they were funny. His favourite was a Skipton one about a fire at a local farm: the fire engine arrived quickly, driven by an Asian immigrant. 'Where are you from, lad?' enquired the farmer. 'Pakistan,' was the reply, to which the farmer commented: 'Thou 'st done well. They're not here from Keighley yet.'

In the last years of his life Iain's appearance belied his personality. He moved slowly and, except when his face lit up in a puckish grin, he looked dour. But his mind was as quick as ever and one never had to underline or emphasize anything. He had registered and often answered the point almost before it had been made. If he was in pain, he could be rude and unsociable, but he was often the gayest and most stimulating of companions and no one could contribute more in company he enjoyed and on a subject in which he was interested. He had great charm when he wished but no small talk and he did not care for social chat, which he considered a waste of time. I remember, after inviting him to dinner, asking whether he would like it to be a party or would prefer to dine with us quietly. He replied: 'It depends on who else in coming, but I'd far sooner have dinner with you on your own or perhaps with one or two others, hand-picked.' On these occasions he always liked to talk about any political issue he was interested in at the time. If the argument was keen and he was in full flight, he would brush aside any interjection with, 'Don't interrupt me at a comma.' He also loved talking about cricket, especially if it was during a test match series. One night when he and Eve and Diana and David Heimann were dining with us to celebrate Diana's engagement, we discussed nothing but cricket and the match then in progress and neither Diana's wedding, about to take place, nor the current political crisis were even mentioned.

Iain loved being at 11 Downing Street and was moved by the experience. He had a family dinner there on June 30th to celebrate his appointment as Chancellor of the Exchequer. At the end of the meal he made a little speech, a tribute to Eve for all her help. She had indeed been a rock of support over the years. As George Hutchinson wrote, 'Her spirit never failed. She was unflinching, sometimes fierce, in defending [Iain] whenever he was under attack. She was always at his side in rough weather.'[2] It was an imaginative gesture on the part of Edward Heath to recommend her for a life peerage and enable her to remain, in her own right, in the world of politics which she had graced for so long. Iain gave Torquil the Bible on which he had sworn allegiance and Diana his scroll of office as Chancellor. He never saw her again because she went into hospital soon afterwards for a serious operation on her back.

Iain Macleod was a straightforward and in some ways a very simple person, although as a politician he was often subtle. He was interested in the exercise of power, but not in the making of money. Perhaps that is

2 The *Spectator*, July 31, 1970.

why he left so little. He was totally honest in all his financial dealings, large or small. He enjoyed the luxuries of life – comfortable surroundings, good food and good wine – but they were not important to him. He had the right values. He was humane and compassionate though he could be intolerant of the stupid, the prejudiced and the hypocritical.

He was a very brave man and his courage was moral and political as well as physical. He never spoke of his pain and one could only tell from sometimes seeing the sweat on his forehead how much he was suffering. He was completely stoical and had learned to live with it. 'I have less pain than President Kennedy had,' he used to say defiantly, 'and I am less crippled than President Roosevelt.'

He was inclined to be intellectually lazy, but he worked hard when he had to and very quickly; nothing was ever skimped or half done. He had a sharp mind with a cutting edge and he was always clear and incisive. He had an endearing gaiety and a keen sense of humour, which could be boyish or dry but was never unkind. There was a volcanic quality about him – a feeling of latent fire. You could love Iain or you could hate him. But you could not be indifferent to him. He was never boring.

He was personally fond of many people whose politics he disliked – Jim Callaghan, Nye Bevan and Alfred Robens were examples. If he didn't like someone, that was that. But he was intensely loyal to his friends and his feelings about them never changed, no matter what they did nor what differences of opinion he might have with them. He did not have many close friends, but those he had he valued and kept till the day he died.

His oldest friends in the higher echelons of the Tory Party were Robert Carr, Reggie Maudling and Edward Boyle, and he was fond of Reggie Bennett and Charles Longbottom, who had worked loyally for him as Parliamentary Private Secretaries. Later he became friends with Ian Gilmour, Humphry Berkeley, Norman St John Stevas, Patrick Jenkin, Terence Higgins, David Howell and Barney Hayhoe. His last Parliamentary Private Secretary, Nick Scott, was a great friend towards the end of his life.

His relationship with Edward Heath was politically productive but not personally close. They worked together in One Nation days and again when Macleod was Shadow Chancellor. Socially they seldom entered each other's houses, or talked at all intimately on any matter unconnected with business. This was not perhaps surprising. Iain had no feeling for either of Ted Heath's interests – music and sailing; he did not understand music and he disliked the sea. Their only common ground was politics;

so they normally saw each other only at meetings of the Cabinet or Shadow Cabinet or latterly, for working discussions in Heath's room at the House of Commons. Macleod did not feel he knew the Prime Minister much better after their twenty years as colleagues than when they had entered the House together on the same day in 1950. But he admired Heath's determination, honesty and strength of character, and was entirely loyal to him from the day of his election as Leader of the Party till the day of his own death.

Outside politics, he was and remained devoted to his old university bridge partner, Colin Harding, and to a fellow rugger enthusiast, John Tallent. And he had a turbulent relationship with Randolph Churchill, which deserves special mention and was well described by Ian Gilmour as: 'Sometimes open war, sometimes armed conflict, occasionally armed peace, but which always had on both sides a solid basis of affection and respect.'[3]

Iain Macleod and Randolph Churchill were well matched, and Iain's essay on Randolph in Kay Halle's book[4] is, like so many in this volume, a revealing study. Randolph was larger than life. He was an aggressive, outrageous eccentric, a brilliant, bloody-minded aristocrat. Iain, with a different background but a better mind, admired Randolph's style and almost relished his rudeness. Both men were intolerant, both were strong and both were brave. Iain wrote that their relationship as editor and journalist was a stormy and affectionate one 'which exactly mirrored our attitude to each other'. It was a friendship of equals, sparring, wrestling, arguing; not intimate but always stimulating.

Macleod described Churchill as 'a great, if somewhat unpredictable journalist', which was an understatement. And again: 'It is a hopeless task trying to explain to people who did not know him how overwhelming was Randolph's charm, and there is no need to those who knew him . . . those who knew him best loved him best.' When Randolph died, Macleod wrote: 'No one can take his place, he was irreplaceable.'

Iain Macleod loved children and they felt instinctively that he was their friend. He met Chris Chataway's son one afternoon going into the House of Commons and, although he had not seen the boy for three years, he greeted him instantly with: 'Hello, Mark, how are you and how is school going?' There had been no prompting. Iain had remembered his face and his name and wanted to express his interest. It was typical of his attitude

3 The *Listener*, July 30, 1970.
4 *Randolph Churchill, the Young Unpretender*, Heinemann, 1971.

to young people. He taught Ian Gilmour's children how to play bridge 'with such humour and lightness of touch that a twelve-year-old thought nothing of doubling his bid of six no trumps. Of course he made seven'.[5]

When he attended Torquil's wedding at Godalming in 1967 the manager of the local hotel where he lunched beforehand was impressed at the prospect of entertaining such a distinguished public figure, but as soon as Iain walked in, Ethne Bannister's youngest son, Thomas, rushed up to him and said in his broad Yorkshire accent: 'Oh, cum quick, Ooncle Iain, there are some fantastic goldfish in the pond,' and, to the manager's astonishment, the Shadow Chancellor took his great-nephew's hand and walked like a lamb into the garden.

Macleod's interest in and influence on the Young Conservatives was especially strong. When he was Colonial Secretary they felt he was expressing their views at the highest level, and he never lost their support and loyalty. He listened to them with tolerance and respect; his humanity and idealism were an inspiration to them and he gave them generous encouragement. My son, who is a Socialist, has always said that only Iain and what he stood for could ever have persuaded him to vote Conservative. Robert Carr, in his address at Iain's Memorial Service at Enfield, thought that this influence 'on a whole generation of younger politicians' would be his greatest legacy 'and it is in them that his talents will live and be amplified'.

In the last few years of his life Iain Macleod became the main inspiration of a new charity which he named 'Crisis at Christmas'. It was organised by the Rev. Nick Beacock and sponsored by the Archbishop of Canterbury and by leading members of all the political parties. Its purpose was to bring some comfort and happiness to those who were cold and hungry and sleeping rough, with no one to help or care for them. Committee meetings were held in an East London vicarage, and Iain and Eve Macleod gave a surprising amount of their time to raising money for it. However cold the weather, Iain was always there to start off and welcome back the members of youth clubs and other organisations who took part in the sponsored walks which were one of its fund-raising activities.

Iain Macleod was a member of many London clubs. Apart from the MCC, he joined Grillion's, a dining club, which he attended whenever he could, and the Beefsteak, where he was a member for only a short time and which he seldom visited. When he became Chairman of the Conser-

5 Ian Gilmour in a broadcast interview, July 30, 1970.

vative Party he also joined the Carlton Club as a duty, but he saw little point in meeting the same people at dinner as he would have seen in the Members' Dining Room at the House of Commons and he did not use it very often. He preferred the Constitutional Club, of which he was a member for a long time and president for the last two years of his life. The club commissioned a portrait of him, painted posthumously from photographs by Alfred Janes, which hangs beside that of Sir Winston Churchill, another former president. But the club he enjoyed most was White's. He joined in 1952 and used it constantly, as an agreeable escape from politics and politicians.

Iain Macleod was in his element, or one of his elements, at White's. It was in a sense a throwback to his Cambridge days. He enjoyed the company of the hard-drinking circle at the bar on the ground floor. Although he was not a social snob, he was attracted by the 'ruling class' world of White's. As J. W. M. Thompson put it: 'He had no time for the class war; yet he was not unresponsive to the glamour of High Toryism. He castigated the Etonian influence upon his party but he was a proud member of White's.' He sometimes suggested that I should join the club and often teased me for being a renegade from the ranks of the Old Etonians.

In the early days of the 1951 Conservative Government, soon after Macleod became Minister of Health and when we were enduring endless all-night sittings in Parliament, he went to play bridge at White's on one of the rare evenings when we were not confined to the House of Commons. He remained all night at the table and returned home at nine a.m. £380 better off. As he explained afterwards to Reggie Bennett: 'I was the only chap present who understood the rules.' Some of the older members were rather scandalised that a Minister of the Crown should sandwich an all-night sitting at cards between two all-night sittings of the House; they considered it irresponsible and talked of it for weeks afterwards.

As the guest of Reggie Bennett, Macleod often dined with the Thursday Club, an amusing collection of wags and wits, with whom he was very popular. Among the members were many of the best script writers of the time and some of the most prominent people in show business. They included Peter Ustinov, James Robertson Justice, Larry Adler, Macdonald Hastings, Arthur Christiansen, Mike Parker and Paddy Campbell, each one of them an outstanding raconteur; but Iain was in the same league and they loved him. He was one of the few non-leftwing intellectuals whom they thought as intelligent and as funny as they were themselves. They used the top floor of Bernard Walsh's Wheeler's restaurant in Soho for their gatherings.

The Thursday Club, which is now defunct, merged into the *soi-disant* Wessex Hunting club, which was merely an excuse for alcoholic evenings in congenial company. The members sometimes met at Reggie Bennett's house at Fareham and one such occasion was during the desperately cold winter of 1962/63. Bennett ensured that the party at least would be a warm one. They began with champagne, drank burgundy during dinner and consumed six bottles of his vintage port after it. They ate Chinese food and only chopsticks were allowed for the purpose. Iain suggested a sweepstake on James Robertson Justice's blood pressure, made possible because Bennett had a blood pressure machine to record it; but they cannot have read this very accurately since, to everyone's astonishment, it revealed the improbable information that Robertson Justice had the blood pressure of a boy of seventeen. Iain was jubilant as he had got the low pool. After the Chinese dishes, Henrietta Bennett had concocted a gooseberry fool but unfortunately it had not set properly. Someone bet Iain thirty shillings to a pound note that he couldn't eat a basinful of it with the aid only of the chopsticks. In the course of doing so he spread the gooseberry fool about a little, but he won his bet comfortably and in the process earned the lasting respect of these hardened campaigners.

One of Iain Macleod's nicest attributes was his loyalty to his friends, especially if they were in trouble and needed his support. When Peter Goldman was defeated at Orpington and, later, Humphry Berkeley at Lancaster, Iain was the first to go to them to console and to sympathise. As Norman St John Stevas put it, Iain 'always forgave an injury, but he never forgot a benefit'.[6] When Berkeley resigned from the Conservative Party in April 1968, Macleod wrote immediately to *The Times* to say, 'I share your view that Humphry Berkeley is a loss to the Conservative Party. I believe he will return.' It was an act of generosity on the part of a member of the Shadow Cabinet to an unpopular figure who had just left the party. When Berkeley did return temporarily to the fold in September 1969, Macleod at once issued a public statement welcoming him back.

George Hutchinson recalls a meeting of the National Executive Committee of the Conservative Party in 1963, shortly after Jack Profumo's resignation: '... one zealot rose to his feet and called on Macleod not only to denounce John Profumo, apparently in the name of the party, but to

6 *Catholic Herald*, July 31, 1970.

do so in a public statement. White-faced and tense, Iain heard him out, and then, in a voice icy with contempt, gave his answer: 'Jack and Valerie Profumo have been friends of my wife and myself for many years,' he said, 'and we're not going to desert them now or ever. They will always be our friends. I have not another word to say."

I ran into some serious constituency trouble in the autumn of 1969 when a right-wing group, dubbed by Harold Wilson 'the skinheads of Surbiton', wanted to run me out of public life after twenty years in Parliament because of my allegedly too liberal views on race relations. They initiated a campaign to replace me as Conservative candidate at the next election by someone who shared the opinions of Enoch Powell. The story broke in a full-page article in *The Times* on Saturday, October 25th. Iain was out of London for the weekend, but he somehow contrived to get a letter to *The Times* which appeared at the top of the correspondence columns the following Monday morning. He was the first of my colleagues to come to my defence. At the same time he wrote me the letter which appears in facsimile opposite page 256.

As soon as I received this letter, I telephoned Iain to thank him and to say that his gesture was of course out of the question; he was the Shadow Chancellor and could not conceivably leave the party. He answered curtly: 'You must know me well enough by now to know that I never write things I do not mean', and he rang off. It was entirely typical of his selfless loyalty and generosity to a friend.

To the public Macleod was best known for his ability as a speaker. He understood the importance of communication and he was a brilliant communicator in any medium – in private conversation, on the television, in the House of Commons, where he was regarded as one of the finest debaters of his political generation, and at public meetings. He knew instinctively how to set alight an audience of thousands and he was at his best at the annual party conference, where almost invariably he made the most inspiring speech of all. He had a gift for words and phrases, as Churchill and Macmillan had, and an exquisite sense of timing. But Macmillan was an actor; Macleod was a poet.

As a speaker, particularly if he was on a platform and at a higher level than the audience, his disability was no disadvantage, because he did not have to raise or turn his head. He always understated his 'minor afflictions'. 'I have one,' he would say, 'that I recommend to all aspiring Tory politicians; I find it very difficult to turn my head to the left.'

7 The *Spectator*, July 31, 1970.

Eve Macleod remembers how he prepared his speeches. She would hear him saying a phrase over and over again till he had the exact inflection and timing. He often composed a speech lying in bed, where he did much of his work of this kind. He would gaze vacantly out of the window, then reach for a scrap of paper and scribble a line or two. Eventually he wrote down six or seven headings and built the speech round them in his mind. His memory did the rest.

He had the jugular instinct in debate and, with his strange, high, rather beautiful, bell-like voice, he could transmit political excitement. In an age when most politicians have adopted a technocratic style of speaking, Macleod was not afraid or embarrassed to talk of duty and principle and vision. He was never dull or pompous. He was one of the few people for whom members sitting in the smoking room would leave their drinks and go into the Chamber to hear. David Watt wrote of him:

> At his best he was a star of the first order. Hunched over the Despatch Box, he would adopt a lucid, pleasant conversational tone for five or ten minutes at a time, then he would trail his coat a little, flicking his opponents with the lightest touch of mockery. There would be an interjection from somewhere below the gangway and slowly the whole of his body would swing round like some great gun being brought to bear, a smile of satanic anticipation would spread across his face and the broadside would blow the opposition out of the water amid a gale of laughter.[8]

No one doubts the ability and determination of Edward Heath's Government to take firm decisions; the criticism is that Ministers do not always succeed in putting the best case for the decisions and may not win the political argument that follows them. As the *Economist* expressed it when Iain Macleod died – if we negotiated our way into the EEC – 'then his real moment of destiny, the time when all his political skill would have been called into play, would have arrived. Mr Heath has acquired authority; Sir Alec has always had respect; Mr Maudling has always been intelligent. But when the day comes for this Government to stand up and declare itself, the European cause will be put the worse to the party and to the country because Macleod will not be putting it.'[8] This was true. Because of the success of Heath's vital meeting in Paris with President Pompidou, and because of Geoffrey Rippon's brilliant negotiations on

8 The *Financial Times*, July 22, 1970.
9 The *Economist*, July 25, 1970.

our behalf in Brussels, Britain got good terms for our entry into Europe; but we felt the lack of Macleod's inspirational advocacy. It did not matter because the Government carried the House of Commons without it, but we should certainly have joined the European Community with greater public enthusiasm and excitement if Macleod had lived to put the case for doing so.

In a Government, the hall-mark of which has been deeds rather than words, it was not only in the Common Market debates that we missed Macleod and I have heard colleagues say again and again: 'How we need Iain now'.

Macleod did not owe his position as a senior member of the Cabinet to anyone. He was there on merit and in his own right, and he was strong enough to put his view and argue his case without fear or favour. In every Cabinet only a few Ministers care to speak before the Prime Minister except on their own departmental subjects – most wait until the Prime Minister has spoken and then say the same thing in different words. In Edward Heath's Cabinet, Macleod, had he lived, would have been one of those who were prepared to speak first. But he seldom intervened during the discussions, and would often reserve his own opinion until he had heard everyone else. J. W. M. Thompson thought 'he was the most interesting man in the Cabinet'.[9]

As I never served in Cabinet, I have had to turn to my senior colleagues for their estimates of Macleod as a contributor at their meetings. They varied and I give them without attributing the sources:

1 'His presentation of a point of view was simple and arresting and he was always listened to. He contributed more as Colonial Secretary and as Shadow Chancellor or Chancellor than at other periods.'

2 'He was very good in Cabinet and, although not a frequent speaker, he was always clear, forceful, strong and wise.'

3 'He was often quiet, almost dormant, in Cabinet.'

4 'He contributed a lot and made strong statements on things he felt strongly about. He was a valuable ally in Cabinet.'

5 'The quality of his advice was erratic and he was not a consistently wise councillor.'

6 'His judgement was good. He expressed himself well and succinctly.'

9 The *Spectator*, July 25, 1970.

7 'When he had a point to make he made it with brevity, relevance and force. If he had nothing new to contribute, he did not speak unless invited to do so.'

In Opposition, Macleod was eloquent and combative; he loved a fight, but it did not satisfy him. As the *Economist* suggested: 'At heart he was a man of government . . . it was the essential process of policy making and political persuasion, conducted from the centre of a governing party, that fascinated him . . . it was for this and not just for a great department that he worked.'

He longed to have his feet under a Whitehall desk again or under the Cabinet table. This, for him and for anyone in public life who has been in government, was what politics are about.

Iain Macleod was a professional and he enjoyed the game. He was adroit and ingenious, with an acute political sense, but he was not devious. He had high ambitions but he seldom compromised to satisfy them and he always put his convictions before his own self-interest. Duty mattered to him. He was steadfast in essential matters and his political integrity was total. 'He possessed a savage tongue, an incisive intellect and a moral passion that is all too rare today.'[10] He had political imagination, though he was never a great innovator. He felt a genuine concern for what ordinary people want, but he always tried to make them want something better.

Macleod had the administrative ability, the intellectual force and the oratorical brilliance, as well as the courage and strength of character, to lead the nation, but he had made enemies in his own party and in the end he had to settle for second place.

The Colonial Secretaryship, more perhaps than any of his other appointments, showed his courage, his determination and his strategic clarity of thought; and his work at the Colonial Office was probably the best and was certainly the most important of his career. He knew that great deeds are not done by stealth and he was always open in declaring his objectives, often at the cost of personal popularity. He understood and sympathised with the problems of the New Commonwealth and of the continent of Africa in particular. Mr Arikpo, the Foreign Minister of Nigeria, was right when he said: 'His death is a great loss, especially at a time when there are signs of impending strain in Commonwealth relations.'

10 *Evening Standard*, July 21, 1970.

Macleod was the spokesman in Cabinet and in the Conservative Party for enlightened Tory radicalism. He could never have been a Socialist because he believed in individual responsibility and disliked state control and allocation. As Ronald Butt wrote in *The Times*[11]: 'He was a Tory by temperament . . . because he had an organic view of society; an understanding of its continuity and its development. He believed in the durability of certain fundamental political ideas and attitudes. That belief made him a Tory. He believed in their capacity for growth. That made him a radical Tory.'

Macleod often quoted Lord Randolph Churchill's maxim: 'Trust the people.' He was essentially a moderate and disliked extremism in any form. He was also a romantic who understood the poetry of politics. He was sensitive to the need for a balance between freedom and order and of the danger to freedom from disorder. He supported the Selsdon Park[12] policy commitments, yet his opponents could never, with any credibility, have accused him of being a 'Selsdon Man' in the sense in which they tried to make political propaganda from the phrase.

Harold Wilson regarded him as far the most dangerous potential Conservative leader from the Labour point of view. 'He was the front-runner of his generation' in Tory politics, yet 'he was nowhere near a contender for the leadership when his generation first really contested it in 1965.'[13] Harold Lever described him as 'the shrewdest and ablest of the modern Tories . . . the House of Commons has lost a great debater and dozens of us on both sides of the House have lost a great friend . . . the Government [has lost] the key-stone in its arch of power.'[14] His early death, like that of Oliver Stanley, Hugh Gaitskell and Aneurin Bevan, diminished the public life of Britain. Looking back, in a *Sunday Telegraph* interview, over his years in politics, Charles Hill named Macleod as one of the three politicians who had made the greatest impression on him. The other two were Macmillan and Butler.

This is a good, strong Tory Government and it was needed, but it looked much more right wing the day after Iain Macleod died than it had looked the day before. 'With the retirement of Lord Butler and more recently of Lord Boyle, Macleod was the natural leader of that feeling and attitude to society in the Conservative Party which is loosely described as

11 *The Times*, July 22, 1970.
12 Selsdon Park Hotel, near Croydon, was the venue for the Conservative Shadow Cabinet conference which made the final decisions on party policy for the 1970 election.
13 The *Economist*, July 25, 1970.
14 *New Statesman*, July 24, 1970.

being left wing, but has its roots in Peel and Disraeli. . . . It will not be easy to replace him as Chancellor of the Exchequer; it is never easy to replace a major figure. What is still more difficult is to see how he can be replaced as a spokesman for the type of enlightened Conservatism which he represented.'[15] The *Economist*'s obituary article made the same point:

> There are many liberal-minded men left in the Conservative Party . . . but without Iain Macleod and also without Lord Boyle in active politics, there is a sense of weakening in the radical Tory ranks, not in the Cabinet but down where the Powellites and near-Powellites are waiting. It ought to be an opportunity for Mr Maudling, in particular, to identify himself, and to be seen to be identified, with those causes which he has always upheld. The left-of-centre Tories are now painfully in need of a leader.[16]

This is true. The same opportunity is open to Robert Carr or William Whitelaw, or, indeed, to the Prime Minister himself. A Conservative government, if it wishes to retain power, must always be managed from a position just to the left of centre. If no one takes this opportunity, the party is unlikely to win the next general election in Britain, because even the best of governments yields the centre ground in politics at its peril. Certainly Macleod, who understood this, would never have allowed it to happen.

The valedictory speeches in the House of Commons the day after his death all stressed his courage, political as well as physical. Harold Wilson singled it out as the hall-mark of his public and personal life: 'It was a courage all of us saw day by day and all of us respected, although he never sought to trade on his disabilities. He asked no quarter, just as he gave none.' And the Leader of the Opposition added that 'His wit could be biting and rough. He enjoyed the fight. But it was strife without malice.'

Jeremy Thorpe, who had just suffered a tragic bereavement through the death in a motor car accident of his beautiful wife, Caroline, came bravely to the House of Commons to pay his tribute to an opponent: 'For me he was one of the most courageous men in Parliament. We can say with Joseph Addison that he had "unbounded courage and compassion joined".' Perhaps the Prime Minister summed up Macleod's career best when he said, quite simply, he was 'a great servant of the State'.

15 *The Times*, July 22, 1970.
16 The *Economist*, July 25, 1970.

The funeral service was held on July 24th. Through the kindness of Air Chief Marshall Sir Charles Elworthy, Diana, still in great pain after her operation, was flown by RAF aeroplane to Leeds and then taken by ambulance to Gargrave. The rest of Iain's family and friends travelled to Yorkshire by train or car. The little church was packed with a congregation which included many Cabinet and parliamentary colleagues, and a crowd of 300 people had gathered outside in the rain. The Prime Minister read the lesson and a moving address was given by the vicar.

Eve had intended to hold the London service at St Margaret's but was told that it would not be large enough and that Westminster Abbey would be more appropriate. On this occasion Harold Macmillan read the lesson and the Bishop of London gave the address. Another service was held next day at Enfield, at which Robert Carr paid tribute to Iain. Despite their close friendship, Carr reflected:

'It was not easy to know him. There was always some further hidden depth to probe. . . . He left a strong presence behind him wherever he went.'

Iain Macleod's body lies near the graves of his parents and sister in the peace of Gargrave churchyard in the Yorkshire dales, but his spirit must sometimes fly to the Western Isles from which he sprang:

There's an isle beyond the sunset in the Western main
Where the dead are done with dying and are young again
And the sun streams softly downwards like an endless rain
In Tir-an-Og.

There they live, the lovely women and the bravest of the men,
There the chiefs of Siol Torquil go out to war again,
And the pipes of the MacCrimmons are waiting in the glen
In Tir-an-Og.

There the sands go dancing downwards to meet the shining sea,
There the great hills rear triumphant heads disdainfully and free,
And all my dreams are haunted and are ever calling me
To Tir-an-Og.

Siol Torquil is Gaelic for 'the seed of Torquil' and refers to the descendants of Torquil, the second son of Leod (born *circa* 1200) and the ancestor of the Macleods of Lewis. Leod's eldest son, Norman, was the ancestor of the Macleods of Skye and Dame Flora Macleod of Dunvegan is directly descended from him. The prefix 'Mac' means 'son of'.

Tir-an-Og is a Gaelic version of Never-never-land.

The poem was written by Iain Macleod at the beginning of the war.

Sanitas Sanitatum
'The Condition of the People'

Text of a lecture by Iain Macleod
delivered at the Conservative Political Centre, 1954.

⟨~~~⟩

IF you are talking about the history of a great political party, or indeed, if you are tracing the origins of any institution in this country, there is always a temptation to fall into Gladstone's error and trace the steam engine back to the tea kettle. I do not want to spend much time doing that: although I am not sure when the Tory faith really started, at least I know, or I think I know, how Tory Democracy started. It is about that that I want to talk to you today, and about its relevance to the modern social problems that we are trying to solve.

The title of my lecture gives the clue to its origins: Disraeli started the idea of the Tory Democracy and Lord Randolph proclaimed it; Lord Randolph's son today is the head of a team of Ministers that is trying to put it into practice. The title comes from a speech of Disraeli's on April 3, 1872, at Manchester:

> A great scholar and a great wit three hundred years ago said that in his opinion there was a great mistake in the Vulgate, which as you all know is the Latin translation of the Holy Scriptures, and that instead of saying 'Vanity of vanities, all is vanity' – Vanitas vanitatum, omnia vanitas – the wise and witty king really said 'Sanitas sanitatum, omnia sanitas'. It is impossible to overrate the importance of this subject. After all the first consideration of a Minister should be the health of the people.

Those were Disraeli's words in 1872: how do they stand up to modern conditions and to the problems of the Social Service State? I said that Disraeli was the inspirer of Tory Democracy and Lord Randolph proclaimed it: and the important words in which Tory Democracy was first formulated come from the article written by Lord Randolph in the

327

Fortnightly Review of May, 1883, when a statue was unveiled to Disraeli:

Some of Lord Beaconsfield's phrases will bear any amount of micro-scopic examination. Speaking at Manchester in 1871, by the alteration of a letter in a quotation from the Vulgate, he revealed the policy which ought to guide Tory leaders at the present time – Sanitas sanitatum, omnia sanitas. Such was the quotation in which a careful mind will discover a scheme of social progress and reform of dimensions so large and wide-spreading that many volumes would not suffice to explain its details. By it is shadowed forth, and in it is embraced, a social revolution which, passing by and diverting attention from wild long-ings for organic change, commences with the little peddling boards of health which occupy and delight the local government department, comprises Lord Salisbury's plans for the amelioration of the dwellings of the poor, carries with it Lord Carnarvon's idea of compulsory National Insurance, includes Sir Wilfred Lawson's temperance propa-ganda, preserves and reclaims commons and open spaces favoured by Mr Bryce, constructs peoples' parks, collects and opens to the masses museums, libraries, art galleries, does not disdain the public wash-houses of Mr Jesse Collings. Public and private thrift must animate the whole, for it is from public thrift that the funds for these largesses can be drawn and it is by private thrift alone that their results can be utilized and appreciated. The expression – Tory Democracy – has excited the wonder of some, the alarm of others and great and bitter ridicule from the Radical Party. But the 'Tory Democracy' may yet exist; the elements for its composition only require to be collected and the labour may some day possibly be effected by the man, whoever he may be, upon whom the mantle of Elijah has descended.

Now that is a very long quotation, and those of us who wrote *One Nation*, when we gave that quotation, added the words that 'Lord Randolph did not live to assume Elijah's mantle and inertia settled on the Tory Party'. That, I am afraid, was true.

That, as I see it, is the blueprint of Tory Democracy; it clothes in words the idea given by Disraeli at Manchester. And it is worth noticing for a moment how up-to-date that article of Lord Randolph's, written in 1883, is today. Indeed, apart from the fact that, as far as I know, temper-ance propaganda plays no particular part in Tory Democracy, the rest of it has either been brought into being or could serve still as an extract from a policy manifesto of today. It is, after all, only a year or two ago that what was described in 1883 as the ideal of compulsory National Insurance has come into being. We are still concerning ourselves with plans for the amelioration of the dwellings of the poor.

But more important than the origins of Tory Democracy is to know what it is. I dare say you all have different views and interpretations about that, so let me give you my own. Tory Democracy depends on three things. First of all it proclaims the duties of man, as against and before the rights of man. Secondly, it believes that if power is given to you, it must be used only in trust to help those who have entrusted it to you. Thirdly – to use the title of a book that Angus Maude, myself and others wrote – Tory Democracy believes that we are 'One Nation'. Perhaps on that last point, of being 'One Nation', I can again turn back to Disraeli and quote to you a word or two from the second great speech at the Crystal Palace which he made a month later. This is what the Tory Party was then, what I hope it is now, and what it must be in the future if it is to live:

> The Tory Party, unless it is a National Party, is nothing. It is not a con-
> federacy of nobles, it is not a democratic multitude, it is a Party formed
> from all the numerous classes in the realm, classes alike and equal before
> the Law, but whose different conditions and different aims give vigour
> and variety to our National life.

A year or two after these two speeches, Disraeli, as Prime Minister, got the chance to put into effect the things he believed in. As you know, in those years from 1874 to 1880, the first really great comprehensive pro-gramme of social reform was put into being. It was described in a sneering phrase, that has become famous, by a Liberal Member of Parliament as a 'policy of sewage'. That, then, is the question which I am going to put to you: should the idea of a sanitary policy, the elevation of the condition of the people, again to use Disraeli's phrase, still inspire our thinking. Is it out of date? And to what extent, in particular, does the provision of universal social services in education, in health, in insurance, alter the emphasis of Disraeli's words?

I hope it will not seem heresy even to invite you to consider such a suggestion. After all, again to use a phrase that you will know, 'Change', we are told, 'is our ally': we ought to consider the implications of modern conditions even on the fundamental principles of Tory belief. *The Manchester Guardian*, commenting on the social policy that we put forward after all the years of study that went into it in the years of opposition in 1945–50, said that the Tory Party had never in its history had, or put forward, such an enlightened policy of social reform. How have we carried it out? To what extent have the social service Ministers been successful in what they sought to do? I am going to take my examples entirely from two fields – first of all *housing*, and secondly *health*.

We have, as you know, left behind our target of three hundred thousand houses a year. We are turning now, through the Rent and Repairs Bill, to consider the even larger question of the preservation of the existing stock of houses. I want you to consider what sort of emphasis we should give to housing in the future, in the light of the success of the past year or two. Perhaps it is easiest if we concentrate on one particular point.

The housing subsidy, as you know, has recently been reduced, as a result largely of the reduction in bank rate and the consequential reduction in rate of interest of the Public Works Loans Board which largely finances local authorities in these fields. What is to be the future of subsidies? Are we to go on as we are now, with one subsidy for all needs, or should we have a differential subsidy which will give emphasis in the sectors of building we want to strengthen? Should we, for example, have a general *needs* subsidy at all? If we do have one, should it be substantially smaller than the subsidy that would be given for slum clearance, or the replacement of overcrowding, or perhaps for one or two other social purposes? If you reduce the general needs subsidy, it might then be possible to give an even larger subsidy to the *social* sector of housing. It is worth remembering that by the middle of the 1930s the only houses that attracted subsidies were those involved in slum clearance, the avoiding of overcrowding, and the provision of houses for agricultural workers: the motive was the same in each case, because they were expected to be, and indeed they were, houses for a low income group. That was, as you see, essentially 'a policy of sewage'. It was a concentration of policy in this most important of all the social service fields, a concentration on those who needed it most.

So the question that naturally arises from what I said earlier is – should we go back to that? Let us be clear about what would happen if we did. If you had, for example, a differential subsidy – with a low subsidy, or even no subsidy at all, on the ordinary council house for the man of ordinary means – it would follow that councils would have to make up the difference; this would be done either through the rates, which would be extremely difficult at their present level, or by charging (as indeed they already have power to do) differential rents to their different council-house tenants. That would mean, in a sense, a means test. Now it may be that we are too much afraid of the term Means Test. It is worth reading, if you want to study the impact of the means test on the social services, a CPC publication called *The Social Services: Needs and Means*, which has just been re-issued. I had a very minor share in the first edition and none at all in the second, which is almost entirely Enoch Powell's work. It may be, too, that we hear a little more than is strictly relevant about the odd case, and I doubt if it is much more than that, of the person in a council house with an income of £2,000 a year and a large car, which he garages round the corner before he returns to his own dwelling. But let us, at least, be clear – whatever view we take on this – what a policy of sewage would mean.

All the early housing legislation, the Cross Acts, the Torrens Acts, the great Act of 1890, derived their powers essentially from sanitary regulations. Indeed before 1949, subsidised housing was only for the working classes, however poorly defined that term may have been. Do we want, then, to go back? At first sight you would answer Yes, without question; if we have gone as far as we have on the road towards provision of new dwellings, it would seem a logical conclusion to turn to the clearance of the slums. Indeed, it is. But does it follow from that that you should abandon the idea of helping, through subsidies, the ordinary person who may still find it difficult to provide the money to buy his own house, and I think we must remember this as we try to make up our minds: it may be that today the priorities are not the same as they were in the 1930s. Then, beyond any doubt, the motive that impelled the Conservative Housing Ministers of the day was the fact of overcrowding and the poverty that overcrowding brought with it. But I would not say today that overcrowding, or indeed poverty or hunger, is the main social problem that we have to face; I should have thought it was old age. Therefore, if it be true that the emphasis has switched, it might be reasonable to expect that policy would switch with it. There might at least be a case – I put this to you as no more than a thought – for encouraging, by differential subsidies perhaps, the provision of accommodation to meet the most hardly pressed sections of the people today.

There are, then, three things we can do: we can go back to the pure milk of Disraelian doctrine, and in fact to the position of the 1930s; we can go on as we are with one subsidy, with no particular emphasis placed on the working classes or on the old people or on slum clearance, as far as financial arrangements are concerned; or we can recast the whole scheme of subsidies to give effect to what we believe are the changes in social priorities.

Perhaps I can sum up what I want to say here in this way: is there a sound argument, and if so what is it, for saying that, whereas education and health and insurance are universal and in some measure compulsory, housing alone of the great social services must remain selective? Well, frankly, I ask the question and I leave it unanswered: partly because it is very difficult, being a Minister, to speculate on what a colleague might do in his own particular field, and secondly, because I think it right that you should seek to come to your own conclusions on this matter and to see, in view of our triumphant success since 1951 in the provision of houses, what the next and the natural step should be.

Now I want to turn to my second example, and to draw my illustrations from health. Again we said in *One Nation*, 'we have at present a service to cure ill-health, we need a service to promote good health'. That again is a sentence in direct descent from the Manchester speech, not in the sense of providing the services only for the poor and having a sort of public assistance Poor Law system, not in the sense that we used to think of public health, in terms of sewage and water and infectious diseases and problems of that nature, but in its literal, original Disraelian sense – 'the elevation of the condition of the people'. The aim therefore, if one remembers the earlier quotation, that the first consideration of a Ministry must be the health of the people, is to do what one can to place much greater emphasis on the preventive rather than the curative side in health matters.

I would like to consider with you why, on the whole (and I am very conscious of my own shortcomings in this respect), we have made so little progress towards such an obvious ideal. Why is there so little in the field of health to put alongside Harold Macmillan's glittering success in the field of housing? Of course it is perfectly true that most of the health graphs are better than they have ever been. But I am bound to say that, by and large, that happens almost every year; it happens, I am glad to say, in spite of politicians, and not in any way because of them. But the real question is whether we are reducing the weight of sickness, and whether we are reducing the demands of sickness on the health service and on the national economy. The answer, I am afraid, without any shadow of doubt, is that we are not. Well, let us see why we are not. We must be clear that the prominence given to housing, and therefore the successes that have come from it, are the result of deliberate Tory social policy.

We said and meant it and have shown we meant it, that housing was the first of the social services, and that education was the second. If you are going to put somebody at the head of the queue, other people have got to fall in in their places behind him.

It is as well to recognise, therefore, that it does follow that we had to give a considerably increased emphasis to housing. I think it was right, and I make no complaint about it at all: I have always advocated it and I advocate it still. But the results, of course, are difficult for a Minister of Health. You see, if you take the years from 1948 to 1952, capital expenditure in education went up from £32 to £64 million (that is by one hundred per cent); housing, in that time, went up by about forty-five per cent, and since then of course has climbed much higher. But capital expenditure in the health service has not gone up at all. I am spending, this financial year, £10 million on capital investment in the health service; but we spent £10 million in 1939, and at present-day prices that would be £32 or £33 million, so that the only advance that we have made after these years of a National Health Service is to be spending, on replacement and on capital investment, about one-third in real terms of what we did in the later years of the despised 1930s. All the same, I want to make it clear again that I have no quarrel with the policy that said that housing must come first and education must come next to it. I am sure it was, and I am sure it is, right.

Now the second reason why it has perhaps been difficult to achieve as much as one would like can be put in the words of the Irishman who was asked the way to Oxford Circus. His reply was, 'Well, if I was going to Oxford Circus, I wouldn't start from here'. It is the same with health. If I was trying to create the sort of service that I want to see, that seems to me in accordance with Tory belief, I would not start from where I am. But of course I have to, and I am also in the position of the Red Queen, who spent so much of her time running to stay where she was that she had no time to go anywhere else. Those really are the problems that confront me at the present time. The whole service and those who run it, including the Minister, are obsessed and hag-ridden with their present problems. We are concerned all the time with the waiting lists and the consequences that flow from the waiting lists. We give far too much attention, and we concentrate far too many of our thoughts, on the one single issue of hospital beds. Indeed, we have got to the point in the health service of expressing everything in terms of beds – we talk about cost per bed, the number of nurses per bed, every single thing is related to the hospital bed. But of course the hospital bed comes in to the picture only when the patient has left his own home, only when probably it has been decided that his illness, or whatever it may be, has gone too far for treatment by the General Practitioner or the out-patient department of a hospital.

In a sense, that sums up the failure of the present system, and you can see that same failure, for example, in the House of Commons, when I am asked questions. If I can tell a questioner that one hundred beds in the speciality – mental deficiency, or whatever it may be – in which he is concerned and on which he is questioning me, are going to be provided in his locality, he is thrilled; he thinks that is absolutely fine. But, of course, it is essentially the wrong approach; we are merely providing more and more beds to cure established diseases and we will never catch up as long as our approach remains essentially curative. I estimate that we are something like a hundred thousand hospital beds, probably more, short in this country. It is a calculation that any of you can make in terms of cost per bed (which runs to three or four thousand pounds): no Chancellor of the Exchequer could look at the figure that you need. I remember saying, I think it was when I opened the International Hospital Congress a year or so ago, that I see little future in providing more and more beds for a population that gets more and more in need of them. That is the way, I think, that we should approach this particular problem. Indeed, although now it is the boast of a Minister of Health that he is opening more beds, the true boast will come when a Minister of Health can say, 'I am closing beds – I am closing five hundred beds in Yorkshire because they are not needed any more.'

Now I do not think that is altogether impossible to achieve. It has been achieved in certain minor fields for example, the infectious diseases have almost disappeared, and as a result many of the old fever hospitals are no longer needed for that purpose and are available to the general pool of beds; they make a tremendous contribution towards the solution of our present problems. It may well be that the sanatoria will be the next large pool that may become available. There are those who think that, within a very few years, tuberculosis will be virtually conquered in this country. Well, I am a layman, and I would not want to prophesy on that. Certainly, no graph, of all the health graphs in this country, is falling as dramatically and as swiftly as that for tuberculosis, and it may well be that we are on the verge of overcoming, if not finally conquering, that particular disease. It may be that as medical science goes forward it will be possible to achieve the ideal of closing hospital beds and not opening them.

But the real problem, as I see it, is this. The health service is out of step because the curative side has got in front of the social side. We have made such great advances in curative medicine, particularly perhaps in surgery, on the one hand, and in chemotherapy – the science of drugs – on the other, that we have rather forgotten about the social side. Here again, the classic example of what I mean is old age. Because we have discovered the antibiotics, because of the new methods of geriatric treatment and so on, we can keep people alive much longer, but in many cases we have no idea what to do with them when we have kept them alive.

Old age provides for health, as I suggested earlier it did in housing, the new and the major problem in all the social services – except, for obvious reasons, in education, In insurance too, of course, it is one problem that overhangs all the others. When we draw up the sum of the cost of old age, and when we look ahead to the twenty years for which the Government Actuary has made his forecast, we see there a sum put down for the cost of retirement pensions, which if you look at it in isolation is frightening. But I would suggest that you do not be too alarmed about that. After all, if we have made the strides that we have in these last five years, through the skill of scientists and surgeons and physicians here and abroad, I see no reason to assume that that progress will stop. Indeed, I think it will go faster, and that we will be able to find, once we realise what the problem is, that we will be able to catch up on the preventive side and on the social side.

It is absolutely essential, in my view, that we should have something of a change of attitude in the hospitals themselves. Because, if it is true, as I said earlier, that to admit somebody to a hospital bed is a confession of failure, if it is also true that there are far more beds available in people's homes than there are in all the hospitals, then what we must do is to see that people do not get as far as the hospitals. It seems, therefore, and this of course is linked to the importance of the preventive side, that we must look for a development in the hospital centre of what might be called the poly-clinics, where people go for diagnosis and treatment and which are linked closely to the out-patients' department. The hospital then, the bed centre, as indeed it might become if one had a Peckham Health Centre approach to the problems of health, would be for those who had to undergo surgery or who had to have a long stay, or who needed more detailed investigation.

That is the problem that confronts me, and I said at the beginning that I am very conscious of how little success I have had although I am pretty clear in my own mind where I want to go. Partly it is because the health service has been behind housing and other services in the calls it can make on our funds; and I do not question that in any way – I am in full agreement with the attitude of the Chancellor of the Exchequer, and his approach to this problem, I have no doubt, is very similar to my own. But it is possible to overestimate, if you like, the lack of success. It is the same sort of thing as you remember in Clough's words:

> For while the tired waves vainly breaking
> Seem here no painful inch to gain,
> Far back through creeks and inlets making
> Comes silent flooding in the main.

And we should not forget, in health, how many powerful allies in fact we have. First of all housing – nothing does more for health than housing, and nothing will contribute more in the long run to my field than Harold Macmillan's success in his. Nothing does more for health, after housing, than food – a substantial variety of good food available to the people of this country. And it is of great importance too, that in times of social distress from whatever cause, the income of a family should be kept up. There, of course, I have as an ally the Minister of Pensions and National Insurance and all the schemes for which he is responsible. And I have too the ordinary growing knowledge of people about such matters as hygiene, which will in due course have their effects on health.

But more than anything, perhaps, the thing that encourages me is the new attitude which I really believe does exist now, and it has only come into being in the last year or two, towards preventive medicine, the new status that it is acquiring in the profession, the new attitude that the General Practitioner has towards the Medical Officer of Health. Now Medical Officers of Health had a difficult row to hoe often enough before 1948, but now, I think, they are becoming increasingly recognised, as they should be, not just as people who are responsible for the sewage of the town or district, but as the natural link between all the health services in that particular area, as the men who, more than anyone else, can bring together the General Practitioner, the hospitals, the health visitors and all the domiciliary services of the local authority.

So, although I am conscious that the pace is slower than I would wish, yet I think the objectives that I put before you are the right ones. I think we are on the right road: I think we are carrying out, in health, the ideals of a true Disraelian policy.

Index

Aberconway, Lord *see* McLaren, Charles, 38

acting, Macleod's love of, 35, 40, 48,

Adams, Sir Grantley, 187, 192

Aden, 154, 181, 185

Adler, Larry, 318

Aldington, Lord 135, 231, 240

Alfrey, Henry, 245

Alison, Michael, 288

Allen, Sir Douglas, 305

Allen, Dr Fraser, 66

Alport, C. J. M. (now Lord), 72n, 76

Altrincham, Lord *see* Grigg, John

Amery, Julian, 72, 164, 187, 194–5, 235, 275

Amory, Derick Heathcoat, (now Viscount Amory), 122

Anstruther-Gray, Sir William (now Lord Kilmany), 238 &n

Arikpo, Okoi, 323

Armitage, Sir Robert, 157

Army Reserve Bill, 207

Assheton, Ralph (now Lord Clitheroe), 61

d'Avigdor-Goldsmid, Sir Henry, 286, 298

Australia, 154, 197, 295, 307

Baker, Kenneth, 288

balance of payments, 132, 204, 219, 268, 277, 291, 292, 298; *see also* economy

Balewa, Sir Abubakar, 165

Balniel, Lord, 207

Banda, Dr Hastings, 152, 156–62, 163, 164, 172, 308

bank rate, 120, 132, 204, 290, 292; *see also* economy

Bannister, Mrs Michael, 317

Bannister, Thomas, 317

Barbados, 187, 190

Barber, Anthony, 302, 305, 306–7

Baron, Leo, 255

Barrow, Sir Malcolm, 157

Baylis, Joan, 250, 251, 257

BBC, 257, 287–8, 303

Beacock, Rev. Nicholas, 317

Beaton, Leonard, 304

Bechuanaland, 84

Beeching Richard (now Lord), 227

Beetham, Sir Edward, 187, 188

Bell, Ingress, 81

Benn, Anthony, Wedgwood, 84

Bennett, Mrs Reginald, 319

Bennett, Dr. Reginald, 129–30, 169, 170, 205, 237, 238, 242, 315, 318, 319

Berkeley, Humphry, 76, 253, 261 &n, 315, 319

Bermondsey Corporation, 75

Beveridge report, 270–1

Bevins, Reginald, 72n

Bevan, Aneurin, 13, 16, 25, 62, 69, 72, 81–3, 84, 85, 87, 89, 90, 92, 96, 99, 103, 108, 324; relations with Macleod, 105–6, 315; and Churchill, 128–9

Beyond the Fringe, 219

Bing, Geoffrey, 73

Birch, Nigel (now Lord Rhyl), 122

Birmingham manifesto on the social services, 279

Bishops' Retirement Act, 75

Black, Sir Cyril, 72n

Black, Thomas, 53

Black, William, 27

Blackburne, Sir Kenneth, 188

Blackwood, Michael, 162

Blake, Quentin, 258

Blakenham, Lord *see* Hare, John

Blenkinsop, Arthur, 101

Blois, Rev. Gervase and Mrs, 43; *see also* Macleod, Evelyn

Blood, Sir Hilary, 184

The Blues in the Night (Staff College revue), 50–1

Blundell, Sir Michael, 145, 147, 148, 149, 173, 196

Blunt, Brigadier, 63

Bonham Carter, Lady Violet, (later Baroness of Yaxborough), 147–8

Boothby, Lord, 73

boxing, Macleod's dislike of, 34

Boyd-Carpenter, Lord, 240

Boyle, Sir Edward (now Lord Boyle), 221, 297, 304, 315, 324, 325; introduction by, 13–23; resigns over Suez, 117; 1963 leadership contest and, 240–1

Boyne, Harry, 205

Bradshaw, Robert, 187

INDEX

'The Harris Hills' (Macleod), 30–1
Hart, Prof. Herbert, *Law, Liberty and Morality* by, 18
Hartley, Anthony, 250, 251
Harvey, Ian, 33, 34
Hastings, Macdonald, 318
Havelock, Sir Wilfred, 145
Hawkins, David, 245
Hawton, Sir John, 87, 104, 105–6
Hayhoe, Barney, 261, 287, 315
Heald, Sir Lionel, 72
health, 62, 330, 332–6; *see also* NHS
Health, Ministry of (Macleod administration, 1952–55), 82, 84–6, 87–106, 107
Heath, Edward, 72, 122, 201, 221, 252, 261n, 262, 269, 278, 306, 317, 321, 333; joins *One Nation* group, 76; appointed Government Whip, 78; and Chief Whip, 108, 135; fights 1965 Finance Bill, 244, 262, 286; put in charge of EEC negotiations, 235; as candidate for leader of party (1963), 136; replaces Home as party leader (1965), 244; Macleod appointed Shadow Chancellor by, 263; presents 'Putting Britain Right Ahead' to party conference, 263; relations between Macleod and, 265–6, 315–16; UDI and, 274–5, 276; 1966 election campaign of, 279, 281, 283; as leader of the opposition, 283–4; takes over chairmanship of EPG, 284; his style of leadership, 284–5; replies to budget proposals, 286; Powell dismissed by, 297; prepares for 1970 election, 301; appoints new Cabinet ministers, 305
Heimann, David, 308, 310–11, 314
Heimann, Diana (née Macleod), 55, 92, 212, 238n, 242, 306, 309–11, 313, 314, 326
Hemingford, Lord, 171
Here Come the Tories (Margach), 56
heroin, banning of manufacture of, 102–4
Higgins, Terence, 263, 285, 288, 315
Hill, Dr Charles (now Lord Hill of Luton), 72, 74, 84, 89, 221n, 324
Hill, Colonel Rowland, 49
Hinchingbrooke, Viscount (now Victor Montegu), 227
Hirst, Geoffrey, 72
Hochoi, Sir Solomon, 187

Hogg, Quintin *see* Hailsham, Lord
Hola Camp disaster, 20–1, 143, 144, 196
Holt, Harold, 295
Home, Earl of *see* Douglas-Home, Sir Alec
'Home Town' (party political b/cast), 96–7
Hone, Sir Evelyn, 173, 174
Hopkinson, Henry (later Lord Colyton), 61, 62, 63
Hornsby-Smith, Dame Patricia, 72, 87, 101, 103, 106, hospitals, 79, 89–90, 91, 94–5, 96, 101–2, 333–5; *see also* NHS
housing, 90, 101; Commons debate on, 16, 62, 63, 90, 101, 301; and Powell's special knowledge of, 76; Tory 300,000 target for, 77, 88, 91; Macleod's views on, 230–2, 336; Heath programme for, 279
Housing (Scotland) Bill, 208
Howard, Anthony, 200
Howell, David, 263, 315
Howitt, Sir Harold, 120n
Hull North by-election, 278–9
Hungarian uprising, 21
Hutchinson, George, 252, 261n, 262–3, 314, 319–20
Hyde, Montgomery, 72n
Hylton-Foster, Sir Harry, 72, 134

immigration, 20, 65, 206–7, 296–7
Industrial Charter, 62, 110–11
Industrial Co-partnership Association, 110
Industrial Court, 126–7, 128
Industrial Relations Act (1971), 72, 111, 112, 115
Industrial Reorganisation Corporation (IRC), 278
inflation, 107, 108, 109–10, 120–2, 125, 131, 135, 268, 303; *see also* economy; reflation
Inglis, Brian, 249
International Monetary Fund (IMF), 294
Israel, 115, 117
Ivanov, Captain, 230

Jack, Prof. D. T., 119
Jagan, Cheddi, 190, 191
Jamaica, 186, 187–8, 189–90
Janes, Alfred, 318
Jay, Douglas, 132–3
Jenkin, Patrick, 263, 285, 288, 303, 307, 315
Jenkins, Roy, 288, 289; as Chancellor of

343

CONT.

as Minister of Health (1952–55), 87–106;
Eve falls ill, 91–2; Bevan's work con-
solidated by, 92–3; his interest in voluntary side of NHS, 93; and mental
health, 93–5; implements NHS charges,
95–6; 'Home Town' broadcast devised
by, 96–7; rapport with medical audiences, 97; and cost effectiveness of GPs,
97–8; concern for disabled people,
98–9; and dental service, 99–101;
hospital building programme initiated
by, 101–2; and Guillebaud Report, 102;
heroin ban controversy and, 102–4; his
political and administrative abilities,
104–5; and interest in sport, 105;
'pairing' with Bevan, 105–6; and work
with Patricia Hornsby-Smith, 106;
Eve's courageous help, 106
as Minister of Labour and National
Service (1955–59), 107–40: wage inflation and, 109–10, 121; favours Workers'
Charter, 110–11; concerned over problem of redundancy, 111–12; and strikes,
112–13, 118–20; abolition of National
Service by, 113–14; Suez crisis and,
114–15, 116–17, 118; social service cuts
recommended by, 121–2; bus workers'
strike, 123–31; debate on unemployment, 132–4; 1st visit to USA, 134–5;
1959 Election manifesto and, 135;
Reading speech, 135–6; re-elected in
1959 election, 136; his new style of
administration, 136–7; and relations
with Ministry officials, 137, 138–9; and
formal speeches, 137–8; his good
relations with journalists, 138
as Sec. of State for the Colonies (1959–
61), 141–98: speeding up of African
independence favoured by, 142–3, 144;
shocked by Hola Camp disaster, 143,
144; 1960 Kenya Conference, 144–8,
150, 171; Kenyatta released by, 150; and
declines to reprieve Poole, 151; meets
Nyerere, 152; and Dar-es-Salaam Conference, 152–3; appoints Ramage Commission, 153; favours African federation,
154, 163; and overseas aid, 154–5; 'One
World' speech of, 155; favours strong
central government in Africa, 156;
visits Mauritius, 156; Dr Banda released

by, 156–61; appoints Glyn Jones as
Governor of Nyasaland, 161–2; and
Nyasaland Conference, 162; and Monckton Commission, 163; and Federal
Review Conference, 164; relations
between Sandys and, 164, 169, 202;
speech to Scarborough Party Conference, 165; N. Rhodesian negotiations
and, 166–74; rift between Macmillan
and, 169; back-bench Tory revolt
against, 170; and Salisbury's denunciation of, 170–3; Maudling takes over as
Colonial Secretary, 174–5; against S.
Africa leaving Commonwealth, 175;
Uganda Conference, 78–81; and independence of Sierra Leone and the
Gambia, 181–2; visits Malta, 184–5; and
South Arabian Federation, 185; visits
West Indies, 187–8; and West Indian
Conference, 188–9, 192; meets Kennedy,
190; and British Guiana Conference,
191; UN Colonial Committee of 24
and, 191; visits New York, 191–2; his
photographic memory, 192–3; Question
Time in House, 193; Dept of Technical
Co-operation created, 193; relations
with staff, 193–5; and with press, 195–6;
and with Labour opposition, 196; his
contribution to building of new Commonwealth, 196–8
as Chancellor of Duchy of Lancaster,
Leader of House and Party Chairman
(1961–63), 199–244: press comment on,
200–1; and public opinion poll, 201;
speeches at Party Conference (1961),
202–3; and Leader's room argument
with Butler, 203; his work as Leader of
House, 204–10; weekly meetings with
lobby correspondents initiated, 205;
Immigration debate and, 206–8; and
use of guillotine by, 208–9; no facilities
for Private Members' Bills granted by,
209; relation with Whips of, 210;
biography of Neville Chamberlain
published by, 210–12; and other writ-
ings of, 212; his work as Chairman of
Party, 213–28; handicapped by unpopularity of Government, 213–14; and
his fighting speeches, 214–16; supports
NEDC, 216–17; his analysis of by-
election results, 217–18, 227; blamed by

Racial Discrimination and Incitement Bill, 209

racing, Macleod's enjoyment of, 33, 37–8, 41, 46–7, 48, 286, 312–13

railways, railwaymen, 88, 118–19, 123, 126, 129, 204, 227, 280, 299

Ramage Commission, 153

Rance, Sir Hubert, 186

Reading, Brian, 285

Reading, Marquis of, 129

Redmayne, Martin (now Lord), 221, 229–30 232, 239n, 241, 243

redundancy, 111–12

Rees, David, 251, 254, 256

Reese, Terence, 38, 41

reflation, 135–6, 218, 219, 220, 226, 292; see also inflation

Reigate, Lord see Vaughan-Morgan, Sir John

Renison, Sir Patrick, 145, 150

Rent and Repairs Bill, 330

The Right Road for Britain (1949 policy document), 63

Rippon, Geoffrey, 135, 321–2

Robertson, Jean, 255

Robbins Report (on higher education), 227

Robens, Alfred (now Lord), 125–6, 127, 128, 129, 267, 315

Roberts, John, 166, 167, 169

Robertson, Sir Dennis, 120n

Robinson, Dr Cedric, 98

Robinson, Joan, 18

Robinson, Kenneth, 96, 97

Rodgers, Sir John, 76

Rogers, David, 261

Ross, Catherine, 306, 307, 308

Ross, Isabella (née Macdonald), 27

Ross, Rhoderick, 27

Ross, William, 134

Roth, Andrew, Enoch Powell: Tory Tribune by, 75

Rothermere, Lord and Lady, 303

Royal Commission (on mental health), 95

Royal Fusiliers, 44

rugby football, Macleod's enthusiasm for, 33, 36, 68, 105, 138, 311, 312, 316

Russell-Smith, Dame Enid, 87, 98, 100, 101, 103, 106

Rutherford, Malcolm, 251

Rutland, 216

Ryrie, William, 307

St Aldwyn, Earl, 239, 243

St John Stevas, Norman, 315, 319

St Kitts, 182, 187

St Monica's Convent School, Skipton, 31

St Ninian's Preparatory School, Moffat, 31–2

Salford caliper, 98

Salisbury, Marquis of, 21, 117–18, 170–3, 199, 233, 273, 274, 275

Sandys, Duncan, 122, 146, 150, 185, 194, 273; as Minister of Defence, 114; relations between Macleod and, 164, 169, 202; visits Welensky in Salisbury, 173; appointed Colonial Secretary, 180; and combines offices of Colonial and Commonwealth Secretaries, 201; supports Home's candidature for PM, 238, 240; demands restriction on Asian immigration, 296

Sanitas Sanitatum ('The Condition of the people': Macleod lecture, 1954), 79n, 327–36

Sayers, Gerald, 63

Scaliscro estate see Lewis, Isle of

Scott, C. P., 249

Scott, Nicholas, 304, 307, 308, 312, 315

Scottish Unionist Committee, 61

Selective Employment Tax (SET), 289–90, 292, 299–300, 302

Seretse Khama, 84

Sewill, Brendon, 285

Shakespeare, Sir Geoffrey, 110

Shakespeare, William, 34, 212, 309

Shanks, Michael, The Stagnant Society by, 219

Shinwell, Lord, 280

shipbuilding unions/industry, 118, 119–20

Sierra Leone, 149, 164, 181–2

Simon, Jocelyn, (now Lord Simon of Glaisdale), 135

Simon, Sir John (later Viscount), 34

Simon, S. J., 40

Singapore, 154, 307

Skipton (and Gargrave), Macleod's early years in, 26, 27–9, 31, 36; 'Home Town' located in, 96–7; Macleod's funeral service in, 326

Smith, Ian, 172n; UDI declared by, 273–6

Smyth, Sir John, 72n

So Rough a Wind (Blundell), 148

Soames, Sir Christopher, 72

INDEX

social services, 60; Macleod's specialisation in, 63, 75, 76; *One Nation* pamphlet on, 76–9; and *The Social Services*, 79–80; cuts in expenditure on, 121–2; Macleod's views on, 270–1, 330–6; Birmingham Manifesto on, 279; *see also* housing; NHS

The Social Services: Needs and Means, CPC pamphlet), 79–80, 270, 331

South Africa, 155, 159, 163, 168, 175,183, 197, 255; arms embargo, 298; and cancellation of cricket tour, 304

South Arabia, 154, 181

South Arabian Federation, 185

Southern Rhodesia, 22, 157, 163, 164, 168, 169, 173, 198, 255; UDI declared, 273–6; *see also* Central African Federation

Soviet Union, 115, 116, 134, 226

Spectator, 108; Macleod articles/reviews in: on D-Day landing, 52; view of Powell, 65; African independence, 142; *So Rough a Wind*, 148n; Macmillan, 232, 234; leadership crisis (1963), 234, 239, 240, 241, 243, 252–4, 262; role of Opposition, 285; immigration, 296; *Notebook* in, 56, 256, 257; Macleod's editorship of, 69, 246–58

Spokes, Ann, 313

Spurling, Hilary, 254–5

Stanier, Sir Alexander, 51

Stanley, Oliver, 88, 186, 324

Statist, 209

Steel, Elizabeth, 272

steel nationalisation, 259–60, 267

Stevens, President, 182

Stevenson, Robert Louis, 309

Stewart, Michael, 293

Stockton-on-Tees by-election, 217, 226

strikes, 19, 112–13, 280; of bus workers (1958), 19, 123–31, 135, 136; of motor-car workers, 111, 113, 118; threat of railway strike averted, 118–19; and shipbuilding/engineering unions, 118–20

Stuart, James (later Viscount Stuart of Findhorn,) 84–5

Suez crisis, 20, 114–17, 118, 170, 232, 275

Summerskill, Dr Edith (now Baroness), 75, 81, 82, 96, 171

Sumner, Donald, 214n

Sunday Express, 208, 219, 222

Sunday Telegraph, 215–16, 324

Sunday Times, 56, 70, 200

Swaffer, Hannan, 39

Swinton Conservative College, 264 &n

Tallent, John, 316

Tanganyika (Tanzania), 142, 143, 152–3, 154, 155, 164, 166, 168, 175

taxation, 58, 107, 109, 135, 220, 292, 298, 299; Macleod's tax reform proposals, 13, 263–5, 269–70, 279, 301–2, 306–7; purchase tax, 204, 299, 302; surtax, 206; corporation tax, 269–70, 299, 302; betting tax, 291; on petrol, 299; capital gains, 301; *see also* SET; VAT

Taylor, A. J. P., 211

teachers, 204, 218, 224

Technical Co-operation, Department of, 193

television and radio, 18, 200, 287–8, 303, 304

Terry, Walter, 200, 205, 220

Test Ban Treaty, 231

Tewson, Sir Vincent, 130

That Was the Week That Was, 219

This is the Road (1950 Conservative Election Manifesto), 63

Thomas, James (later Lord Cilcennin), 62

Thompson, J. W. M., 251–2, 318, 322

Thorneycroft, Peter (now Lord), 120–2, 201

Thorpe, Jeremy, 26, 221, 325

Thurlow, Henry, 28

Thursday Club, 318–19

Tilney, John, 72n

Time and Tide, 208

The Times, 55, 138, 139, 170, 205, 212n, 225, 299, 319, 320; on Macleod's maiden speech, 74; review of *The Social Services* by, 79–80; on Macleod's appointment as Leader of House and Party Chairman, 200–1, 203, 207, 208; Macleod's letter on racial discrimination to, 297; and obituary, 324

Transport and General Workers' Union, bus strike and, 123–31, 132

Transport Bill, 208

Transport Tribunal, 131

Trend, Sir Burke, 227

Trevor, Meriol *see* Macleod

Trinidad, 186, 187, 188, 189, 190

Truman, President 281 &n